Essential Readings On
Jewish Identities, Lifestyles & Beliefs
Analyses of the Personal and Social Diversity of Jews by Modern Scholars

Essential Readings On
Jewish Identities, Lifestyles & Beliefs
Analyses of the Personal and Social Diversity of Jews by Modern Scholars

Edited by
Stanford M. Lyman

Gordian Knot Books

A Division of Richard Altschuler & Associates, Inc.

ISBN 1-884092-60-8

Library of Congress Control Number: 2003100777

Cover Design: Josh Garfield

Distributed by the University of Nebraska Press, Lincoln

Printed in the United States of America

In Memoriam

Stanford M. Lyman
June 10, 1933—March 9, 2003

This book is dedicated to the memory of Stanford—an extraordinary scholar, wit, and creative writer who made an immeasurable contribution to the social sciences and supported Gordian Knot Books from its inception. We were honored to have him as editor of this book. Although he will be missed dearly, his more than one-hundred articles in refereed journals and twenty-five books, replete with groundbreaking insight, will ensure his presence in the lives of social scientists everywhere well into the twenty-first century.

Contents

Part I: The Core Concepts for Understanding Jewish Diversity

Part II: Understanding Jewish Diversity Through Sociological, Historical, and Philosophical Studies

Part III: Understanding Jewish Diversity Through Social-Psychological and Psychological Studies

Part IV: Understanding Jewish Diversity Through Community and National Studies

About the Authors

Mark E. Blum, Ph.D., is Professor of History at the University of Louisville, Louisville, Kentucky.

Warren J. Blumenfeld, Ph.D., is Visiting Assistant Professor at Colgate University, Department of Educational Studies, Hamilton, New York, and former editor of *The International Journal of Sexuality and Gender Studies*.

Karina Bodo, Ph.D., is Adjunct Professor of Environmental Health at Concordia University College of Alberta, Alberta, Canada.

Dennis W. Carlton, Ph.D., is Professor of Economics at the University of Chicago Graduate School of Business, Chicago, Illinois, and a Research Associate at the National Bureau of Economic Research.

Jean Endicott, Ph.D., is Associate Professor of Psychiatry, New York Psychiatric Institute, Columbia University, New York, New York.

Abby L. Ferber, Ph.D., is Associate Professor of Sociology, Director of Women's Studies, and Assistant Vice Chancellor for Academic Diversity and Development at the University of Colorado at Colorado Springs, Colorado.

Martin Fiebert, Ph.D., is a Professor of Psychology at California State University, Long Beach, Long Beach, California.

Joshua A. Fishman, Ph.D., Distinguished University Research Professor, Social Sciences, Ferkauf Graduate School of Psychology, Yeshiva University, New York, continues to teach at the University's Albert Einstein College of Medicine campus and is also a Visiting Professor at Stanford University and at New York University.

Steven Friedman, Ph.D., is Professor of Psychiatry at S.U.N.Y. Downstate Medical Center, Brooklyn, New York.

Nancy Gibson, Ph.D., is the Department Chair of Human Ecology at the University of Alberta, Edmonton, Alberta, Canada.

Nathan Glazer, Ph.D., is Professor Emeritus of Sociology and Education, Graduate School of Education, Harvard University, Cambridge, Massachusetts, founding coeditor of *The Public Interest*, and coauthor of *The Lonely Crowd.*

Marci Gluck, Ph.D., is a postdoctoral research fellow in the NY Obesity Research Center at St. Luke's/Roosevelt Hospital, Columbia University College of Physicians and Surgeons, New York, New York.

Allan Geliebter, Ph.D., is a Research Scientist in the NY Obesity Research Center, Departments of Psychiatry and Medicine at St. Luke's/Roosevelt Hospital, Columbia University College of Physicians and Surgeons, and Professor of Psychology at Touro College, New York, New York.

Irving Louis Horowitz, Ph.D., is the Hannah Arendt Distinguished Professor of Sociology and Political Science at Rutgers University, New Jersey, and recipient of the National Jewish Book Award in Biography for his memoir of a Harlem childhood, *Daydreams and Nightmares*.

Arnold A. Lasker, D.H.L, was rabbi of Congregation Beth Torah in Orange, New Jersey, prior to retiring in 1977. He passed away in 1996.

Judith N. Lasker, Ph.D., is NEH Distinguished Professor of Sociology and Anthropology at Lehigh University, Bethlehem, Pennsylvania.

Seymour Martin Lipset, Ph.D., is Hazel Professor of Public Policy at George Mason University, Fairfax, Virginia, a senior fellow at the Hoover Institution, Stanford, California, past president of the American Sociological Association and the American Political Science Association, and recipient of the MacIver Prize for *Political Man.*

Stanford M. Lyman, Ph.D., was Robert R. Morrow Eminent Scholar in Social Science and member of the Holocaust and Judaic Studies Program at Florida Atlantic University, Boca Raton, Florida, and recipient of the Herbert Mead Award for lifetime contributions to the study of social psychology, given by the Society for Symbolic Interaction. He passed away Sunday, March 9, 2003.

Yvonne D. Newsome, Ph.D., is Associate Professor of Sociology at Agnes Scott College in Decatur, Georgia.

Lisa D. Robinson, MBA, EdD. is an adjunct faculty of Business at Webster University and Women's Studies at the College of Charleston, Charleston, S.C.

Donna Shai, Ph.D., is Associate Professor of Sociology at Villanova University, Villanova, Pennsylvania.

Ira M. Sheskin, Ph.D., is Associate Professor of Geography and Director of The Jewish Demography Project of the Sue and Leonard Miller Center for Contemporary Judaic Studies at the University of Miami, Coral Gables, Florida.

Rita J. Simon, Ph.D., is a University Professor in the School of Public Affairs and the Law School at American University in Washington D.C.

Ben Z. Sorotzkin, Psy. D., is a clinical psychologist in private practice in Brooklyn, New York.

David G. Stern, Ph.D., is Associate Professor of Philosophy at the University of Iowa, Iowa City, Iowa, and co-editor, with, Bela Szabados, of a collection of essays entitled *Wittgenstein Reads Weininger: A Reassessment* (Cambridge University Press, forthcoming).

Elizabeth Sublette, M.D., is Attending Psychiatrist at Long Island Jewish Hospital, Queens, New York.

Laurence Thomas, Ph.D., teaches in the Department of Philosophy and the Department of Political Science in the Maxwell School at Syracuse University, New York, where he is also a member of the Judaic Studies Program.

Phyllis Brooks Toback, Ph.D., is a Supervisor of Clinical Pastoral Education and a staff chaplain at Advocate Christ Medical Center in Oak Lawn, Illinois.

Brian Trappler, M.D., is Director of Outpatient Services at Kingsboro Psychiatric Center, Brooklyn, NY, and Associate Clinical Professor in Psychiatry, S.U.N.Y., Brooklyn, NY.

Avi Weiss, Ph.D., is the Chief Economist and Deputy General Director of the Israel Antitrust Authority, and Associate Professor of Economics at Bar-Ilan University, Ramat-Gan, Israel.

Publisher's Preface

In the vast literature on the Jewish people, this book represents a rare publishing event—a rich collection of scholarly studies on Jewish identities, lifestyles, and beliefs by leading thinkers in more than a dozen different disciplines: sociology, psychology, history, economics, education, business, philosophy, psychiatry, geography, demography, political science, public policy, and religious studies.

Collectively, the articles in this book not only cast a penetrating light on the subject of Jewish diversity, from ancient to modern times, but provide a "prism" that refracts the light, and thereby enables the reader to see facets and nuances of Jewish life impossible to perceive through the limited lens of a single author, ideology, or religious orientation.

Inherent in the scholarly approach to the study of Jewish identities, lifestyles, and beliefs—as with the scholarly approach to any phenomena—is the author's attempt to be dispassionate, i.e., to view the subject matter as objectively as possible in the search for the truth, or at least the most plausible explanation or interpretation of an event or situation investigated.

This scientific approach—which tempers the human desire to ignore, alter, or overemphasize data or viewpoints solely to "make a case"—is especially important in the study of both religion *per se* and religiously-related subject matter—such as the "spirit," "soul," "Creator," and "hereafter"—where emotions often prevail among adherents of a particular denomination, way of life, or belief system.

Indeed, it is safe to say that the vast amount of published work by adherents of Judaism is fueled by the spiritual fervor of the authors. Their enthusiasm, and often love of the Jewish religion and people, pervades the sacred texts and books, articles, and poems that compose the literary corpus of Judaism. In this regard, writings about Jews and Judaism are not unique, of course. The same can be said about the literature written by proponents of any religion, including Christianity, Buddhism, Hinduism, and Muslimism.

While such literature undoubtedly satisfies the emotional needs of longtime religious adherents, new converts, and "seekers" in need of sudden solace, it is not intended to satisfy any needs they may have for impartial analyses of religion; and, of course, this literature largely or totally fails to satisfy the intellectual needs of both scholars involved with the study of religion and individuals outside of academia who hardly, if at all, observe religious practices, hold religious beliefs, or have a religious identity.

Until now, those who have sought dispassionate analyses and empirical studies about Jewish subject matter have had to rely almost exclusively on a relative handful of academic journals, out of the thousands of such journals published each year. Our search on the major academic databases for English-language journals since 1990 showed less than one-thousand articles on Jewish identities, lifestyles, and beliefs! And about two-thirds of these were written by authors in countries other than America, especially Israel, Britain and Australia. The number of books in print with a scientific approach to this subject matter is much smaller; and of these, almost every one has been written by one or a few authors, who necessarily convey a limited viewpoint.

This book therefore fills an important void in the Jewish literature, by presenting in one convenient volume twenty-four authoritative studies on Jewish identities, lifestyles, and beliefs, by thirty-one leading thinkers from diverse scientific disciplines. Collectively, they dispel stereotypes about Jewish men and women, by revealing the wide range of cognitive, affective, and behavioral differences among Jews with respect to sex and sexuality; marriage, intermarriage, and divorce; childbirth; religious practices; the Torah and other sacred texts; Jewish and African-American relations; mental and physical illness; Zionism, Israel and Palestine; body image and eating behaviors; and death, suicide, and euthanasia, among many other topics central to Jewish life.

The facts, perspectives and insights contained in *Essential Readings On Jewish Identities, Lifestyles & Beliefs* make this book a vital resource not only for Jews and students of Judaism, but for all individuals concerned about issues involving identity, assimilation, acculturation, conflict, and discrimination among members of minority groups in multicultural societies.

Richard Altschuler
May 2003

American Jewry or American Judaism?

Nathan Glazer

Abstract: *The author contends that there is no danger to the physical existence of Jews in the United States, but he considers whether there will be a corporate survival of those carrying a Jewish identity and a Judaic religious meaning. The analysis proceeds in the context of the viewpoints of three scholars who have written important books on Jewish identity and assimilation: Stephen M. Cohen (*American Assimilation and Jewish Revival*), who believes neither intermarriage nor low fertility will reduce the largest Jewish community in the world; Leonard Fein (*Where Are We? The Inner Life of America's Jews*), who advocates a Judaism of liberal concern; and Charles S. Liebman (*Deceptive Images: Social Science and the Study of American Jews*), who supports traditionalism or Orthodoxy. Ultimately, the author concludes that Jews will assimilate, and that their identity will continue, but without serious content.*

Between "American Jewry" and "American Judaism" there exists a peculiar tension of which most American Jews, I believe, are not aware. By "Jewry" I mean simply the total body of American Jews and everything they do and stand for. American Jews are predominantly businessmen and professionals; their children overwhelmingly go to college; they are concentrated geographically in major cities, and retire very often to Florida; their average income is high; and they vote Democratic, and even when they vote Republican they vote for liberal Republican politicians. By "Judaism" I refer to something more specific: the religion of the Jews, not just any religion that Jews, defined by descent, practice but a historical complex, one that has evolved and become different things at different times and that is still evolving, but that can be transformed to the point where, although it may still be the religion of Jews or of Jewry, it is no longer Judaism. Arguments over just what that point is can be intense. Without settling that matter, we can generally agree what is "closer to" or "farther from" the Judaism of our fathers and grandfathers, or from normative, traditional Judaism.

    A related distinction is that between "Jewishness" and "Judaism." "Jewishness" is what Jews do; but suggests, as against "Jewry," some connection with a distinctive Jewish past, a culture, some involvement in activities with a specific Jewish component, social, cultural, political, or religious. Thirty years ago, I entitled one chapter in my book *American Judaism*

"Jewishness and Judaism." The chapter dealt with American Jewish life between the two world wars, and in it I described the very vigorous Jewish life of the areas settled by immigrants in the big cities in the 1920s and 1930s. I pointed out how much of that life was specifically antagonistic to Jewish religion, to Judaism, while it was positive about some other aspects of Jewish life. This seems strange to us now, but in the 1920s and 1930s one could find, for example, antireligious Zionists, secular Jewish schools that were anti-religious, Yiddish culturalists, anarchist, socialist, and communist Jewish organizations for different age groups and with varied objectives, all of which could have been described as atheist and "anti-judaist." Things are very different today. It is assumed—and is indeed true—that those who support one manifestation of Jewish life tend to be supportive of all the others. We do not find, as we did fifty years ago, Reform synagogues that are strongly anti-Zionist, or Jewish organizations of whatever kind that are strongly anti-religious or anti-Judaist. In the chapter following "Jewishness and Judaism," I described the very different situation that emerged after World War II, as Jews moved to the suburbs, as the dense Jewish immigrant quarters of the big cities were broken up, and as the synagogue became, from only one Jewish institution struggling against others, the central Jewish institution of the new Jewish communities. Great numbers of synagogues were built, Jewish schools became part of the synagogue complex, the synagogue became the place where every Jewish issue found a home.

This chapter was entitled "The Jewish Revival." In view of the weight I am putting on the distinction between Jewishness and Judaism, could it not have been entitled "The Judaist Revival?" But that would not have been quite right; there was an ambiguity to this Jewish revival. The religious element was rather thin, despite that institutionally the synagogue was the bearer of the revival. But I argued, as did others at the same time, that what we were seeing in the building boom of new synagogues was less an expression of religiosity than ethnicity. Jews wanted to remain Jews, wanted their children to remain Jews, wanted them to marry other Jews, but one would have been hard put to find a strong overtly religious impulse.

The Jewish revival, it hardly need be said, had nothing in common with the kind of "revivalism" we are familiar with from the history of American Protestantism. There were no radio rabbis, no mass conversions, no fervent public commitments at mass revival meetings to observe the commandments. What we saw was something like an institutional explosion. Will Herberg had made the argument in his book, *Protestant-Catholic-Jew,* that the religious revival which, of course, affected more than Jews, in the United States in the 1950s, had little to do with faith and religious impulses and it seemed primarily concerned with ethnicity; that is, with the desire of people to maintain communities based on ethnic attachment. In the America of the 1950s, this required taking the institutional form of religion. Ethnicity then was embarrassing and backward-looking; religion was respectable and American. I agreed, at least as far as Jews and the Jewish revival were concerned. I quoted one rabbi who wrote: "[The congregants] invariably imply, and often explicitly state: We need you as our representative among the non-Jews, to mingle with them, to speak in their churches, to make a good impression. We do not need you for ourselves. Well, for the old people, perhaps, and for the children, yes, once a week, but for the Gentiles most of all." It seems that Jews did not need rabbis for religious purposes. I wrote that the common feeling "among large numbers of Jews was that the institutions of the Jewish religion were useful because they contributed to the continued existence of the Jewish people. The ancient notion that Israel existed to serve the law was here reversed: It was argued the law existed to serve Israel."

Secular Jewishness in almost all its institutional forms has declined almost to the vanishing point. Even nonreligious Jewish institutions have become in terms of observance more Judaist. They do not meet on Friday night or Saturday, serve kosher food, or give an honored place to prayers and rabbis. One would think the story of this conflict, this tension, is at an end. Why bring it up now? But it has revived in a somewhat different form in the last few years to lead a most vigorous life in dispute and controversy that has given rise to new and confusing dichotomies. After all, the argument between Jewishness and Judaism was how would the Jews survive in the United States: as a people simply bearing the ethnic label, Jews, or as a religion? The conclusion of the argument in the 1950s was that the Jews would survive as a religion. The new conflict is over what kind of religion is surviving as the vehicle of survival? Further, if the only function the religion is serving is survival, what kind of religion is that? Indeed, if the only content of the religion becomes survival, can it even serve that single function?

We saw the argument flare up a few years ago in discussions and reviews of *A Certain People* by Charles Silverman. Recently it has again become the focus of discussion of several books. Among them are *Leonard Fein's Where Are We? The Inner Life of America's Jews,* Charles S. Liebman's *Deceptive Images: Social Science and the Study of American Jews,* and Steven M. Cohen's *American Assimilation and Jewish Revival.*

A cluster of dichotomies ask the same questions, and point to the same problem. What is the nature of Jewish life in the United States; and how, and in what form, will it continue? To put it more crudely, will the Jews survive in the United States, and if so, how? But I must point out that neither I nor these writers mean continuation in a physical form. None of the writers I have referred to see any danger to the physical existence of Jews in the United States.

While the word "survive" reminds us, properly, of the Holocaust and of the permanent threat to the security of Israel and of the survival of Jews there, that is not the problem for the Jews of the United States.

These writers are speaking of a corporate survival carrying a Jewish identity, and even more, carrying a religious identity and a religious meaning. When Leonard Fein, Charles Liebman, and Steven Cohen ask what is the future of American Jews, will they survive, and how, they are asking, what will be the content of Jewish life? They divide between what we may call an optimistic view, a pessimistic one, and something in between and all three positions are of interest.

Steven Cohen, from whose earlier work Charles Silberman drew heavily in his optimistic book *A Certain People,* is the typical representative of this viewpoint. He has allies, perhaps more optimistic than even he is, in Calvin Goldscheider and Alan Zuckerman. The optimist tells us, that, first of all, the Jews will survive physically because neither intermarriage nor low fertility will substantially reduce what is now the largest Jewish community in the world. Further, he tells us—and on this point all agree—that the expectation of straightline assimilation held by Jewish sociologists of an earlier day, the expectation of a steady weakening of Jewish identity, commitment, loyalty, and observance with each passing generation, was exaggerated. Previously, Will Herberg made great use of Marcus Hansen's essay on the return of the third-generation immigrant. He turned this provocative thesis into "Hansen's Law," which said: "What the children want to forget, the grandchildren want to remember." Indeed, those of us who grew up in immigrant homes, and who are aware of how far many of us have moved away from Jewish learning, tradition, and religious observance have been surprised that our children have not moved the same distance from our practices and beliefs, but have, to some extent, "returned." The empirical data shows signs of "return," in the form of greater regular observance of some religious rites (Seder on Passover, and Hanukkah candles), and no decline in synagogue membership among third generation Jews.

The most controversial element of this optimistic scenario deals not with these empirical points, but with interpretation. The Jewish commitment continues, the optimists tell us; Jewish religion continues. Jewish schools continue to teach, and children go to them. The pessimists say, hold on. Charles Liebman calls his book *Deceptive Images,* and before I read it, I wondered where the deception was. The deception that he is talking about is this claim that American Judaism is healthy. To present this picture of health, one must accept whatever Jews do as Judaism. If they have become increasingly remote from tradition, if they observe only two commandments out of the 613, and these mostly for the children, why that is alright. Jews are still Jews, Judaism survives, it is only that it has become transformed. These "transformation-ists"—as Liebman dubs those who interpret the condition of American Judaism as healthy—argue that Judaism has always changed through the ages. The Judaism of the first century would have been unrecognizable in the tenth, as that of the tenth century would have been unrecognizable in the nineteenth; and so, in the twentieth century of American life, moving into the twenty-first, Judaism is something else again, but Jews are still Jews. This is a somewhat crude view of the "transformationist" position, but it gets to the essence of the controversy.

One of our difficulties in coming to terms with this controversy is that Jews do not speak easily about religion; that is, religion as it is understood in divinity schools. Indeed, Jews find something a little Christian and un-Jewish or un-Judaic in such things as a catechism of beliefs, confession of faith, fervent prayers to a living god; they are happier with practices. Indeed, as they move further from tradition it is not that their beliefs change, it is their practices that change. When the Orthodox criticize most Jews for straying from tradition, they refer to their practices, not their beliefs.

This characteristic of Judaism makes it easy for us to take the position that nothing essential has changed in Judaism, it is simply adapting to American life and to modernity, as it once adapted to Mesopotamia, to Spain, or to Poland. But I think this is too simplistic; Judaism has indeed changed. Its change is of sufficient gravity to at least raise the question of continuity. But perhaps a more important question is what role can Judaism play for Jews and Jewish life when its religious content is radically reduced?

That reduction is indicated, for example, in some of the data on recent surveys Leonard Fein presents in his book, *Where Are We?* Consider: In a recent survey, 91 percent of Jews agree that "without Jewish religion, the Jewish people could not survive." On the other hand, two-thirds disagree with the statement: "To be a good Jew, one must believe in God."

But even to ask such a question in a survey is rare. Surveys of Jews, as we know, ask about practices, not beliefs. "We know considerably more about ritual practice than about religious belief. Two out of five do not fast on Yom Kippur, four of five don't observe the dietary laws, only ten percent attend services more than once a month. But 84 percent attend a seder, 82 percent light Hanukkah candles."

We have known for at least twenty years, since Marshall Sklare and Joseph Greenblum's studies of Lakeville, that "to the average American, a good Jew is someone who does good things: contributes to Jewish causes, aids the poor, doesn't lie and steal, obeys the law, and the like." He is certainly a good man, but is he a good Jew?

Fein quite properly worries about this. If the meaning of a Jew is to be good, then what do we tell our children, and what is the point of a Jewish corporate survival? As we know, there is an answer to this, but it is not one that satisfies the pessimist (Liebman) or Fein, whom I will place between the pessimists and optimists. The answer is that the Jews survive in order to survive. "Survival" has become the rallying cry not only for the Jewish people, and for any people there is no more important one, but also for the Jewish religion, and that does raise a problem. Surveys and experience suggest that the content of the Jewish religion as a system of belief, as an orientation to the world is remarkably reduced. If we examined what Jews wrote in their magazines, books, and newspapers, what they were told from the pulpits in sermons, and to what they responded in their synagogues, temples, and organizations, one would conclude that Judaism now deals with only one overwhelming concern, the physical survival of the Jews. First, of course, is the memory of the Holocaust, the mass destruction of European Jews in Nazi death camps: the outpouring of books and educational materials, and the building of museums and memorials. The themes addressed in this huge effort vary: "Never again"; "Our children must be taught"; "The world must be taught"; "We must not let the world forget"; or "We cannot allow the reality of what happened to be denied." Nothing arouses Jews as much as denials that it occurred, or agitates them as much as the fear the denial will be believed. As Leonard Fein writes: "We engage in a veritable orgy of Holocaust museum construction . . . and learn that it is far easier to raise money for the construction of such museums than it is, say, to offer higher wages to the often scandalously underpaid teachers in Jewish schools. The Simon Wiesenthal Center for Holocaust Studies, in Los Angeles, an institution that at the time of its creation was widely viewed as being entirely redundant with existing efforts, has become by far the most successful solicitor of contributions of any domestic Jewish organization."

Linked with the Holocaust is the other great survival concern, the overwhelming fear for Israel's safety, the threat of the destruction of the Third Commonwealth. And there are the lesser survival concerns to which we have referred: intermarriage, low fertility, the assimilation of Russian or American Jews.

The Jewish religion, Judaism, has become the religion of survival. It has lost touch with other values and spiritual concerns. No one has to argue in favor of survival; there is nothing else if one does not survive. We do not have to ask further, if we are in Israel, why Israel wants to survive; or ask further, if one is a Jew in the United States, why the Jews want to survive. But we should ask why the corporate community of Jews in the United States wants to survive, and why it wants to do so in the form of a religion, when the traditional content of that religion, it would seem to me, and to any observant Jew, has been quite reduced. What has replaced it? On the one hand, the common content of a universal ethic, which has nothing distinctively Jewish about it, and on the other, survival—remember the Holocaust and save Israel. That is what Judaism comes down to if we question Jews about it, and that is what the pessimists—Liebman calls them "traditionalists"—find inadequate. The "transformationists," on the other hand, by discovering what Judaism has become, see good reasons for the singular focus of Judaism. It maintains a distinctive identity for Jews. What more is needed?

Leonard Fein probably would not want to be grouped with the "traditionalists," but he is certainly critical of the transformationist view. "Here we have one of the world's great religious civilizations," he writes, "yet if a child comes home and asks his/her parent, 'What does it mean that we are Jews?', odds are the answer will not be about belief, or about ritual, or about shared language or shared culture or even shared history. Odds are the answer will one way or another focus on our shared fate, on the horrid prospect that when 'it' happens again, we will all again be lined up together."

"What happens," he writes further, "when Jewish identity is reduced to a response to anti-Semitism? What happens is this: Those embattled few who have made the welfare of the Jews their mission look out upon a Jewish community whose members are Jewishly available only to protect a right they themselves do not (and do not want to) enjoy, only to defend a way they do not (and would not) walk. And so anti-Semitism becomes a motive, perhaps the motive, for Jewish life." Fein insists that there must be more than warmth of ethnic ties to Jewish life. It must have a meaning, because he wants to regard "the Jewish community as a means rather than an end in itself."

I would modify this conclusion somewhat. The Jewish people does not need a purpose, just as an animal species does not need a purpose. It has evolved through nature and history, and life is an ultimate value. But the Jewish religion is another matter. That can only be an end if we truly believe it is the word of God; but how many of us believe that? If we do not, the religion has to be a means to an end. It has to carry values, to lead to something of worth; can that value, that worth, for a transcendental religion, be the maintenance of the Jewish people?

It seems problematic that this transcendental and universal religion has become the chief workhorse and ally of national survival: Good enough if one has a purely instrumental attitude to religion. But a religion does not survive on instrumental value alone. If one stands outside of religious faith, one can see its instrumental value and support it for that reason alone. Religion, in general, helps maintain families; keeps children from drugs, crime, and premature sexuality; and, in the case of the Jews, as we know, religion is a major mainstay of the state of Israel (also a major trouble for the State). The more religious

American Jews—that is the Orthodox and the devout Conservatives—are more committed to Israel's defense, care more about it, may go to live there, even though Israel is still in many ways more secular than religious. But if one stands within religion, one cannot see it as simply instrumental: "I believe because it is useful." There is a paradox about religion's instrumental value. Religion has to be believed, for its own sake, to serve instrumentally. If it is not believed, it loses even its instrumental value. Yet, the element of noninstrumental faith in American Judaism is now radically reduced.

There are two proposals to give American Judaism some transcendent value, something of the power of the traditional faith. Neither of these two proposals is new. Leonard Fein makes a powerful plea in his book for a Judaism of liberal concern. Judaism is meant, he says, to repair the world not solely to save Jews. Repairing the world means helping the poor, the deprived, and the welfare state. It also means attention to the non-Jewish poor and the deprived, as there are certainly immeasurably more non-Jews in the world than there are Jews.

He almost answers his own proposal; rather, he agonizes over his own answer, and is not fully satisfied with it. The main reason he is not fully satisfied is that liberalism (along with its variants to the left) has come into conflict with the other crucial aspect of Judaism, its particularism, its concern for the Jewish people and the state of Israel. I need not go into this increasing split between what liberals and progressives consider right, and the interests and fate of the state of Israel and the Jews who live there. Nor is this conflict simply one with the present government; even if the government were to take the most liberal position that is compatible with Israel's survival, that would not satisfy most of those who criticize it from what generally is called the left. There is the deep suspicion among Jews that many of those who criticize the state of Israel from the liberal-left-progressive position are not much concerned with its survival. Fein's aim of replacing part of the lost traditional content of Judaism with a universalistic liberalism comes in many variants, from that of classical Reform to various kinds of Jewish radicalism, to Leonard Fein's new formulation.

And then there is the second great answer: traditionalism or Orthodoxy. Charles Liebman, in *Deceptive Images,* seriously considers the Orthodox alternative, because Orthodoxy has shown a strength in the last thirty years that is, indeed, surprising.

One of the chief pieces of evidence against the old thesis, that assimilation was inevitable among American Jews, is that Orthodoxy has not declined in the past thirty years and, indeed, by various measures, has become stronger. Liebman makes the interesting point that this generation is the first in two hundred years in which Orthodoxy has not declined. The relationship of this to our general problem is complicated: On the one hand, the resistance of Orthodoxy would seem to give strength to the optimists, the transformationists; on the other hand, Orthodoxy not only survives and grows stronger, it also becomes increasingly resistant in its consideration as an intrinsic part of a variegated Jewish community, the great majority of whom do not observe the commandments. It is increasingly ready to cut itself off from connection with the greater part of American Jewry. In other words, Orthodoxy rejects the Judaism to which the transformationists point to support their claim that American Judaism is healthy.

Even Orthodoxy, upon examination, does not escape the radical reduction of the religious element in Judaism. If the Orthodox Jew tries to account for his distinctiveness, there is not much that we would consider spiritual, referring to higher values, to transcendent values, or even to God. We will once again hear only one thing: survival. Fein argues: Concerning "the rationale of the Jewish endeavor," the "what for?" "the sobering truth is that even the Orthodox, in making their case, are not very likely to argue from God: Like almost all others, they rest their case on the idea of survival itself. When young people are asked to 'stay' Jewish, they are not asked to do so for God's sake or for their own but in the name of Jewish survival."

I believe this to be true. Another recently published work, Jeffrey Gurock's interesting history of Yeshiva University, *The Men and Women of Yeshiva,* can be searched in vain for what we might consider a spiritual element to the Orthodox revival. Perhaps I define "spiritual" and "religious" too narrowly, or perhaps I am influenced by Christianity and by American Protestantism. I may be looking for something in American Judaism that is not there because it is not Jewish. The dominant theme in the history of Yeshiva is survival; of course, that is the dominant theme in the history of any college, university, or institution. I do not refer to Yeshiva's survival; rather, Yeshiva's argument for its own survival is that it helps in the survival of the Jews.

Consider this: In describing the expansion of the University's programs into the fields of social work and communal service, which created some controversy as it was against the classic and essential mission of educating rabbis, Gurock tells us that "it was assumed that these workers would use their combination of professional training and 'deep appreciation of spiritual values', learned at Yeshiva, to promote positive Jewish identity among their clients. An unspoken but implicit additional agenda was that these social workers would promote, with the lightest touch, interest in Orthodoxy." One struggles to give content to the phrase, quoted from some official document, "deep spiritual values." The only content one can give it is the maintenance of some of the distinguishing observances of Orthodoxy, but it is not clear just what their spiritual content is. The only clear content we can give these observances is that they preserved the distinctiveness of the Jews and their separation from others, and, in the contemporary context, their own separation from other branches of Judaism. But Gurock himself struggles with the question of what was being served: "Was Yeshiva's overwhelming concern, however lofty, with the problems of survival of their particular religious or ethnic group, appropriate for an American university?" Samuel Belkin, president of Yeshiva, found the justification of this primary insistence on survival in the philosophy of cultural pluralism as developed by Horace Kallen and used by his predecessor Bernard Revel. Ironically, the philosophy that justified the maintenance of the distinctive Orthodox strand had to come from what was really a secular sociology.

Charles Liebman, exploring in a hardheaded manner the reasons for Orthodoxy's success—let us be reminded that it is a modest success, a largely institutional success, and it has not transformed the faith or practice of American Jews, among whom only 10 percent or less can be considered Orthodox—also cannot find what I would call religious or spiritual reasons. Orthodoxy's current influence is due to a number of factors. The most important one is the sense of many non-Orthodox Jews that Orthodoxy is the voice of Jewish authenticity, a sense shared by many Conservative and Reform Jews (including rabbis) and at least some leaders of secular Jewish organizations; although they are not Orthodox and don't want to be Orthodox, they regard the Orthodox as better Jews.

The sense that Orthodoxy is "the voice of Jewish authenticity" may stem from the fact that Orthodoxy is a legitimate expression of the Jewish tradition by everyone's standard whereas Orthodoxy denies that status to Conservatism and Reform. Most important is that Orthodoxy speaks with a sense of confidence about its Jewishness that the non-Orthodox lack.

Liebman states that "the influence of Orthodoxy may also be attributable to the feeling among many of the non-Orthodox that the Orthodox are the real Jewish survivors. They are the ones least likely to assimilate." Survival has become the theme of Jewish life, and the theme of Jewish religion. Leonard Fein finds it not enough, and indeed most thoughtful observers of American Judaism find it not enough. But what else is there? Liberalism is a weak reed. It was not enough for classical Reform, which has returned to particularism even while it tries to maintain its weak attachment to general social reform. I don't think it will be enough for American Jews. There are too many contradictions between a political stance, even a good and compassionate one, and the particularistic interests and needs of the Jewish people. Orthodoxy is increasingly confident, but its religious content has become to my mind ossified, and if it has a living motive, that motive is also survival. "We survive better than you do," the Orthodox tell us; indeed, on the basis of what I see around me, in a hundred years only a fragment of American Jews who are Orthodox will survive fully as Jews; while American Jews, in general, affected as they are by intermarriage and a secular society, and not easily influenced by religious themes, will preserve only a hazy identity as Jews.

The Holocaust and Israel are the contents of American Judaism forty years after the establishment of the state and the end of the Holocaust. Can one imagine that they can continue to play this role and maintain American Judaism forty years from now? Or that they can be supplemented with a stronger general liberalism and progressivism? Or that that can be replaced by a renewed traditionalism? Those are the alternatives available. But when one reviews them it seems that earlier sociological projections of the Jewish future in America had a substantial measure of truth. Jews will assimilate; however, that assimilation will not take the form of the disappearance of Jewish identity. The identity, without much content, of Jews will continue. But neither traditional religion—Orthodoxy—nor the transformed religion, whose major theme is survival and liberalism, seem strong enough or appropriate enough for our conditions to be sustained. What sustains them now is the fear of physical destruction, a reality in the past, and a reasonable possibility in the future. That gives us our agenda today, and perhaps for many years to come. But it is a different agenda, I believe, from that of two thousand years of Jewish history, and not one that has the staying power of the religion of the past.

References

Readings Suggested By The Author:

Cohen, Stephen M. *American Assimilation and Jewish Revival.* Bloomington, Ind.: Indiana University Press, 1988.

Glazer, Nathan. *American Judaism.* Chicago: University of Chicago Press, 1957.

Fein, Leonard. *Where are We? The Inner Life of America's Jews.* New York: Harper and Row, 1988.

Gurock, Jeffrey S. *The Men and Women of Yeshiva.* New York: Columbia University Press, 1967.

Goldscheider, Calvin and Alan S. Zuckerman. *The Transformation of the Jews.* Chicago: University of Chicago Press, 1984.

Goldscheider, Calvin. *Jewish Community and Change: Emerging Patterns in America.* Bloomington, Ind.: Indiana University Press, 1986.

Liebman, Charles S. *Deceptive Images: Social Science and the Study of American Jews.* New Brunswick, NJ: Transaction Books, 1988.

Silberman, Charles E. *A Certain People: American Jews and Their Lives Today.* New York: Summit Books, 1988.

Minimalism or Maximalism: Jewish Survival at the Millennium

Irving Louis Horowitz

Abstract: *In his Keynote Address at an international workshop held during the approach of the 50th anniversary of Israel, titled "Jewish Survival—The Identification Problem at the End of the Twentieth Century," the author analyzed challenges to the stability of the Jewish identity and the survival of Judaism, against the backdrop of the Holocaust and the creation of the state of Israel. The issue 25 years ago was the blending of Jewish life into Israeli society. Today the issue is opposite, as Jewish life flourishes without Israel being the center, and with Israel experiencing problems of secularization and national identity. While concentrating on the belief that Jewish people are committed to the existence of Israel, the author argues that Israel was formed for a moral purpose, and thus neither Israeli citizens nor Jewish people elsewhere can accept it being a complete democracy. The study of Jewish survival, however, must consider the state of Israel with a democracy set up in the British pattern; the influence of the Torah, a divine moral and ethical guide to the Jewish people over centuries; and the Jewish culture that has remained intact al though Jews have been scattered throughout the world. To understand these complex forces, the author uses a minimalist view of the relationship between Jewish life and Israel.*

By common consensus, the two most extraordinary events of twentieth-century Jewish history were the destruction of European Jewry in the Holocaust, and the construction of the State of Israel. They bracket the 1940s, and they define Jewish parameters in the 1990s. Whatever the interpretations of these events, they clearly conjure up powerful and contradictory emotions: defeat and victory, peripheries and centers, helplessness and heroism, and of spirit and matter itself. The purpose of this article is to identify Jewish survival prospects in a post-Holocaust world, and in a world in which Israel is soon to celebrate the first half-century of its existence as a modern nation-state.

How the Jewish religion, national integration, and cultural identity are forged in light of these two immense events is at the core of this analysis. It is evident from any close examination of the subject of Jewish survival that contradiction is far more characteristic of Jewish life than consensus. This was the case in the past and remains so in the present. Struggles between orthodoxy and reformism, nationalism and cosmopolitanism (for want of a better word), Israeli national interests and Jewish universalistic claims, and capitalist individualism and socialist collectivism, have all hardened into postures rather than been resolved over the course of the century. Add to this mix such volatile private concerns as intermarriage, conversion, ethnic heritage, secularization, and the task of analysis appears daunting, while that of synthesis seems well nigh impossible.

Policy makers repeatedly claim that even were Israel not to exist, conflict among Arab and Moslem interests would continue to fester. Dare one add in reverse that even were Arab hostilities toward Israel and Moslem animosities toward Jews magically to dissolve, conflict among Jewish interests—political and religious—would continue in force? Urgent questions have been raised about generational concerns: the evolution of Israel as a national entity with "normal" state proclivities to monopolize force, and the prospect that Judaism may become a minority religion even within Israel, much less within the context of most open societies. It behooves the social science community to answer whether Judaism is any different than other world class religions, and what constitutes Judaism as a frame of reference in national and cultural terms with nominal regard to issues of religious observance or theological discourse.

There is also the thorny, if largely unspoken, issue of how strategies of becoming Jewish enhance or impede principles of scientific research. Concerns for Jewish survival strongly imply that such survival is a positive value. But whether a moral center of gravity, much less a teleological purpose, can be deduced from the history of religions as a sociological concern merits examination. Within these heavy domains of relevance I should like to consider minimal and maximal approaches to Jewish survival. To be sure, the topic of Jewish survival in the period ahead is so broad and pervasive that the potential for saying something new, much less presenting a startling set of findings or conclusions is more presumptuous than ambitious. Yet, it is in the nature of human nature to persist in lurching forward, no matter how slightly, and to seek closure no matter how tentative.

I take as my text a highly personal point-counterpoint: the collection of my essays published a quarter century ago under the rubric: *Israeli Ecstasies and Jewish Agonies,* and the work I have pursued in the intervening years called *Taking Lives.* Risking a digression before addressing the wider issue of Jewish survival directly, I ask the reader's indulgence on how I view my own work in tandem, as book-ends separated by a quarter century.

The purpose of *Israeli Ecstasies and Jewish Agonies* was to explain how a dialectical set of relationships emerged as a result of a new centrality for Jewish life, Israel; and the evolution of a new periphery as well, in North America. For what seemed to be at stake in the late ·1960s and early 1970s was the serious weakening of Jewish life as an entity of value apart from the existence of Israeli society. Now, the situation is curiously reversed. There is a widespread recognition of the work of Jewish life and a growing skepticism of the centrality of the Israeli center! My intentions in *Taking Lives* were somewhat less global: to develop a social scientific framework for understanding the Holocaust in terms of state legitimacy, or more specifically, variables of class, status and power familiar to those who work in the Weberian tradition. Curiously, we have a huge literature based on personal testimonials and biographies, and only a slightly smaller amount of writings exploring theological and religious considerations that emerged from the Holocaust. Yet the social analysis of this monumental tragedy is only now receiving its proper due.

What makes the study of Jewish identity complex is that we are not dealing with a unilinear phenomenon, but one more akin to a multiplexed phenomenon moving in a variety of historical as well as structural directions. To discuss the Jewish condition is to examine religiosity, nationality, and culture all at once as well as one at a time. Indeed, to separate these elements of Judaism, results in distortions and reductions that can, and sadly enough often does, lead to little light and much heat.

To be sure, the arguments between those who emphasize issues of class stratification on one side, and cultural identity on the other, indicate that exaggerated claims for any one sort of social scientific method are likely to result in frustration and futile argumentation. I turned from a study of Israeli-Jewish relations to an examination of the deeper roots of the Jewish condition as such, because the explosion of literature on the Holocaust led to serious distortions in the intellectual landscape; and no less important, the social scientific accounts, while attempting to repair distortions resulting from a variety of reductionists in the popular literature, introduced a few new sins of their own.

We have an astonishing amount of personal narratives (some serious, others self-serving) providing eyewitness reports of horrors and human degradation, but failing to place the Final Solution in any larger context. So what we are left with is a series of uplifting or depressing stories of living with the past, or getting beyond horror and degradation. On the other extreme are what might be called the theological exegeses, in which issues of an ultimate sort are examined: from questions like, "Can we believe in God's goodness after the Holocaust?" to a variety of messages, intentional or otherwise, that serve as Providential warning signals for those who fall from grace. Again, the quality of such human examinations of Providential intentions shift from profound to trivial-and worse.

Because they constituted a collective unit, the Jewish people were uniquely singled out for total and complete annihilation; Christian and Hebrew scholars alike have tried to interpret the Nazi war on the Jewish people in Biblical, revelatory terms; frequently laced with reflections on the historical status of Jews living in a Christian world, and extending into the particular economic drives, political motives, and cultural longings of each world religion in relation to the other.

In the midst of these larger trends—what we may call the biographical and the theological, respectively—a third trend has emerged: the empirical study of how the Holocaust took place, what happened when, where it did, and why it surfaced in relation to the Jews of Europe. The major and admittedly bowdlerized answers given are: first, Germans have a unique propensity for racial purity and animus toward strangers in their midst who do not share in the national value system; and second, it is not the nation but the system, the Nazi-Fascist system that created the foundation for implementing the final solution.

I do not want to enter a polemic with other viewpoints, or argue issues examined at length in the text of *Taking Lives*. Rather, I want to note emphatically that my own view is that, however multiple the sources of anti-Semitism, and however broad the base of emotive support for the Final Solution, the actual implementation and execution of the Holocaust was a function of state power, of the legal and military monopoly of power that resided in the hands of the National Socialist state, which allowed for the Holocaust to move ahead in its grinding, vicious wholeness. The emergence of Israel as a state implicitly recognized as much. It made Jew and non-Jew alike aware of the modern as well as ancient sources of power and authority. The monopoly of power rather than the beneficence of rulers became the touchstone of Jewish life after the Holocaust. It provided the grounds of legitimacy for the Jewish State of Israel.

However "banal" the perpetrators of the Holocaust may have been as private persons, they acted in concert as part of a killing machine, comprised of a hugely expanded and swollen bureaucracy dedicated to surveillance, a military establishment that dwarfed anything hitherto known in the annals of European armed force, and a disciplined political party apparatus that had as its exclusionary membership mission the extirpation and destruction of Jewish life wherever Nazism held sway, including occupied zones and lands not known in earlier eras for anti-Semitism as national preoccupation. In this sense, *Taking Lives* is an effort to concretize the work of political sociology, of the interaction between state and society. It is also a way to lay claim to the fact that the very act of taking lives and counting bodies is the sociological equivalent to locating the essential variable by which a society and a state are to be judged.

The analysis of Jewish survival in post-Holocaust terms is immediately made complex by its triadic nature. We must simultaneously deal with the state of Israel, its model of democratic rule rooted in Westminster; a divinely inspired Torah pasted on to Jews over centuries and millennia as a guide to ethical and legal behavior; a Jewish culture filtered through many nations and conventions and languages that are encapsulated in an adherence to some form of community living; and certain personality characteristics. Add to this mixture the relationship between persons who claim a common adherence to Judaism in philosophic terms, and any ensuing analysis of the Jewish condition becomes numbingly complex. But we have set ourselves the task of clarifying these relationships; we are seeking to establish an analytical model rather than a clerical muddle. Essentially, I do this by taking a minimalist, rather than maximalist view of the Jewish-Israel relationship. Along with Abba Eban, I assume that being a Jew implies commitment to the fate and fortune of Israel, and to a community of like-minded souls. Whether being an Israeli implies, in reverse, a commitment to the fate and fortune of world Jewry, is a question perhaps best left in abeyance for the present. Let me immediately note that this minimalist approach carries risks. Marginalization within Jewish religious life can, and often does, readily translate into complete secularization, or as is sometimes the case, into varieties of alternative civil religious persuasions.

Before we examine current struggles, it might be useful to remind ourselves how military matters stood only a quarter century ago. It might help explain why I entitled my work *Israeli Ecstasies and Jewish Agonies.* In the period that followed the euphoria of the Six-Day War in 1967, it is understandable that a dominant wing of Israeli leaders could argue, as David Ben-Gurion had earlier, that commitment to Zionism could have no validity without Jewish immigration to Israel. Without such a pioneer vision, Jewish life in the Diaspora was bankrupt.

> I don't know how long it will take, whether ten years or fifty years, but in time, America will be a unitary nation, just like any other nation. It is entirely different with Jews in Israel. The roads in this country are Jewish roads, they were built by Jews. The houses that you see here were built by Jews. The trees are Jewish trees; they were planted by Jews. The railway is a Jewish railway; it is conducted by Jewish workers, by Jewish engineers. The papers are Jewish. We do not live a group life. Here we are living a national life. There is another difference between Israeli Jewry and Diaspora Jewry. We are also an independent factor in international life. We appear like any other free people at the United Nations. We meet with representatives of large and small states on an equal footing. We do not need *shtadlanim* (intercessors) any more.

Those amazingly proud words uttered in the glowing aftermath of military victory now appear quaint, inspiring more response than regard. As a consequence of military struggle, one which resulted in a political stalemate, redefinitions of Israeli realities topped the agenda. Claims of sovereignty and autonomy have been tempered by a renewed realization of the special relationship between Israelis and Jews, without much outward concern for who is preeminent in this interaction network. Thus, in a new book by Geoffrey Wheatcroft on *The Controversy of Zion* we have a summary of arguments against Zionism that have become as strident as they are commonplace.

> It is the very absence of the kind of ethnic nationalism and cultural homogeneity exemplified by Israel which has made possible their own triumphant story. What Jews outside of Israel have come to recognize very clearly is not only that Israel is not their home, but that the Israelis, however much they admire them, are no longer their people. . . . The final paradox might be that Zionism has succeeded in everything but its ostensible purpose; to resolve the Jewish Question by normalizing the Jewish people and to end their chosenness. . . . And yet the Jews remain in some manner chosen. . . . Today there is a Jewish state which is a source of healing pride for millions of Jews, but also a source of anxiety. Should they defend the religious zealots and right wing settlers who play an ever larger part in Israeli life? Or is Israel increasingly irrelevant to the fabulous success story of the Jews of America?

More contradictory general propositions on Israeli-Diaspora relations are hard to envision. But we need to determine whether such varied sentiments represent something deeper than the changing fortunes of warfare and statecraft. Do these two ideological frameworks define, not only the limits of Israeli existence, but the survival capacities of the Jewish people as a whole? In exploring this question, we must confront a reality in which a center (Israel) remains relatively weak while a periphery (American Jewry) is relatively powerful.

Israel's geographical rationalization, in the current period, and the Arab countries' own continuing struggles between tradition and modernity, have led to a renewed search for religious, ethnic, and cultural elements within Judaism. Do the political and social structures that divide Jews along national lines permit unity or fusion in religious and cultural terms? I suspect that even posing the issue in this way makes a positive answer possible. Definitive political and theological responses cannot be concluded with respect to Israeli-Jewish relationships. Dialectical people have a habit of maintaining long-standing differences, broken in moments of crisis by tactical synthesis. This certainly characterizes the present condition of Jews and Israelis. The state of Israel is an irreducible fact, one that Jews must live with—even those who might not celebrate such a fact. In this sense, Zionism and anti-Zionism are less policies than postures in present-day Israel. National realities now seem indifferent to internationalist ambitions.

In a broad series of stages, the Arab effort to convert Jews into a pariah people, and Israel into a pariah state, have failed. This is no small accomplishment in its own right. Beyond these, a series of issues within Judaism were also resolved in the past quarter century. Arabic adversaries, by ceaselessly questioning the legitimacy of Israel as a "settler state," provided the foundations for wide-ranging reexamination of the contemporary state of Jewish affairs, culminating in relatively successful efforts by Israel to come to terms with its position in the Middle East. Again, no small achievement for a land that felt far more tied to Europe than the Middle East only a quarter century ago. Such self-exploration might be a constant in Jewish affairs without external pressures, but with them, the sense of immediacy takes on dramatic proportions.

The repudiation of the Zionist-as-racism canard, not without the firm support of Western democracies, was coupled with a series of negotiated arrangements starting with Egypt and Jordan, and now expanded to include Palestinians and Syrians. A variety of diplomatic as well as military arrangements have modified the sense of Israeli estrangement. The question however remains whether weakening the threat to Israel as a pariah State translates into a weakening sense of identification of Jews with the fate and fortune of Israel. More bluntly, do Jews now view Israel as a place to visit archaeological sites and go scuba-diving rather than a place to restore political commitments or make an issue out of vigilant support?

Debate about whether Israel is central or peripheral to the Jewish experience in the United States or elsewhere in the Diaspora is only one half the essential paradigm. The other half is whether Judaism is central to Israeli political integration. It might well be that underlying these questions is whether Judaism is central to Jews wherever they are. Posing the issue in these admittedly harsh terms is not an exercise in dialectics, but an effort to examine the empirical state of affairs that makes the issue of Israeli sovereignty profoundly meaningful. For example, if migration from Israel to America far exceeds Jewish-American immigration to Israel, does this weaken or strengthen world Jewry? If one believes in the organic incompleteness of Jewish life outside Israel, the answer is self-evident. But for those who believe that the Jewish nation resides wherever a Jewish congregation exists, temporal problems of the state of Israel are of only limited significance to what Herzl called "the Jewish company." The extent to which orthodox positions on Israeli centrality have broken down is best illustrated by the current demographic situation. At least 10 percent of Israelis, or approximately 450,000 of Israel's citizens, are currently living in the United States on a relatively permanent basis. Beyond that, new migrants to Israel from Russia are often interested in moving to the United States, Canada, New Zealand, or Australia, what might be referred to as the Anglo-democracies, rather than staying in Israel. Whatever the explanations offered—hardships of settlement in Israel, limited knowledge about or interest in Jewish religious life, fears of new military hostilities, oppression of tax burdens, or limits to upward mobility and career opportunities—Jewish dedication to Israel remains highly questionable under present-day circumstances.

Whenever the existence of Israel has been threatened by hostile, military dominated states, and the survival of the Jews of Israel is clearly imperiled, Jewish solidarity has been evident and made near total by the "facts on the ground." Witness the outpouring of international Jewish support for Israel in the 1967 and 1973 Arab-Israeli conflicts or, most recently, the solidarity of Jews against Iraq, Libya and Iran—the so-called terrorist states. Ultimate questions about survival always obviate niceties of discussion and disputation. The choice between social life and death, like individual life and death, makes intellectual hairsplitting seem fatuous. To the extent that the Jewish fate has, from its inception, been engaged in a survival-crisis-response syndrome, one can speak with confidence of the centrality of Israel to the Jewish experience.

However, when minimum conditions of Israeli security are met and, in consequence, the needs of a large portion of Jewish peoplehood are met, the question of the centrality of Israel to Jewish life becomes thorny. When Israeli survival is not in jeopardy, but to the contrary, relatively normalized, conventional distinctions between socialism, nationalism, and religiosity slip back into the rhetoric ordinarily employed by Jews inside and outside of Israel. The state of normality thus unleashes national rather than overseas concerns. The relative lack of such normal, peaceful, conditions in the Middle East since the founding of Israel has obscured real differences between Jews in the Diaspora and in Israel with respect to a variety of issues affecting the international Jewish community. The data indicate some clear guidelines in this respect.

First, Reform Jews, adults and youth, who are presumably representative of American Jewry as a whole, rate the relationship of American Jews to Israel as very important; but only a quartile agree with the statement that Israel is the center of contemporary American Jewish life. As orthodoxy continues to hold sway in Israel, and Reform and Conservative religious movements inside Israel are confronted with problems of legitimacy, even that figure may be inflated. Second, regional studies of American Jews reveal noticeable differences in the strength of Zionism between fathers and sons. Fathers scored significantly higher on indicators of Zionist persuasion. For the most part, all available data support the argument that the Zionism of American Jews is less an intent to migrate than a general belief in Israeli claims. Pro-Israel sentiment is directly linked to perceived threats to the survival of the Israeli state. Third, American Jewish attitudes vary significantly depending on whether Middle East wars are perceived to have negative consequences for the United States. Thus, the reaction of American Jews to the Six-Day War of 1967 was more favorable than their attitudes toward the Yom Kippur War of 1973 or the Lebanese adventure of 1982 precisely because the synergy and consistency of American and Israeli interests in the earlier war did not hold true for the later conflicts.

Israel has registered genuine achievements in various spheres of life-science and medical research, cyberspace technology, humanistic education in kibbutzim, folk music and dance, basic agricultural self-sufficiency, army efficiency and *esprit,* and so forth. Beyond these areas, the caliber of Israeli society is not notably higher than say, Western Europe. In politics, academic life, industry, labor leadership, religion, *belles lettres,* the media, the dramatic and fine arts, Israel, while surely not lagging too far behind other developed countries, is far from producing standards of excellence sufficient to inspire its own citizens or the Jewish Diaspora. As long as the relationship of the Diaspora to Israel is strictly financial, with no genuine joint responsibility in planning for Israel's development, or real accountability to contributors abroad for the funds collected, one cannot (outside the religious clusters) expect thoughtful Jews around the world to express a sustained sense of personal involvement in Israel at the intimate, or subjective level.

It may be argued that an adequate reexamination of Israeli-Diaspora relations should begin by understanding Israel as both a Third World entity and a European democracy operating in a unique context. Perceived in this way, tendencies toward growing separation of Jewish life in the Diaspora from identification with Israeli society might be seen as part of a long-term secular trend distinguishing nationhood from religiosity and ethnicity. Diminishing Jewish involvement with Israel may have long-term benefits as well as costs for center and periphery alike. For Israel, such secularization could lessen overseas pressure in the formation of national and international policies, and hence permit Israel greater flexibility in its decision-making processes. For Diaspora Jews, such a distinction might compel greater attention to Judaism as such, to the role of religion, culture, and ethnicity in the contemporary West, apart from concerns about military annihilation currently shrouding Middle Eastern affairs. Evolution of the debate over Israeli centrality and Diaspora marginality has moved a considerable distance beyond inherited Zionist and anti-Zionist shibboleths.

The question of Israel's centrality to Jewish life cannot be resolved by the wave of a magic wand. The inner reality of Jewish life is tripolar, it is not simply manifested in choices dictated by State considerations. Judaism has had its own special religious Trinitarianism: Israel, the Torah, and God. Corresponding to that, in secular terms is first, Israel as a state (in the Hobbesian sense of retaining a monopoly power). Second, peoplehood, in which the sacred documents are invested in the Jewish people as a whole, a legal entity without a physical nation, but a national people. Finally, there is the Hebrew God, in which a collection of moral sentiments, legal precepts, and cosmological concepts are joined and fused to make Judaism a religion.

The centrality or marginality of American Jews to the Israeli experience can similarly be broken down into a kind of tripartite arrangement. Survey data have repeatedly shown that American Jewry's response to Israel depends on whether Israel is being talked about as a nation-state, as part of a worldwide communion of Jewish people, or as a theological-religious phenomenon having transcendental as well as immanent goals. When Israel is physically threatened by military activity, there is a high degree of international Jewish mobilization. But it is hard to imagine any responsible American Jewish leader calling on the Jewish people of the world to respond exclusively to Israeli needs as a state power in the Middle East, or for that matter even to urge support of the specifics of everyday life in Israel.

The historian Melvin Urofsky, who has done significant research on American Zionism, put the matter of Jewish response to Israeli appeals forcefully. Being Jewish is not the central concern of most American Jews: being American is. With the exception of one or two "gut" issues, such as anti-Semitism or Israel, American Jews are divided, indeed fragmented on every other question. They want to consider matters relating to religion as private; secular issues, even those which might affect Judaism, are to be treated in a secular, an American manner. Another way to express this same opinion is to observe that Jewish communities are themselves seriously affected by the centrality of American society and economy as a whole to the continued existence of Israel. In this sense, to the extent Israel as a society remains peripheral to American centrality, Israel compromises its claims for cultural or religious centrality with respect to Jews, especially those who live in the United States.

The notion of centrality, or the direct impact of Israel on a peripheral Jewish population, has three distinct frames of reference: the state of Israel, the Jewish people, and the Hebrew religion. This is a critical differentiation inherent in the history of Judaism. Its tripartite character underscores a great deal of ambiguity in Jewish life. But it also gives Jewish life considerable strategic resilience. What falsifies a great deal of data and statistics on who is or is not a Jew, or *when* a Jew becomes a non-Jew, and so on, arises precisely within the American context, where this kind of tripartite structure becomes intolerably manifest. National Jews, ethnic Jews, and theological Jews all confront each other as total ideological solutions (i.e., assimilationist or survivalist) to fragmented political frameworks. As a result, contemporary Judaism exemplifies a feeling of pluralistic peoplehood that involves many diverse elements. Judaism cannot easily be destroyed or eliminated: but neither can it be easily synthesized into a single supreme frame of reference. The universalism, or if one prefers, the very porosity of Judaism, even if it causes moments of grief to Israel's particular concerns, provides residual strength to Jewish survivalist impulses. One indicator of this strength is the multiple problems encountered in conversion efforts. The source of so many failures in evangelical efforts to "convert" Jews is the narrow fundamentalist definition of what constitutes Jewishness. Christian fundamentalism tends to limit its interests in Judaism to one of theology. To the extent that Islamic theology also sees Judaism as exclusively a religious faith, it has the same interpretive problems as the Christian West. Consequently, their efforts to eliminate Judaism via theological conversion have had limited success. Jewish strength resides in its plurality, clerical and secular alike. The gigantic historical ambiguity involving God, ethnicity, and nation is a positive and healthy factor in Judaism's survival. But it also makes it exceedingly difficult to reach a definitive answer to the question of how central Israel is to Jewish life.

In the past, Israeli centrality has implied Jewish marginality. The ideological bridge between Israel and Jews is much more heavily traversed in one direction: from the Diaspora to Zion. Yet in demographic terms, the bridge carries more traffic from Zion to the Diaspora. Increasingly, an older pattern, in which Jewish leaders are frequently asked to define the role of Israel in the life of the individual American Jew, is being replaced by a newer pattern, in which Israeli figures must begin to explain the role of Diaspora Jews in the life of individual Israelis.

As this pattern of intellectual cross-fertilization ripens, the foundations of Zionism themselves undergo scrutiny. The totality of the destruction of the European Jewish communities that thrived between 1789 and 1939 served to vindicate classical Zionist persuasions. But the continued vitality of Jewish life in Anglo-American democracies has, with equal force, compelled reconsideration of Zionist ideological tenets. Earlier maximalist demands that Diaspora Jews resettle in Israel have reduced themselves to a minimalist approach. Now the duraility, permanence, indeed, the absolute necessity of a viable Diaspora replaced older, more religious-oriented visions of a return to Zion. What this does to Israel's centrality in the lives of world Jewish communities becomes a question of some urgency.

Do Conservative and Reform varieties of the Jewish religion have anything to contribute to Israeli society or theological attitudes in Israel? To ask this question is to ignore the most pronounced tendency in present-day Israeli

society itself, the manifestly weak levels of religiosity and religious participation in Israeli society. Israel's secularization approximates secularization in
other modernizing societies. Regular synagogue attendance is probably lower
than Sunday morning churchgoing in American society. Indicators such as
worship in a synagogue may prove little, by themselves, but at least they help
make quite plain the differences between support for Israel and active par-
litripation in Jewish community or religious experience.

We need to confront uncomfortable questions within both Jewish life
and Israeli society. To what degree can one have American Jewish
identification with Israel that corresponds to a highly secular Israeli society?
This is a more difficult question than whether one identifies with Israel in a
strictly crisis scenario. Here the touchy issue becomes under what global
conditions might support for Israel not be forthcoming by American Jewry? For
example, what kinds of military action or capabilities would make it
permissible or even theologically mandated to withhold support of Israel by
Jewish communities? We witnessed the beginnings of this sort of distinction in
the Israeli-Lebanese struggles during the early 1980s. Israeli military victories
in the field were greeted with far more unease than were the threats that
confronted Israeli society in earlier periods.

Such extremely sensitive questions are being raised with increasing
frequency. If Israel enters a period of protracted political stalemate, in which
it is part of pluralistic goals, and dynamic development in the Middle East as
a whole, the capacity for quick mobilization of world Jewish support will
diminish. As the war-peace syndrome recedes, stagnation-growth issues
emerge. In such a scenario, matters taken for granted between Jews in the
Diaspora and Israelis in Zion, are far fewer and less compelling than in the
grand dialogue of the formative period of Israeli existence.

Whether the Jewish question rather than the Israeli question has once
more become central is the thorny problem of the present decade. Throughout
the twentieth century, every decade has thrown up a master problem which has
occasioned realignment, reshuffling, and rethinking. Old alliances tend to
dwindle with a decade's end. Those who found themselves united around
opposition or support for the Vietnamese conflict in the 1960s, found old
alliances sharply curtailed during the 1970s under the impact of the Middle East
crisis. This is not to say that new forms of association between Jews as an
"interest group" and other social movements cannot be forced, only that the
foundation of such associations tend to be more domestic than global concerns.

The American experience has become more intertwined with Jewish
experience than at any time in the past. Quite apart from military support to
Israel, whether posed in terms of integration of Russian Jews, Jewish
settlements in the West Bank, or impact of Latin American and South African

Jewish communities on new immigration patterns, all become central considerations for those charged with rethinking democratic premises in American Jewish organizational affairs. The special concerns of Israel must somehow be placed within a Jewish context so that policy choices are not reduced to Israel's impact on America, but rather on the more complex issue of Israel's reflection of, no less than impact upon, the so-called Jewish question.

The existence of Israel has led to a realignment of forces. Because of the compelling fusion of objective circumstances and subjective sentiments, the Jewish people are no longer the people they were between the Anschluss and Auschwitz. Jews no longer exhibit the same circumscribed commercial concerns or the same focus on survival. Whether or not this shift from economic survival to political participation is celebrated, the fact that the Jewish question has become central to international debates in the 1990s is incontrovertible. It is profoundly intertwined with problems ranging from energy supplies to military preparedness, to profound reconsideration of the Holocaust and the behavior of nations under stress. Within this global context, the Israeli issue is profoundly meaningful to all peoples and parties. Outside of that context, Israel is of special meaning primarily to the Jewish peoples.

Given the plural status of Jewish identification, what then should be the posture of the individual Jew toward the question of national allegiance to Israel and political participation in matters of importance to Israel? This question is specifically anguishing for the American, Canadian, and West European Jews (in that order) since there is only limited potential for full citizen participation in Latin America, South Africa, Russia, Eastern Europe, and portions of the Third World where Jews exist in large numbers. Past Jewish participation in these home countries of the Diaspora has been at the economic and social levels. As a result, the problem of dual or multiple political allegiance remains, for such people, largely an abstraction.

Diaspora participation in affairs of state in Israel is limited to rhetorical flourishes and editorial anguishes. It is true that certain key leaders in the American Jewish community have some marginal voice in Israeli life. But this is primarily a consequence of philanthropic and monetary power; not any special policy-making acumen that is essential to Israeli political affairs. Prominent wealthy American Jews have the same input into Israel as the International Monetary Fund does in any Third World country. A central problem in consequence is the extent to which Jewish solidarity, in times of Israeli military crisis, can or should be brought to bear on one's own country or countries. Jewish mobilization in support of Israel by no means violates their citizen obligations to the United States or anywhere else in which they have a vote as well as a voice; but the United States is particularly sensitive to large interest-group pressures.

The arguments which have raged concerning divided loyalties of American Jews are largely chimerical if not entirely fictitious. Certainly, throughout the relatively brief history of the state of Israel, Jews have never surrendered political loyalty to another state. If anything, Jewish communities have drawn closer to the American political mainstream as Israeli interests have become intertwined with those of the United States. In the absence of any impulses in the opposite direction, the issue of dual loyalties remains of marginal importance. Only in special circumstances, such as the Pollard spy case, are uncomfortable issues of any relevant sort introduced.

While conceptually possible, it is empirically unlikely to envision a condition under which American and Israeli interests diverge so sharply as to compel Jews to confront the pluralistic premises of this viewpoint with the monistic requirements of choosing between either the United States or Israel. At such a time, the very essence of the American commitment to pluralism or, perhaps, the Israeli commitment to democracy, would be sorely strained. And in such moments, abstract guidelines must yield to historical specifics; such is the character of decision making in times of national strife. The great advantage of Israel is its explicit commitment to limited democratic government and pluralistic outlooks, presumably a milder form of commitment than Americans have to the United States. If this delicate equilibrium breaks down on either side, a decision might be forced. But to presume so on *a priori* grounds would represent an extreme form of unwarranted historical pessimism.

Jews have traditionally lived in a partial, fragmented world. Tensions and polarities are built into the substance of Jewish lifestyle. Marginality is a consequence of a people dispossessed, displaced, and well traveled. More pointedly, marginality is also a condition that makes it possible to face world problems with a maximum amount of objectivity and a minimum amount of undiluted fanaticism or ideological investment. Perfect integration into any national system, even that of Israel, could well represent negation of positive Jewish values. It would also signal a collapse of the pluralistic sources of American politics and traditions. Presently, neither of these outcomes seem imminent. Jewish concerns can remain largely focused on positive solutions to practical issues, including the status of Israel. But as Charles Liebman has rightly pointed out, given Israel as a state with a moral purpose, neither Israelis nor Jews can quite accept the theory—much less the practice—of unlimited democracy. As a result, conservative values coexist in uneasy alliance with liberal politics.

What seems to have taken place is a huge shift in cultural fault lines, a transformation of values that has seen the emergence of problems of secularization and national identity that are characteristic of emerging free societies the world over. While concerns about individualism and identity clearly enlist the sympathies of Jews the world over, they do not exhaust the *Geist* or *Weltanschauung* of the Jewish people at century's end. Varieties of specifically Jewish clerical belief, from pragmatic reconstructionism to cabalistic mysticism abound. If the current situation hardly permits euphoria or ecstasy, the processes underway in Israel do serve to refocus Jewish energies and enlarge its visions. That so much change has occurred in the past quarter century is a tribute to the maturation of Israel, but perhaps more generically to the survival capacities of Judaism as such. Israel is the preeminent example in our times on how political and emotional flexibility are special characteristics of small new nations and big historic peoples.

References

Ben-Gurion, David. 1962. "How is Israel Different?" *Jewish Frontier* 21 (Aug.), as quoted in Howard M. Sachar, *A History of Israel: From the Rise of Zionism to Our Time.* New York: Alfred A. Knopf, pp. 718-719.

Horowitz, Irving Louis. 1974. "Israeli Imperatives and Jewish Agonies," pp. 3-36 in *Israeli Ecstasies and Jewish Agonies.* New York and London: Oxford University press.

Wheatcroft, Geoffrey. 1996. *The Controversy of Zion.* London: Sinclair-Stevenson Publishers, pp. 342-43.

Suggested Readings

Ben-Sasson, H.H. 1976. *A History of the Jewish People.* Cambridge, MA: Harvard University Press.

Dashevsky, Arnold and Howard Shapiro. 1974. *Ethnic Identification among American Jews.* Lexington: D.C. Heath.

Deshen, Charles, S. Liebman and Moshe Shokeid. 1995. *The Sociology of Religion in Israel: Israeli Judaism.* New York and London: Transaction Publishers.

Eisen, Robert. 1997. "Jewish Mysticism: Seeking Inner Light." *Moment,* 22, 1: 38-43.

Eisenstadt, Shmuel N. 1992. *Jewish Civilization: The Jewish Historical Experience in a Comparative Perspective.* Albany: State University of New York Press.

Elon, Amos. 1971. *The Israelis: Founders and Sons.* NY: Holt, Rinehart, and Winston.

Ezrachi, Yaron. 1997. *Rubber Bullets: Power and Conscience in Modern Israel.* New York: Farrar, Strauss and Giroux.

Harrison, Bernard. 1996. "Talking Like a Jew: Reflections on Identity and the Holocaust." *Judaism,* vol. 45, no. I (Winter): 3-28.

Heilman, Samuel C. 1992. *Defenders of the Faith: Inside Ultra-Orthodox Jewry.* New York: Schocken Books.

Horowitz, Irving Louis. 1974. *Israeli Ecstasies-Jewish Agonies.* New York: Oxford University Press.

——. 1997. *Taking Lives: Genocide and State Power* (Fourth edition). New York and London: Transaction Publishers.

Liebman, Charles and Steven M. Cohen. 1990. Two *Worlds of Judaism: Israeli and American Experiences.* New Haven, CT: Yale University Press.

Sachar, Howard M. 1976. *A History of Israel: From the Rise of Zionism to Our Time.* New York: Alfred A. Knopf.

Scholem, Gershom. 1971. *On the Kabbalah and its Symbolism.* New York: Schocken.

Segre, Dan V. 1980. *A Crisis of Identity: Israel and Zionism.* New York and Oxford: Oxford University Press.

Sklare, Marshall. 1971. *America's Jews.* New York: Random House.

Seltzer, Robert M. 1980. *Jewish People, Jewish Thought.* New York: Macmillan, London: Collier Macmillan.

Sobel, B.Z. 1974. *Hebrew Christianity: The Thirteenth Tribe.* NY: John Wiley & Sons.

Urofsky, Melvin I. 1976. "Do American Jews Want Democracy in Jewish Life?" *Inter-Change. vol. 1,* no. 7: 1-7.

Waxman, Chaim I. 1976. "The Centrality of Israel in American Jewish Life: A Sociological Analysis." *Judaism,* vol. 25, no. 2.

Wheatcroft, Geoffrey. 1996. *The Controversy of Zion.* NY: Sinclair-Stevenson.

Some Thoughts on the Past, Present and Future of American Jewry

Seymour Martin Lipset

Abstract: *In this article, which is based on the author's remarks at the annual meeting of the Association for the Social Scientific Study of Jewry, December 20, 1993—where he received the Marshall Sklare Award for Distinguished Scholarship—Lipset analyzes why Jewry in America is exceptional among the world's Jewrys, much as the U. S. is an exceptional country. Jews won acceptance as equal citizens here earlier than elsewhere, and have been exceptionally successful in intellectual, business and political endeavors. The dominant ethos of American culture has been congruent with Jewish values. However, success in both America and Israel seemingly undermines the conditions for survival, as it encourages intermarriage and cultural assimilation.*

I am obviously extremely pleased to receive the first Marshall Sklare Memorial Award for a career of distinguished scholarship in the study of Jewry. I am most pleased to so honor Marshall's memory, yet, I must say it is also a sad event. Just as parents should not outlive their children, professors should not outlive their students. As we all know, Marshall died much too young. In terms of professor and student relationship, the only consolation is that the age difference between Marshall and myself was not very great. I started as a member of the graduate faculty at Columbia when I was quite young, and he had other careers before he turned to academe, which kind of equalized the age factor. I could spend all of my time going into a discussion of Marshall and his work. His doctoral dissertation, the classic book *Conservative Judaism* (Sklare 1955), is, I think, one of the most important sociological studies of denominationalism done in the United States. His most recent work (Sklare 1993), a collection of his essays, gives one a clear impression of the contributions which Marshall made over time to the study of the Jewish community and of Jews in America.

The first article I ever wrote (Lipset 1955) dealing with Jews *per se* discussed "Jewish Sociologists and the Sociologists of the Jews." In that essay, I made a point which in part has been answered. I raised the question why were there so many Jewish sociologists and so few sociologists of the Jews. The fact was that in the fifties and earlier, many of the Jewish sociologists were uninterested in Jews either in ethnic or religious terms. But even if they were personally involved as Jews and/or practiced Judaism, they avoided studying Jews per se. Their neglect had a very negative impact on our scholarly understanding of the Jewish situation in America. Non-Jews in the social sciences, with very rare exceptions, also tended to ignore the Jews. In part, I think, they did so because there were so many Jews in the discipline who could analyze their own community that they felt there was no need for them to do research on Jews. There were plenty of other groups and situations they could work on. However, as I just noted, the Jews around them did not study Jews. Of course, the growth of this organization, the Association for the Social Scientific Study of Jewry, attests to the fact, as does Marshall's career, that the concern that there are few Jewish sociologists studying Jews is no longer as serious a problem as it once was. There is now an abundant literature: general books about Jews in America, specialized studies, Jewish demography, the National Jewish Population Survey (NJPS) and the work going on around it. All of these attest to the existence of a large number of Jews working in the field. Hence, my earlier article is rather out of date. In any case, I want to talk today briefly on the future of American Jewry.

To attempt an exercise in futurology is, of course, a daunting task. If one were to go back to any time before 1930 and ask what people would have said then about the future of the Jews, they obviously would have erred greatly. Indeed, there is almost no period in which social scientists or others have been able to predict with any degree of accuracy where a community or a nation is heading (Lipset 1980).

To understand American Jews it is important to recognize that they are exceptional among the world's Jewrys. Their experience on this continent differs qualitatively from that of their coreligionists in other countries (Lipset 1989). Jews won acceptance as fully equal citizens earlier here than elsewhere. They have faced much less discrimination in the United States than in any other Christian nation. Although never more than 3.7 % of the population and now only about 2.5%, they tend to be given one-third of the religious representation. In many public ceremonies one sees a priest, a rabbi and a minister. Currently there are thirty-three Representatives and ten Senators in Congress, many of them represent areas that have few Jews in the population.

As Goldscheider and Zuckerman (1986: 183) note, "the pace of socio-economic change and the levels of occupation and income attained are exceptional features of Jews compared to non Jews." Various national surveys, including those conducted by Steve Cohen (1989) and by the various demographers involved in NJPS as well as others, all point to the fact that Jewish income is much higher than that of nonJews, perhaps twice as high. Kosmin and Lachman (1993:260) report that Jews have the highest median annual household income, $36,700, among thirty different religious groups. An analysis of the four hundred richest Americans as reported by *Forbes* finds that two fifths of the wealthiest forty are Jews, as are about a quarter of the total list (Kosmin 1988).

Jews are disproportionately represented among many sections of elites which are largely drawn from the college educated. A study of leading intellectuals found 45% are Jewish (Kadushin 1974); something approaching 30% of professors at the major universities are Jewish (Lipset and Ladd 1971); among high level civil servants, 21%; among partners in the leading law firms of New York and Washington, 40%; among reporters, editors, and executives of the major print and broadcast media, 25%; and among the directors, writers and producers of the top fifty grossing motion pictures from the sixties to the eighties, 59 %, the same percentage of people involved in two or more prime time television series (Rothman, Lichter & Lichter, forthcoming).

These achievements, which are extraordinary, given the proportion of Jews in the population, are related, of course, to their scholastic accomplishments. At the beginning of 1990, about 85 % of college-age Jews were enrolled in higher education as compared to two-fifths for the population as a whole. Moreover, as is the case for Jewish faculty, they are heavily located in the better, more selective, schools. An American Council of Education survey of college freshmen found that those with Jewish parentage have significantly higher secondary grades than their gentile counterparts in spite of the fact that a much larger proportion of Jews were going to college. Moreover, Jews seemingly perform better as undergraduates as evidenced by their disproportionate membership in Phi Beta Kappa.

It has been argued that the ability of Jews to do so well in America reflects the fact that Jewish characteristics and values have been especially congruent with the larger national culture (Feingold 1982: 189). The sociologist Robert Park (1950: 354-355), who is not Jewish, once suggested that Jewish history be taught in the schools so that Americans could learn what America is about. Park argued that in their drive and achievement, the Jews were quintessential Americans. That is, Park believed that if you examined all the ethnic groups in America, including those of English background, the most American group, the group which embodied American values most, was the Jews. Thus, if you want to understand America you would do it better by studying the Jews than by analyzing the English or the Germans or any other group. I am not arguing that Park was necessarily correct. I think he may have overstated the point. Nevertheless, I think there is some point to Park's notion. Furthermore, some evidence in support of such assumptions can be found in Max Weber's analysis of the relationship between the Protestant ethic and the spirit of capitalism in America, in East European Jews' reaction to Benjamin

Franklin, and in the contemporary links between Margaret Thatcher, the capitalist reformer, and British Jews.

Weber (1935:54-55), in explaining the economic success of the United States, notes that the Puritans brought with them the religiously derived values conducive to capitalism: rationality, hard work, savings, a strong achievement drive. These values were expressed in the secular writings of Benjamin Franklin whom Weber quoted as the quintessential expression of the capitalist ethic. Franklin's values not only appealed to Americans, they found an enthusiastic audience in Eastern Europe among Jews to whom they also resonated as consistent with their religious beliefs and secular culture. Franklin's writings were translated into Yiddish around 1800 and were read devoutly and discussed in Talmudic discourse fashion by young Jews in Poland and Russia after they had completed their daily religious studies in the yeshivas (Lebeson 1975). Indeed, Weber (1968: 622-623) himself pointed to the kinship of Puritanism and Calvinism with Judaism. Weber noted Puritans felt their similarity to Judaism. Jews were welcome in Puritan areas. In the United States, for example, they were admitted without much ado whatsoever.

The linkage of Protestant sectarian and Jewish values to the bourgeois market ethic and the classic laissez faire liberalism of Americanism is to be noted in the closing decades of this century in the relationship which Margaret Thatcher (Blond 1988: 14-15) has had to British Jews. She admires them as hardworking, self-made, people who believe that God helps those who help themselves. She chose to represent the most Jewish district in Britain, Finchley, and appointed five Jews to cabinet posts at different times. She also designated the Chief Rabbi, Immanuel Jakobovits, as a member of the House of Lords. In commenting on the latter action, various British publications noted that she much prefers the tough minded self-help work-oriented values of the Chief Rabbi to the soft Tory welfare emphasis of the Archbishop of Canterbury.

Moreover, Margaret Thatcher detests the aristocracy and especially the Queen. The differences which newspapers reported from time to time between her and the Queen were not just an argument between two ladies who somehow did not like each other. They were a disagreement between one, the Queen, who represented the essence of Tory *noblesse oblige* and aristocratic values, and another, who embodies the essence of bourgeois egalitarian competitive values, norms which Thatcher found prevalent in America and among Jews. As a classical liberal, she strongly emphasized these values and saw them practiced by Jews (Thatcher 1993).

From its origins, America has been a universalistic culture, slavery and the black situation apart (a big "apart"). Nevertheless, it is true. America has been the purest example of a bourgeois society, one that has followed capitalist market norms uninterfered with by beliefs derived from feudalism. These norms assume, and America as the purest market economy or society embodies, an emphasis on the values of meritocracy, on a society open to talent, open to the most efficient, to the most competent. As the self-conscious center of liberal and increasingly populist revolutions from 1776 on, the United States has been viewed by Americans and others as open to newcomers. One becomes an American by joining the party, accepting the Creed. This, of course, is what Jews were able to do here. Americans encouraged Jews to play an equal role. This is explicit in George Washington's message to the Jews of Newport in 1790. In it, he said that in the United States all possess alike the liberty of conscience and the immunities of citizenship. Even more significantly the first President emphasized that the patronizing concept of toleration of one class of people by another has no place in America. Jews are as much American, and on the same basis, as everyone else. Washington (1895: 91-92) was condemning the idea of tolerance in 1790, saying that it is an invidious concept, that if Jews are "tolerated" they are inferior. At a time when Jews had no rights anywhere in the world except perhaps in the emerging French Revolution, Washington recognized that the concept of tolerance denotes second class citizenship. Jefferson and Madison also noted that America was different from Europe, that the discrimination against Judaism prevailing there did not exist here. In Jefferson's words all were on an equal footing in the United States. Jefferson rejoiced over the presence of Jews in the country because they would ensure the religious diversity which in his judgement is the best protector of liberty.

One can describe many events in American history which reflect the positive relationship between Americanism and Americans on the one hand and Judaism on the other. John Adams, our second President, was a Zionist long before there were many Jewish Zionists. One of the most amazing laws enacted in America or any other place was passed in 1810, the Sunday Mails bill, which provided that the mails be delivered on Sunday and that certain government offices be kept open on that day (Rohrer 1987). The law was much debated of course. Yet, in 1836, a Senate majority reaffirmed that, as they put it, "Jews, Mohammedans, Infidels and Atheists have the same rights as Christians in the United States." Some Senators, among them some deeply devout Protestant sectarians, noted that the idea that America is a Christian country is wrong, that every religious group is equal in this country. Of course, I do not mean to imply we have had no anti-Semitism here. We obviously have. There have been serious waves of anti-Semitism. One of the worst occurred in the 1930s. However, scholars agree that on the comparative scale there is no country which has been as open and as accepting of Jews as the United States has been. I think one can safely say that the State of Israel would not be in the situation it is in today if it were not for the help and the support it received, and continues to secure, from the United States. While many can debate as to why the United States has been supportive of the State of Israel, it is important to recognize that in diplomatic discourse which long preceded the founding of the State of Israel the United States repeatedly evinced a concern for the position of the Jews. A book which came out in the 1940s dealing with the diplomatic memoranda or concerns of the United States about Jews in the rest of the world reports that starting in 1840, with respect to the persecution of Jews in Syria, down to the 1920s, the State Department often and consistently sought to intervene on behalf of Jews against anti-Semitic activities (Adler and Margalith 1943). From the time that Czarist pogroms became a public issue in the 1880s, the State Department sent memos almost every year to Russia complaining about the treatment of Jews. There are memoranda from Secretaries of State to ambassadors to Romania and Russia and other places which instruct them that it has been the historic and consistent policy of the United States to be concerned with the position of the Hebrew people and to demand that they receive the same rights as everyone else. These efforts to protect or support the Jews in Eastern Europe could not be explained by the existence of an AIPAC or its equivalent. To the contrary, they reflected the sense of identity which many American Protestants felt with the Jews and their outrage about persecution. The eventual concern of the United States for the State of Israel may be viewed as a continuation of this pattern.

It is, of course, true that the record of the United States with respect to the Holocaust and persecution of the Jews in the 1930s was not a good one. One should not respond to this with any degree of denial. It is a fact. The only thing that can be said is that the record of all other countries was as bad, in many cases worse. There is a book about Canada, *None Is Too Many* (Abella 1983), documenting Canada's record. It would not admit a single Jew during the 1930s. However, as significant as the failure of the nations of the world to help Jews is, the fact is the Yishuv in Palestine did not have a great record for saving East European Jewry either. Ben Gurion and others did not put a great priority on rescuing the Eastern European Jews.[1]

Thankfully, the problem of survival facing Diaspora Jewry in the West is not one of persecution. In America it is assimilation, a process which goes back to colonial days and continues down to the present. It is interesting to note, for example, that there were 250,000 German Jews in the United States in 1880, before the East European migration. If these people had all stayed Jewish, millions of their descendants would be Jewish today. But they are not. Their numbers did not decline because they were persecuted. They fell off because they intermarried. Indeed, if you trace the descendants of colonial families, as Earl Raab and I report in a recently completed book on the American Jewish Community, you will discover early Jewish settler families in Georgia and other places who remained Jewish for a long time, but are now Christian. For example, there are the Sheftalls of Georgia. The family is still there; there are people of that name. If you interview them you discover they know their ancestors were Jewish. However, by some point in the nineteenth century or earlier, many of them ceased being Jewish. The fact of intermarriage, of assimilation, has reduced the number of Jews in the American population.

At the present time, we have a community which has five or six million members, but which is on the whole secularized. While the majority of Jews do adhere in one way or another to a Jewish denomination, they have a lower rate of synagogue attendance and of religious observance than the Christian community. Jews, as NJPS has documented, currently have an extremely high rate of intermarriage. Depending on which analysis of the data is used, somewhere between 50 and 57 percent of marriages involving Jews in the five year period between 1985 and 1990 were with non-Jews. Moreover, the rate of conversion by non-Jews married to Jews has not been increasing. Indeed, it has been going down. Furthermore, while the majority of Jewish partners in intermarried couples tend to look on their families as Jewish, their children are less involved, less committed, less likely to be Jewishly educated (Lipset 1994). Thus, the pattern of assimilation into the larger community which undermined the German Jews in America is now happening to those whose families came from Eastern Europe.

There are two factors, other than religious commitment, which have operated in this country to keep Jews Jewish: one, is anti-Semitism, or more correctly foreboding about anti-Semitism and relations with the larger community; the second is commitment to the state of Israel and the role which Israel plays in the commitment of American and other Diaspora Jews to Jewishness. As many have said, Israel has become the religion of the Jewish people, a secular one of course.

These two secular conditions are declining, weakening considerably. First, in spite of the fact that we have periodic incidents of antiSemitism, which I think are over dramatized, anti-Semitism has continued to decline in this country. As Lucy Dawidowicz (1982: 51) once pointed out, there is almost no position that is not open to Jews in this country. Some of the statistics noted above are an indication of such openness, as are public opinion data showing a steady fall in acceptance of anti-Semitic sentiments. Second, as the Middle East moves towards peace, the anxiety which American Jews have had about Israel should decline and their commitments to Jewish organizations which their concerns inspired will also fall off. In fact, data from NJPS indicates that the proportion of Jews who say they are committed, or, in the terms the survey used, anxious or concerned about Israel, declines sharply with age. Younger Jews are much less dedicated than older ones. Projecting an America which is even less anti-Semitic and a world in which Israel is much more secure provokes the question what will keep American Jews Jewish, what will prevent them from melting in the melting pot.[2]

It is difficult for any group to maintain its identity unless it has a solid core. Fortunately, Jews do have such a core, one which has maintained them. For the most part, of course, that core has been religion. However, religious identification has grown weaker. Thus, we have to recognize that in the future we are going to be dealing with a remnant. Of course, such a problem has beset Jews of all generations. In the past, many Jews stopped being Jewish for good reasons, if you consider assimilation good, or for bad ones such as persecution. Hence, a great concern has developed among Jewish philanthropists, scholars, community leaders and others who care about Jewish continuity to identify what might be done to improve the possibilities for the maintenance of a sizeable Jewish community.

It is necessary to be realistic in this regard. We have to recognize that unless conditions turn very bad, unless there is a serious revival of anti-Semitism and/or serious threats to the State of Israel, a sharp decline in the number of Jews is likely.

In closing, I would like to just raise an issue for further study. Perhaps it goes beyond the sociology of the Jews per se. The question was raised for me by a judge in Washington who inquires every time I meet him, "How many people are there in the United States who are of Jewish ancestry and know it?" I always promise to get the answer for him, but, in fact, I never have. My best guess is that it would be in the order of 10 million. Does it make any difference to these people that they are of aware of their Jewish ancestry? There is some evidence that it does. They are not Jews by any criterion commonly used to determine who is a Jew. Nevertheless, having a Jewish background in the American context is not viewed negatively, as it once was everywhere in the Diaspora. Here and now part-Jews can feel proud of their ancestry, and tell their children about their Jewish background. Many read books about Jews and have some sense of interest and involvement in things "Jewish." I think such a background plays a positive role. I suspect it affects political opinions. Thus, we should be interested not simply in the question of who is a Jew and how do Jews behave but in the Jewish impact on American society, I suggest the next population survey should also look at people who are part Jewish. It should do so not because we want to identify them as Jews, but to understand the contribution Jews have made to America.

Notes

1.   I think one of the problems is that during the 1930s, neither Jews nor non-Jews really believed the Holocaust was happening. It is true they were all told about it. It was described in horrific detail by eyewitnesses who came to Washington and to Palestine. However, I think the reaction of everybody, including Jews, was: "Of course it is terrible. Terrible things are happening. People are being killed, but it is impossible for anyone to believe that there is a systematic effort to wipe out all Jews in Europe." The reports were not dismissed, they were ignored because the dominant view was that the most important task was to defeat the Nazis. The notion that six million would be killed was so unimaginable that leaders ranging from Franklin Roosevelt to David Ben Gurion could not really accept it. They did not act as if they believed it. Nevertheless, the failure to act is a very negative aspect of record.

2.   I should note here parenthetically that all the talk about the extent to which the revival, supposed revival, of identity and multiculturalism is upsetting the melting pot is exaggerated. Of course, feelings about the position of Blacks have led to strong concern, discussion and interest in the idea of maintaining the culture of ethnic groups. Yet, the intermarriage rates among whites show there is almost a random distribution of groups intermarrying. Eighty percent of the Irish are married to non-Irish; the majority of Japanese Americans are wed to people of non-Japanese background; the majority of Catholics are married to non-Catholics. Jews, with an intermarriage rate of 57%, in the five years preceding the 1990 NJPS, tend to be less intermarried than some other groups, but the percentage is going up. The United States is a country in which there is "melting," in which whites are "melting." The most rapidly growing ethnic group in the United States in terms of identification is "European American." One-third of all Americans when offered choices of what their identity is, say, "European." Of course, this response may be a counter-reaction to the idea of "African American." If there are "African Americans," then them must be "European Americans." However, it is also a reaction to the fact that many have a mixture of Irish, Italian, and Jewish grandparents and do not know what to call themselves other than "European."

References

Abella, Irving. 1983. *None is Too Many: Canada and the Jews of Europe, 1933-1948.* New York: Random House.

Adler, Cyrus and Aaron M. Margalith. 1943. *American Intercession on Behalf of Jews in the Diplomatic Correspondence of the United States 1840-1938.* New York: American Jewish Historical Society.

Blond, Anthony. 1988. "The Jews and Mrs.Thatcher." *The Sunday Telegraph.* December 11.

Cohen, Steven M. 1989. *The Dimensions of American Jewish Liberalism.* New York: American Jewish Committee.

Dawidowicz, Lucy S. 1982. On *Equal Terms: Jews in America* 1881-1981. New York: Holt, Rinehart and Winston.

Feingold, Henry L. 1982. A *Midrash on American Jewish History.* Albany: State University of New York Press.

Goldscheider, Calvin and Alan S. Zuckerman. 1986. *The Transformation of the Jews.* Chicago: University of Chicago Press.

Kadushin, Charles. 1974. *The American Intellectual Elite.* Boston: Little Brown.

Kosmin, Barry A. 1988. "The Dimensions of Contemporary Jewish Philanthropy." Unpublished paper, North American Jewish Data Bank: City University of New York.

Kosmin, Barry A. and Seymour P. Lachman. 1993. *One Nation Under God: Religion In Contemporary American Society. New* York: Harmony Books.

Lebeson, Anita Libman. 1975. *Pilgrim People.* New York: Minerva Press.

Lipset, Seymour Martin. 1955. "Jewish Sociologists and Sociologists of the Jews," *Jewish Social Studies.* 17: 177-178.

—. 1980. "Predicting the Future of Post-Industrial Society," Pp. 2-35 in *The Third Century: America as a Post-Industrial Society* edited by S. M. Lipset. Chicago: University of Chicago Press.

—. 1989. "A Unique People in an Exceptional Country." Pp. 3-29 in *American Pluralism and the Jewish Community* edited by S. M. Lipset. New Brunswick, NJ: Transaction Books.

—. 1994. *The Educational Background of American Jews.* Boston and Los Angeles: The Wilstein Institute.

Lipset, Seymour Martin and Everett Carl Ladd. 1971. 'Jewish Academics in the United States: Their Achievements, Culture and Politics,' *American Jewish Year Book* 72: 87-128.

Park Robert E. 1950. *Race and Culture.* Glencoe, IL: The Free Press.

Rohrer, James R. 1987. "The Sunday Mails and the Church-State Theme in Jacksonian America." *Journal of the Early Republic* 7: 53-115.

Rothman, Stanley, Robert Lichter and Linda Lichter. Forthcoming. *Elites in Conflict: Social Change in America Today.* Westport, CT: Greenwook/Praeger Press.

Sklare, Marshall. 1955. *Conservative Judaism: An American Religious Movement.* Glencoe, IL. The Free Press.

—. 1993. *Understanding America's Jews* edited by Jonathan D. Sarna. Hanover, NH: University Press of New England.

Thatcher, Margaret. 1993. *The Downing Street Years.* New York: Harper Collins Press.

Washington, George. 1895. "Washington's Reply to the Hebrew Congregation in Newport, Rhode Island." *Publications of the American Jewish Historical Society.* No. 3: 91-92.

Weber, Max. 1935. *The Protestant Ethic and the Spirit of Capitalism.* New York: Scribner.

—. 1968. *Economy and Society I.* Berkeley: University of California Press.

Zuckerman, Harriet. 1977. *Scientific Elite: Nobel Laureates in the United States.* New York: Columbia University Press.

Postmodernism and the Construction of Ethnocultural Identity: The Jewish-Indian Theory and the Lost Tribes of Israel

Stanford M. Lyman

Abstract: *Ten of the original 12 tribes that comprised the ancient Hebrew people disappeared from conventional history and other secular annals in 722 B.C.E., when the Northern Kingdom of Israel was overrun by the Assyrians and its people sent into exile. However, sacred histories and biblical prophecies held that the 10 Lost Tribes would be reunited with their tribal brethren descended from the Southern Kingdom of Judea in the coming messianic age. A quest for the descendants of the lost tribes has begun many times, usually associated with the resolution of immediate, local, secular, or sacred issues that emerged in a particular era and at a particular place. Various peoples (e.g., the Falasha of Ethiopia, the Lemba of Zimbabwe, the Pachucans of Mexico, the imperial family of Japan, the British Israelites) have proclaimed themselves to be, or have been designated as, the saving remnants of the lost tribes. Among these are the aborigines of Ecuador, Florida, western Georgia, and New England, each group of which has been the subject of occasional intensive and always controversial identification as Jews. In the processes entailed in the rise, vicissitudes, and fall of the Jewish-Indian theory is revealed a proto-postmodern mode of ethnoreligious group construction and collective identity formation.*

"What we call serious criticism," wrote Sanford Budick (1996:6) in a discussion of the crises attending the current interest in alterity, "is occasioned when something formerly considered significant has been lost or cut off in our understanding, so that a separation (or clarification) and decision must be made." Of such things said to be cut off and long missing, one may include the fate, real and imagined, of the lost tribes of Israel, that is, the tribes of Reuben, Simeon, Dan, Naphtali, Gad, Asher, Issachar, Zebulon, Ephraim, and one half of the tribe of Manasseh. These tribal groups comprised the biblically identified Hebrew denizens of the Northern Kingdom of Israel who were exiled and dispersed from their homeland when it was conquered and despoiled by the Assyrians in 722 B.C.E. From that date forward, the mystery of the disappearance of the 10 tribes from history has inspired very few scholarly inquiries but much questing in search of its solution.

Modernist Jewish historians, as well as most secular investigators of

antiquity (Grant 1984:121,164, 272), appear to have accepted as unchallenge-
able truth a conclusion that severs from the annals of the peoples descended
from Judea (i.e., the kingdom that did not succumb to the Assyrians) the
oblivion into which the 10 tribes are alleged to have sunk. As Erich Kahler
(1885-1970) put it, "The Assyrians, who ... destroyed the North Kingdom, . . .
carried . . . the vanquished into exile. The majority of them . . . dispersed and
. . . merged with other populations, sharing the fate of many peoples and realms
which perished in the turmoil of human history" (1989:xvi). For Kahler, it is the
later exile from Judea that convokes the beginning of a Judaic community as
well as the onset of anti-Jewish modernity: "The characteristic and recurring
hostility toward Judaism has its origin in the decisive downfall of 586 B.C. For
the fall of Judea as an independent state means the rise of Judaism" (P. xvi). It
was the Babylonian rather than the Assyrian exile, Kahler asserted, that gave
the Jewish community its peculiar coherence:

> This community . . . began to establish itself on a new symbolic plane
> without losing its connection with the old tribal cult, with the
> promised homeland, and, indeed, with the advent of a concrete day of
> fulfillment. (P. xvii)

However, religious prophecy holds that the 10 tribes must have
survived and that one day they will be reunited with the descendants of their
Judean coreligionists in a reconstituted Jewish state. Ancient Zion had been the
geocultural center of a theocratically driven civilization established by the
Hebrews, a patriarchically organized people. At an earlier time, the Hebrews
had fled Egypt under Moses and, after wandering in the desert for 40 years,
defeated the peoples of Canaan, settling on a land vouchsafed to them by God
(Elazar 1995:155-160; Walzer 1985). As settlers they were not inclined to
become permanent bedouins. As a leading scholar of the latter, Anatoly M.
Khazanov (1994), has observed, "There is no reason to look upon the
inhabitants of the steppe, [including such peoples as] the . . . ancient Jews . . .
as real nomads" (P. 98). Rather, they remained a spiritual, land-rooted
peoplehood who, since the beginning of their diaspora, are in quest of a return
to their homeland (Kahler 1989:1-30). To sacred historians, the 10 tribes (here,
I transpose words describing the effects of the later Roman assault on Hebraic
culture to the alleged response of the earlier exiles from the Northern Kingdom)
are credited with having carried the "culture of the Land . . . into the great
Diaspora, where it was preserved in the minds of Jews who for [more than] two
thousand years truly inhabited a cerebral version of the Land" (Erlich
1995:199). That "cerebral version of the Land" and its putative representatives
are the topic of this investigation.

The Texts of Israelite Survival

In one sense, this study is a particularistic elaboration of Tamar Garb's (1995) postmodern approach to The Jew in the Text in that, like Garb, I seek

> to focus attention on a number of specific instances in which a complex, sometimes contradictory construction of Jewishness, Jewish history, or Jewish memory either forms the central theme or motif of a work or problematizes its very mode of address. (P. 29)

However, whereas Garb and her colleagues drew their conclusions from the many and varied representations of Jews in the 19th- and 20th-century Occident, I have turned my attention to the "texts" proclaiming a postbiblical and non-Occidental Jewish presence that is hidden away in the modern world. In this study, I examine the conjectures, histories, and theosophies of those who see the descendants of the lost 10 tribes of Israel in the countenances, culture, and color of 17th-century Ecuadorean Indians. In the centuries since that time, other peoples have been singled out as descendants of the 10 tribes (e.g., the entire nation of Japan or, alternatively, its imperial rulers; various peoples of Africa and Asia; and the self-proclaimed "British Israelites." These are, however, only a few of the numerous peoples said to descend from the people exiled from the Northern Kingdom. In all of these assertions, two basic theses are being proclaimed: (a) that a prophetic promise and eschatological prediction are about to be fulfilled in defiance of insurmountable odds and (b) that a peoplehood of antiquity has persevered in a separate diaspora (Avichail 1990) that parallels that of the Jews in the Occident (Keller 1969; Sachar 1995; E. Levine 1986). Moreover, in the contexts in which Israelite ancestry claims are put forward (e.g., identifying such peoples as South American Indians, the imperial family if not the entire nation of Japan, American priests of British Israelite Christian identity, or others from various parts of the African and Asian world as epigoni of the long-lost Israelites) there are also to be found pursuits of a decidedly inner worldly and secular character; in the case of the Ecuadorean aborigines, an attempt to influence Lord Cromwell and gain the repeal of England's ban on Jewish immigration; in the case of the Japanese nation, the rescue of thousands of European Jews from the Nazi Holocaust; in that of the British Israelites-Christian Identity movement, the murder of Medgar Evers, attempts on the lives of American Jewish leaders, and the formation of the Aryan Nation; and in that of the several Afro-Asian designates, the right to settle in the modern state of Israel. In this essay, I discuss only that of the Ecuadorean Indians.

The Charisma of Nonlinear Time and Space

Assertions of lost Israelite identity entail an instantiation of the ambivalence contained in Fredric Jameson's (1991:297-418) conceptualization of "disjunctive social time." Jameson's idea has been reframed by Homi K. Bhabha (1984:217):

> There is, on the one hand, a recognition of the interstitial, disjunctive spaces and signs crucial for the emergence of the new historical subjects . . . However, . . . Jameson disavows the temporality of displacement which is, quite literally, its medium of communication. For Jameson, the possibility of becoming historical demands a containment of this disjunctive social time.

In the cases of the several putative inheritors of lost tribes identity, however, the disjunction involves a displacement of both social time and social space (Bammer 1994), as well as a "containment" that somehow attaches the newly recognized identity onto the corpus of conventional history. All this is made difficult by the claim that the habitats at which one or another of the remnants of the lost tribes are alleged to reside consist not only of specific places of landed settlement, but also of such "nonplaces" as in Mormon belief (Brough 1994), to take an outstanding example, on an unknown planet, in an undiscovered cave or volcano, or at the North Pole, thus making these tribal survivors, if nothing else, an appropriate topic for the "anthropology of supermodernity" (Augé 1995) and a strategic situs on which to construct alternative ethnocultural maps of meaning (Jackson 1994).

   The 10 tribes of Israel have been lost from—and lost to—conventional modes of secular temporal historiography. They thus present those scholars who enquire after them with a special problem: how a prophetic cosmology of survival, remembrance, and ultimate reunification can be fitted into the widely accepted and conventional knowledge of events past and present (Handelman and Katz 1995:75-85). In fact, however, the sense of *duree* that stands behind claims of the continued existence of Israel's lost tribes belongs not to what Maurice Natanson (1968:172-177) once referred to as "Big History"—that is, the metanarratives that postmodernists claim to have evicted from their place in hegemonic Occidental scholarship—but rather to what Carl Becker noted is the "kind of history that has [the] most influence upon the life of the community[:] . . . the history that common people carry around in their heads" (Snyder 1958:61; Zerubavel 1995:3). Such modes of history have their own tracks of time (Lyman and Scott 1989:35-50) and their own topologies of space (Lyman and Scott 1989:22-34, 51-59, 182-190), and these do not—and need not—necessarily correspond to the accepted linear or cyclical time-and-space dimensions of authorized histories. At present, in the case of the lost tribes of Israel, the spatiotemporal accounts and conjectures of their allegedly living descendants partake of a dual cosmology: one, inner worldly, for example, entitling those such as the Beta Israel of Ethiopia (Leslau 1969; Ashkenazi and Weingrod 1987; Kaplan 1992), who are recognized as legitimate heirs of the ancient Hebrew peoplehood (or, more generally, to be authentic Jews), to settle in the modern state of Israel under its "Law of Return" (Isaacs and Olitzky 1995:212-226); the other, eschatological, fulfilling biblical prophecy and heralding the coming of a messianic age (Avichail 1990:56-62). In either perspective, understanding the present entails interpreting the past, that is, grasping the nomothetic through the prism of the idiographic (Hay 1990: 20-37). Whether inner worldly or esoteric, each perspective maintains a belief in destiny, in a particular teleology. The latter belief at first seems to stand against the postmodern opposition to and deconstruction of preordained futures, but ultimately—eschatologically, that is—embraces what Mikhail N. Epstein (1995) has described as the central temporal feature of the futurology of the *nouvelle vague:*

> The future was thought to be definite, attainable, and realizable; in other words, it was given the attributes of the past. Postmodernism, with its aversion to utopias, inverted the signs and reached for the past, but in so doing, gave it the attributes of the future: indeterminateness, incomprehensibility, polysemy, and the ironic play of possibilities. . . . Postmodernism announced an "end to time," but any end serves to open at least a crack in time for what is to come after and, thus, indicates the self-irony of finality, which turns into yet another beginning. (Epstein 1995:330-331)

The quest for the lost tribes of Israel focuses on one or another present-day people, prismatically perceived as a survivor of a lost past and serving to predict and fulfill a foreordained future.

However, each time a specific claim of lost tribe identity is put forward, it produces what the sociological historiographer Frederick J. Teggart (1925:82-86, 107-149, 180-194) called an "intrusion." An intrusion operates on conventional history by challenging its spatiotemporal horizon, forcing into liminality a hitherto buried consciousness that the latter's pregiven unquestionableness can no longer be accepted as such (Schutz 1966:93-98), or with the same effect that an ethnomethodological experiment is likely to have on its unwitting subjects (Garfinkel 1967)—namely, it interrupts the flow of happenings as they are understood in the prevailing but implicit hermeneutic of everyday life and brings to the surface of perception an epistemologically piercing moment. In the case of the lost tribes, the veil of history is torn and its less than secure bases exposed. From that moment (often experienced as crucial, decisive, or a turning point—a reconfiguration of both history and historiography—one that incorporates or coopts the newly recognized lost tribes) is, at the very least, entertainable. As is shown in what follows, recognizing a people as one or all of the lost tribes of Israel is one of those rare but significant moments that thematizes the idiographic horizons of the *Lebenswelt* (Schutz 1966:116-132), that requires a reconceptualization of past, present, and future. Indeed, such an event opens a fissure in the spatiotemporal world, or widens one that has already been noticed but uncontained.

The Indians of the Americas as Lost Israelites

Christopher Columbus's 15th-century Caribbean encounter with the people now known as Tainos (Rouse 1992; Keegan 1992) introduced a crisis in biblically based European cosmology. That crisis could only be resolved by insisting that these "Indians," as Columbus miscalled them, be regarded as descendants of some prehistoric migrants from Eurasia or Africa (Huddleston 1967), that is, the land base from which humankind originated. Although over the centuries since Columbus's voyages there have been many claimants to the title of Amerindian forefatherhood—and at least one hypothesis of reverse migration from ancient America to Asia, Africa, and Europe (Lyman 1990:22-75)—one that had a brief but portentous effect on future events was presented in epistolary form to a Protestant divine on November 25, 1649, by the rabbinical leader of Amsterdam's Jewish community, Menasseh ben Israel (1604-1657; Roth 1934:176-273). The letter—replying to the storm of curiosity that had arisen in England and The Netherlands over Menasseh's earlier recounting of the story brought to him by Aaron Levi de Montezinos, a crypto-Jew, to the effect that one part of the remnants of the lost tribe of Reuben now dwelt beyond the Cordillera mountains in the interior of the Spanish colony of New Granada (Ecuador) and that the tribe of Joseph lived on an island nearby (Roth 1934:176-181)—promised publication of a treatise in which the learned rabbi would

> handle of the first inhabitants of America which I believe were of the Ten Tribes; moreover, that they are scattered also in other Countries, that they keep their true Religion, as hoping to returne againe into the Holy Land in due time. (Roth 1934:184).

Thus, in this letter is contained each of the elements of a historical-hermeneutic intrusion: A disputed thesis of ancient Jewish history is offered not only as factual, but also as proved to be so by the proffered fact that at least one of the tribes had survived expulsion, global dispersion, and the travails of more than 2,000 years of exile with its culture and belief system still intact. Further, the prophetic promise of homeland return and redemptive reunification with both the other surviving Israelite remnants as well as the descendants of the people derived from the Southern Kingdom, the latter in diaspora since 70 C.E., seemed about to be fulfilled. In its 17th-century appearance, the "Jewish-Indian theory"—which would reappear in the 18th and 19th centuries and have disparate effects on aspects of Jewish (Feingold 1974:3-5, 25-27, 65-67), Christian (Even [1861] 1977), and secular political thought and praxis (Adair [1775] 1930; Spence [1914] 1994)—also provided the basis and the occasion for Menasseh ben Israel's bold attempt to reshape England's immigration policy. In force since 1290 C.E., an English royal edict had banned Jews from its soil (Roth 1934:225-273). Menasseh's version of the Jewish-Indian theory thus became an (unsuccessful) instrument for bringing about the revocation of a centuries-old discriminatory statute, a feat the Amsterdam rabbi nearly accomplished by inserting both Jewish and Christian eschatologies into Cromwell's secular national policy considerations.

Menasseh's book-length version of the lost tribes' history not only incorporated Montezino's Ecuadorean Indian thesis into the religious cosmology on the matter, but also took care to allow for a diasporic dispersion to have placed the several long-lost tribes in virtually every part of the, world. Thus, after asserting that

> I . . . doe finde no opinion more probable, nor agreeable to reason, then that of our Montezinus, who saith, that the first inhabitants of America, were the ten Tribes of the Israelites. . . . who . . . (as God would have it) hid themselves behind the Mountaines Cordillerae.

Menasseh went on to observe that, in his own disquisition on the subject,

> I [shall] also shew, that as they were not driven out at once from their Country, so also they were scattered into divers Provinces, sc. into America, into Tartary, into China, into Media, to the Sabbaticall River, and into AEthiopia. (Ausubel 1975:520-521)

Their supposed dispersion over most of the Earth was of crucial importance to Menasseh's twofold purpose: to divulge new proofs that biblical prophecy was being fulfilled and to argue that only England's edict prohibiting Jewish immigration stood in the way of their biblically foretold global dispersion. Once completed, the worldwide Jewish diaspora would herald the beginning of the much hoped-for messianic era.

As to the first issue, prophetic eschatology, Menasseh pointed out that he could

> prove that the ten Tribes never returned to the second Temple, that
> they yet keepe the Law of Moses, and our sacred Rites; and [that he
> could predict with confidence that they] at last shall return into their
> Land, with the two Tribes, Judah and Benjamin; and shall be
> governed by one Prince, who is Messiah the son of David. (Ausubel
> 1975:521)

However, to succeed in his political, this-worldly goal, the repeal of England's anti-Jewish immigration edict, Menasseh sought to insert his religiocosmological time-and-space hermeneutic of the 10 tribes into conventional and contemporary English historicopolitical beliefs and practices. Moreover, he appeared to be ecumenical in his outlook, merging Judaic with Christian messianic prophecies in a manner that would win the support of Oliver Cromwell's Puritan regime. In this regard, Menasseh was aided not only by the fact that in England he was already regarded as "the principal exponent of Jewish science" (Roth 1934:65), but also by a parallel, development of the Jewish-Indian theory among Protestant divines and English missionaries to the New World. There was, in addition, growing support among Cromwell's Puritan admirers for the exhibition of a greater tolerance toward the once despised Jews, "the people of God" (Roth 1934:191-202), than was then being expressed by their Spanish Catholic rivals for an American imperium.

Although such English ministers of the gospel as Thomas Thorowgood and John Durie took to embellishing their own view that the Indians of the Americas were Jews—making contact with Menasseh and adding their support to his thesis, but perceiving it as an added proof of their own belief that the Jewish Indians were divinely destined to receive the blessings of conversion to Judaism's successor religion, Christianity—Menasseh found the linchpin for his own practical project in the homiletic he put forward as the appropriate Christian, as well as Jewish, interpretation of a prophecy found in Daniel 12.7: "When he shall have accomplished to scatter the power of the holy people, all these things shall be finished." However, precisely because it was possible to translate the phrase *scatter the power to breaking the power* (Tanakh 1985:1492), Menasseh could not rest his case on the ambiguity contained in that biblical utterance. Hence, he turned to a verse in the Book of Deuteronomy, 28.64, wherein it is written "And the Lord shall scatter thee among all people, from one end of the earth even unto the other" (Roth 1934:207). Seizing on this phrase and combining it with that of the prophecies in the Book of Daniel, Menasseh contrived an argument that held that Cromwell's Puritan republic was the land referred to by the Hebrew Deuteronomic term *Kezeh ha-Arez*, often translated into French as *angle-terre*, or the *end of the earth*, that is,

England. As Menasseh presented the matter, now that Montezino had found Jews among the Indians of the New World, only the admission of Jews into England was necessary to fulfill the Lord's promise of a completed global Jewish dispersion, the prelude to the coming of the messianic age.

Building on this thesis, Menasseh was eventually able to convince Lord Cromwell to convoke a council to deliberate on the matter of the repeal. The council did not act in the way he desired, however, and Cromwell, though he sought to connive at it in a different way, never issued the proposed edict of repeal.

Nevertheless, Menasseh's proposal proved to be prescient. His petition was an early appeal not only for toleration with respect to Jewish entrance to England—which, incidentally, was granted to the Jews in 1663, after the restored monarch bestowed it on them in gratitude to those other Dutch Jews who, opposed to Menasseh's approach, had aided the deposed Prince Charles during his period of continental exile (Roth 1934:274-284)—but also for a communally based form of surveilled civil rights. For Menasseh had used his Jewish-Indian thesis to request that Jews be readmitted to England not merely as alien settlers but as a communally recognized people equal to others in English law. To secure these rights, he proposed

> that all laws against them should be repealed; that the principal public officers . . . be made to take an oath to defend them; that public synagogues . . . be permitted in all parts of the English dominions, as well as cemeteries outside the cities for the burial of the dead; that they . . . be granted free full liberties of trade; and that the privilege of internal jurisdiction (subject to the right of appeal to the civil judges) . . . be conceded to the heads of the community for the time being. (Roth 1934:231-232)

Further, and in a promise of fealty to the English polity, Menasseh's petition to Cromwell required that those Jews who chose to emigrate to England would "swear allegiance to the government and . . . [allow themselves to] be kept under the strictest surveillance" (Roth 1934:232). Despite Menasseh's 20th-century biographer's belief that what he was proposing "was one of those closely controlled, semi-autonomous communities of the sort tolerated in . . . Hamburg or Leghorn" (Roth 1934:232), and that if his petition had been granted, "With the slightest modification in public opinion, the Ghetto might have been introduced in all of its German or Italian severity" (Roth 1934:283), it is worthy of note that—Menasseh's petition having failed to be accepted—the very same debate over Jewish identity, loyalty, religion, and destiny that had marked and marred Cromwell's councillors' sessions (Roth 1934:225-273) was renewed in England in the 19th century as a part of that country's determination to remain a Christian nation and its leaders' worry over the effects of increasing tides of Jewish immigration from eastern Europe (Gartner, 1960; Aris 1970; Feldman 1994; Bermant 1970, 1975).

English suspicion of the Jews continued through the first half of the 20th century. England would be in the forefront of those Occidental polities that did little to save continental Jews from the Nazi Holocaust (Wasserstein 1979; Penkower 1983; Abella 1982). Indeed, England's World War II Jewish policies spoke loudly about but did nothing to ameliorate the plight of Jews then desperately in search of the kind of haven that Menasseh had sought so earnestly, and had sought to build on the basis of an extraordinary claim of a Jewish connection to the pre-Columbian aborigines of America. In fact, while England and America dawdled (Wyman 1984, [1968] 1985; Morse 1983; Feingold 1970; Dinnerstein 1982), in Fascist Italy (Caracciolo 1995) and militaristic Japan (Sugihara 1995; Tokayer and Swartz 1979; Levine 1996) efforts to rescue Jews from the terror of Hitler's Holocaust proved quite effective.

The Jewish-Indian Theory in America

Although the Jewish-Indian theory proved neither necessary nor sufficient to effect Menasseh's immigration project, once having been enunciated it became sedimented in the arcana of lore about the Israelites. However, Menasseh was not the originator of the claim that ancient Jews had somehow gotten to America; rather, he was the first Jew to adapt it to Jewish sacred and secular interests. The theory appears to have originated among Iberian commentators on the encounters of Columbus and later Spanish conquistadores with the aborigines of America and the Caribbean (Huddleston 1967:33-40, 128-138). Menasseh's treatise on the subject went through numerous editions and several translations, *The Hope of Israel* having appeared in English as recently as 1901 and in Spanish in 1929 (Huddleston 1967:131). If nothing else, its continued popularity calls attention to the instability of racial and ethnoreligious categories of classification that are still in use and that have become grist for the postmodernists' critical mill.

However, as Simon Schama (1995:24) has pointed out, "Unstable identities are history's prey." Such has been the case with the Jewish-Indian theory. In the centuries since Menasseh's death, it has been revived intermittently, almost always in service to Jewish or Christian eschatological interests as well as mundane secular interests. Thus, in 1775, in the most well-known instance, James W. Adair, an 18th-century historian of the American Indians, put forward no fewer than 23 arguments in support of his claim that the aborigines of Florida, with whom he had lived for several years, were descendants of the lost tribes and that, because of this, their territory ought to be wrested from Catholic Spain and its anti-Jewish Inquisition by means of an Anglo-Indian alliance (Adair [1775] 1930:16-230, 481-497). To evangelical Protestants, seeking converts among the Indians, as Bernard W. Sheehan (1974) has pointed out, "Coupling the Indians with the Jews yielded obvious theoretical advantages. . . . [For, because] the European man had his spiritual origin in Israel, it would certainly improve the anomalistic situation of the Indian to find his historical beginnings there."

However, biblical exegetes among the missionaries to New England worried over the contradictions that a close reading of their sacred literature seemed to suggest. Insistent on their belief in a Puritan variant of what is now known as flood ethnology (Numbers 1992), pious evangelists of colonial New England knew that the Indians could not be autochthonous to America, but they worried over whether the aborigines they encountered were descendants of the accursed son of Ham (Jordan 1968:17-20, 35-62, 84, 111, 158, 243, 246, 525) and, therefore, perhaps beyond salvation; or whether, as offspring of the long-lost tribes of Israel, they might be unwitting instruments of a much" sought-after millenium (Bozeman 1988:202-259, 271-280). Ingenious casuistries seeking to affirm or set aside a Jewish-Indian genealogy were written and preached throughout the 17th-century, some linking the American aborigines to Scythians, others to Judaeans, and still others seeking to give them either a Semitic origin or an absolution from the Hamitic curse (Canup 1990:55-87). One paradigm initially proved to be attractive: designating the Indians as "Canaanites," thus Hamitic in origin, Canaan being the patronym of the accursed son of Ham who was said to be the progenitor of the seafaring Phoenician people (Aubet 1996:8-20, 121-129, 290-293). However, although such a perspective might speak to the Puritans' self-conceived mission as biblically directed conquerors in service to the settlement of the "New-England-Israel," a new Promised Land, a Hamitic identification of the Indians opened up the question of whether the "accursed" aborigines were to be subjugated and ostracized or made whole again by being drawn into the commonwealth of converted believers (Canup 1990:79-85).

Ultimately, however, neither the Jewish-Indian thesis nor the Canaanite-Indian genealogy could be made commensurable with the aims and interests of either the Puritan divines or their more materialist-minded settler coreligionists. Cotton Mather, a subscriber to the belief that the Indians were unsalvageable Scythians, was, as John Canup (1990:73) observed, "reluctant to honor them by assuming that they were the long-lost Tribes of Israel, the ancient people of God [who] would have to be gathered in before the climax of Christian history." As a matter of fact, Canup (P. 73) concluded, "When Cotton Mather thought of Indians, he thought more often of Satan than of Christ."

Sacvan Bercovitch (1978: note 75), who held that the lost tribes identification of Native Americans was not as prevalent among the Puritans as some others have supposed, claimed that

> by the time King Philip's War broke out the Indians were unequivocally identified with the doomed "dark brothers" of Scripture—Cain, Ishmael, Esau, and above all the heathen natives of the promised land, who were to be dispossessed by divine decree of what really belonged to God's chosen [i.e., the Puritan settlers].

However, in the 19th-century, it was precisely their continuing anomalous situation in America that gave rise to disparate programs directed at their redemption through a renewed lost tribes identification. The North American tribe selected most prominently for either salvation through conversion to Christianity or reclamation through Judaism was that of the Cherokees. Exemplary of the former approach were the efforts of Elias Boudinot, a sometime member of Thomas Jefferson's cabinet and the founder of the American Bible Society. In 1816, Boudinot published his premillenial magnum opus, *A Star in the West*, proving by means of comparing evidence of language, customs, traditions, and religious practices that there existed a more than coincidental cultural similarity between the contemporary Cherokees and the ancient Israelites (Sheehan 1974:59-60). As Israelite descendants, the "Indians are perfect republicans," he observed; "they will admit of no inequality among them but what arises from age, or great qualifications for either council or war" (Sheehan 1974:111). They were also ripe for evangelization. To this end, Boudinot adopted and converted a young Cherokee man, Buck Watie, who in turn married a White woman, took the name of his adoptive father, and rose to become the controversial go-between and remarkably accommodating negotiator during the struggle over Cherokee removal (McLoughlin 1992:277-278, 367-403, 416-417, 450-451; Prucha 1994:178-181). Regarded as a traitor to his people, the younger Boudinot was assassinated by members of his tribe on June 22, 1839 (Williams 1993:150 note 32). Although the descendants of the Watie-Boudinot family would continue to play important roles in Cherokee politics, in later years the Cherokee-Israelite theory seems to have lost its significance in both Indian and Protestant circles (McLoughlin 1993).

In the same era, a Jew, Mordecai Noah (1785-1851), an erstwhile U.S. consul in the Barbary States during James Madison's presidency (who had been recalled from his post in April 1815 because, in Secretary of State James Monroe's cryptic account, "it was not known that the Religion which you profess would form an obstacle to the exercise of your consular function," Feingold 1974:55) made the decision to end his coreligionists' diaspora by establishing a Jewish homeland on American soil. Although the modern emancipation of the Jews had been announced by Napoleon a decade and a half earlier—when the future emperor had paused 25 miles away from Jerusalem to urge, "Israelites arise! Now is the moment . . . to claim your political existence as a nation among nations!" (Grose 1983:8)—the major result in America had been a Protestant call for a new Christian crusade to the Holy Land: "Rise, American ambassadors," cried Albany's Chapel Street Presbyterian pastor, John McDonald, "and prepare to carry the tidings of joy and salvation to your Saviour's kinsmen [i.e., the Jews] in disgrace" (Grose 1983:9).

Having begun to encourage an increase in Jewish immigration to America on his return to the United States, and aware of other Jewish attempts to develop enclaves in Florida and west of the Mississippi River, Noah proposed that the New York legislature permit him to establish "a colony for the Jews of the world," a homeland that, given his surname, he not coincidentally called Ararat, on Grand Island, a 17,000-acre tract in the Niagara River. His petition attracted the interest of the German *Verein für Kultur and Wissenschaft der Juden* (Sachar 1992:45-48) and, in its early years of development, that society and other European and American Jews began to invest capital in the scheme (Diner 1992:40-42, 153). Noah's conception of Jewish identity encompassed more, however, than the Jews of Europe. To the dedication ceremony of his ultimately abortive plan to carry forth, in a hitherto unimagined way, the project envisioned by the biblical prophets of zionism (Clements 1989:163-184, 203-226)—held on September 15, 1825, in the city of Buffalo's Episcopal Church of St. Paul—Noah invited Red Jacket as well as several other Indian tribal chiefs, explaining that he fully subscribed to the belief that they and their fellow tribesmen and women were descendants of the 10 lost tribes of Israel and, as such, were, like the Jews from Europe, being called to become full-fledged members of the immediately proclaimed "Jewish nation [that he had established] under the auspices and protection of the constitution and laws of the U. S. of A." (Feingold 1974:66; see also Lipset and Raab, 1995:112-113).

The Jewish-Indian Theory in Postmodern Thought

At the present time, the claim that the Indians of the Americas are descendants of the lost tribes of Israel has for the most part been relegated to folklore (Faulkner 1992) and to the "little histories" (Natanson 1968:172-177) that exist at the edges and in the interstices of a complex culture. Yet, the thesis that the lost tribes are still living somewhere in the modern world has not entirely disappeared, nor has it been altogether disavowed. Recently, for example,

Pierre Vidal-Naquet (1996:250), while recounting his life as a Jew under France's pro-Nazi Vichy regime, recalled

> making the acquaintance of an austere and mystical lady from Dieulefit who belonged to a famous family of pastors, the Atgers. She explained to me at length that the ten tribes of Israel had spread across the world, including Denmark, as its name, which came from the tribe of Dan, proved.

Even more recently, Bernard Lewis (1995:70), a noted authority on the history and sociology of Jewish-Muslim relations, in the course of a wide-ranging commentary on how the designation and classification of the continents and their peoples are sociocultural constructions that have become legitimated through widespread usage and acceptance, admitted, "I do not know at what stage or by what processes the descendants of the Aztecs and the Incas came to understand and accept their identity as Americans." Whatever the stage or process, however, the credence given to their identification as Jews and, more particularly, as descendants of the lost tribes of Israel, is, at present, quite insecure. Indeed, it has been removed from most serious discussions of either people and has become a source of bitter humor, most pointedly in Mel Brooks's 1974 film *Blazing Saddles*.

However, it is not altogether a departure from its locus in culture to find the Jewish-Indian theory today to be a feature of dark comedy. For, in all of its usages, the thesis that there still exists a cultural peoplehood that conventional and secular historians insist could not have survived exile and dispersion acts to ironize and displace the accepted limits of the latter claim. In America, where the canon of its authenticated history has only begun to be called into question by the protagonists of a multiethnic multiculturalism (Taylor et al. 1994), but where the older Jewish Question no longer occupies as central a place as it once did in either modernist or proto-postmodernist works of scholarship, an older situs of the expression of Jewish mordant humor (Schiff 1982; Erens 1984), Hollywood (Gabler 1988; Heinze 1990:203-218) becomes one venue for raising the issue of the theory's relevance and meaning, its place in the time-space continuum. Some of today's movies, perhaps less so than television, speak to "that rupture-point in human history [that has emerged] between the decline of the now-passé age of sociology and the upsurge of the new world of communications" (Kroker and Cook 1991:272).

About this situation, Homi K. Bhabha (1984:152) has observed, "the national culture comes to be articulated as a dialectic of various temporalities—modern, colonial, postcolonial, 'native'—that cannot be a knowledge that is stabilized in its enunciation." As Mel Brooks's film illustrates, however, it is a kind of knowledge that can be articulated in the form of comedy, in the supposedly "unspeakable images" (Friedman 1991) that unresolved ethnicity has evoked.

Using a satire on the Jewish-Indian theory, *Blazing Saddles,* provides its viewers with a postmodern glimpse of a culture that is simultaneously modern and traditional, colonial and postcolonial, national and fragmented, with peoples who are mainstream and marginalized—a pastiche, a collage. The "entire film," observed Lester D. Friedman (1982:227), "reverberates with the Jewish sense of alienation that leads Brooks to focus on the problems faced by outsiders in the Old West, those segregated by race, color, or religion." In a memorable scene, Brooks essayed a complex variant on what Herbert Marcuse (1969:25-26) once called the desublimation of repression, presenting a band of Indians, whose chief is portrayed by Brooks himself in "redface," speaking Yiddish to one another. Compounding this send-up of the Jewish-Indian theory, Brooks's Indian parodies what is, in fact, the common epithet used when American Jews talk among themselves about American Blacks. "Schwartzers?" his Indian inquires incredulously as he and his men come upon a wagonload of African Americans being transported across the plains. One critic has interpreted that scene to be benevolently universalizing: "black and white interchange—and, at bottom, all men—even Indians are secretly Jews" (Pinsker 1983:250). But American Indians had been said to be Jews for hundreds of years. So also had the so-called Falasha (now called Beta Israel) of Ethiopia; the inhabitants of Kaifeng, China; the people of Japan; the Pathans of Afghanistan; the Shin-Lung people on the Burma-India border; the Knanites in Southern India; the Pachucans of Mexico; and many others (Avichail 1990:63-176).

Perhaps the sociological lesson of *Blazing Saddles,* a message of some aspects of postmodernism, is that all our systems of classification are simultaneously necessary and arbitrary, and in fact are ethnomethodological experiments (Lyman 1993:379-393) that always suffer from the fact that there is no escape from Garfinkelian rules, only one of which is "let it pass" (Garfinkel 1972:312, note 3).

Conclusion

The lost tribes of Israel have passed through and beyond most of the peoples of the world. They epitomize a combination that Simmel (1950:402-408) did not foresee: a permanent synthesis of traveler and stranger, a wandering body of Jews that reminds people of how malleable their conceptions of time, space, and character—and peoplehood—are. "Thus," observed Rudolf Glanz (1986:116), "the wandering Jew . . . filled the full function of the Jew in American folklore, viz., being a known phenomenon to provide a standard to be applied to the unknown that so often seemed to pose a threat." With *Blazing Saddles,* the unknown comes into its own. "Somehow," wrote Lester D. Friedman (1982:228), "it seems comically appropriate that the West's most conspicuous outsider, the Indian, should speak in the tongue of history's traditional outsider, the Jew."

In effect, once having been ensconced in *Blazing Saddles'* postmodern comic frame, the debate over whether the Jewish-Indian theory has any validity has entered the realm of what Jean-Francois Lyotard (1988:xi) called the *differend:* "A differend would be a case of conflict between (at least) two parties that cannot be equitably resolved for lack of a rule of judgment applicable to both arguments." The query "Are (some or all) American Indians descended from the lost tribes of Israel?" cannot be given an unequivocal answer, one, that is, that would satisfy both a rational modernist historian and a New Age postmodern investigator. For, as David J. Hess (1993:37) has pointed out,

> New Agers incorporate and rework the research of anthropologists, physicists, philosophers, and other scientists and scholars to legitimate a discourse that also sanctions crystal healing, channelers, astral bodies, goddess religion, and other beliefs and practices generally associated with popular culture.

Jewish eschatological esoterica, or at least that part of it that quests for the lost tribes, like so much else of what modernist secularists consider paranormal, has become a part of that popular culture, a part, that is, of the "nostalgic aesthetic of postmodern movies known as *a la mode retro*" (Hess 1993:37). Like Karl Marx's (1983:287-323) quest to discover the real Napoleon III, Mel Brooks's postmodern placement of the lost tribes of Israel in Hollywood's American West turned mythic history into mundane farce.

References

Abella, Irving. 1982. *None Is Too Many: Canada and the Jews of Europe, 1933-1948.* New York: Random House.

Adair, James. [1775] 1930. *Adair's History of the American Indians,* edited by S. C. Williams. New York: Promontory Press.

Aris, Stephen. 1970. *But There Are No Jews in England.* New York: Stein and Day.

Ashkenazi, Michael and Alex Weingrod, eds. 1987. *Ethiopian Jews and Israel.* New Brunswick, NJ: Transaction.

Aubet, Maria Eugenia. *1996. The Phoenicians and the West: Politics, Colonies, and Trade.* Translated by M. Turton. Cambridge, England: Cambridge University Press.

Augé, Marc. 1995. *Non-Places: Introduction to an Anthropology of Supermodernity*. Translated by J. Howe. London: Verso.

Ausubel, Nathan, Ed. 1975. *A Treasury of Jewish Folklore*. New York: Crown.

Avichail, Rabbi Eliyahu. 1990. *The Tribes of Israel: The Lost and the Dispersed*. Translated by M. Gross. Jerusalem, Israel: Amishav.

Bammer, Angelika, Ed. 1994. *Displacements: Cultural Identities in Question*. Bloomington: Indiana University Press.

Bercovitch, Sacvan. 1978. *The American Jeremiad*. Madison: University of Wisconsin Press.

Bermant, Chaim. 1970. *Troubled Eden: An Anatomy of British Jewry*. New York: Basic Books.

— 1975. *London's East End: Point of Arrival*. New York: Macmillan.

Bhabha, Homi K. 1984. *The Location of Culture*. London: Routledge.

Bozeman, Theodore Dwight. 1988. *To Live Ancient Lives: The Primitivist Dimension in Puritanism*. Chapel Hill: University of North Carolina Press.

Brough, R. Clayton. *1979. The Lost Tribes: History, Doctrine, Prophecies, and Theories About Israel's Lost Ten Tribes*. Bountiful, UT. Horizon.

Budick, Sanford. 1996. "Crises of Alterity: Cultural Untranslatability and the Experience of Secondary Others." Pp. 1-24 in *The Translatability of Cultures: Figurations of the Space Between*, edited by S. Budick and W. Iser. Stanford, CA: Stanford University Press.

Canup, John. 1990. *Out of the Wilderness: The Emergence of an American Identity in Colonial New England*. Middletown, CT: Wesleyan University Press.

Caracciolo, Nicola. 1995. *Uncertain Refuge: Italy and the Jews During the Holocaust*. Translated and edited by F. Rechnitz Koffler and R. Koffler. Urbana: University of Illinois Press.

Clements, R. E., Ed. 1989. *The World of Ancient Israel: Sociological, Anthropological and Political Perspectives*. Cambridge, England: Cambridge University Press.

Diner, Hasia R. 1992. *A Time for Gathering. The Second Migration, 1820-1880*. Baltimore: Johns Hopkins University Press.

Dinnerstein, Leonard. 1982. *America and the Survivors of the Holocaust*. New York: Columbia University Press.

Elazar, Daniel J. 1995. *Covenant and Polity in Biblical Israel: Biblical Foundations and Jewish Expressions*. New Brunswick, NJ: Transaction.

Epstein, Mikhail N. 1995. *After the Future: The Paradoxes of Postmodernism and Contemporary Russian Culture*. Translated by A. Miller-Pogacar. Amherst: University of Massachusetts Press.

Frens, Patricia. 1984. *The Jew in American Cinema*. Bloomington: Indiana Univ. Press.

Erlich, Avi. 1995. *Ancient Zionism: The Biblical Origins of the National Idea*. New York: Free Press.

Even, Charles. [1861] 1977. *The Lost Tribes of Israel, or the First of the Red Men*. New York: Arno Press.

Faulkner, Charles H. 1992. *The Bat Creek Stone. Miscellaneous Paper No. 15*. Knoxville: Tennessee Anthropological Association.

Feingold, Henry L. *1970. The Politics of Rescue: The Roosevelt Administration and the Holocaust, 1938-1945*. New York: Holocaust Library.

— 1974. *Zion in America: The Jewish Experience From Colonial Times to the Present*. New York: Hippocrene Books.

Feldman, David. 1994. *Englishmen and Jews: Social Relations and Political Culture, 1840-1914*. New York: Yale University Press.

Friedman, Lester D. 1982. *Hollywood's Image of the Jew*. New York: Frederick Ungar.

— Ed. 1991. *Unspeakable Images: Ethnicity and the American Cinema*. Urbana: University of Illinois Press.

Gabler, Neal. 1988. *An Empire of Their Own: How the Jews Invented Hollywood*. New York: Crown.

Garb, Tamar. 1995. "Introduction: Modernity, Identity, Textuality." Pp. 20-30 in *The Jew in the Text: Modernity and The Construction of Identity*, edited by L. Nochlin and T. Garb. London: Thames and Hudson.

Garfinkel, Harold. 1967. *Studies in Ethnomethodology*. Englewood Cliffs, NJ: Prentice-Hall.

— 1972. "Remarks on Ethnomethodology." Pp. 301,-324 in *Directions in Sociolinguistics: The Ethnography of Communication*, edited by J. J. Gumperz and D. Hymes. New York: Holt, Rinehart and Winston.

Gartner, Lloyd P. 1960. *The Jewish Immigrant in England, 1870-1914.* London: Allen and Unwin.

Glanz, Rudolf. 1986. "The Wandering Jew in America." Pp. 105-118 in *The Wandering Jew: Essays in the Interpretation of a Christian Legend*, edited by G. Hasan-Rokem and A. Dundes. Bloomington: Indiana University Press.

Grant, Michael. 1984. *The History of Ancient Israel*. New York: Scribner's.

Grose, Peter. 1983. *Israel in the Mind of America*. New York: Alfred A. Knopf.

Handelman, Dan and Elihu Katz. 1995. "State Ceremonies of Israel: Remembrance Day and Independence Day." Pp. 75-85 in *Israeli Judaism: The Sociology of Religion in Israel*, edited by S. Deshen, C. S. Liebman, and,M. Shokeid. New Brunswick, NJ: Transaction.

Hay, Cynthia. 1990. "What is Sociological History?" Pp. 20-37 in *Interpreting the Past, Understanding the Present*, edited by S. Kendrick, P. Straw, and D. McCrone. New York: St. Martin's Press.

Heinze, Andrew R. 1990. *Adapting to Abundance: Jewish Immigration, Mass Consumption, and the Search for American Identity*. New York: Columbia University Press.

Hess, David J. 1993. Science in the New Age: The Paranormal, Its Defenders, and American Culture. Madison: University of Wisconsin Press.

Huddleston, Lee Eldridge. *1967. Origin of the American Indians: European Concepts, 1492-1729.* Austin: University of Texas Press.

Isaacs, Ronald H. and Kerry M. Olitzky, Eds. 1995. *Critical Documents of Jewish History: A Sourcebook*. Northvale, NJ: Jason Aronson.

Jackson, Peter. 1994. *Maps of Meaning: An Introduction to Cultural Geography*. London:. Routledge.

Jameson, Fredric. 1991. *Postmodernism Or, The Cultural Logic of Late Capitalism*. Durham, NC: Duke University Press.

Jordan, Winthrop D. 1968. *White Over Black. American Attitudes Toward the Negro, 1550-1812*. Chapel Hill: University of North Carolina Press.

Kahler, Erich. 1989. *The Jews Among the Nations*. New Brunswick, NJ: Transaction.

Kaplan, Steven. 1992. *The Beta Israel (Falasha) in Ethiopia: From Earliest Times to the Twentieth Century*. New York: New York University Press.

Keegan, William F. 1992. *The People Who Discovered Columbus: The Prehistory of the Bahamas*. Gainesville: University Press of Florida.

Keller, Werner. 1969. *Diaspora: The Post-Biblical History of the Jews*. New York: Harcourt, Brace and World.

Khazanov, Anatoly M. 1994. *Nomads and the Outside World. 2nd edition*. Translated by J. Crookenden. Madison: University of Wisconsin Press.

Kroker, *Arthur and David Cook. 1991. The Postmodern Scene: Excremental Culture and Hyper-Aesthetics*. 2nd edition. Montreal, Quebec, Canada New World Perspectives.

Leslau, Wolf, ed. and trans. 1969. *Falasha Anthology: The Black Jews of Ethiopia*. New York: Schocken Books.

Levine, Etan, Ed. 1986. *Diaspora: Exile and the Contemporary Jewish Condition.* New York: Steimatzky-Shapolsky.

Levine, Hillel. 1996. *In Search of Sugihara: The Elusive Japanese Diplomat Who Risked His Life to Rescue 10,000 Jews From the Holocaust.* New York: Free Press.

Lewis, Bernard. 1995. *Cultures in Conflict: Christians, Muslims, and Jews in the Age of Discovery.* New York: Oxford University Press.

Lipset, Seymour Martin and Earl Raab. 1995. *Jews and the New American Scene.* Cambridge, MA: Harvard University Press.

Lyman, Stanford M. 1990. *Civilization: Contents, Discontents, Malcontents, and Other Essays in Social Theory.* Fayetteville: University of Arkansas Press.

— 1993. "Marginalizing the Self: A Study of Citizenship, Color, and Ethnoracial Identity in American Society." *Symbolic Interaction* 16:379-393.

— 1995. "History and Sociology: Some Unresolved Epistemological Problems." *International Journal of Politics, Culture and Society* 9:29-56.

Lyman, Stanford M. and Marvin B. Scott. 1989. *A Sociology of the Absurd.* 2nd edition. Dix Hills, NY: General Hall.

Lyotard, Jean-Francois. 1988. *The* Differend. *Phrases in Dispute.* Translated by G. Van Den Abbeele. Minneapolis: University of Minnesota Press.

Marcuse, Herbert. 1969. *An Essay on Liberation.* Boston: Beacon Press. Marx, Karl. 1983 [1851]. "The Eighteenth Brumaire of Louis Bonaparte." Pp. 287-323 in *The Portable Karl Marx,* edited by E. Kamenka. New York: Penguin Books.

McLoughlin, William G. 1992. *Cherokee Renascence in the New Republic.* Princeton, NJ: Princeton University Press.

— 1993. *After the Trail of Tears: The Cherokees' Struggle for Sovereignty, 1839-1880.* Chapel Hill: University of North Carolina Press.

Morse, Arthur D. 1983. *While Six Million Died. A Chronicle of American Apathy.* Woodstock, NY: Overlook Press.

Natanson, Maurice. 1968. *Literature, Philosophy, and the ;Social Sciences: Essays in Existentialism and Phenomenology.* The Hague, The Netherlands: Martinus Nijhoff.

Numbers, Ronald. 1992. *The Creationists: The Evolution of Scientific Creationism.* New York: Alfred A. Knopf.

Penkower, Monty Noam. 1983. *The Jews Were Expendable: Free World Diplomacy and the Holocaust.* Urbana: University of Illinois Press.

Pinsker, Sanford. 1983. "Mel Brooks and the Cinema of Exhaustion." Pp. 245-256 in *From Hester Street to Hollywood. The Jewish-American Stage and Screen,* edited by S. B. Cohen. Bloomington: Indiana University Press.

Prucha, Francis Paul. 1994. *American Indian Treaties: The History of a Political Anomaly.* Berkeley: University of California Press.

Roth, Cecil. 1934. *A Life of Menasseh ben Israel: Rabbi, Printer, and Diplomat.* Philadelphia: Jewish Publication Society of America.

Rouse, Irving. 1992. *The Tainos: Rise and Decline of the People Who Greeted Columbus.* New Haven: Yale University Press.

Sachar, Howard M. 1992. *A History of the Jews in America.* New York: Alfred A. Knopf.

— 1995. *Diaspora: An Inquiry into the Contemporary Jewish World.* New York: Harper and Row.

Schama, Simon. 1995. *Landscape and Memory.* New York: Alfred A. Knopf.

Schiff, Ellen. 1982. *From Stereotype to Metaphor: The Jew in Contemporary Drama.* Albany: State University of New York Press.

Schutz, Alfred. 1966. *Collected Papers III: Studies in Phenomenological Philosophy,* edited by I. Schutz. The Hague, The Netherlands: Martinus Nijhoff.

Sheehan, Bernard W. 1974. *Seeds of Extinction: Jeffersonian Philanthropy and the American Indian.* New York: W. W. Norton.

Simmel, Georg. 1950. "The Stranger." Pp. 402-408 in *The Sociology of Georg Simmel,* Translated and edited by K. H. Wolff. Glencoe, Ill.: The Free Press.

Snyder, Phil L., Ed. 1958. *Detachment and the Writing of History. Essays and Letters of Carl L. Becker.* Ithaca, NY: Cornell University Press.

Spence, Lewis. [1914] 1994. *North American Indians.* London: Studio Editions.

Sugihara, Yukiko. 1995. *Visas for Life,* edited by L. Silver and E. Saul. Translated by H. Sugihara et al. San Francisco: Edwards Brothers, Inc.

Tanakh: The Holy Scriptures—The New JPS Translation According to the Traditional Hebrew Text. 1985. Philadelphia: Jewish Publication Society.

Taylor, Charles, K. Anthony Appiah, Jürgen Hakermas, Steven C. Rockefeller, Michael Walzer, and Susan Wolf. 1994. *Multiculturalism: Examining the Politics of Recognition,* edited by Amy Gutman. Princeton, NJ: Princeton University Press.

Teggart, Frederick J. 1925. *Theory of History.* New Haven: Yale University Press.

Tokayer, Marin and Mary Swartz. 1979. *The Fugu Plan: The Untold Story of the Japanese and the Jews During World War II.* New York: Paddington Press.

Vidal-Naquet, Pierre. 1996. *The Jews: History, Memory, and the Present,* translated and edited by D. A. Curtis. New York: Columbia University Press.

Walzer, Michael. 1985. *Exodus and Revolution.* New York: Basic Books.

Wasserstein, Bernard. 1979. *Britain and the Jews of Europe, 1939-1945.* London: Institute of Jewish Affairs and the Clarendon Press of Oxford.

Williams, David. 1993. *The Georgia Gold Rush: Twenty-Niners, Cherokees, and Gold Fever.* Columbia: University of South Carolina Press.

Wyman, David. 1984. *The Abandonment of the Jews: America and the Holocaust, 1941-1945.* New York: Pantheon.

—— [1968] 1985. *Paper Walls: America and the Refugee Crisis, 1938-1941.* New York: Pantheon.

Zerubavel, Yael. 1995. *Recovered Roots: Collective Memory and the Making of Israeli National Tradition.* Chicago: University of Chicago Press.

The Influence of Austrian Humanism in Theodor Herzl's Vision of a Jewish State

Mark E. Blum

Abstract: *Theodor Herzl's thought was a product of an Austrian political and humanist culture. His political values were formed within a multinational, cameralist tradition that at its best bred a tolerance for differing persons and cultures but isolated the private individual from a responsible role in his or her own governance. The problem of governmental power in relation to the members of its society became for Herzl a conundrum whose solution was a redistribution of that power downward. Herzl's depiction of the future Jewish state in his 1896* The Jewish State *and in his 1902 novel* Old-New Land *offers the vision of a privatized society in which each citizen may eventually become a cooperative owner. An examination of Herzl's vision reveals a thread of Austrian humanistic concepts and values that have characterized social-economic thought in Austria since the Enlightenment.*

Theodor Herzl's thought, which produced the spark that led to development of an effective Zionist movement eventuating in the state of Israel, is more than historical artifact. Its socioeconomic vision is still fecund for present nations. Herzl's Zionist project was intended not only as a solution for the plight of Jews in Europe but rather as a model for all nations: "The New Society can exist anywhere—in any country" (Herzl, 1960b, p. 291). In our present age where political economists call for a deconstruction of government and for privatization of services, Herzl's notion of a nation as "not a State, but a cooperative association" (1960b, p. 288) is still timely. The continuing significance and currency of Herzl's thought lies not in the specific elements of his political-economic sketches, which were never meant as precise blueprints, but rather in high insight into forms of human association that were and are feasible within the existing patterns of Western culture.

Discerning potentialities in the existing attitudes and skills of a populace that could be directed into new institutional designs was a traditional strength in Austrian thought. From the Enlightened administrative public policy of Joseph von Sonnenfels through the myriad efforts of the late nineteenth and early twentieth centuries to maintain the multinational integration of the Austrian state, Austrian political-social thinking was alive to the unique and challenging character of geopolitical diversity. The fluctuating boundaries of the Austrian Hapsburg Empire, its multiple ethnicities, and its mixture of urban and rural economies called constantly for new political-economic designs to maximize the stability and productivity of its peoples.

Central to every political-economic plan was attention to the affects of policy on the motivational and behavioral norms of its citizenry. The extraordinary attention given to the influence of public policy on human relationships may have been occasioned by the rich diversity of its populations which negated the effectiveness of abstract measures designed "to fit all." Austrian humanism was a perspective that fleshed out every rational measure with attention to its consequences for human will, emotion, and the quality of resultant interdependent relations. The furthering qualities of Austrian humanistic concepts contributed to every field in the arts and the sciences that required attention to human motivation and consequent action. Some discussion of the nature of Austrian humanism and its relation to Western humanism, in general, is required at this point.

Western humanism since its origins with the Greeks has been an attitude and practice within a culture that seeks to make "man the measure of all things." This statement of Protagoras highlighted the Greek conception of a cultural education that stressed the importance of balancing the technical progress of civilization with a just, human proportion. The just, human proportion situated *techne* and other specialized knowledge in the arts and sciences within the locus of human needs and human dignity. Aristotle in particular spoke to the importance of integrating specialized knowledge into understanding and action for the good of humankind (see Aristotle, 1941, pp. 1027-1028, 188-189). Humanism broadly is an attempt to establish a society that constantly improves its foundation for nurturing the spiritual and material needs of its populace with ever greater insight into the human condition. Science is central to the humanist vision as the human is and lives within nature. Humanism is a mode of thought that has emphasized that in any act of inquiry into nature there be a corresponding insight into oneself. However, as we will see particularly in Austrian humanism, objective analysis of nature must precede and constantly complement the subjective appreciation of its significance for human culture. Nature is not simply "other" than oneself; rather it is a mirror for one's own organic nature. One becomes informed about the conditions of his or her humanity and arrives at self-definition through a study of the organic, inorganic, and social environs in which one dwells. The advances of *techne* must also be informed by this reference to the human condition if the artist or scientist is to be a humanist. Thus, a physicist, sculptor, sociologist, philosopher, architect, poet, or biologist can be a humanist if in his or her inquiry conclusions are drawn not only about the subject matter but also about the implications for human cultural existence.

The Austrian humanists more than their counterparts in other European cultures brought an Aristotelian foundation to their ideation.[1] Ideas that explained human culture were generated through the events of human relationship. Ever new explanatory principles could be forged if the events warranted a necessary reformulation of the concepts that heretofore were used to interpret human behavior. There was not an eternal table of ideas to which human conduct must conform. Conceptions of human practice were the considered result of countless hours of behavioral observation. Causal categories could be formulated that endured over time but only through insight into the actual interactions of persons.

Perhaps the most metaphysical aspect of Austrian humanism was its tendency to see extended patterns in behavior rather than each event as somehow a singular accident. Aristotle's formal cause or entelechy was the chief causal perspective (see Kauder, 1958, pp. 418-419).[2] Human actions were seen as fulfilling certain patterns that developed over time. A entelechy existed in human behavior that guided appetite and action toward the realization of characteristic designs. The pattern could be discerned from the evidence of single words or gestures, and its developmental stages predicted. Thus, the interactions of individuals, small groups, or large groups each had differing outcomes depending on the patterns that each was fulfilling. At its best, this focus helped the Austrian policy maker establish a differentiated approach to the multiple ethnicities of Austria. We will see how Herzl approaches the diverse characters of peoples both Jewish and non-Jewish in his emigration plans through the lens of this appreciation for separate destinies of peoples. The challenge to the statemaking art of the Austrian policy maker and of Herzl was to establish a pattern that could permit divergent values and destinies while maintaining a coherent, integrated society.

Other Austrian humanist characteristics that will be mentioned in this study include several traits of the Austrian mind discussed by the Austrian intellectual historian, William M. Johnston: the significance of interpersonal dialogue among all affected parties in arriving at mutual solutions, the focus on *Gemeinschaft* (community) rather than an impersonal society, and the primacy of nature in bringing its own solutions rather than a too artificial intervention into human affairs.[3]

Herzl's thought reflects these humanist characteristics, but as with every creative thinker, it also innovates within the range of these characteristics. Herzl addressed a growing problem in Austrian political life with his inherited humanism that touched not only on the Jewish problem and its Zionist outcome but on the continuing dilemma of Austrians even without the Jews. This problem was citizen participation in government. Although absolutist government had been ameliorated by the post-Metternichian statist policies of Franz Joseph—there were many suffrage increases and a constitution—nonetheless, ministers were still chosen by the emperor without consultation with Parliament in the era of Herzl's youth and maturity. The private individual was distanced from self-directed, responsible participation in his or her own governance. The problem of governmental power in relation to the members of its society became for Herzl a conundrum whose solution ultimately was to be a redistribution of that power downward. Herzl's depiction of the new Zion in his 1896 pamphlet *The Jewish State* and in his 1902 novel *Old-New Land* offers the vision of a privatized society in which each citizen may eventually become a cooperative owner.

The radical quality of Herzl's dissolution of the nation-state into a cooperative society of individuals may be traced to the importance given to the individual in his or her particular actions and environ by the Austrian humanist tradition. Cooperative will mean more than abstract institutional rule when considering social reality. Perhaps being ruled by one family, the Hapsburgs, for half a millennia enabled the Austrian to discern the king and not the clothes. Institution, station, and role became primarily the person and his or her actions. For the Austrian humanist, reality had its sole locus in the immediacy of human relations. This rootedness of reality in the sensual particulars of actual interactions gave even public events a semiprivate character because of the emphasis of motivation, will, and immediate personal effects. I will relate Herzl's thought to three Austrian humanist predecessors, in particular, in tracing the roots of his cooperative social solution to participation in governance—the cameralist public policy of Joseph von Sonnenfels, the political economy of Carl Menger, and the literature of Adalbert Stifter.

Theodor Herzl had the intellectual and literary tools for imparting the humanist vision to any subject he took up. He had a visual imagination and thus could impart abstract ideas in terms of the sensual particulars that were evidence of these ideas. He was a gifted writer as a youth. Several of his dramas were produced by one of the most prestigious theaters of Europe, the *Hofburgtheater* in Vienna, and he became a successful *feuilleton* writer for the Viennese press (Bein, 1941). Drama and the *feuilleton* were mediums where the character of a person or the implications of a plan of life must be shown with the pregnancy of the single word or gesture. Herzl's maturity gave him an exceptional vantage point for comprehending the behavioral patterns of his contemporary culture: he became a political correspondent for the prestigious *Neue Freie Presse* of Vienna as well as the chief editor of its *feuilleton*.[4] Herzl was always conscious of the role of a poetic imagination in the comprehension of world affairs. He wrote to a friend during his first year as a Paris correspondent: "Poetry deals with a higher abstraction than politics: the world.

And can he who is able to grasp the world be incapable of comprehending politics?" (Schorske, 1980, p. 153). As I examine Herzl's vision of the Jewish state, especially in his novel *Old-New Land,* the role of the poetic narrative will be a factor in discerning how the Austrian humanist tradition informed and guided his projected improvement of culture. Poetic prose was able to grasp the human attitudes and motives that were implicit in the basic assumptions of a political economic analysis.

Herzl's social-economic vision of an improved Western culture was discounted in his own time by economists who saw him merely as a *feuilleton* writer (Zweig, 1943). Even as the state of Israel became a reality, Herzl's view of how this state might be developed has generally been treated as a utopian sketch. Herzl himself sought to avoid the onus of being treated as a utopian. He writes in his preface to *The Jewish State* (1946, p. 71):

> I shall not be lavish in artistically elaborated descriptions of my project, for fear of incurring the suspicion of painting a Utopia . . . .
> If I describe future circumstances with too much caution I shall appear to doubt their possibility. If, on the other hand, I announce their realization with too much assurance I shall appear to be describing a chimera. I shall therefore clearly and emphatically state that I believe in the practical outcome of my scheme without professing to have discovered the shape it may ultimately take.

Herzl voices an aesthetic guideline for himself that typifies the Austrian humanist tradition. He wishes to create the Aristotelian formal cause—the "shape" to be fulfilled—without prematurely describing the exact content that will be the flesh of that shape. He wishes to project forms of potential interdependence that grow out of actualities without distorting the model by too much concreteness. An entelechy must be suggested, but allowance must be made for the model's realization in the contingent uncertainties of future experience. These criteria called for a genre of social narrative that had few predecessors if it was to find the new path between the either/or of utopianism or premature concreteness. Herzl studied the pragmatic plans of other utopian thinkers of the early nineteenth century in an effort to learn from their ideas and undoubtedly the pitfalls of their style of presentation (Herzl, 1960b, p. 148). *The Jewish State* fails in some ways to fully express his intentions. It is too concrete in its plans and falsely conveys the impression of a strange oxymoronic solution to the future society that combines the statist realities of the late nineteenth century with entrepreneurialism. David Herman (1994, p. 243) has written an eloquent think piece to guide one's approach to Herzl's utopianism in *The Jewish State.* He points out that Herzl's 1896 pamphlet wrongly strained to avoid a richer poetic texture to its socioeconomic rhetoric in its effort to be taken as a serious project. Herman argues that Herzl's imagination, in the best sense, is nonetheless present in the text. Herman (1994, p. 240) quotes Ernst Bloch in defining Herzl's imaginative strength: "the imagination of the utopian function combine(s) the already existing facts in a random manner, but carries on the existing facts toward the future potentiality of their otherness." It is this potentiality that is more thoughtfully worked out through poetic discourse in Herzl's 1902 novel *Old-New Land.* Yet Herzl (1960a, p. 13) had a novelistic approach to the Jewish problem in mind at the same time he wrote *The Jewish State:* "How I proceeded from the idea of writing a novel to a practical program is already a mystery to me, although it happened within the last few weeks. It is in the realm of the Unconscious." Recognition of this poetic depth in his initial formulations of a new cultural solution for European Jews (and Western culture in general) is important in appreciating the constant presence of Austrian humanism in Herzl's vision.

1

Herzl's *agon* with Zionism provided him with a crucible in which to clarify his thought and own what was truly his own mind and heart, rather than what he merely imbibed in the problem-filled norms of his milieu. Stefan Zweig (1943, p. 107) reports a conversation with Herzl that testifies to the creative focus Zionism afforded Herzl:

> In the two thousand years of our history we Jews have not had any practice in creating anything real in this world. One must first learn unconditional devotion, and I myself have not yet mastered it, for I still keep on writing *feuilletons, I* am still the *feuilleton* editor of the *Neue Freie Presse,* whereas it would be my duty to have only one thought and not to put another pen-stroke on paper for anything but that one thought. But I am on the way to improve myself. I must first learn unconditional devotion.

Between 1895 when he actually composed *The Jewish State* and 1902 when he completed *Old-New Land,* he arrived at a reformulation and refinement of his political, social, and ethical values. One must carefully track the movement of his thought from the inception of his Zionist ideation until the completion of the Zionist novel to adequately understand his ultimate vision. His political values before Zionism were a composite shared by most educated middle-class Austrians—a respect for the cameralist heritage of Joseph II as well as adherence to the constitutional principles of democratic-republican governance that gradually brought empowerment to the common people. As he engaged in the effort to plan an effective means to realize the Zionist state, Herzl shed these inherited values. By 1902 Herzl refocused the discussion of political-social liberty and progress within parameters that departed from the traditional tension between the aristocratic and democratic-republican sovereignty principles. By 1902 he will postulate a vision of government free of a concept of sovereignty that implies either an initial "contract" that distributes that authority or even a "state" that exercises that authority. In *The Jewish State sovereignty* is defined chiefly as a "subjective basis" of authority that exists in the people rather than the "objective basis" of land (Herzl, 1946, p. 137). One is reminded of Themistocles assertion during the Persian War that the people of Athens were the polis, not the territory that had been abandoned. The people themselves do not derive their sovereignty from any legal precedent; rather it is a constant anthropological given that a person's autonomous will is sufficient to justify the right of an individual to decide how he or she will participate in governance. John Locke's vision of sovereignty as an inalienable human right separate from any legal authorization may be seen as a precedent for Herzl's treatment of the concept.[5] In fact, Locke's view of the commonwealth as simply a guarantor of the private rights of persons will be close to Herzl's vision of a cooperative society.

Herzl (1946, p. 137) compares the future sovereignty of the people of the Jewish state to the situation of the Pope, whose "sovereignty . . . has no objective basis at all." He will describe the Jewish state as no state in the traditional sense, discarding the concept of sovereignty entirely in *Old-New Land* (Herzl, 1960b, p. 288).

His rejection of the traditional concept of sovereignty as a legally derived right based on a social contract between parties potentially liberates the political-social polemics of Western thought from considering government and community as the same (cf. Locke, 1988, p. 114). By not confounding the justification of community with the inherited range of governmental options, Herzl is able to free twentieth-century political thought from the classic *aporia* of aristocratic versus republican, or even republican versus democratic, principles of sovereign authority. Governmental authority will be recentered in the fluid will of cooperating individuals, who will be careful not to burden themselves with the traditional political structures. Herzl will formulate a set of principles based solely on cooperative wills that not only moves beyond the notion of state sovereignty but dissolves the classic dichotomy of the public and the private spheres of society into a new fusion to be known as a "cooperative association" (Herzl, 1960b, p. 288). The cooperative groups that will be the foundation of human relations in the new land are not an idea fashioned "from whole cloth." Undoubtedly Ferdinand Tönnies's *Gemeinschaft and Gesellschaft* (1887) and Otto von Gierke's exhaustive study of the ancient German community, *Das Deutsche Genossenschaftsrecht* (1868-1873), the latter which increasingly influenced political-economic thought even as far as England in the 1890s, were known to Herzl.[6] The Austrian humanist bias for establishing dialogue among all participants in common events and thus creating a communal discourse made the thought of Tönnies and von Gierke especially fecund for Herzl.

Herzl wrote a deeply revealing and complex reflection in his diary on June 8, 1895, as he composed the pamphlet *The Jewish State*, that may be seen as the entering wedge between his inherited world that sought political freedom in terms of sovereignty and a new world that steps beyond the locus of the sovereignty principle (Herzl, 1960a, p. 41): "Rousseau believed that there was such a thing as a *contrat social*. There is not. In the state there is only a *negotiorum gestio*. Thus *I* conduct the affairs of the Jews without their mandate, but I become responsible to them for what I do."

Jacques Kornberg has recently discussed this diary entry as evidence of Herzl's embeddedness in the Austrian cameralist tradition (1993, pp. 166-167). Cameralism is governance by administration. It was the aristocratic alternative to parliamentary action as a vehicle for bringing progress to a commonwealth. The Josephinian spirit of enlightened, absolutist monarchy created progress in society from above through state planning. Herzl's expression of this perspective lies in his dismissal of a social contract between the ruler and the ruled and his substitution of the Roman legal notion of *negotiorum gestio*. The *negotiorum gestio*, which existed in the Austrian civil code, allowed a person who had no legal obligation or contractual engagement with certain parties to act in their interest without their consent in cases of their absence or incapacity. As a principle extended to a political realm it expressed the notion of "both political guardianship and accountability" (Komberg, 1993). Komberg points out that Herzl's use of the *negotiorum gestio* would allow a *Gestor* to plan and carry out activities that could make the resettlement of the Jews in a new nation possible in the transitional absence of any forum by which the affected peoples could articulate their own will. The Society of Jews, the organization Herzl conceived as the planning and administrative body to settle the Jews in Palestine, would be the governing agency until a state with responsible institutions could be created.

Herzl (1964, p. 139) points out in *The Jewish State* that the *negotiorum gestio* exercised by the Jewish Society is a transitional necessity as no forum exists for the dispersed Jews to make concrete decisions.[7] Kornberg emphasizes that Herzl's preference for decision making prior to and apart from the will of the projected Jewish peoples was not only a necessary pragmatic step but an indicator of a political ideology in Herzl that favored cameralist government. Herzl admired Bismarck's state building and the Austrian statist liberalism of his era. There is evidence in Herzl's diary in 1895 of his aristocratic pretensions as an Enlightened state builder. Herzl (1960, p. 196) writes in his diary on July 5, 1895: "If there is one thing I would like to be, it is a member of the old Prussian nobility." He follows this thought on July 9 by quoting Rousseau on the decisive power of a prince to resolve public policy (1960a, p. 198): "If I were a prince or a legislator I would not waste my time telling what ought to be done; I would do it, or keep silent." On July 23, 1895, he considers whether the Jews will accept "a predetermined Constitution" (1960a, p. 211). And the form of that Constitution composed in his diary entry of July 23, 1895 is clearly statist. Yet, if one tracks the movement of Herzl's thought from *The Jewish State* to *Old-New Land*, the cameralist heritage will be seen as dross, an atavism whose only merit was its concern for the welfare of the populace. Herzl rejected the opportunity to be a counselor to Count Badeni chiefly because it made him into a supporter of the traditional cameralist principle that separated the nonaristocrat from authority in one's own governance (cf. Herzl, 1960a, p. 266).[8]

Herzl's vision of the statist constitution for the future Jewish state that he articulates in 1895 must be considered as an atavism that will be shed in his mature Zionistic thinking. There is a counterwill to the statist, cameralist thought even in this draft that potentially redistributes state power to the people (Herzl, 1960a, p. 211):

> Full autonomy for the communities in all parish-pump politics. Let the gabbers play parliament to their heart's content. But only one Chamber of Deputies which cannot overthrow the government but only deny it particular resources. This will suffice for a public control. One-third of his Chamber will be named by the ruler upon the recommendation of the government (a lifetime appointment, for only nobility and property will be hereditary). Another third will be elected by the learned academies, the universities, schools of art and technology, chambers of commerce, and trade associations. The final third will be elected by the community councils (an election commission to examine authorizations), or perhaps by the provinces after a scrutiny of voting lists.
>
> The ruler will name the government. It remains to be considered, however, how the ruler's arbitrariness may be kept in check. For, since the Chamber is not supposed to overthrow the government, a ruler could surround himself with straw men. Perhaps this three-fold composition of the chamber will suffice to prevent the abuses of the Palais Bourbon, and the Chamber could be given the right to overthrow the government. To be considered carefully and discussed with state jurists.

Herzl's reflection that the Chamber has the right to overthrow the government is the Lockean element that will increasingly become dominant in his thinking. The commonwealth as a society of persons constituted only for the procuring, preserving, and advancing their own civil interests, and thereby needing a minimum of governmental interference, is articulated by Kingscourt in *Old-New Land* (Herzl, 1960b, p. 273): "Legalism and Europeanism obscure your vision. One can get along with very little governmental authority. If you had lived and loved, as I did, in America, you would know better."

In Herzl's mature vision of *Old-New Land* the seemingly cameralist *negotiorum gestio* is clearly depicted as a temporary vehicle, as merely one moment in the creation of a self-governing populace. The Jewish Company and the Jewish Society as *gestors* for the Jews were as early as 1895 conceived as private enterprise corporations with stockholders, rather than as a bureaucratic executive (Herzl, 1946, p. 98). Herzl trusted free-market principles to interest both Jewish and non-Jewish investment in what was to be both a profitable and facilitating organ for Jewish resettlement. The deconstruction of the *negotiorum gestio* into a cooperative, self-governing commonwealth is described in *Old-New Land* as the *gestor* executive Joseph Levy recounts the transformation of the Jewish Company and the Jewish Society, which functioned as the *gestors* for the Jews of Europe (Herzl, 1960b, pp. 197, 199):

> *Levy:* The former New Society and the present one are the same organization, and yet different. Originally, it was a stock corporation, and now it is a co-operative. The co-operative is the legal heir of the stock corporation. . . .
>
> *Kingscourt:* Did the stockholders give their money away? If that's the idea, it's all a fairy tale.
>
> *Levy:* It will be clear to you in a moment, Mr. Kingscourt. . . . You need only distinguish between the various legal entities involved. We have here three judicial or abstract persons. Number one comprises the endowed foundations which had a combined capital of twelve millions sterling in 1900. Number two was a joint stock company organized with a capital of ten millions by London financiers who became interested in our cause when the grant of the charter was assured. Number three was the co-operative association of the colonists. The latter were represented by their chosen leaders. These leaders set the masses in motion only after an agreement had been reached with the joint stock company that it would later become a cooperative association. . . . You see how we were able to transfer the land to the commonwealth. The stock corporation came into the possession of the co-operative which, from then on, was officially called the "New Society."

One must see Herzl's thought from the point of view of the Austrian humanist formal cause or entelechy. His plan is always one that has stages of development.

2

Nonetheless, it is valuable to consider Jacques Kornberg's cultural assertion that Herzl's thought had cameralist roots. One of the chief figures of Enlightenment Austrian cameralism was Jewish—Joseph von Sonnenfels. The conversion of Sonnenfels' family to Christianity allowed him to become one of the bureaucratic elite in the courts of Maria Theresa and Joseph II. The German nobleman Adalbert von Konigshof in Herzl's *Old-New Land,* who changes his name to Kingscourt after experiencing the nonbureaucratic life in America and who finally decides to become a citizen of Jewish New Society, may be seen as a transformation of Sonnenfels back to his Jewish roots.[9] One cannot doubt that von Sonnenfels was a figure well known to Herzl. It is instructive to see Sonnenfels as an Austrian humanist model whose activities in Enlightenment Austria created a model that informed Herzl, even as Herzl separated himself from this cameralist heritage.

Joseph von Sonnenfels (1733-1817) was named the first Austrian professor of cameral science *(Staatswissenschaft)* in 1763 at the University of Vienna (Ingrao, 1994). He articulated the message to Maria Theresa, Joseph II, and the Austrian bureaucracy that "a society's productivity—and its tax base—grew in direct proportion to the size, living standards, health, and happiness of its people" (Ingrao, 1994). The concept of state planning emerged in the era of Sonnenfels. The German expression *Kammerziele* (treasury goals) became current (Grimm and Grimm, 1873-1889, vol. K, p. 132). Sonnenfels formed plans and means for their realization in his effort to improve conditions in Austria. His plans were structured according to the Austrian humanist principle of the formal cause—a pattern that guides the steps that lead to its fulfillment. As Herzl later put it, the shape of what one plans for must be given but not so much concreteness that it frustrates the interface of the plan and reality. Such plans were deemed best when flexible, following Plato's dictum that true knowledge of a situation is when "one is neither too far ahead, nor too far behind events themselves" (Plato, 1961, p. 412). This reflected the Austrian humanist notion of allowing nature to speak as the best guide in addressing affairs. In fact, the entire notion of planning was still suspect in the German as well as the Austrian culture, as Grimm's dictionary conveys in its citing of Goethe and Schiller in regard to plans that were *gescheitert, vernichtet, verietelt,* or *verworfen* (Grimm and Grimm, 1873-1889).

In a play Sonnenfels (1764) composed in the late 1750s and early 1760s, *Xerxes der Friedsame* (Xerxes the Peaceful), produced for an audience on April 23, 1764, he illustrates how a cameralist minister behaves as he constructs a plan and the extent to which he depends on the goodwill of the entire populace as that plan is put into effect. Ataphernes, the uncle of the brothers Xerxes and Artemenes, as a minister of state is charged with determining which of these two youths will become the next king of Persia. He deliberates through five acts, taking his time in order to allow the protagonists as well as the populace to demonstrate their separate characters. His plan is to name a ruler who has certain characteristics that will be sufficient in integrating the common people and the army. He waits in part in order to be certain that these characteristics are demonstrated by either Xerxes or Artemenes in their everyday behavior. This pretest of a plan reminds one of Herzl's critical analysis of Baron Hirsch's Argentina experiment, as well as the constant interface of critical commentators in the narrative of *Old-New Land* as the full extent of his final plan is fleshed out. A quick decision, one that is influenced by a sudden turn of events or some other salient pressure, is suspect. Xerxes comments on the *unwillkommenes Licht* (the unwelcome light) of a momentary insight that distorts rather than clarifies. In order to judge correctly one must take time to be personally in touch with the live presence of others so that false motives are never inferred. What seems to be the case in this moment must be weighed also against the history of and expectations toward the parties involved (Sonnenfels, 1764, p. 42). In other words, time is conceived morphologically, as a durational development, rather than as a singular epiphany. Throughout Herzl's *Old-New Land* the reader is reminded of the historical efforts of European thinkers to create ideal communities, and his own effort is cast within the scope of this history (Herzl, 1960b, pp. 74, 148-150). The characteristics that are mentioned for the just and effective ruler will include such a measured response to events, enabling the administrator of a state to weight each event in the light of the actual conditions and the entire range of the plan as it has been conceived.

Besides developmental thinking, the effective ruler, according to Sonnenfels (1764, p. 11), must exhibit *Sanftmuth* (good temper or gentleness), *vertrauliche Herablassung* (intimate or familial condescension), and *Wohl* (attention to the common good) capable of bringing the cooperation of "the poorest among the people." Xerxes gives evidence of each of the characteristics in his treatment of his family and vassals. One must note that "condescension" was not a pejorative term in the age of aristocracy. The common people for Sonnenfels still had the ultimate voice because of the natural fact that they were the nation, Ataphernes says (Sonnenfels, 1764, p. 73): *"Das Volk hat den Auspruch gethan, den ihr meiner freyen Wahl überliesset. Xerxes ist durch die allgemeine Stimme zum Könige ausgerufen*" (The people have spoken, to whom I have freely given over my choice. Xerxes is by the common voice called to be King). Sonnenfels had faith in populist absolutism and in that faith challenged the feudal constitution with his attention to the real demand of the entire nation (Ingrao, 1994). In this he laid the groundwork for a redistribution of power toward the voice of the people that Herzl further made possible in the form of the assembly of cooperatives.

David Littwak, who will finally become the president of the New Society in *Old-New Land,* replicates the personal characteristics of Sonnenfels's Xerxes. David's "condescension" is that of a natural elite among those with whom he has shared destiny. Herzl could never shed his sense of superiority, although he did move from "popular absolutism" to a genuine populism in his projections of the future society. David Littwak lives high on a hill in a villa called *Friedrichshof.* The name of his villa calls to mind Frederick the Great. Littwak has a Negro footman. This unfortunate racist stereotype can be seen as a vestige of Herzl's fantasies of old, teutonic nobility. Nonetheless, Littwak as a name is a play on the Eastern European Jews—the common herd—yet their spiritual heritage and potent greatness. David and his family were "little people" at the beginning of the novel, literally beggars in the streets.

David Littwak is a man of peace as is Xerxes. The New Society will not have a military to pursue foreign wars (Herzl, 1960b, p. 79); Xerxes pictures a Persia that remains small, concerned with its own domestic issues, raising no challenge to other nations (Sonnenfels 1764, pp. 21-24).

One of the most marked commonalities between Sonnenfels and Herzl is their mutual tolerance for continuing differences in thoughts and values among the populace of the imagined states. The multiethnic realities of Austria, of course, are a background for toleration. In Sonnenfels's play, a remarkable closing scene sees Xerxes pardoning those who plotted against him, giving them their freedom, and when even they object this is too lenient, Xerxes bolsters their self-image so that they may accept their self-worth. Differences do not disturb the political leaders of Herzl's New Society because, as it is an amalgam of cooperatives, each largely self-governing, no one need become the same in values. The conflict of ideas enriches the whole. The kaleidoscope of character difference merely is proof of the healthy range of humanity that makes up the whole. The loving positivism of Sonnenfels's Austrian humanism that embraces difference with open-armed acceptance helps one see the enduring roots of what some have criticized in Herzl as wooden, naive writing (cf. Stewart, 1974). When the protagonists of *Old-New Land* are asked for the essential trait that has brought the New Society into being, David Littwak says "love and pain" (Herzl, 1960b, p. 295).

3

Considering Carl Menger's Austrian humanistic influence on the political-economics of Theodor Herzl may have a strange ring to the historically and institutionally minded economist. Menger as an economic thinker; his influence on Herzl is attested to by others (Stewart, 1974). But Austrian humanism? It is Emil Kauder's appreciation of Austrian humanism in Menger's economics that first stirred my interest in the significance of Austrian humanism in Herzl. Kauder points out the Aristotelian thought in Menger's economics, especially the formal causal pattern integral to his notion of marginal utility. In this vein he calls Menger's economics a "social ontology" (Kauder, 1958, pp. 416-419). Ontologically, the state is an interdependent humanity with a distinct anthropological character. The economist must discern the fundamental human needs of a society and work to establish a public policy that can institute and fund public and private means to satisfy those needs. The range of needs will be felt in differing degrees by the diversity of the population at differing times because of variations in age, class, skills, and interests. Marginal utility is a way of identifying and charting the fluctuating assessment of needs perceived by individuals and groups in the general population (Kauder, 1958; Johnston, 1972). The ontological unfolding of the people is continual, but it remains in a constant pattern because of the essential, enduring character of the species-needs. One can predict the form the state as a whole must maintain in order to enable each generation of persons the freedom to realize their individual lives.

Menger (1840-1921) expresses in this theory an aristocratic populism that recalls Sonnenfels's cameralism and reflects the actual Austrian liberal statism of his early maturity and middle years. He was a tutor to the Crown Prince Rudolf of Austria in 1876. Menger's lectures to Rudolf found a balance between cameralist responsibility and the capitalist thought of Adam Smith (Menger, 1994). The state is given the responsibility for cultivating the public and private recognition of the range of needs that comprehends the "social ontology" of the Austrian lands.

Menger's stress on free enterprise within a state oversight is halfway to the populist political-economic authority Herzl will finally institute in his projected Zion. By focusing economic policy within the stated desires of a populace, authority in establishing and directing economic policy is ultimately a function of that populace. This authority is exercised by the demand of people for certain goods and services. Herzl's plan for the establishment of the Jewish state began with the private needs of the Jews—freedom from discrimination (Herzl, 1946, pp. 85-87). The vehicle chosen to begin the solution to the problem was private enterprise. The Jewish Company and the related Society of Jews are conceived as joint-stock companies in the model of England East India Company (1946, p. 98; 1960b, p. 199). Colonial construction through the agency of private enterprise was seen by Herzl as both a pragmatic necessity to gain the support of European nation-states and the most adequate model for the nature of effective state building in light of human drives. [10] It is this private foundation that will make possible the transition of a form of cameralist decision making in the early stages of the Jewish settlement to complete populist control by the development of the mature New Society. The Jewish Company and the Society of Jews as cameralist-type decision makers empowered by the legal concept of *negatio gestor* become in the spirit of free enterprise a self-eliminating, transitional body as they sell their stock to the settlers of the New Society (1960b, p. 197).

Yet as an Austrian humanist Herzl can never eliminate the old completely. The spirit of private corporatism will live on in the ability of the cooperative associations within the New Society to form "trusts" or "syndicates" (1960b, pp. 290-291). The new and the old are linked by ancestry and thus organic development. Within the cooperative associations a common oversight must exist in order to maintain the infrastructure that each group will necessarily draw on. Water, transportation, education, housing—these are common needs in a society. While denying in *Old-New Land* that the New Society is in fact a state, Herzl does require a national assembly of cooperatives and a president to regulate the whole. The integration of public and private forms for furthering economic life will always reflect the trials, errors, and successes of past political-economic organization. David Littwak (Herzl, 1960b, p. 91) remarks on the relationship between old and new forms of political economy in the New Society: "It is, if you choose to call it so, a patriarchal relation, but one expressed in ultra-modern forms." Herzl (1960b, p. 289) expresses the Austrian humanist sense of a developing social organism that never completely denies its roots:

> Something Dr. Marcus said lately about the coexistence of things has been running through my mind. Old institutions need not go under at one blow in order that new ones may be born. Not every son is posthumous. Parents usually live along with their children for many years. It follows that an old social order need not break up because a new one is on the way. Having seen here a new order composed of none but old institutions, I have come to believe neither in the complete destruction nor the complete renewal of a social order. I believe—how shall I put it?—in a gradual reconstruction; of society. And I also believe that such a reconstruction never comes about through systematic planning, but as the need arises. Necessity is the builder. We decide to alter a floor, a staircase, a wall, a roof, to install

electricity or water supply only as the need arises, or even when some new invention wins its way. The house as a whole remains what it was.

Herzl's metaphor of the house that is the alpha and omega within which change is gradually made captures Menger's notion of the enduring state that is in constant organizational flux as it attends the signals for change the theory of marginal utility puts into focus. The nature of state planning in Menger's political-economic thought preserves the Austrian humanist characteristic of flexibility and attention to natural solutions. Let the voice of the populace articulate its life needs. Herzl in the above passage confirms this perspective of allowing need to dictate action.

Menger's conception of a social ontology driven by the voiced needs of an entire populace is, as stated, a formal causal conception. In ordinary terms, conventions and habits function as mechanisms to channel and move the small expressions of will among millions into the unfolding but constant pattern these conventions and habits themselves configure. Herzl (1946, p. 135) describes the power of the habits and customs of a culture to function in this manner: "For these little habits are the thousand and one fine delicate threads which together go to make up an unbreakable rope." "Thus," says Herzl (1946, p. 135), "when we journey out of Egypt again we shall not leave the fleshpots behind." Indeed, Herzl encouraged the establishment of European theater, restaurants, and even enabled the transfer of private wealth to support social distinctions and the accompanying material benefits bred in the European world he wished to leave. Herzl believed the civilizing elements of these habits and conventions outweighed the social abuses. The thousand and one habits and customs are what another Austrian humanist, Adalbert Stifter, called *das sanfte Gesetz* (the soft law) by which civilization was formed and sustained (Stifter, n.d.).

4

Kauder linked Stifter's "soft law" to Carl Menger's fellow Austrian economist F. von Wieser. Kauder (1958, p. 423) referred to Wieser's text *The Sociology of Power,* which argued an economy must be based on charity and not power. The strength of love for one's fellows was seen by Wieser as the most objective basis for a healthy economy because it recognized the essential interdependence of peoples. The soft law was the effect of each individual act of charity in its cumulative outcome for the whole nation. Each act that recognized and provided for the need of another multiplied throughout a culture was an empowerment of the whole from below, as it were. Agency in such a society was in each ordinary person and their immediate intentions to care for others as well as for themselves. In such a society the dynamic leader who intervened with force to establish new directions would not be needed. Cause for change would be the manifold charitable wills of everyone (Kauder, 1958, p. 424). Kauder (1958, p. 424) at this point, in an aside to the reader, attempts to soften the nonscientific appearance of such statements: "It is easy to sneer at the dream of triumphant love, yet he who does so misses the meaning of Wieser's and Stifter's social message. The final triumph of brotherly love forms the goal, for which the statesman is striving in spite of power politics, labor unrest, and all that misery which existed in Old Austria." Sonnenfels's conclusion to *Xerxes, Der Friedsame* is a testimony to the seriousness given by Austrian cameralist policy to the value of charity as the binding leaven of the state. The final page of Herzl's *Old-New Land* has a similar reconciliation of all differences. Ten individuals with diverse points of view are reconciled by dint of a mutual openness that melds them to each other and the New Society. Literary critics might call both Sonnenfels's and Herzl's endings a comic narrative resolution. Cooperation as an economic motive, however, is more than a narrative ploy in the Austrian tradition: it is the Leibnizian sense of preestablished harmony, with a preplanning that seeks to ensure Adam Smith's notion of the invisible hand that integrates separate wills.

Kauder might have associated Stifter's humanism in the form of the "soft law" with Menger's theory of marginal utility. While love and charity are integral to the dynamic of Austrian humanism, there are a plethora of values that operate within Stifter's notion of the soft law. Menger's marginal utility is based upon the idea of a range of differing values that each spend themselves in a human gesture that reaches for satisfaction. As with Leibnitz's "rational appetite" (Leibnitz, 1969, p. 644) the ordinary person desires what will fulfill an element of the idea that will bring him into harmony with everyone else. There is no one dominant value or action that can bring progress to the state or health to the economy but rather a series of interrelated demands coming from all quarters of the state. The art of governance is seeking equilibrium or in some cases tilting activity toward the most salient new demands. Thus the soft law or marginal utility, if I may be permitted this working construct, is the interrelated dynamic of each associated action and reaction—a formal causal pattern of moments rather than some intrusive efficient cause. In order to fully appreciate how Herzl shares this notion of economic activity and creates the foundation for it in the agencies that monitor the whole society, it is valuable to look at Stifter's (n.d., pp. 13-15) description of the soft law in more detail:

The light movement of the wind, the rippling of the water, the growth of the wheat, the billowing of the sea, the greening of the earth, the shining of the heavens, the shimmering of the stars, I hold as great [in significance]: the magnificent storm that draws one into it, the lightning which splinters houses, the gale that drives a conflagration, the mountain that spills fire, the earthquake that disintegrates the ground, I do not hold to be greater than the above appearances, indeed I hold them as less, as they [too] are only effects of much higher laws, [yet] they occur only in single instances, and are the results of one-sided causes.

The force which causes the milk in the poor woman's crock to rise up and overflow is like that which drives forth the lava from the volcano, and leaves it on the surface of the mountain to flow down. Only the latter appearance is more obvious, compelling the glance of the uninformed and the inattentive. . . . And as it is in outer nature, so is it also in the inner [nature] of humankind. An entire life full of justice, simplicity, self-control, understanding, effectiveness in one's circle, admiration of the beautiful, united with a calm, resigned dying, I hold as great: powerful movements of disposition, frightful manifestations of anger, the desire for revenge, the inflamed spirit that strives for activity, and in its excitement, compels, disturbs, and even throws away its own life I hold not as great, rather as less significant, since these things are only manifestations of single and one-sided forces as the occurrence of storms, fire-spilling mountains, and earthquakes.

We will seek the soft law, through which humankind is led. There are forces which intend the enduring of the individual. These forces are receivers and bestowers of everything necessary for the endurance and development of the person. They secure the stability of the individual, and thereby all individuals.

The soft law as revealed in the above passages is a process whereby organic and inorganic nature, and the human spirit, develop and manifest themselves. This is on the one hand an ontological process, for the being of nature and the human spirit are described in their goals and operation; on the other hand, however, the soft law is for the human an epistemological process, for the manner in which a person knows the events of his own and external nature conditions what he may see and what he himself becomes.

Ontologically, we may state the following characteristics of the soft law:

1. It is a universal process made up of many separate laws, wherein a unity of effect is achieved that is quiet and ceaseless.

2. It appears most evident in small, unobtrusive phenomena that are widespread rather than in unique, overwhelming expressions of nature.

3. It is beneficent as it encourages and sustains growth and maintenance of nature and humankind, yet united in it is a calm, resigned dying that is part of its nature.

4. The "dying" is an expression of the morphological nature of being. Each moment of existence spends itself for the sustenance of the whole. The phenomenon's shape may change in the various phases of its development, but the process of the law itself remains a constant.

Epistemologically, there is one major principle for identifying the soft law and making public policy to facilitate its presence in human institutions—*gelassenheit* (letting be). One must as a midwife birth only what wills life. One must allow nature to announce its plans.

Herzl articulates both the ontological and the epistemological dynamic of the soft law in a passage in Old *New Land* where Joseph Levy's brilliant ability to identify the necessary fundamentals of the potential society are described. Levy is able to institute the necessary infrastructure to attract colonists and give them the needed support to enable their own separate and interrelated drives to flourish. Each separate activity interfaces with another for the good of the whole. Although competition may create failures in some cases, the free enterprise that is engendered within a planned range of goods and services leads to a beneficent outcome. Herzl (1960b, p. 212) calls the interrelated dynamics of growth the new *Had Gadya: "Had Gadya! Had Gadya!* (One Kid! One Kid!) was a serio-comic legend in the book of the Seder service. The cat ate the kid, the dog mangled the cat, the stick beat the dog, the fire consumed the stick, the water extinguished the fire, the ox drank the water, the slaughterer killed the ox, the Angel of Death carried off the slaughterer, while above all was God. . . . That's how . . . the story of the New Society runs. The ox is replaced by the coal, and the coal by the water."

Herzl's novel *Old-New Land* has several protagonists like Joe Levy who comprehend the fluctuating interests within a state that the theory of marginal utility puts into focus and who support the political-social planning that addresses these fluctuating needs. Adalbert von Königshof is one; another is the narrator, Friedrich Loewenberg. The ancestor of this quasi-public and quasi-private perspective is the more public absolutist populism of Sonnenfels (and Adalbert Stifter, who in 1848 supported the authority of the beneficent emperor). However, Adalbert von Königshof and Friedrich Loewenberg (who is "captured," as it were, by the elder Baron) are of an older school of thought, more related to the absolutist populism of the Austrian past. David Littwak, the real hero of *Old-New Land,* represents democratic populism, albeit with adequate community planning.

There is a Stifter (n.d.) short story in *Bunte Steine* (colorful gemstones) whose hero reflects the meaning carried by David Littwak. "Limestone"

(Stifter, 1990) is the story of a "little man" who at least after 1815 becomes the typical hero in the Austrian humanist tradition (Johnston, 1972). The little man of "Limestone" exists at the bottom of the social scale and despite his humble, insignificant, and virtually invisible existence, has the intelligence and persistence to be a community planner. "Limestone" is an allusion to the manner in which this rock is formed: limestone is a consequence of the artifacts left behind by millions of small sea creatures who gave the fruit of their existence to the whole. Over time the many generations of such lives create the bedrock on which communities may settle and thrive. The little man of "Limestone" helps bridge a dangerous stream by standing in its current, so children can reach school, and leaves his small inheritance for the construction of a school on safe ground. His planning is successful because he acts toward the needs most apparent in his community with a personal gesture. He does not rely on public agencies; rather he effects change through private enterprise. His very body fills the watery hole that is a public danger, and any monies he accrued beyond his modest needs and the balance of his material remains were directed toward the good of the whole.

David Littwak, the eventual president of the New Society, is a little man, a waif who is son of a street beggar. David Littwak's "letting be" as a conscious policy in relation to his community is expressed by his belief in private enterprise and competitive *laissez faire*, balanced by the cooperative *ethos* of the soft law. He promoted profit sharing with his workers, and his public service is without ambition, a simple willingness to offer his acquired intelligence for the good of his community. Without running for president he is elected overwhelmingly. As the little man of Stifter's "Limestone," a million David Littwak are the bedrock of a civilized world.

One may hope that Theodor Herzl's Austrian humanist political-economic vision will be considered as relevant to contemporary issues by public policy makers as the Hapsburg multiethnic experience that was its matrix. Even the most well-meaning public authority must disperse its functional authority to the populace that is its sole rationale. The well-meaning cameralist state could not sustain its oversight when its educated populace sought to express its own political will. Even the democratic-republican state distances its citizens from real participatory decision making. Herzl's recognition that a society could have its locus of power within private interests that nonetheless appreciate the commonwealth of all may be one model that informs the current desire to deconstruct government and privatize society.

Notes

1.   See Emil Kauder's (1958) article on the centrality of Aristotle to Austrian thought.Kauder's aritcle focuses on economic thought in particular, but his appreciations are for Austrian intellectual norms in general. The most thorough study of the "Austrian Mind" in recent years has been Johnston (1972). Johnston stresses the formative influence of Leibnitz on modern Austrian thought in the arts and the sciences. However, the marked influence of Aristotle on Leibnitz could have occasioned Johnston to a greater appreciation of the former's influence on the Austrian mind. Leibnitz discusses the significance of Aristotle for his thinking and the modern philosophy of his day in his letter to Jacob Thomasius, April 20/30, 1669; see Leibnitz (1969, p. 93-104).
2.   Aristotle's formal cause or entelechy is central to Leibnitz's notion of the individuating monad that *fulfills* its idea (Leibnitz, 1969, no. 18, p. 644).
3.   See Johnston (1972, pp. 214-221, 20-23, 89-92, 223-229) on these respective characteristics in Austrian thinking. The openness to natural solutions is called by Johnston "therapeutic nihilsm."
4.   A testament to the incisive, intelligence of Herzl's vision as a *feuilletonist is* given by Zweig (1943, pp. 101-109) in his autobiography. As an editor of the *feuilleton* Herzl helped cultivate profound intellects such as Zweig and Hugo von Hoffmansthal.
5.   See the discussion of Locke's concept of sovereignty by Peter Laslett in Locke (1988, pp. 113-115). Laslett sees the central concept of state building for Locke as trust rather than a legal basis. The notion of subjective trust is a weak form of Austrian humanism's anthropological notion of the fundamental interdependence of human existence.
6.   The influence of Otto von Gierke on English thought at the turn of the century is conveyed by Maine (1889) and Maitland's (1990) introduction of Gierke to an English audience in his essays and translations.
7.   Herzl (1946, p. 139) writes: "The Jewish people are at present prevented by the Diaspora from conducting their political affairs themselves. Besides, they are in a condition of more or less severe distress in many parts of the world. They need, above all things a *gestor*.
8.   Herzl (1960a, p. 266) writes on November 6, 1895: "A deeply discouraging day. Community Councillor Stern and others came to the office. They are all people who expect salvation to come from the government and who go on bended knee to the ministers. Therefore, they would have believed in me if I had become Badeni's journalistic right-hand man. And so now I have no authority with them."
9.   As Kingscourt leaves "Friedrichshof" in the New Society in a limousine accompanied by a Negro footman, the horn reminds him of "the good old days. The postilion with his horn" (Herzl, 1960b, p. 116). In this vein of literary interpretation, where characters are overdetermined symbols for attitudes, Joseph Levy, the *gestor* of the New Society, can be seen as an alter ego of Kingscourt and a reincarnation of Joseph von Sonnenfels. Joseph Levy is like Joseph in Egypt or Joseph in the court of Maria Theresa and Joseph II—an effective administrator. He is only heard through a record he leaves behind (Herzl, 1960b, p. 188).
10. Oskar K. Rabinowicz (1960, pp. 37-48) discusses Herzl's practical wisdom in the light of the foreign policy of England in casting the Zionist movement within a corporative enterprise modeled on the East India Company.

References

Aristotle. (1941). "Nicomachean Ethics" (pp. 1027-1028, 1140a-1140b). "Topica" (pp. 188-189, 100b-101a). In *Basic Works of Aristotle,* ed. by Richard McKeon. NY: Random House.

Bein, Alex. (1941). *Theodore Herzl: A Biography*, Translated by Maurice Samuel. Philadelphia: Jewish Publication Society of America.

Gierke, Otto von. (1868-1873). *Das Deutsche Genossenschaftrecht*. City: Publisher.

Grimm, Jacob and William Grimm. (1873-1889). *Deutches Wörterbuch*. Leipzig: S. Hirzel.

Herman, David. (1994). "Zionism as Utopian Discourse." *Clio* 23(3), 234-246.

Herzl, Theodor. (1946). *The Jewish State: An Attempt at a Modern Solution of the Jewish Question*. New York: American Zionist Emergency Council.

Herzl, Theodor. (1960a). *The Complete Diaries of Theodor Herzl*, edited by Raphael Patai and translated by Harry Zohn (vol. 1). New York: Herzl Press and Thomas Yoseloff.

Herzl, Theodor. (1960b). *Old-New Land* ("Altneuland"), translated by Lotta Levensohn. New York: Block Publishing Company and Herzl Press.

Ingrao, Charles. (1994). *The Hapsburg Monarchy 1618-1815*. Cambridge: Cambridge University Press.

Johnston, William M. (1972). *The Austrian Mind: An Intellectual and Social History 1848-1938*. Berkeley: University of California Press.

Kauder, Emil. (1958). "Intellectual and Political Roots of the Older Austrian School." *Zeitschrift für Nationalokonomie* 17(4), 411-425.

Kornberg, Jacques. (1993). *Theodor Herzl: From Assimilation to Zionism*. Bloomington: Indiana University Press.

Leibnitz, Gottfried Wilhelm. (1969). *Philosophical Papers and Letters*, translated and edited by Leory E. Loemker (2nd ed.). Dordrecht, Holland: Reidel.

Locke, John. (1988). *Two Treatises of Government*, edited by Peter Laslett. Cambridge: Cambridge University Press.

Maine, Henry Sumner. (1889). *Village-Communities in the East and West: Six Lectures Delivered at Oxford*. New York: Holt.

Maitland, Frederic William. (1900). *Political Theories of the Middle Age*. Cambridge: Cambridge University Press.

Menger, Carl. (1994). *Carl Menger's Lectures to Crown Prince Rudolf of Austria*, edited by Erich W. Streissler and Monika Streissler and translated by Monika Streissler with the assistance of David Good. Brookfield, VT: Elgar.

Plato. (1961). "Cratylus." In *The Collected Dialogues of Plato*. Bollingen Series 71. Princeton: Princeton University Press.

Rabinowitcz, Oskar. (1960). "Herzl and England." In Raphael Patai (ed.), *Herzl Year Book*. New York: Herzl Press.

Schorske, Carl. (1980). *Fin-de-Siecle Vienna: Politics and Culture*. New York: Knopf.

Sonnenfels, Joseph von. (1764). *Xerxes der Friedsame*. Vienna: Kraussischen Buchladen nächst der K.K. Burg.

Stewart, Desmond. (1974). *Theodore Herzl*. Garden City, NY: Doubleday.

Stifter, Adalbert. (n.d.). *Bunte Steine*. In *Stifter Werke in Zwei Bänden* (vol. 1). Salzburg/Stuttgart: Das Bergland Buch Verlag.

Stifter, Adalbert. (1990). "Limestone." In *Brigitta with Abdias, Limestone, The Forest Path*, translated by Helen Watanabe-O'Kelly. London: Angel.

Tönnies, Ferdinand. (1887). *Gemeinschaft and Gesellschaft*. City: Publisher.

Zweig, Stefan. (1943). *The World of Yesterday: An Autobiography*. Lincoln: University of Nebraska Press.

Interwar Eastern European Jewish Parties
And the Language Issue

Joshua A. Fishman

Abstract: *Four factors (language [Yiddish/Hebrew], socialism/capitalism, Zionism/ Diasporism, and secularism/religion) defined the political space of interwar Polish Jewry. Language ideology was highly implicational vis-a-vis Zionism/Diasporism, but even in this connection there were exceptions, resulting in Yiddishist/Zionist combinations. Socialism/capitalism and secularism/ religion were less implicational, resulting in a substantial number of unique political combinations and an unusual number of small parties in addition to the few major ones. Although the political significance of language can be fully appreciated only in terms of its linkages to other major issues, some of these linkages are quite idiosyncratic and, therefore, nonimplicational.*

1. Introduction

Sociolinguistics has constantly illuminated the proposition that stable multi-lingual populations use their several languages in a functionally complimentary and orderly way, related to extralinguistic considerations, rather than in isolation from such considerations or at random. The present paper will try to examine a related point with respect to the ideologies or "issues" that concern stable multilingual populations when their hitherto unideologized languages become politicized. The case to be examined in detail is that of interwar Eastern European Jewry in general and of Polish Jews most particularly.

Poland, in its interwar boundaries, had the proportionally largest Jewish population (viewed as a percentage of the total population) of any country in the world (3.5 million or 10%). By the outbreak of World War II, Jews had already lived in Poland for roughly a thousand years and had developed there a quintessentially Jewish culture, both along traditional and along modern lines. Polish Jewry is in many ways comparable in importance, authenticity, and creativity to such prior great Jewish centers as those that had existed in Moslem and Christian Spain before the Reconquista and the Inquisition, or in Babylon during the first millennium after Christ, or even in the Holy Land itself, before most of its inhabitants spread throughout the circum-Mediterranean Diaspora.

However, Polish Jewry was also unique in many ways and one of these ways was its internal political and ideological diversification (see Table 1). The juxtiposition of traditional and modern life styles and beliefs, on the one hand, and intensive political participation (both intramurally and at times extramurally, when these parties participated in Polish elections to the national *sjeym* or city councils), on the other hand, was particularly noteworthy among Polish Jews during the interwar years. One of the major dimensions of contention was the language issue itself (Table 1, factor i), each political party positioning itself on either one side or the other of the Yiddish and/or Hebrew debate. But the foregoing debate was itself only part of a larger one, pertaining

Table 1. *Inter-war Eastern European Jewish parties in 4-factorial space*

Party / Ideol. complex	Factor i		Factor ii		Factor iii		Factor iv	
	Y	H	Soc	Cap	Z	Dias	Rel	Sec
GZ								
3		x/p		x	x			
Miz								
4		x/p		x	x		x	
RPZ								
6	x ?	x	x		x a	x ?		x
LPZ								
6	x	x	x		x a	x		x
ShHa								
4		x	x		x a			x
Territ								
4	x					x a t	x ?	x
AgYis								
5	x ?	x		x		x	x	
PagYis								
5	x ?	x	x			x	x	
Folk								
3	x					x		x
JLB								
4	x		x			x		x
Row T								
44	7	7	5	3	5	7	4	6
Fac T		14		8		12		10

Key to Table 1:
Factors
i. Language: Yiddish (Y) and/or Hebrew (H).
ii. Socialism (S); Capitalism (C).
iii. Zionism (Z) and/or Diasporas (Dias).
iv. Religion (Rel) and/or Secularism (Sec).

Parties
GZ   General Zionists[a] (1929)[b].
Miz   Mizrakhi (1902): "Eastern," i.e. focused on Zion.
RPZ   Right Poaley Tsiyon (1906)[c]: "Workers of Zion": right wing.
LPZ   Left Poaley Tsiyon (1923): "Workers of Zion": left wing.
ShHa   Shomer Hatsayir (1916): "Young Gaurd."
Territ   Teritorialists (1905)[b]:Favoring a suitable (unsettled and uncontested) territory
         for Jewish resettlement outside of Zion.
AgIs   Agudes Yisroel (1912, 1921): "The Union of Israel".
PAGIs   Poaley Agudes Yisroel (1922)[d] "Workers of the Union of Israel."
Folk   Folkistn (1918): "Folkists" (i.e. for the rank and file, all-inclusive).
JLB   Jewish Labor Band (1897): "Jewish Labor Alliance."

p   favors acquisition of Polish for citizenship functions (found only among
        two parties that oppose Yiddish)
a   favors agricultural settlements in Palestine
t   favors a territory less contested than Zion
?   uncertain or fluctuating support

a. Another political party, Zionist Revisionists (1925), had the same ideological profile
as the General Zionists and differed from them only in its insistence that "strong
measures" (possibly including terrorism) might be necessary in order to take control of
the Land of Israel from the British "occupants." It is not listed in this table in order to
avoid redundancy and so as not to designate "terrorism" as a separate factor, since it is
ideologically limited to only one party.
b. Date of beginning of functioning in Poland is not clear.
c. "Right"/"left" differentiation began in 1923.
d. Founded in Poland but functioned mostly elsewhere.

to socialism/capitalism (factor ii), Zionism/Diasporaism (factor iii), and
religion/secularism (factor iv). It was the involvement of language in all of
these issues for most of the parties that made language such a key factor in
Polish Jewish life. Language was implicational as well as all-pervasive in
political affairs. And Polish Jewry's example in connection with all of these
issues was closely monitored and emulated in the neighboring Baltic States and
in Rumania; and had the Soviets permitted, it would have been emulated in
Russia, Belarussia, and the Ukraine as well (and, indeed, still was frequently

emulated well into the mid and even late 1920s).

II. The Parties

Ten distinctive political parties that were active during this period will be examined.[1] They subdivide into two major and quite different clusters. A smaller semicluster that shares some features of both major ones may also be recognized.

a. The Zionist/Hebrew Cluster

Five out of the ten parties were Zionist in orientation. They looked forward to the implementation of the Balfour Proclamation (1917), in accord with which "Palestine" would be "looked upon with favor" (by the British government) as "a home for the Jewish people." These parties fostered first and second-language Hebrew acquisition and language-spread efforts even before members left to resettle in the Middle East. Hebrew was viewed as particularly appropriate for reactivating the ancient spirit of independence, justice, and morality that had characterized the Jews in their original homeland. Note that Hebrew advocacy is the only other common feature shared among all the Zionist parties, even though two of them also found room for Yiddish in their programs. In matters of socialism/capitalism and religion/secularism the Zionist parties were quite disunited. Even in connection with a favored type of settlement pattern within Palestine itself, some favored the establishment of agricultural/rural settlements there, while others saw nothing amiss in continued urban life, both in the Holy Land and in the Diaspora. Even the inevitability of continued Jewish concentrations in the Diaspora per se was acceptable to some Zionist parties (those that were also favorable to Yiddish).

b. The Diaspora/Yiddish Cluster

The remaining five parties were Diasporist in orientation (counting the Territorialist in this cluster, since their hoped-for territory was, of necessity, outside of Zion). All of these five were pro-Yiddish, a language that had been born in the Diaspora and that was the vernacular of Ashkenaz,[2] although the two religious parties in this cluster were also pro-Hebrew, counterbalancing the two Labor Zionist parties in the previous cluster that were also pro-Yiddish and pro-Diaspora. With respect to the other two factors, socialism/capitalism and religion/secularism, this cluster is quite diverse (as was the previous cluster). Diasporist parties differed from one another in connection with the latter two factors, while those two themselves were only weakly related to each other.

C. Straddlers: The More Complex "Parties in the Middle"

Given that there are two strongly implicational factors and two nonimplicational ones, those few parties that straddle the stronger factors may be considered as atypically mixed types. The two pro-Yiddish religious parties and the two pro-Yiddish Labor Zionist parties all support Hebrew as well and the latter two parties straddle the Zionist/ Diasporist divide as well. These four parties therefore have above-average *ideological complexity scores* (if their "?" ratings hold up, i.e., turn out to be x's, under further scrutiny). It is this greater complexity that differentiates between the various religious parties (e.g., between the Agudas Yisroyel-related parties and the Mizrakhi) as well as between the various socialist parties (e.g., between the Bund and Left Poaley Zion). The average complexity score for the six simplex parties is 3.5, but the above-named straddler parties have average complexity scores of 5.5.

III. The Issues

A. Language: Hebrew, Yiddish and/or the Co-Territorial Language

In premodern times, language had not been a conscious issue among Jews. Even the holyness of Hebrew was not much stressed and there is no "commandment" to speak or safegaurd (or even pray in) Hebrew. The modernization and the political ideologization of both Yiddish and Hebrew occurred at approximately the same time and even, to an appreciable extent, among the same writers and intellectuals during the last decades of the nineteenth and the first decades of the twentieth century. The latter part of this period is referred to as "the language war," and by the outbreak of the First World War (and certainly by its conclusion) it left Hebrew victorious in Palestine and Yiddish victorious in Poland and in the Diaspora more generally. Writers who had previously written in both languages now began to choose sides, some going one way and some the other way. Separate ideological/practical World Conferences were convened for each language. Each language was proclaimed to be "the" (in the case of Hebrew) (or at least "a," in the case of Yiddish) "national Jewish language" by at least some of its respective adherents. Neither side vigorously protested the strongarm tactics (burning of kiosks displaying publications in the "wrong" language, legal prohibitions, the hurling of public insults at individuals daring to speak the "wrong" language, interruption of lectures via raucous protest demonstrations, expulsion of individuals from party membership, arrests, print prohibitions, theater prohibitions, etc.) implemented on its behalf, while strongly condemning those implemented against it (see Figure 1). While the most serious conflicts took place in the Soviet Union and in Palestine, those in the diaspora led to the formation of an American-based "League for the Defense of Yiddish in the Land of Israel" and contributed to the splintering of the Labor Zionist movement into a right and left wing on three continents. Younger generations began to be educated in supplementary and full day schools (attended in lieu of public education at government expense) that provided absolutely no knowledge of the "other language" or its literature. When such world-class authors as Sholem Aleichem and Y. L. Perets were translated from Yiddish into Hebrew, no mention was often even made that the original had been written in Yiddish.[3]

The entanglement of each language with its own cluster of parties contributed to the formation and adoption of its own associated myths. Hebrew was touted as the language of a "new Jew," one who was not only freed from Diasporal fear of and servitude to non-Jews but, in secular Hebraist circles, freed from false "medieval" beliefs and "meaningless" rituals, while in Hebraist religious circles, it was hailed as bringing one closer to God and to the spirit of the ancient rabbis and prophets. For both groups, their use of Hebrew legitimated

Figure I. `A Weak Position for a Strong Complaint'. Hebrew writers in Palestine (under the British Mandate) suppress Yiddish while protesting the suppression of Hebrew in the Soviet Union. (`Der groyser kundes', August 30, 1926)

their return to the Homeland and for both of them it symbolized the potential ingathering and unification of a greater Jewish world than that of Eastern Europe alone: including the Jewries of North Africa, the Near East, and Asia (where many males were Hebrew-literate), as well as the dejudaized Jews of Western Europe and the Americas (for most of whom it could serve as their one and only Jewish language, since they knew no Yiddish). Among Secular Zionists, Hebrew also stood for "absorption" and "integration" into a new and proud experience in which Jews were physical workers, in factories and on farms, rather than primarily Yeshiva students, middlemen, and intellectuals. For the Religious Zionists, speaking Hebrew was part of "the beginning of the flowering of our redemption" and of the "first steps of the coming of the Messiah."

While spoken Hebrew remained rather elitist and sidestream in comparison with the massive mainstream of Yiddish-speaking Polish Jewry the two religious parties that clung to Yiddish did so out of ancestral piety and traditional practices as well as due to the prohibition of their rabbis against profaning (i.e., speaking) Hebrew ("the holy tongue") before the coming of the Messiah. The latter view was also part and parcel of their overriding prohibition against reclaiming the Holy Land (via political activity and organized settlement) since that too was a messianic prerogative. This view left the Agudas Yisroyel parties with no option but to champion Yiddish as the vehicle of daily life and as the constant auxiliary language for the traditional study (via translation and argumentation in the vernacular) of sacred texts. In secular circles traditional study was entirely dispensed with and soon became totally unknown to the young. Here too, the creation of a "new Jew," one unencumbered by centuries of physical fear and mental "obscurantism," was aspired to, particularly where a new socialist order was hoped for. Yiddish was the main vernacular tool of political organization and of secular education at every level, in schools that were frequently sponsored by political parties or their educational surrogates. In secular circles, Yiddish developed a new written standard for literary and scientific publications and soon boasted a vibrant secular culture, led by teachers, writers, journalists, actors, philosophers, and political spokespersons, with no rabbinic presence whatsoever. Jews were reconceived of as a modern, secular people among whom religion was (at best) a private matter [4], to be totally separate from state or party concerns.

It is apparent that modern Hebraist and Yiddishist goals and attainments were quite similar, one developing in Palestine and the other in the Diaspora; one making a virtue of starting history all over again in Palestine, after resettlement, the other of starting it all over again, after the revolution, in the Diaspora. Only one branch of Secular Zionism (Labor Zionism) even conceived of supporting both languages and both venues, just as only one branch of the religious world (Agudes Yisroyel) conceived of using both languages in the Diaspora. Generally speaking, the culture that had once given birth to religious monism was now overwhelmingly of the view that the "new Jew" should be monolingual insofar as Jewish identity was concerned. As far as the co-territorial non-Jewish languages in the Diaspora, only the bourgeois Zionists made a point of insisting on their importance (partially also in furtherance of their anti-Yiddish position), but for purposes of civic identity. In the Land of Israel itself, French and English were preferred "foreign languages," but the curriculum then in place for such languages produced scant fluency, being fully in tune with the reading and translation emphases of the times. From being a multilingual (often trilingual) people up until the twentieth century, Jews became increasingly monolingual in the early twentieth century period that we are reviewing, fully in accord with the Central European Herderian romantic view of "one people, one language." Furthermore, with the exception of the Orthodox Religious wings and minor left-wing Zionist efforts, the three separate party goals for intra-Jewish monolingualization were mutually exclusive and the Czarist view of forced "state monolingualization" was clearly an unacceptable means toward a desirable end.

b. A Land for the Jews

The territorial basis of Jewish life was, as we have already seen, fully implied by (and implicational of) politicized ideologies with respect to language. This was true both for those parties that held monolingual language views and those that held bilingual language views. Even those Zionist parties that emphasized the co-territorial language (in addition, of course, to Hebrew) actually did so at the expense of Yiddish and even of serious efforts regarding Aliyah (personal settlement in the Land of Israel). The ultra-Orthodox Agudes Yisroel parties firmly believed that Jews would ultimately return to Palestine but refused to activize this issue, since such return was to occur only when God considered it appropriate to begin the Messianic age and should not be undertaken before then by mere mortals. As a result, these two parties concentrated on Diasporist efforts to assure acceptance, knowledge, and observance of the complex scruples of Orthodoxy. Similarly, the ideologically complex Labor Zionist parties could not totally ignore Jewish proletarians in the Diaspora, certainly not as long as most Jewish proletarians resided in the Diaspora (where, by the way, they were constantly appealed to in Yiddish for funding support, at the very same time that Yiddish was being denied any overt public role at all in Jewish Palestine). Similarly, the non-Zionist Territorialists were constrained to being Diasporist on threefold grounds: by their Yiddish emphases by their anti-Palestinism, and by the fact that they really had no alternate Territory "in hand."

All in all, though many Jews viewed the resettlement issue as the most fundamental and the most urgent issue facing Polish Jewry (particularly as the dangers from Polish and from German anti-semitism grew by leaps and bounds during the mid-1930s), ultra-Orthodoxy, bourgeois Zionism, pluralistic Labor Zionism, and secular socialism kept most Polish Jews from migrating as their legal and economic position in Poland steadily deteriorated. Had they migrated out of Europe, they would have had a better chance to avoid the Nazi genocide that overtook them in Poland. Of course, the British prohibitions against Jewish resettlement in Palestine during the 1930s (not to mention America's tiny quota for immigrants from Poland) were also bars to resettlement abroad. As a result of all of these circumstances, internal and external to the Jewish fold, precious little pre-Holocaust resettlement actually occurred, even though most Jewish parties and ideologies favored resettlement of one kind or another. Most of the parties that opposed leaving Poland were pro-Yiddish, and the opposition to Yiddish in the Land of Israel (as well as in the USSR) may also have subtly played a part in their reluctance to find an alternative home.

c. Socialism/Capitalism

The issue of socialism was another important divisive factor for interwar Polish Jewry. Nevertheless, attitudes toward socialism are not implicational and scatter across both the Zionist/anti-Zionist dimension and across the Hebrew/Yiddish dimension. The ideologically more complex parties are more likely to include socialism than are the ideologically simplex parties, but that is largely a redundant observation, since the more ideologically complex parties are more likely to include each of the other factors as well. Nor are the five socialist parties necessarily closely related to each other either, except for the two that are also Labor Zionist (in which the smaller one [LPZ, with its firmer pro-Yiddish and pro-Diaspora views] arose as the result of a schism within the larger one). On the other hand, a schism also produced the other complex duo [AgYis and PAgYis], but in this case the break came precisely over the issue of socialism.

Finally, it should be pointed out that socialism was actually stronger among Polish Jews than our tabular lineup reveals, since there was also a sizable number of Jews in the Communist Party and in the Polish Socialist Party. We do not list these parties here because they were general political parties rather than specifically Jewish ones. The Communist party as a whole was outlawed in Poland during most of the period we are considering. Its

"Jewish Section" ("Yevsektsiye") in the USSR remained nominally pro-Yiddish through to the beginning of the Second World War, although anti-Yiddish acts (closures of schools and newspapers) had already begun, due to accusations that they fostered Jewish nationalist goals. All in all, however, the intellectual influence of socialism was quite noticeable among Polish Jews in interwar Poland, and through it they felt united with modern progressive Western sentiments on behalf of a more just allocation of resources. In addition, socialism almost always also implied secularism (the Poaley Agudas Yisroyet being the only exception).

d. Religion/Secularism

The final factor, religion/secularism, is also nonimplicational. While it may seem that the religious parties are quite a bit more often pro-Yiddish than is the case among the pro-Hebrew parties, this impression is exaggerated by the apparently pro-religious stance of the Territorialists. In actuality, some of the leaders of the Territorialists were personally religious,[5] but the party as such adopted no religious position in its platform. While it was certainly open to both religious and nonreligious Jews, its programs and the bulk of its membership were definitely secular. If we set the Territorialist aside as too ambiguous to classify with respect to the religious/secular factor, then there is one religious party in the Zionist/Hebraist camp and two in the Diasporist/Yiddish camp. Thus, religion is the least implicational factor with respect to the other self-definitions of pre-Holocoast Jewish parties in Poland. Nevertheless, its importance (as well as the importance of its rejection among secularists) surpasses by far its systematic implicationality. The notion of "chosenness" and the obligations that it placed upon Jews, on the one hand, and the Western anticlerical (particularly French) views of religion as outdated and as barred from political involvement in civilized contexts, on the other hand, were intensely held, respectively, by those who subscribed to them. Secularism was another mark of identity with the Western concept (anchored to both the American and the French revolutions) of the separation of Church and State. Religion was buttressed by firm belief in continued Jewish exceptionality, even in the modern world.

IV. So Near and Yet So Far

The Jewish parties and their respective ideologies often seem to be so similar factorially that it bears considering whether they were enabled thereby to function in a unified fashion or at least to display some kind of "canonical unity" within certain clusters. Actually, there was little if any such unity except on severely and openly threatening occasions and during the collective mass rallies, protest, or self-defense activities that were organized in connection with them. The parties that arose via schisms cooperated rarely if at all with their "parental" parties. Similarly large and painful was the language divide. As a result, Yiddishist and Hebraist parties rarely if ever found a common language via which to cooperate, even if they otherwise were more similar than different (e.g. Shomer Hatsair and the Jewish Labor Bund). Since language was so implicational of Zionist/non-Zionist ideology there was, of course, no cooperation across those lines either. Thus, though the Left Labor Zionist complex ideology fully accepted all of the points espoused by the Jewish Labor Bund, nevertheless they rarely cooperated on an organizational level. The various Zionist parties cooperated little if at all with each other, primarily because of differences with respect to religion and socialism. Within the Secular Yiddishist block (Folkists, Bund, and even Poaley Tsiyon), there were more cosponsored activities, particularly of a Yiddish literary nature. Territorialists and Folkists also often attended such cosponsored events, but, even here, the religious/ secular issue and the language divide normally kept the Agudes Yisroyel parties and the Shomer Hatsair from attending. Thus, little differences meant a lot, whether they were implicational or not, and there was generally very little socialization and coparticipation across party lines. Even factors that were relatively less frequently on party platforms (for example, the issue of socialism/capitalism was absent from the Territorialist and Folkist platforms) were no less divisive for all that than were the most frequently politicized factors. Each party was relatively self-contained, in its political operations and in its community-service activities, although news about the activities and views of other parties was easily obtainable, particularly in the larger cities and towns, both via the press and by word of mouth. The functional divide between the Mizrakhi and the Revisionists (see note at the end of Table 1), with no major differences on any of our four factors, was just as great as that between the Mizrakhi and the Bund, which have not a single point of programmatic agreement.

V. The Illustrative Case of Nathan Birnbaum

The importance of the link between language and party ideologies may be helpfully illustrated by the interesting case of Dr. Nathan Birnbaum (1864-1937). His first published articles about Yiddish were rather negative, and during the late decades of the nineteenth century, when he was an early (perhaps the earliest) and leading Zionist, he definitely championed Hebrew as the language that would be instrumental in bringing Jews closer to the high ethical ideals of their greatest prophets. This view of Yiddish was quite predictable also on the basis of his German (Viennese) childhood environment and education. In those circles it was common for Yiddish to be looked down upon (by Jews themselves) as ungrammatical and simply "bad" or "inferior" German. Nevertheless, he slowly became impressed by the full-blooded and authentic Jewishness of Eastern European Jews and began to write more positively about their language. Indeed, he was arguably the only leading Western Zionist to do so.

After the First Zionist World Congress (at which he was chosen to be the Secretary of the newly founded World Zionist Organization, 1897), he withdrew from the organization he had just helped to establish and threw himself into efforts on behalf of Yiddish and Jewish cultural autonomy within the multiethnic Austro-Hungarian Monarchy. With the help of Jewish students at the University of Vienna (where he had founded a youth group for Yiddish literature, the first such university-based youth group in all of Europe), Birnbaum convened the First World Congress for the Yiddish Language (1908, in Tshernovits [then Bukovina, now Moldova]) where Yiddish was declared to be "a [but not "the"] national language of the Jewish people." He was selected to be the first Secretary of the organization that the Congress then founded in order to carry forward cultural efforts on behalf of Yiddish.

When the First World War broke out and two of his sons were drafted into the Austro-Hungarian army (and one was seriously wounded but survived), he experienced a religious awakening, becoming ultra-Orthodox as a result. After the War he served for a few years as Secretary of the renewed Agudes Yisroyel organization (1919). He strongly supported its affiliated Beys Yankev Yiddish Schools for Girls but also wrote again in German on Orthodox religious topics that would not have been accessible to German Jews in any other language. He continued publishing and speaking in Yiddish and in German, living mostly in Berlin until his death, near Amsterdam (to which he had fled when the Nazis came to power). Thus we see that in each of his "phases" he utilized the language that was most appropriately identified with a particular Jewish movement, whether on ideological or practical grounds. Most Polish Jews did not experience any such ideological odysseys. They were ideologically more consistently unidirectional and chose Yiddish, Hebrew, or both in accord with their interlocked convictions on all four dimensions.

Language and Ideology in Jewish Eastern Europe During the Interwar Years

Most adult Eastern European Jews, particularly the males, were either trilingual or bilingual when the nineteenth century closed. By the end of the First World War, their intragroup bilingualism was narrowing and their intergroup bilingualism was expanding. Yiddish, the vernacular of Ashkenaz since its inception as a self-sufficient Jewish civilization in the Rhineland at the turn of the millennium, also had traditional functions within the pale of sanctity as the language of translation and argumentation in the study of sanctified Hebrew and Judeo-Aramaic texts. In addition to its textual functions, Hebrew was also the language of important written records and rabbinic writings. Yiddish traditionally also had a few written functions in connection with popular literature or translations of sacred or rabbinic texts. In the nineteenth century, both Yiddish and Hebrew increasingly began to acquire modern literary, journalistic, and letter-writing functions. Initially, the majority of those who wrote for publication in Yiddish also did so in Hebrew as well, and many (though not most) readers were similarly bilingual. With the development of modern political parties at the end of the nineteenth century, both languages modernized virtually simultaneously and took on definite and often mutually exclusive ideological overtones.

The modern political ideologies and their political parties were polarized along four axes: (a) preferred Jewish language, (b) attitude toward Zionism vs. Diasporaism, (c) socialism vs. capitalism, and (d) religiosity vs. secularism. In all cases, the parties opting for Hebrew alone (or Hebrew plus the co-territorial language) were also Zionist in orientation, whereas those opting for Yiddish alone were Diasporist in orientation. Ideologically more complex or pluralistic parties/ideologies existed within both the secular and the religious camp, such that both of these languages were espoused. In both instances, however, schisms had occurred, in one case over the vehemence of the support for Yiddish and in the other case over the support of Socialism. Although socialism and secularism were not themselves implicational of other ideological principles, they were both extremely important for one another and in ruling out the possibility of cooperative efforts with parties that lacked these characteristics.

Although Nathan Birnbaum learned all three of his languages during his childhood and youth, he alternatively fostered and stressed one or another of them as he changed his party allegiance in adulthood. The more politically active and adept secular blocs rendered normative the association between Yiddish, Socialism, and Diasporaism, on the one hand, and between Hebrew and Zionism on the other hand, although exceptions to these rules of thumb can easily be noted, particularly within the more pluralistic parties. The more ideologically complex parties particularly underscore the fact (a fact that the others illustrate as well) that although within the Eastern European Jewish fold language is frequently ideologically implicational, it is not implicational when both Yiddish and Hebrew are advocated.

Implicational or not, language is never an issue all by itself. Language does not function within society in a societal vacuum. It is part of an entire complex of issues (in the Eastern European Jewish case: Zionism/Diasporaism, socialism/capitalism, and secularism/religionism), ethnic identity per se often being among them, not to mention romantic Herderianism, Marxism, and Western anticlericalism as Zeitgeist motifs that linked Jews in interwar Poland to the world of modern ideas and modern political causes. As the world has learned at considerable expense, language can either powerfully unite or divide, both within and across cultures, as language convictions co-occur with other major societal fissures. In Jewish Eastern Europe, it was definitely a major issue, as it was for non-Jews as well, when minority-majority issues came into play in that ethnically most diverse corner of Europe. Its importance depended precisely on its manifold linkages to other crucially important issues and ideologies.

These conclusions may well be applicable elsewhere as well and an array of case studies will be needed to test their limits and their generalizability.

Notes

1. Parties came into and went out of existence during this period. At various particular times, fewer than ten may have been competing with one another. Although all of the major parties are included in this report, only the most contrastive minor ones are included.

2. "Ashkenaz" is the collective name applied to the Jewish civilization that developed in the Germanic and Slavic lands. Although it is originally a biblical place name, it began to be applied to the German lands proper early in the second millennium after Christ, and to Jews in those lands and eastward by the fifteenth century or earlier.

3. This has remained an ongoing complaint reiterated by Yiddishists in Israel to this very day.

4. The treatment of religion as a "private (i.e. individual rather than societal) matter" by the secularist was repudiated by the religionists as being as ludicrous as would be treating socialism as a private rather than a societal matter. To this very day, most Jewish religious parties in Israel cannot conceive of the Jewish religion other than on a societal basis (particularly "in a Jewish country").

5. Two such leaders were Nathan Birnbaum (about whom see section V), during the interwar period (when he was in his religious phase) and I. N. Shteynberg (Steinberg), 1888-1957, primarily during the postwar period.

References

Astour, Michael C. (1967). *Geshikhte fun der fi ayland-lige un funem teritorialistishn gedank.* Buenos Aires and New York: Frayland lige.

Bacon, Gershon C. (1996). *The Politics of Tradition: Agudat Yisrael in Poland, 1916-1939.* Jerusalem: Magnes.

Elichai, Joseph (1993). *Tenuat haMizrakhi beFolin hakongresait, 1916-1927.* Tel-Aviv: Moreshet.

Fishman, Joshua A. (1974). *Shtudyes vegn yidn in poyln 19/9/1939; Studies on Polish Jewry, 1919/1939.* New York: Yivo Institute for Jewish Research.

Johnpoll, Bernard K. (1967). *The Politics of Futility: The General Jewish Workers Bund of Poland, 1917-1943.* Ithaca: Cornell University Press.

Kantorowicz, N. (1968). *Di tsionistishe arbeter-havegung in poyln, 1918-1939.* New York.

Lewin, Isaac and Michael-Gelber, Nahum (1990). *A History of Polish Jewry During the Revival of Poland, 1918-1945.* New York: Shengold.

Melzer, Emanuel (1997). *No Wav Out: The Politics of Polish Jewry, 1935-1939.* Cincinnati: Hebrew Union College Press.

Mendelsohn, Ezra (1981). *Zionism in Poland: The Formative Years.* New Haven: Yale University Press.

Netser, Shlomo (1980). *Maavak yehude polin al zekhuyvotehem haezrakhiyot vehaleumiyot (1918-1922).* Tel-Aviv: Universitat Tel-Aviv.

Oppenheim, Israel (1989). *The Struggle of Jewish Youth for Productivization: The Zionist Youth Movement in Poland.* Boulder, Co: East European Monographs.

Schaary, David (1990). *Misetam tsiyonut letsiyonut kelalit: ikhud ufilug bereshit darkah shel hatsiyonut hakelalit, 1929-1939.* Jerusalem: Reuven Mas.

Weinbaum, Laurence (1993). *A Marriage of Convenience: The New Zionist Organization and the Polish Government, 1936-1939.* Boulder, Co: East European Monographs.

International Issues and Domestic Ethnic Relations: African Americans, American Jews, and the Israel-South Africa Debate

Yvonne D. Newsome

Abstract: *In examining the relationship between international issues and domestic ethnic relations between African Americans and U.S. Jews, it is noted that long-established ethnic groups sustain or develop economic, political, or social ties to their ancestral lands. These ties are often manifested in the identities, ideologies, and politics of diaspora groups. International issues may stress or strengthen African American–Jewish relations, depending on the political posture each group assumes. Using case studies, the author shows that both African Americans and U.S. Jews seek the return of national territories and work toward an end to persecution and oppression of minority ethnic and religious groups in other nations. In the international arena, African Americans often support other Third World people with whom they identify, while U.S. Jews tend to side with the Jewish diaspora and Israel. As a consequence, when Africa and Israel clash, new conflicts erupt or existing ones are exacerbated between African Americans and Jews.*

Introduction

Although it is recognized that world political and economic conditions influence emigration patterns, sociologists give little attention to how events in homelands affect relations between immigrants once they become established ethnic groups in third countries. Long-established ethnic groups, like new immigrant or sojourner groups, may sustain or develop economic, political, or other social ties to their ancestral lands. These ties are often manifested in the identities, activities, and ideologies of diaspora groups, and especially in politics. For example, ethnic Americans attempt to influence United States foreign policy by directing their efforts "toward the fruition of national hopes, retaining or seeking the return of national territories, winning and preserving national independence, and cessation of persecution and oppression of minority ethnic and religious groups in other nations" (Gerson 1977, pp. 54-55).

There are documented cases wherein homeland politics have affected African Americans' relations with other US ethnic groups. Italy's 1935 invasion of Ethiopia, for instance, reveals the African American identification with

Africa, the Italian American identification with Italy, and the significant impact that international events can have on US ethnic relations. African Americans responded to Italy's invasion by establishing fund-raising organizations to support Ethiopia, lobbying in national and international bodies as well as other countries, holding mass protest rallies, performing military exploits for Ethiopia and training its air force, and volunteering to serve in the Ethiopian military (Franklin 1967, Shack 1974; Challenor 1977, Shankman 1978; Keller 1984; Magubane 1987).[1] While Mussolini's invasion of Ethiopia eroded his support among most Americans, the Italian American community continued to back him until Italy invaded France in 1940. For Italian Americans, "Mussolini still symbolized progress and power for Italy," and for a time most of them remained "indifferent to Fascism" (Martinelli 1982, p. 222).

The Italian-Ethiopian war had a negative impact on Italian American-African American relations across the country (Drago 1978; Shankman 1978). In July, African Americans organized a campaign to boycott Italian American businesses in New York. Windows were smashed and continuous riots broke out in adjoining Italian and African American neighborhoods. Eventually, a delegation of seven African Americans and Italian Americans filed a joint petition to the acting secretary of state requesting the US to defend Ethiopia against the fascist aggression.

A more familiar, contemporary case is the effect of international issues on African American-Jewish relations, which is the focus of this study. There are several examples of international or "homeland" issues which have provoked conflicts between African Americans and American Jews.[2] These include Jewish reactions to statements on the June war of 1967 made by the Student Nonviolent Coordinating Committee (SNCC) and the Black Panther Party, Jewish anger over Andrew Young's meeting with a member of the Palestine Liberation Organization (PLO) in 1979, Jewish disapproval of Jesse Jackson's support of a Palestinian homeland in the 1984 presidential election campaigns, African American anger at Israel's refusal to break economic and military ties with South Africa, and Moshe Dayan's racist assessment of the intelligence of African Americans in the US military in November of 1980. The next section discusses how international issues have been perceived and addressed in the literature on African American-Jewish relations.

International Issues in Previous Studies

In the late 1960s there was a rash of publications on what most writers describe as a sudden rupture in a civil rights alliance between African Americans and American Jews. In these early works, international issues were rarely considered to be legitimate contributing factors to escalating hostilities between the two groups. Geltman (1970, p. 177), for example, insists that "neither ancient nor recent troubles of Israel are important to the study of the Jewish-Negro confrontation in the United States." Geltman takes an extreme position in arguing that any African American opposition to Israeli policies is a product of "black anti-Semitism." In contrast, Berson (1971) acknowledges the importance of international issues to the alliance's demise, but she is patronizing in her assessment of African American criticism of Israeli policies and Zionism. She states, "If the state of Israel stands as a model of what can be accomplished, it also serves as a reminder of painful Negro deficiencies. Jewish achievements seem so beyond the technical ability of the Negro people that they inspire anger and hostility" (Berson 1971, p. 170). She also alleges that African Americans identify with the Third World because they are being courted by Arab and other Third World leaders: "The social acceptance by world figures has been repaid by an emotional identification with them and their causes: anti-colonialism and anti-Israelis" (Berson 1971, p. 171). In short, neither Geltman nor Berson recognizes the ideological and social bonds that African Americans, like Jews, have to their ancestral land and its diaspora.

Cruse (1967, p. 490), however, argues that African American-Jewish relations were affected by the very creation of Israel. He writes,

> (T)hese relations now become colored by the incipient clash of two ideologies—Black Nationalism and Zionism. These nationalisms, totally dissimilar in most respects, share one essential motivation: a yearning for national redemption through regaining a 'homeland' that was lost. But Zionism and Black Nationalism have undergone historical conditionings peculiar to themselves, and have never, to my knowledge, confronted each other on any domestic or international issue. *But today things are different, and Black Nationalism, Zionism, African affairs, and Negro civil rights organizations are intimately interlocked on the political, cultural, economic and international fronts* . . . .

Likewise, Washington (1984, p. 14) claims that "the rising level of nationalism within each group, especially the concern with Israel by the one and the concern with the independence of Africa . . . of the other, drives a deep wedge of resentment between Jews and Afro-Americans. The national implications of this rift are unsettling, and they hardly contribute to healthy international prospects."

Other recent publications acknowledge that international factors influence African American-Jewish relations (K. Cohen 1988; Weisbord and Kazarian 1985; Labovitz 1975; Weisbord and Stein 1970), but some tend to underestimate the long-term effects these factors could have on interethnic harmony or discord (Brown 1987; Gelb 1980).

The purpose of this study is to ascertain how relations between Israel and Africa affect their diasporas in the United States. I conclude that Israeli-African relations have consequences for the political, economic, and ideological relations between African and American Jews.

This study by no means attempts to assert that international issues are the sole or always the most important cause of tensions between ethnic groups. Instead, it tries to demonstrate that currently and historically international issues affect US ethnic relations and argues that their effects should be explored as an empirical possibility rather than be *assumed* inconsequential.

The first section reviews the historical relations between African Americans and American Jews up to the 1960s. The second provides support for the contention that African Americans identify with Africa and American Jews with Israel. The third section begins by analyzing the Israeli-South African connection and concludes with an analysis of its effects on African American-Jewish relations. The final section discusses the implications of these findings for the study of racial and ethnic relations in the United States.

Historical Relations Between African Americans And American Jews

In the early 1900s, American Jews, like African Americans, confronted discrimination in housing, education, and employment. It was therefore advantageous for Jews to support the civil rights efforts of African Americans (Diner 1977). Jewish involvement in the civil rights movement culminated after World War II, when the Holocaust made Jews more aware of their own vulnerability not only in Europe, but also in the United States (Labovitz 1975).

African Americans and Jews first came into extensive contact after 1915 in Northern cities (Diner 1977). In 1915, African Americans began their Great Migration northward to fill industrial jobs left vacant as the great wave of Southern, Central and Eastern European immigrants ended and the US entered into World War I. These African Americans usually moved into old Jewish neighborhoods where Jews retained ownership of property and ran businesses. As a result, African Americans and Jews first interacted in unequal status relations which sometimes fostered economic tensions between them (Labovitz 1975).[3]

African American-Jewish relations were affected when anti-Semitism and nativism surged following the immigration of thousands of poor Eastern European Jews to Northern cities between 1880 and World War I (Lieberson

1980). In 1915, Leo Frank, a Jewish pencil factory manager convicted for the murder of a young white girl, was lynched by a white mob after the governor of Georgia commuted his death sentence to life imprisonment. Also, by the mid-1920s the Ku Klux Klan had millions of members, and it was active in almost every state (Berson 1971). Overall, the number of anti-Semitic organizations in the US multiplied from 14 in 1915 to more than a hundred by 1941 (Diner 1977; Feagin 1989).

These developments prompted Jews to organize, and they may have also contributed to the disproportionate Jewish involvement in the African American civil rights movement in comparison to other whites. Three prominent Jewish civil rights organizations were established during this period: the American Jewish Congress (1918), the Anti-Defamation League (1913), and the American Jewish Committee (1906). The founding of these organizations was contemporaneous with the birth of the National Association for the Advancement of Colored People (1909) and the Urban League (1917). Jews played a prominent role in founding, leading, and financing these and future African American organizations. For example, in the 1920s Jews made up at least one-third of the executive board of the Urban League (Stevenson 1988).

The African American-Jewish alliance revolved around political, union, legal, and civil rights matters until the 1960s (Diner 1977; Gelb 1980). However, Diner (1977) argues that events occurred in or around 1935 which initiated the alliance's disintegration. First, a national Democratic political coalition formed during the New Deal successfully convinced African Americans to switch from the Republican to the Democratic party, making them a large voting bloc in Northern cities. Second, the Committee on Industrial Organizations of the American Federation of Labor began a major effort to recruit African Americans, becoming the first US union to do so. Third, in 1936 the US Supreme Court's decision in *Missouri v. Canada* helped to undercut the "separate but equal doctrine" which had stood since *Plessy v. Ferguson* in 1896.

Also, by 1935 other whites supported the civil rights struggle in greater numbers, making African Americans less dependent upon Jewish support. African Americans became more assertive in demanding leadership roles in civil rights organizations. For example, the NAACP elected its first African American board chairman in 1934 and A. Philip Randolph's Brotherhood of Sleeping Car Porters was finally recognized by the Pullman company in 1935 (Diner 1977).

Significantly, the status of Jews had improved by this time, despite the rise in anti-Semitism. By 1920 there were eleven Jews in the House of Representatives. In addition, Louis Brandeis was appointed to the US Supreme Court by Woodrow Wilson in 1916 despite strong objections from the Senate, and by 1939 two other Jews had been appointed. Oscar Straus was appointed secretary of commerce and labor by Theodore Roosevelt in 1906 and Henry Morgenthau, Jr. became secretary of the treasury under Franklin D. Roosevelt in 1934.

Race was a factor that gave Jews rights for which African Americans were to struggle for decades. As whites, Jews had the vote, and they used it to gain political clout and move up the social and economic ladder (Lieberson 1980, p. 51). As whites Jews were also elected to influential positions in localities where they lacked demographic strength. In contrast, African Americans were "obliged to pursue a variety of political goals that could more or less be ignored by the new European groups" but which were "prerequisites for reaching the level of political potential available much earlier" to Jews (Lieberson 1980, p. 100). The lack of political power severely crippled African Americans' efforts to advance socially and economically.

American Jews could now afford to pursue political objectives which did not parallel those of African Americans. After the Holocaust, Jews increasingly focused their energies on their own survival, and with the creation of Israel in 1948, their "quest for security and survival became wrapped up" in the new Jewish homeland (Diner 1977, p. 242). Yet Jewish civil rights activists and attorneys continued to lobby and file legal briefs to end housing and education discrimination against African Americans until the 1960s (Labovitz 1975).

Racial conflicts surfaced in the civil rights movement when frustrated African Americans initiated new strategies to end racial discrimination. Sit-ins, freedom rides, and protest marches began to overtake the litigation and lobbying tactics of an earlier generation. By the 1960s, there was urban rebellion in the North and West. Young nationalists demanded self-determination and "Black Power" as groups like SNCC and the Congress of Racial Equality (CORE) stepped to the forefront of the movement. Voicing concerns that had been long suppressed, some African Americans derided liberal whites (many of whom were Jews) for their "paternalism" and questioned whites' commitment to African American liberation (Marx and Useem 1971). Lieberson (1980, p. 116) writes that inherent conflicts between African Americans and liberal whites were suppressed until the passage of the 1954 *Brown v. Board of Education* decision ending school desegregation, the civil rights acts, and the Voting Rights Act of 1965. These decisions initiated the decline of legally sanctioned discrimination in the South, allowing African Americans to direct attention to correcting social injustices in the urban North. No longer could diverging interests between African Americans and Northern white liberals be ignored or suppressed.

In addition, in the early 1970s political, economic, and legal clashes erupted after the passage of affirmative action legislation designed to end centuries of discrimination against African Americans. For the first time African Americans were in direct competition with middle-class Jews and whites for jobs and college admissions spots. While some writers conclude that Jews broke away from the coalition because of "black anti-Semitism" (Geltman 1970; Halpern 1971) or African American frustration with Jewish "paternalism" (Cruse 1967), it seems most likely that conflict erupted when African Americans fought for control of the movement and vied with Jews for political and economic power (Labovitz 1975; Diner 1977; Gelb 1980).[4] By the 1960s the social status of African Americans and Jews diverged so much that the issues which once drew them together now propelled them apart. The world political scene was changing also, and in the late sixties and seventies international issues became a focus of conflict between African Americans and Jews. The brief period of harmony and cooperation between independent Africa and Israel had ended, igniting new tensions between their diasporas in the United States.

Ethnic Identity and the Homeland

African Americans and Africa

African American identification with Africa, both in its political and psychological aspects, is not new, but the currency and nature of such iden-tification varies through time (Challenor 1977). Kilson and Hill (1971, pp. 3-4) state "Africa for the American Negro was and is a great dilemma. . . . It is essential to consider Negroes' feelings toward Africa as an aspect of their struggle for survival and citizenship in America." As is often true of oppressed and exploited groups, African Americans' perceptions of Africa—whether in the US, Africa and elsewhere—have often been influenced by the negative images of that continent propagated by the dominant white society (Erikson 1965). Yet various incidents and issues related to the continent demonstrate that the African American's "subterranean world possesse(s) enough kinship with Africa to be stirred by a nationalist defense of her name" (Emerson and Kilson 1965).

Africa has always been a symbol of freedom and hope for some African Americans, and most African Americans believe their fate is intertwined with that of Africans (Keller, 1984). African American interest in Africa is largely manifested in three ways: in "(1) the tendency to call oneself African and to incorporate the word African into the titles of associations, (2) interest in emigrating to Africa, and (3) attempts to influence U.S. policy toward Africa and otherwise influence the course of African affairs" (Challenor 1977, p. 142). Historically African Americans have exemplified interest in Africa by agitating against the slave trade and European imperialism, undertaking missionary work on the continent, maintaining discourse with African leaders, organizing colonization schemes for emigration to Africa, training African students in black colleges, and attending and implementing pan-African conferences with African leaders. For example, African Americans organized several African colonization schemes, with the most active period lasting from 1816-1865 (Clarke 1985; Bracey, Meier, and Rudwick 1970). Liberia was founded by African American emigrants, who declared its independence from the US in 1847. Between 1821 and 1867, 20,000 emigrants settled in Liberia, 13,000 of whom came from the US. These emigrants retained strong ties to African Americans in the US (Harris 1972).

Political and cultural pan-Africanism thrived in the early 1900s. W.E.B. DuBois, a Harvard-trained sociologist, was prominent among African American intellectuals who organized and participated in several Pan-African Congresses. The first Pan-African conference was held in London in 1900 and subsequent Pan-African Congresses were held in 1919 (Paris), 1921 (London), 1923 (London and Lisbon), 1927 (New York), 1945 (Manchester), and 1974 (Dar es Salaam). Cultural pan-Africanism was manifested in the works of prominent African American, African, and West Indian writers like Alaine Locke, Langston Hughes, Countee Cullen, Leopold Senghor, Aimé Cesaire, and Claude McKay.

Garveyism was perhaps the most widely embraced pan-African social movement. Marcus Garvey established the United Negro Improvement and Conservation Association and African Communities League (UNIA) in Jamaica in 1914 and opened a Harlem branch (the world headquarters) in the US two years later. The UNIA advocated self-determination for blacks, race pride, African liberation and development, and the establishment of commercial networks between Africans and the African diaspora. The UNIA operated several business enterprises including a newspaper and a shipping line.

The UNIA's popularity is demonstrated by its active membership and support from the African American masses. A UNIA convention held in New York in August 1920 drew thousands of delegates from every state and "more than a score of countries on three continents" (Cronon 1973, p. 8). Africa was well-represented even though the Negro World, the UNIA newspaper, had been banned by colonial officials in many parts of that continent. Garvey boasted that by 1919 his organization had branches in 30 US cities and a membership of two million. By August 1920, UNIA membership reached 4 million[5] (Garvey 1973, p. 25).

Garvey was convicted of mail fraud in 1923 and deported to Jamaica in 1927. He died in London in the 1940s, but his legacy lived on in the platforms and ideologies of African nationalists and African American protest leaders for decades to come.

World Wars I and II brought about domestic and international changes that significantly affected African American ideologies and the civil rights movement (Kilson and Hill 1971). First, African Americans were embittered when their second-class status persisted in the US despite their valiant fight for democracy abroad. Second, a growing number of African Americans began to link their plight in the US to global imperialism, and they perceived an interdependency between the liberation of Africans, other Third World peoples, and themselves (Franklin 1967; Carmichael and Hamilton 1967; Harris 1972, Allen 1973).

African independence struggles inspired African Americans to revolt against racism in the US (Allen 1973; Blauner 1972; Emerson and Kilson 1965), and contributed to the "militant stage" of the civil rights movement that began in the 1950s (Kilson and Hill, 1971, p. 346). For instance, James Forman of SNCC "came to militant protest through the study of postwar African nationalism" (Kilson and Hill 1971, p. 346).

By the 1950s, African American consciousness of Africa reached new heights (Magubane 1987, p. 232). This consciousness swelled in the 1960s, taking on new political, cultural, and ideological dimensions. This broadening African identification is in part directly attributable to the African independence movement, since "it is one thing to be the descendant of a slave born in a colonial country of an allegedly barbaric continent, and another to be linked racially to a continent suddenly peopled with independent states making a strident and impressive entry into the world's affairs" (Emerson and Kilson 1965, p. 642). In addition, improved communications, higher educational levels, and the proliferation of published materials on Africa that resulted from the rise of black studies programs better informed African Americans about their homeland (Challenor 1977; Magubane 1984).

Data from the 1979 and 1980 National Survey of Black Americans indicate that African Americans generally feel a closeness to Africa (Thornton and Taylor 1988). In all, 21.8 percent of respondents said they felt "very close" to Africa; 35.4 percent felt "fairly close"; 26.7 percent felt "not too close"; and 16.1 percent felt "not close at all" (Thornton and Taylor 1988, p. 146). Currently, an estimated 13 million African Americans observe Kwanzaa, a seven-day festival in December which honors their African heritage. Anosike (1982, cited in Thornton and Taylor 1988, p. 148) suggests that the television miniseries "'Roots' and events in South Africa have provided black America with a greater awareness of its links to Africa and made identifying with Africa more acceptable."

Since the late 1800s, African American churches have sent missionaries to South Africa, trained South African students in American church schools, and maintained personal ties with South Africans (Drake 1984, p. 25). In addition, African Americans have always drawn parallels between the racial situation in America and that in South Africa (Magubane 1987). For instance, South Africa and Namibia were the subjects of discussion at the Pan-African Congresses of 1900 and 1923 respectively. In 1915 the Pan-African Association sent a petition to the British crown protesting the forced labor, segregation, and pass systems enacted against Africans in South Africa and Rhodesia. In 1939 the Council on African Affairs was formed by African Americans to promote Africa's liberation and to provide economic assistance to black South Africans. And "in 1962 Dr. Martin Luther King (Jr.) and Chief Albert Lutuli, President of the African National Congress . . . issued a joint statement appealing for the imposition of international sanctions against the white minority regime of South Africa" (Magubane 1987, p. 216). More recently, a 1986 Gallup poll reveals that African Americans are much more likely to follow events in South Africa than are whites. Seventy-two percent of African Americans said they follow these events either "very" or "fairly" closely as compared to 54 percent of whites and 68 percent of "non-whites" (*Gallup Report* 1986). Earlier surveys support these findings (Thornton and Taylor 1988, p. 139).

Challenor (1977) predicts that African American identification with Africa will be long-lived since most African states have gained independence, African Americans are more informed about Africa and have enough voting power to influence political candidates, and there are now extensive contacts between Africans and African Americans.

American Jews and Israel

While Zionism was never widely embraced in the United States, American Jews have always had a "strong emotional, religious, and ethnic attachment" to Israel (Gilboa 1987, p. 247). The term *pro-Israelism* best describes American Jewish support for Israel. Waxman (1976, p. 177) defines the pro-Israeli American Jew as one "who lives in the United States and who supports Israel economically, politically, and even emotionally, but whose primary source of Jewish identification is derived from, and oriented to, the American Jewish community." By contrast, Zionists perceive Israel as the cultural and spiritual center of world Jewry as well as the focus of their identities, personal lives, and existence. Herman (1989) also argues that American Jewish support for Israel reflects pro-Israelism rather than Zionism. He writes "Zionism is more than the expression of a positive attitude to Israel. . . . Zionist ideology represents an all-encompassing approach to the problems of the Jewish people" (Herman 1989, pp. 120-21). While some American Jewish support for Israel may be rooted in "nostalgia" for the homeland, few American Jews hold *aliyah*—or return to Israel—as an ideal (Waxman 1976). Furthermore, there is serious debate about how Zionism should be defined and applied to American Jews. Since one purpose of this paper is broadly to gauge how American Jews' support for Israel affects their relations with African Americans, Waxman's definition of pro-Israelism is used to avoid the ambiguities and limitations that arise if Zionism is used as a measure of identification with Israel.

Opinion poll and survey data from the period of Israel's establishment reveal overwhelming Jewish support for an independent Jewish state (Gilboa 1987). In a September 1945 Roper poll of American Jews, 80 percent of respondents approved and 10 percent disapproved of the following statement: "A Jewish state in Palestine is a good thing for the Jews and every possible effort should be made to establish Palestine as a Jewish state or commonwealth for those who want to settle there." Furthermore, 80 percent of the respondents disagreed with the statement that "Jews are a religious group only and not a nation, and it would be bad for the Jews to try to set up a Jewish state in Palestine or anywhere else." Gallup found 90 percent of American Jews supporting a Jewish state in Palestine. Clearly these results show that strong pro-Israeli sentiments existed among the masses of American Jews before the birth of the state.

A few Jews did oppose the establishment of a Jewish state. After World War II some upper-class German Jews, such as those represented by the American Jewish Committee (AJC), believed that European refugees should be returned to their home countries. They suggested that those who could not return be resettled in the US, Australia, or even Palestine. Members of the American Council for Judaism (ACJ), a small group of Reform Jews who broke away from the AJC in 1943, maintained that Judaism is a religion, and not a nationality. The ACJ strongly opposed the creation of a Jewish state in the belief that it would incite charges of dual loyalty against American Jews. It held that Palestine should become a land in which Jews, Moslems, and Christians shared equal responsibility in building a democratic government (Mendes-Flohr and Reinharz 1980). Few Jewish organizations or synagogues ever endorsed the position of the ACJ.

Perhaps the Holocaust was and remains a factor in the strong support for a Jewish state. Mark Cohen (1988, p. 98) writes that the need for a national sanctuary became "self-evident" to Jews after World War II. Unfortunately there are no reliable pre-Holocaust survey data expressing Jewish opinions on the establishment of a Jewish state in Palestine (Gilboa 1989). There is, however, evidence that the Middle East conflicts have induced fears of Israel's destruction or a second Holocaust in the minds of many Jews, Israeli and diaspora (Herman 1989).

American Jews also demonstrate pro-Israelism through their actions. After the war, "the role assigned the American (Jewish) faithful was to send money and foster a supportive climate for Israel in the U.S." (M. Cohen 1988, p. 98). In the 1940s, American Jews contributed millions of dollars to the United Jewish Appeal (UJA) to help establish the state and fund relief efforts for European Jews. The UJA raised $101 million in 1946, $117 million in 1947, and $148 million in 1948 before contributions began to decline (Glazer 1957). After 1948, American Jews began to identify Israel as a territorial homeland and became firmly committed to its continued existence as a haven for the Jewish diaspora (Diner 1977, p. 242). The creation of the new state actualized the Jewish quest for security (Labovitz 1975; Halpern 1971, Cruse 1967).

Jewish support of Israel has been relatively consistent through the decades. In 1983 the National Survey of American Jews found that 78 percent of the Jewish public and 90 percent of their leaders agreed that "'Caring about Israel is a very important part of my being a Jew'" (Gilboa 1987, p. 245). An estimated one-quarter of the $3.5 billion American Jews gave to charity in 1986 went to Israel, with less than $400 million going by way of the UJA. Jewish political action committees (PACs) exert a strong influence on US foreign policy in the Middle East. As of 1990 there were over eighty pro-Israel PACs in the United States. PAC contributions to political candidates rose from $85,000 in 1980 to more than $7 million in 1986 (Rubin 1990). The effectiveness of the pro-Israel PACs is seen in the success they have had in gaining congressional and executive support for Israel. From 1978 to 1982, Israel received nearly half of all US military aid and 35 percent of its economic aid to foreign countries.

Many American Jews' support for Israel is so strong that "virtually all Israeli policies and practices are treated as *if* to evaluate or criticize them would, in fact, call Israel itself into question" (Holden 1984, p. 205). With such ties to their ancestral homeland, it should come as no surprise that many American Jews have been angered by African Americans' criticism of Israel's domestic and foreign policies. The next section evaluates the impact of Israeli-African relations on African American-Jewish relations.

Pro-Israelism, Pan-Africanism and the
Israel-South Africa Debate

Israeli-South African Relations

Chazan (1984, p. 148) asserts that "Israel has appeared to relinquish the cause of liberation in Southern Africa at precisely the same time as an international consensus has coalesced on the obsolence of white domination in that area." Israel's relations with South Africa has soiled its image in the Third World, especially among African states and African Americans. Once an avid and vociferous opponent of the apartheid system, the Israeli government has in recent years established military, political, economic, and cultural ties to South Africa which seriously challenge the sincerity of its antiapartheid rhetoric. There is also a certain irony in the relationship in that "the present leaders of South Africa . . . were often Nazi sympathizers during the Second World War" (Hellyer 1975, p. 3).

Israel's relations with South Africa have evolved through four phases (Chazan 1984). From 1948 to 1961, Israel maintained moderate diplomatic ties to South Africa. South African leader Jan Christian Smuts played a crucial role in convincing Britain to support a Jewish homeland in Palestine, and South Africa was one of the first countries to recognize the new state. There was also an exchange of visits by state officials, with Israeli Foreign Minister Moshe Sharrett visiting South Africa in 1950 and South African Prime Minister Daniel Francois Malan reciprocating with a visit to Israel in 1953.

But the rise of nationalism following World War II affected Israeli-South African ties. In 1955, Arab states succeeded in banning Israel from participation in the Bandung Conference of Third World states. They also enlisted African and Asian support in calling for the human rights of Palestinians (Beshir 1982). More importantly, in 1960 seventeen newly independent African states, none of which had a say in the decision to partition Palestine, gained a voice in the United Nations. This figure reached thirty-two (excluding South Africa) in 1963 (Harris 1972). Because of this turn of events, Israel became "concerned with her own diplomatic need to seek African friendship in an attempt to outflank Arab diplomatic initiatives in Africa" (Hellyer 1975, p. 6). In 1958, in a strategy to gain African support in the Middle East (Ojo 1988), Israel began to provide training to African military personnel, technical assistance to agricultural and development projects, and subsidies to train Africans in Israel. Africans, themselves struggling for liberation, perceived Israel as "a shining example of national achievement by a liberated people of a poor country" (Sklar 1984, p. 371), and they readily accepted Israeli aid. From 1958 to 1970, 1,948 of the 3,483 Israeli experts who served abroad were in

Africa. In addition, over half of the 13,790 foreign students studying in Israel (most from three to four weeks) were from black Africa.

The second stage of Israeli-South African relations lasted from 1961 to 1967. During this period Israel became outspoken in its opposition to apartheid. In 1962 it supported an UN General Assembly resolution calling for sanctions against South Africa, but simultaneously abstained from a clause which called for South Africa's expulsion from the organization. Israel supported similar resolutions in subsequent years, and in 1963 it recalled its diplomatic representative from South Africa. Three years later it supported a UN initiative to end South Africa's mandate over Namibia.

Stage three lasted from 1967 to 1973. These years saw a warming of relations between the two countries, as South Africa established a consulate in Israel and attempted to reestablish commercial and trade connections. During the June war of 1967, Israel crossed onto the West Bank of the Suez Canal. Traffic through the canal was effectively obstructed until 1971. As a result, many East African countries suffered economically. Ojo (1984) estimates that East African states lost $125 million a year in export trade during the closure. Cargo was forced to pass through the Cape of Good Hope—raising shipping costs—and Africans were angered that South Africa benefitted economically from the closure.

In contrast to the Organization of African Unity (OAU), whose member countries were angered by Israel's "preemptive" strike against its neighbors and its occupation of Arab (especially Egyptian) land, South Africa was effusive in its praise of the Israeli victory in the June war of 1967. In 1968, the OAU ministerial council passed a resolution which called Egypt "'the victim of Zionist aggression' and demanded the 'immediate and unconditional withdrawal' of Israeli troops" (Ojo 1988, p. 25). However, the resolution was softened at the OAU's next summit meeting, with the pan-African body reemphasizing its support for Egypt but calling for Israeli withdrawal in accordance with UN Security Council resolution 242. Beshir (1982, p. 79) argues that "the silence of the majority of African countries on the issue implied either indirect support for Israel or fear of economic retaliation." Whichever the case, Israeli-African relations were further chilled when the OAU rejected an Israeli donation in 1971.

A chain of events in 1973 concluded this period. The October war and the Arab oil embargo altered Israel's relations with other countries. Also, Egypt claimed that it had shot down a Mirage fighter jet of South African origin during one of its battles with Israel, although the veracity of this claim is disputed (Adams 1984). The Egyptian accusations raised suspicion, that Israel had failed to comply with a 1963 UN Security Council resolution which it had supported—one calling for an arms embargo against South Africa. Perhaps most damaging to its relations with black Africa, since December 1973 Israel has generally opposed or abstained from voting on antiapartheid resolutions in the UN (Weisbord and Kazarian 1985). By year's end only four African states maintained diplomatic ties with Israel. In retaliation, Israel broke bilateral relations with these states.

Israel's increasingly close relations with the racist South African government aggravated Israeli relations with black Africa and threatened its influence in international forums. Chazan (1977, p. 169) alleges that "the resolution of the General Assembly, condemning Zionism as a form of racism and racial discrimination akin to apartheid, is the most serious result to date of the general tendency to juxtapose Israel with South Africa." On 14 December 973 the General Assembly passed resolution 3151 G (XXVIII) which condemned "the unholy alliance between Portuguese colonialism, South African racism, zionism (sic) and Israeli imperialism." Also, UN resolution 3379 (XXX), passed on 10 November 1975, determined "that zionism (sic) is a form of racism and racial discrimination." Three months earlier the OAU had passed a resolution proclaiming that "the racist regime in occupied Palestine and the racist regimes in Zimbabwe and South Africa have a common imperialist origin, forming a whole and having the same racist structure and being organically linked in their policy aimed at repression of the dignity and integrity of the human being" (Stevens and Elmissiri 1977, pp. 199-200). Arab efforts to pass similar resolutions had failed in previous years.

The most significant turning point in Israeli-South African relations began in 1974 when Israel appointed an ambassador to Pretoria. In 1975, following passage of the UN resolution equating Zionism with racism, South Africa sent an ambassador to Israel. Trade relations expanded. African states were outraged when in April 1976, Prime Minister B. J. Vorster was welcomed by Prime Minister Yitzhak Rabin on the first official state visit by a South African to Israel. As a result of this visit, the two states signed a pact covering "a range of commercial, trade, cooperative, fiscal, and, in all probability, military spheres" (Chazan 1984, p. 152). Thus, at a time when other states were imposing economic and military sanctions against South Africa, Israel was building stronger ties with South Africa than at any time in its short history.

Perhaps most damaging is Israel's training of South African military personnel and its sales of military hardware to that country. Exact figures are not available to the public, but Israeli arms exports to South Africa are estimated to have multiplied significantly from the $20 million figure in 1960. In 1980, South Africa accounted for 35 percent of Israeli arms exports. This collaboration has only inflamed rumors that Israel is providing nuclear technology to the South Africans and has been involved in joint testing of nuclear weapons. In accordance with the 1977 UN resolution calling for an arms embargo against South Africa, Israel supposedly had no "official" dealings with the South African military (Adams 1984). Since the late 1970s other nations have accused Israel of violating the 1968 Treaty on Non-Proliferation of Nuclear weapons by collaborating with South Africa. In addition, there have been reports of "hundreds of Israelis . . . working on secret projects in South Africa, some of them scientists with military background, working in South Africa's most sensitive nuclear programs" (Weisbord and Kazarian 1985, pp. 109-110). On 22 September 1979 an orbiting satellite picked up what was suspected to be a nuclear flash over the southern Indian Ocean, and world leaders alleged an Israeli-South African nuclear collaboration. In sum, Israel's relations with South Africa seem to have tarnished its image even further in the eyes of Africans and, similarly, African Americans.

The Impact on African American-Jewish Relations

Many analysts of African American-Jewish relations fail to devote serious attention to African Americans' repugnance for Israeli-South African ties. For example, in discussing African American opinions on Israel and the Arab-Israeli conflict, Gilboa (1987) grants a single paragraph to the important issue of Israel's relations with South Africa. Like many other scholars who underestimate the significance this issue has to African Americans, Gilboa asserts that the Israel-South Africa relationship has been exaggerated since other countries have also maintained close ties to South Africa (cf. Weisbord and Kazarian 1985 and Chazan 1984). Instead he writes, "Israel was singled out by the Arabs as the closest and the most important ally of South Africa. These allegations have affected the attitudes of some American blacks toward Israel" (Gilboa 1987, p. 274). Such arguments ignore the political interests of African Americans in Africa and the Middle East and belittle their ability to formulate opinions on world issues.

      African Americans' identification with Africa and American Jews' identification with Israel have implications for their relations in the United States. Yet, tensions aroused by Israeli-South African ties cannot be understood independent of African American and Jewish responses to other international and domestic issues.[6] Consequently, this analysis must be placed in the context of other historical processes that have occurred since Israel's creation and Africa's liberation.

      African Americans' opinions of Israel have been shaped by their "relations with American Jews, perceptions of American and Israeli foreign policy, and racial solidarity with the Third World" (Gilboa 1987, p. 272). Historically most African Americans have empathized with the centuries of Jewish oppression and the Jewish quest for self determination and a homeland. Before 1948, African Americans were among the staunchest supporters of an independent Jewish state. Also, in the 1950s and 1960s, liberal Jewish involvement in the civil rights movement and Israeli-African nations gave Israel a favorable image among African Americans (Beshir 1982). In return for financial backing and support, civil rights organizations supported Jewish foreign policy positions (Miller 1981).

Despite current identification with Egypt, most African Americans did not react strongly to Israel's part in the joint French, British, and Israeli invasion of Egypt during the Suez Crisis of 1956 (Weisbord and Stein 1970). Exceptions were the Nation of Islam (Black Muslims), which has consistently taken an anti-Israeli stance since 1956 (Weisbord and Stein 1970; Young 1972) and the Harlem-based Asian-African Drums Association which organized a rally to show solidarity with Egyptian President Gamal Abdel Nasser (Challenor 1977) In contrast, the African American press depicted Israel as either an imperialist pawn or a tiny, brave nation fighting for survival, whereas France and Great Britain were depicted as the aggressors (Weisbord and Stein 1970; Weisbord and Kazarian 1985). But some African Americans did question the wisdom of Israel's involvement, while others praised Nasser's defiant seizure of the canal from European imperialists. Indeed, this event may have sparked a new African American interest in Egypt and the Middle East (Weisbord and Kazarian 1985).

This identification with Egypt influences African Americans' perceptions of Israeli policies. For example, Kitty Cohen (1988, p. 65) found that African Americans "identify not only with blacks in South Africa, but with other Third World nations and with all other colored peoples, including Arabs." For many African Americans and "black" Africans, Egypt is not an "Arab" land but an African one. In fact, Egypt is a leading member of the OAU and it has historically supported pan-Africanism. Cohen (1988, p. 65) concludes, "The fact that Egypt is part of the African continent has led some to the perception that Israel has attacked the African homeland. A foreign policy issue is thus colored by ethnic identification and, for the small Black Moslem community, also supported by religious belief. Similarly, Drake (1984, p. 24) states that "if we are to fully understand why (since 1956) there has been a tendency for some politically conscious people everywhere to sympathize with Egypt when it is disputing with Israel, we must be aware that one of the triumphs of African and Afro-American scholarship during the last thirty years has been to reclaim the history of Egypt for the black world." Furthermore,

> the deep-seated belief that Egypt is a part of the black world that Europeans are repeatedly trying to 'whiten' reinforced political

Pan-Africanism. But even without any emphasis upon its blackness, the fact that Egypt is in Africa has made it a crucial Pan-African symbol. Israel attacked Egypt in 1955 and then joined France and Britain in further attacks. Africans have never forgotten these preemptive strikes (Drake 1984, p. 24).

The June 1967 war was perhaps the turning point in African American perceptions of Israel. After the war, "Jews began to be seen as victors—and presented by their detractors as 'aggressors'—rather than as victims to be pitied" (Herman 1989, p. 89). For the first time the plight of the Palestinians received widespread media attention and African Americans, like their African kin, were appalled by what they learned about the seizure of Arab territory in the West Bank, Golan Heights, Sinai, and Gaza. The younger, radical leadership of African American organizations such as SNCC and the Black Panthers openly criticized Israeli treatment of Palestinians and Sephardic (many of whom are North African) Jews. Like many Third World leaders of the day, these young activists defined Zionism as racism. In their view, the Middle East conflict was another episode of the encroachment of an imperialist or "settler" white world against darker Third World people. Ultimately, disagreement over this issue broadened the schism between the older, more moderate leadership of the "integrationist" wing of the civil rights movement and the younger pan-Africanist and black nationalist arm. Integrationist leaders had worked with American Jews in the civil rights struggle, and they expressed loyalty to Jews who had backed them politically and financially. For example, Roy Wilkins of the NAACP and Whitney Young of the Urban League accused SNCC of anti-Semitism when it published a newsletter containing an anti-Zionist and allegedly libelous account of Israel's treatment of Palestinians. The younger leaders felt no such obligations. Instead they believed their interests to be more aligned with those of other Third World peoples. But despite the sincerity of the moderates' support for Israel, Young (1972) concludes that reliance on Jewish financial contributions may have made moderate African Americans hesitant to criticize Israeli policies and that these same African Americans were often unaware of Israel's ties with South Africa.

Two ads which appeared in 1970 issues of the *New York Times* illustrate the divergent viewpoints expressed by "radical" and "moderate" African Americans on Israel's role in the Middle East. On 28 June the A. Philip Randolph Institute printed a full-page ad entitled "Appeal by Black Americans for United States Support of Israel." The ad was signed by prominent African American entertainers, politicians, educators, writers, and elected officials, among others. The signers described Israel as "the most democratic country in the Middle East" and urged the US government to ensure its security (Young 1972, p. 71). In response to this appeal, a group of African Americans calling themselves the Committee of Black Americans for the Truth About the Middle East ran a full page ad on 1 November with the heading "An Appeal by Black Americans against United States Support of the Zionist Government of Israel." This ad charged that Israel was created on "stolen" Arab land and compared it with South Africa as a white settler-state. It also called Israel an imperialist outpost of the United States (Young 1972, p. 71).

In comparison, Jews rallied to Israel's defense. Most American Jews had always perceived Israel as a bastion of democracy—a tiny, embattled nation fending off "implacable" Arabs (M. Cohen 1988, p. 98). They were overjoyed by Israel's victory over its Arab neighbors in the June war of 1967. Since the war, pro-Israel organizations such as the American-Israel Public Affairs Committee (AIPAC) and the Conference of Presidents of Major Jewish Organizations (Presidents Conference) lobbied feverishly to increase American foreign aid and the arms sales to Israel (Trice 1977). The war had created a new "selling point" for the lobbyists: "Spartan Israel as a strategic asset of the United States" (M. Cohen 1988, p. 98). In general, AIPAC interacts between Jewish organizations and Congress while the Presidents Conference works between the Jewish community and policy makers in the executive branch. Congress has been more responsive to the lobbyists than has the executive branch, however Congress has often succeeded in convincing each administration to support Israel (Trice 1977).

The 1967 war helped to erode an already tenuous coalition in which African Americans had begun to question the legitimacy of liberal white leadership in "black" civil rights organizations. Beshir (1982, p. 96) argues:

> The UN Resolution on Zionism as a form of racism in 1975, Vorster's visit to Israel in 1976, and the subsequent growing relations with South Africa and the withdrawal of the liberal Jews from the Civil Rights movement because they could not 'stomach its concern with power and other minorities' contributed to the changes in the attitude of Black Americans toward Israel. The emergence of Black Moslems (sic) as a force in Black American society contributed to the increased sympathies towards the Arabs and Palestinians.

African American opinions of Israel continued to transform as conditions in the Middle East changed. Between 1970 and 1974 there was evidence of a growing sympathy among African Americans for the Arab cause in the Middle East conflict (Newby 1981, p. 50). The American Jewish Congress found that during the October 1973 Middle-east conflict African American newspapers mainly took either a pro-Israeli or an "evenhanded" stance toward the war (Weisbord and Kazarian 1985). But a January through February 1975 Yankelovic poll of grass roots African American leaders found conflicting results. While these leaders expected Israel to continue as a state, two thirds believed that it made no difference to African Americans whether it did so or not. Moreover, 41 percent expected African Americans to support the Arab nations in a conflict with Israel (Weisbord and Kazarian 1985).

A growing number of African Americans had become aware of warming Israeli-South African relations by the mid-1970s, and it "was being discussed in Black American circles with increasing frequency and no little emotion. At that juncture it was clear that Afro-Americans were becoming increasingly involved in the Middle East dispute. Black American-Jewish American relations would be influenced in turn" (Weisbord and Kazarian 1985, p. 55). In 1979 two-hundred African American leaders demanded that American Jews exert pressure on Israel to sever its ties with the repressive South African and Rhodesian regimes. Even Bayard Rustin, director of the pro-Israel, African American organization known as Black Americans in Support of Israel (BASIC), expressed concern over these ties. In addition, the *Bilalian News* and *Pittsburgh Courier* saw South African Prime Minister Johannes Vorster's visit to Israel in 1976 as "confirmation of the United Nations condemnation of Zionism as racism" (Weisbord and Kazarian 1985, p. 103).

Jews were angered by African American accusations of Israeli-South African ties. The American Jewish Congress has announced its opposition to apartheid on several occasions, but on 6 September 1976 the Congress responded to African American criticism by releasing a study naming nineteen black African countries which had trade relations with South Africa. The author, Moshe Decter, asserted that the study was conducted to "expose the double standard" that was applied to Israel (Stevens and Elmessiri 1977, p. 11). Among the countries named were several southern African states which are dependent on the South African economy due to an "exploitative imperial-colonial legacy" (Stevens and Elmessiri 1977, p. 11). The study argued that the Israeli economy was similarly dependent on that of South Africa, and that breaking economic ties would be harmful to Israel. African Americans were unconvinced by this argument, and the study only sparked more furor.

The Anti-Defamation League has also spoken out against apartheid and in 1989 it held an anti-apartheid protest on the first day of Hanukkah in front of the South African embassy. Since 1984, many Jews have also marched in demonstrations conducted in Washington, DC by the Free South Africa movement *(American Jewish Yearbook* 1987). But some Jewish organizations disagree with African American calls for divestment from South Africa and claim that "American-run companies often played a liberalizing role and that their departure might actually destabilize the South African government" *(American Jewish Yearbook* 1987, p. 124).

Some Jews have expressed concern about Bishop Desmond Tutu's visits to the US. Tutu has been critical of Israelis' treatment of Palestinians and has accused them of exercising "the arrogance of power" in their influential lobbying efforts in the United States *(American Jewish Yearbook* 1987, p. 124). The most recent antagonism between African Americans and Jews developed around Jewish criticism of South Africa's African National Congress (ANC) leader Nelson Mandela's long-time friendship with PLO leader Yasser Arafat. During his 1990 visit to the US, Mandela praised on ABC-TV's "Nightline" program, Fidel Castro, Muammar Gadhafi, and Yasser Arafat for their long-time support of the ANC. Jews accused Mandela of ignoring these men's human rights records when he contended that he lacked the time to investigate the internal politics of other countries and that they did not concern him. Once again, African Americans resented the suggestion by some Jews that anyone who is pro-Palestinian rights is also anti-Semitic or anti-Israel *(New York Times* 29 July 1990).

By the late 1980s the Israeli-South African relationship had become the "most divisive issue in black-Jewish relations" (Cohen 1988, p. 65). African Americans have difficulty understanding why Israel perceives a need to maintain contact with South Africa and why so many American Jews are slow to criticize Israel's stance. A study by the World Jewish Congress revealed that African American Congress members believed that the African American-Jewish alliance "had deteriorated during the year as a result of some Jewish opposition to affirmative action and Israel's relations with South Africa" *(American Jewish Yearbook* 1987, p. 125). In 1985, fifty-nine percent of African American state senators believed that Israel's ties to South Africa had a negative impact on African American-Jewish relations in the United States (K. Cohen 1988*)*. Only 11 percent said it had a positive influence, 14 percent said it had no influence, and 16 percent did not know or would not comment.[7] However, their opinions did not seem to have a significant effect on their support of foreign aid to Israel. Twenty-six of the 56 state senators interviewed favored extensive aid to Israel, 22 supported limited aid, two opposed aid, and six did not comment. But much of this support was qualified by suggestions that aid should be conditional. For example, many argued that the US should continue aid to Israel but be more critical of its policies. Other comments suggested that aid should be contingent upon Israel's breaking ties with South Africa, its treatment of the Palestinians, its involvement in the Jonathan Pollard spying incident, and the needs of poor Americans and developing nations.

Jewish support of Israel is more steadfast than that of African Americans, but there has always been a small minority of Jews who publicly object to Israel's policies. Intellectuals such as Irving Louis Horowitz *(*1974*)* engage in mild criticism relative to "New Left" or "Left Radical" critics like Michael Lerner and Noam Chomsky who engage in harsher criticism. Chomsky *(*1983,

p. 3), for instance, has charged Israel with "repression and state terrorism." Chomsky also accuses the Anti-Defamation League of attempting to suppress criticism of Israel's policies, and he castigates Jews who debate the "legitimacy" of criticizing those policies.

After the 1982 Israeli invasion of Lebanon, Jews the world over began to reassess their almost unmitigated support of Israel (Adams 1984). Many Jews "now suggest that the lobbies should become more involved in the politics of Israel and support those groups that will maintain liberal traditions and oppose those individuals who, they feel, are not representative of Jews around the world" (Adams 1984, p. 138). Since the 1982 invasion, Jewish community federations have toned down their requests for aid to Israel for fear that "Israel's bad press has made her less attractive, to donors" (Elazar 1990, p. 178). In addition, a 1988 survey revealed that 41 percent of American Jews would accept a peace plan which exchanged territory for guaranteed peace compared to 31 percent who would not. In 1988, two-thirds of American Jews also indicated that Israel should talk with the PLO if it recognized Israel and renounces terrorism (Lipset 1990). Similar results were found after Yasser Arafat met these demands in December of 1988.

In recent years, American Jews who disapprove of Israel's policies have taken steps to organize and make their voices heard. Friends of *Yesh Gvul*[8] provides family and emotional support for *sarvanim,* Israeli Defense Forces (IDF) reservists who refuse to serve in the occupied territories. The new Jewish Peace Lobby (JPL) describes itself as an alternative to the more conservative AIPAC.[9] Americans for Peace Now is the US branch of an Israeli organization which supports the exchange of land for peace. Established in 1986, *Tikkun* bills itself as "the liberal alternative to *Commentary* magazine and the voices of Jewish conservatism." Perhaps this growing willingness to publicly censure Israeli policies will make American Jews less sensitive to criticism from other ethnic groups, and it may also help ameliorate some of the tensions which currently exist between African Americans and Jews.

It would be remiss to conclude that all or even most African American opposition to Israel's policies is due to anti-Zionism or anti-Semitism. African American opposition to Israeli policies is complex and involves feelings of comradeship with Africans and other Third World people, especially if they are seen as oppressed or struggling for liberation. On the one hand, recent studies show a trend for African Americans to be more sympathetic toward the Palestinians than Israel as compared to American whites (Weisbord and Kazarian 1985). On the other hand, there appears to be some ambivalence in African Americans' opinions on the Middle-East conflict. Their pro-Palestinian stance does not preclude any pro-Israel sentiments. For example, African Americans and their leaders were outraged by rumors of an Arab plot to expel

Israel from the United Nations General Assembly in 1975. In addition, the Congressional Black Caucus has consistently taken a pro-Israel stance on legislation granting aid to Israel and has opposed the sale of F-15 fighter planes to Saudi Arabia. BASIC, an organization of 250 prominent African Americans which arranges trips to Israel and "educates" African Americans on Israel and Zionism, was founded in the mid-1970s by activists Bayard Rustin and A. Philip Randolph. Gelb (1980, p. 11) asserts that the "continued Black support for 'Jewish' interests (particularly in the Middle East), despite concern over disproportionate resources being diverted from domestic areas is especially noteworthy and undoubtedly related to continued Jewish support for Black politicians and causes." It is quite possible that African Americans identify with Arab and Jewish quests for survival since such is the legacy of the African in America.

In comparison, most American Jews "oppose any political or intellectual act that appears to threaten Israel" (Holden 1984, p. 204). Many Jews express anger at African Americans' criticisms of Israeli policies. For example, Jews were offended when African Americans spoke out on the Middle East, insisting that what happens in the Middle East should be of no interest to African Americans (Gelb 1980). In a Philadelphia survey, 67 percent of the rabbis and 20 percent of secular humanists in respective Jewish organizations said they would withhold support from African American groups that held pro-Arab or anti-Israel sentiments (Labovitz 1975, pp. 80-81). Brown (1987) found that Jewish university students invariably chose Israel and the equating of Zionism with racism as the issues they most wanted their African American peers to understand. But despite a tendency to align themselves with the Palestinians, African American students insisted that they did not question the Jewish right to a homeland and, they were eager to learn more about the Jewish perspective. Jewish students, on the other hand, tended to "romanticize" Israel in a way which prevented them from understanding "legitimate Black concerns about Palestinian rights" (Brown 1987, p. 21). In addition, many Jews equate African American criticism of Israel with "black anti-Semitism'" (Labovitz 1975).

Discussion and Conclusion

As this paper demonstrates, a valid discussion of African American-Jewish relations cannot focus on domestic issues to the exclusion of international affairs. International issues may alternately strain, or strengthen African American-Jewish relations depending upon the political stance each group takes on an international issue and the combined effects of intervening factors such as their positions on domestic matters. Both African Americans and American Jews work toward "retaining or seeking the return of national territories, winning and preserving national independence, and cessation of persecution and oppression of minority ethnic and religious groups in other nations" (Gerson 1977, pp. 54-55). When pursuing their international interests, African Americans often take the side of Africans and other Third World peoples with whom they identify. In a similar vein, American Jews tend to side with the Jewish diaspora and Israel. Consequently, when Israel and Africa (and sometimes even Arabs) clash, new conflicts erupt or old ones are exacerbated between African Americans and American Jews.

These findings have implications for race and ethnic relations theories in general. The findings demonstrate that studies of ethnic relations must go beyond analyses of group prejudice to incorporate the important issues of an ethnic group's position in the domestic and global social structures, its interests, and its identification with the homeland. These factors must be addressed for a full understanding of current relations between these and possibly other ethnic groups.

Ethnic relations theory has been peculiarly myopic in its tendency to assume that ethnic conflict can be explained as a manifestation of the internal political and economic dynamics of a country. Despite the evidence that ethnic groups retain international interests specific to their homelands, this factor is only alluded to or marginally incorporated into ethnic relations theory. For example, there is discussion of how ethnic hierarchies are structured in the internal colonialism model or how middleman minorities' love of their homeland foments charges of dual loyalty from members of the host society.

Ethnic relations theory should be broadened to recognize that ethnic groups may take a particular stance around an international issue and that this in turn may affect their relations with other ethnic groups. Just as sociology is beginning to recognize that ethnic relations cannot be explained by analyses limited to case studies in the United States, it must also recognize that ethnic politics now transcend international boundaries, affecting domestic ethnic relations in turn (Said 1977). This is especially important today in the United States as the ethnic population continues to diversify with the immigration of various peoples scarcely represented in this country before the mid 1960s.

Consequently, there is a need for additional studies to determine under what conditions international issues influence interethnic dynamics and how common a phenomenon this actually is. The case of African Americans and Jews is a contemporary one which has received much media coverage. Undoubtedly there are historical cases where this has been true as well, such as the African American and Italian American clashes in New York City following Italy's invasion of Ethiopia in 1935. A second, current example is the hostility that arose in 1990 between African and Cuban Americans in Miami after city officials refused to honor South Africa's ANC leader Nelson Mandela with an official welcome. Cuban American city officials, who view Fidel Castro as an oppressor of human rights, were offended when Mandela expressed appreciation for Castro's long-time support of the ANC. African Americans have responded to the "snub" by cancelling plans for conventions in the city. They have also gained the support of groups like the National Organization for Women and the American Civil Liberties Union. As a result, by January of 1991 the city had lost an estimated $5 million to $12 million in tourist revenue *(Chicago Tribune,* 27 January 1991). Other contemporary examples include American Jewish-Arab American relations in light of Middle East tensions or the dynamics between Southeast Asian refugees as they become established ethnic populations in the United States.

The Ethiopian-Italian and the Israeli-South African cases offer strong support for the argument that homeland politics affect their diaspora populations in the US, thereby impacting relations between ethnic groups. Moreover, these findings dispute Yancey, Ericksen, and Juliani's (1976) overstatement that ethnicity in the US has little to do with conditions in the homeland. African Americans and Jews have always linked their fates with those of their ethnic kin in other parts of the world, whether this be their homelands or the diaspora. This reality is recognized by the Israeli government, which has sponsored studies exploring African Americans' perceptions of Israel. It has also initiated discussion of African American-Jewish relations in its meetings with US officials (Young 1972). This study demonstrates that each group is quick to mobilize around international issues when it perceives a threat to its homelands' interests or survival. Each group willingly challenged a diaspora population of their homeland's enemies, even when it disrupted previously harmonious relations with that population.

It is possible that the Persian Gulf War will have a damaging effect on African American-Jewish relations. To date most African Americans seem to express ambivalence or disapproval of the US decision to declare war on Iraq. In comparison, most American Jews lean toward supporting the US attempts to unseat Saddam Hussein, especially since Iraq began its scud missile attacks on Israel. As of this writing, Israel has restrained from retaliating against Iraq's attacks. However, should Israel be drawn into the conflict and Arab leaders refuse to fight alongside Israel in its attacks on an Arab country, African Americans and Jews may once again be forced to take stands which place them on opposite sides of an international issue. It would be rash to make a definitive prediction of the effects of the war on African American-Jewish relations since it is impossible to know whether Israel will respond to Iraq's provocation and whether key Arab countries will maintain their coalition with the West. A more crucial factor to consider may be how the issue of Palestinian self-determination is handled after the war. There is a strong potential for disagreement between African Americans and American Jews if the UN, Israel, and Arab representatives do not take immediate measures to resolve the Palestinian predicament in the occupied territories following Iraq's forced withdrawal from Kuwait.

It is also difficult to assess the long-term effects that international issues have on US ethnic relations in general. In the case of African Americans and Jews, international and homeland politics have caused serious conflicts since the late 1960s. However, we might be better able to answer this question if similar studies are conducted of relations between other ethnic groups. Such studies will be increasingly important as the diverse groups of newer US immigrants become established ethnic groups.

Acknowledgments

An earlier draft of this paper was presented at the annual meeting of the American Sociological Association, Washington, DC, 1990. The author wishes to thank Charles Payne, Charles Ragin, Bernard Beck, Aldon Morris, Arlene Kaplan Daniels, Yuval Yonay, Mary Kate Kinney, Mahmoud Sadri, and Stanford Lyman for their comments.

Notes

1. The State Department denied passports to most African Americans who volunteered to fight for Ethiopia.
2. The earliest evidence that I could locate of international issues straining African American-Jewish relations involved African American anger over B'nai B'rith's protesting the pogroms in Russia and Rumania in 1903. African Americans accused American Jews and the US government of hypocrisy, since there was no mass Jewish or government reaction to the lynchings of thousands of African Americans in the United States (Foner 1975).
3. There was no special bond between African Americans and Jews before this period. For most of the antebellum years, Northern Jews were no more likely to be abolitionists than were other whites, and Southern Jews were often slave owners and active members of the Confederacy (Korn [1961] 1973; Bender 1969; Dinnerstein and Palsson 1973).
4. It is often debated whether such an African American-Jewish alliance ever existed. Cruse (1967), Stevenson (1988) and Halpern (1971) insist that the alliance was limited to a small, intimate network of "mostly middle to upper class (sic) black and Jewish professionals and intellectuals who were especially concerned with their peoples' ability to eventually (sic) assimilate into American society . . ." (Stevenson 1988, p. 9). Similarly, Labovitz (1975, p. 7) states that there is "a general tendency to romanticize the relationships and overemphasize the extent to which Jews and Blacks have worked harmoniously."
5. DuBois put the figure at 300,000 dues-paying members at a time when the UNIA claimed a membership of 3 million. Both figures may reflect bias, however, especially since Garvey and DuBois, although both pan-Africanists, were archenemies.

6.   Weisbord and Stein (1970, p. 110) write that "while Israel has added a new dimension to relations between blacks and Jews in America, the seemingly insoluble Middle East enigma cannot be disentangled from ghetto frictions or from black attitudes toward the United States and its white populace."

7.   It is important to keep in mind that respondents were aware that their interviewer was an Israeli Jew.

8.   The Hebrew phrase *Yesh Gvul* translates into "There Is a Limit"

9.   The JPL currently has a membership of 1,500 compared to approximately 50,000 for AIPAC.

References

Adams, James. 1984. *The Unnatural Alliance.* London: Quartet Books Limited.

Allen, Robert. 1973. "Black Liberation and World Revolution." Pp. 247-70 in *Contemporary Black Thought: The Best from the Black Scholar,* edited by R. Chrisman and N. Hare. Indianapolis: Bobbs-Merrill.

American Jewish Committee and the Jewish Publication Society. 1987. "Report on Intergroup Relations." Pp. 117-36 in *American Jewish Yearbook.* Scranton, PA: The Haddon Craftsmen.

Bender, Eugene I. 1969. "Reflections on Negro-Jewish Relationships: The Historical Dimension." *Phylon* 30: 56-65.

Berson, Lenora E. 1971. *The Negroes and the Jews.* New York: Random House.

Beshir, Mohamed Omer. 1982. *Terramedia. Themes in Afro-Arab Relations.* London: Ithaca Press.

Blauner, Robert. 1972. *Racial Oppression in America.* New York: Harper & Row.

Bracey, John H. Jr., Augusts Meier, and Elliott Rudwick. 1970. *Black Nationalism in America.* Indianapolis: Bobbs-Merrill.

Brown, Cherie R. 1987. *Face to Face. Black-Jewish Campus Dialogues.* New York: American Jewish Committee.

Carmichael, Stokeley and Charles W. Hamilton. 1967. *Black Power The Politics of Liberation in America.* New York: Random House.

Challenor, Herschelle Sullivan. 1977. "The Influence of Black Americans on U.S. Foreign Policy Toward Africa." Pp. 139-74 in *Ethnicity and U.S. Foreign Policy,* edited by A. A. Said. New York: Praeger Publishers.

Chazan, Naomi. 1977. "Israel's Shortsighted Policy on South Africa." Pp. 168-70 in *Israel and South Af ica: The Progression of a Relationship,* edited by R. P. Stevens and A. M. Elmessiri. New Brunswick, NJ: North American.

— 1984. "The Fallacies of Pragmatism: Israeli Foreign Policy Toward South Africa." Pp. 148-81 in *Jews in Black Perspectives: A Dialogue,* edited by J. R. Washington, Jr. Cranbury, NJ: Associated University Presses.

Chomsky, Noam. 1983. *The Fateful Triangle: The United States, Israel and the Palestinians.* Boston: South End Press.

Chicago Tribune, 27 January 1991.

Clarke, John Henrik. 1985. "African Americans and the Berlin Conference." *TransAfrica Forum* 3: 61-69.

Cohen, Kitty O. 1988. Black-Jewish Relations: *The View from the State Capitols.* New York: Cornwall.

Cohen, Mark P. 1988. "American Jewish Response to the Palestinian Uprising." *Journal of Palestine Studies* 17: 97-104.

Cronon, E. David, ed. 1973. *Marcus Garvey.* Englewood Cliffs, NJ: Prentice-Hall.

Cruse, Harold C. 1967. *The Crisis of the Negro Intellectual.* New York: William Morrow.

Drake, John Gibbs St. Clair. 1984. "African Diaspora and Jewish Diaspora: Convergence and Divergence." Pp. 19-41 in *Jews in Black Perspectives: A Dialogue,* edited by J. R. Washington, Jr. Cranbury, NJ: Associated University Presses.

Diner, Hasia R. 1977. *In the Almost Promised Land: American Jews and Blacks, 1915-1935.* Westport, CT: Greenwood Press.

Dinnerstein, Leonard and Mary Dale Palsson, eds. 1973. *Jews in the South.* Baton Rouge: Louisiana State University Press.

Drago, Edmund L. 1978. "American Blacks and Italy's Invasion of Ethiopia." *Negro History Bulletin* 41: 883-884.

Elazar, Daniel J. 1990. "Developments in Jewish Community Organizations in the Second Postwar Generation." Pp. 173-92 in *American Pluralism and the Jewish Community,* edited by S. M. Lipset. New Brunswick, NJ: Transaction Publishers.

Emerson, Rupert and Martin Kilson. 1965. "The American Dilemma in a Changing World: The Rise of Africa and the Negro American." Pp. 626-55 in *The Negro American,* edited by T. Parson and K. B. Clark. Boston: Beacon Press.

Erikson, Erik H. 1965. "The Concept of Identity in Race Relations: Notes and Queries." Pp. 227-53 in *The Negro American,* edited by T. Parson and K. B. Clark. Boston: Beacon Press.

Feagin, Joe R. 1989. *Racial and Ethnic Relations.* 3d ed. Englewood Cliffs: Prentice Hall.

Foner, Philip S. 1975. "Black-Jewish Relations in the Opening Years of the Twentieth Century." *Phylon* 36: 359-67.

Franklin, John Hope. 1967. *From Slavery to Freedom: A History of Negro Americans.* 3d ed. New York: Alfred A. Knopf.

Gallup Report. March 1986. Report #246. Princeton, NJ.

Garvey, Marcus. 1973. "From Jamaica to New York." Pp. 19-26 in *Marcus Garvey,* edited by E. D. Cronon. Englewood Cliffs, NJ: Prentice-Hall.

Gelb, Joyce. 1980. *Beyond Conflict: Black-Jewish Relations, Accent on the Positive.* New York: Institute on Pluralism and Group Identity of the American Jewish Committee.

Geltman, Max. 1970. *The Confrontation: Black Power, Anti-Semitism and the Myth of Integration.* Englewood Cliffs, NJ: Prentice Hall.

Gerson, Louis L. 1977. "The Influence of Hyphenated Americans on U.S. Diplomacy." Pp. 46-58 in *Ethnicity and U.S. Foreign Policy,* edited by A. A. Said. New York: Praeger Publishers.

Gilboa, Eytan. 1987. *American Public Opinion toward Israel and the Arab-Israeli Conflict.* Lexington, MA: D.C. Heath and Company.

Glazer, Nathan. 1957. *American Judaism.* Chicago: University of Chicago Press.

Halpern, Ben. 1971. *Jews and Blacks: The Classic American Minorities.* New York: Herder and Herder.

Harris, Joseph E. 1972. *Africans and Their History.* New York: New American Library.

Hellyer, Peter. 1975. "Israel and South Africa: Development of Relations, 1967-1974." London: Palestine Action.

Herman, Simon N. 1989. *Jewish Identity: A Social Psychological Perspective.* 2d ed. New Brunswick, NJ: Transaction Publishers.

Holden, Matthew, Jr. 1984. "Reflections on Two Isolated Peoples." Pp. 182-211 in *Jews in Black Perspectives: A Dialogue,* edited by J. R. Washington, Jr. Cranbury, NJ: Associated University Press.

Horowitz, Irving Louis. 1974. *Israeli Ecstasies l Jewish Agonies.* New York: Oxford University Press.

Keller, Edmond J. 1984. "Black Americans and US Policy Toward the Horn of Africa. *TransAfrica Forum 2:* 15-25.

Kilson, Martin and Adelaide Hill. 1975. *Apropos of Africa: Afro-American Leaders and the Romance of Africa.* Garden City: Doubleday.

Korn, Bertram Wallace. [1961]1973. "Jews and Negro Slavery in the Old South, 1789-1865." Pp. 89-134 in *Jews in the South,* edited by L. Dinnerstein and M. D. Palsson. Baton Rouge: Louisiana State University Press.

Labovitz, Sherman. 1975. *Attitudes Toward Blacks Among Jews: Historical Antecedents and Current Concerns.* Saratoga, CA: R & E Research Associates.

Lieberson, Stanley. 1980. *A Piece of the Pie: Blacks and White Immigrants Since 1880.* Berkeley: University of California Press.

Lipset, Seymour Martin. 1990. *American Pluralism and the Jewish Community.* New Brunswick, NJ: Transaction Publishers.

Magubane, Bernard M. 1987. *The Ties that Bind: African American Consciousness of Africa.* Trenton: Africa World Press.

Martinelli, Phylis Cancilla. 1982. "Italian-American Experience". Pp. 217-32 in *America's Ethnic Politics,* edited by J. S. Roucek and B. Eisenberg. Westport, CT: Greenwood Press.

Marx, Gary T. and Michael Useem. 1971. "Majority Involvement in Minority Movements: Civil Rights, Abolition, Untouchability." *Journal of Social Issues* 27: 81-104.

Mendes-Flohr, Paul R. and Jehuda Reinharz, eds. 1980. *The Jew in the Modern World A Documentary History.* New York: Oxford University Press.

Miller, Jake C. 1981. "Black Viewpoints on the Mid-East Conflict." *Journal of Palestine Studies* 10: 37-49.

Newby, Robert G. 1981. "Afro-Americans and Arabs: An Alliance in the Making?" *Journal of Palestine Studies 10:* 50-58.

New York Times, 29 July 1990.

Ojo, Olusola. 1988. *Africa and Israel. Relations in Perspective.* Boulder, CO: Westview Press.

Rubin, Lawrence. 1990. "The Emerging Jewish Public-Affairs Culture." Pp. 193-201 in *American Pluralism and the Jewish Community,* edited by S. M. Lipset. New Brunswick, NJ: Transaction Publishers.

Said, Abdul Aziz. 1977. "A Redefinition of National Interest, Ethnic Consciousness, and U.S. Foreign Policy. Pp. 1-15 in *Ethnicity and U.S. Foreign Policy,* edited by A. A. Said. New York: Praeger Publishers.

Shack, William A. 1974. "Ethiopia and Afro-Americans: Some Historical Notes, 1920-1970." *Phylon* 35: 142-55.

Shankman, Arnold. 1978. "The Image of the Italian in the Afro-American Press, 1886-1936." *Italian Americana* 40: 30-49.

Sklar, Richard. 1984. "Africa and the Middle East: What Blacks and Jews Owe to Each Other." Pp. 132-47 in *Jews in Black Perspectives: A Dialogue,* edited by J. R. Washington, Jr. Cranbury, NJ: Associated University Presses.

Stevens, Richard P. 1977. "Zionism, South Africa and Apartheid: The Paradoxical Triangle." Pp. 57-73 in *Israel and South Africa: The Progression of a Relationship,* edited by R. P. Stevens and A. M. Elmessiri. New Brunswick, NJ: North American Press.

Stevens, Richard P. and Abdelwahab M. Elmessiri, eds. 1977. Rev. ed. *Israel and South Africa: The Progression of a Relationship.* New Brunswick, NJ: North American, Inc.

Stevenson, Marshall Field, Jr. 1988. "Points of Departure, Acts of Resolve: Black-Jewish Relations in Detroit, 1937-1962." Ph.D. Dissertation, University of Michigan.

Thornton, Michael C. and Robert J. Taylor. 1988. "Black American Perceptions of Black Africans." *Ethnic and Racial Studies 11 (2):* 139-50.

Trice, Robert H. 1977. "Domestic Interest Groups and the Arab-Israeli Conflict: A Behavioral Analysis." Pp. 117-38 in *Ethnicity and U.S. Foreign Policy*, edited by A. A. Said. New York: Praeger Publishers.

Washington, Joseph R. Jr. 1984. *Jews in Black Perspectives: A Dialogue*. Cranbury, NJ: Associated University Presses.

Waxman, Chaim I. 1976. "The Centrality of Israel in American Jewish Life: A Sociological Analysis." *Judaism* 25: 175-87.

Weisbord, Robert G. and Richard Kazarian, Jr. 1985. *Israel in the Black American Perspective*. Westport, CT: Greenwood Press.

Weisbord, Robert G. and Arthur Stein. 1970. *Bittersweet Encounter: The Afro-American and the American Jews*. Westport, CT: Negro Universities Press.

Yancey, William L., Eugene P. Ericksen and Richard N. Juliani. 1976. "Emergent Ethnicity: A Review and Reformulation." *American Sociological Review 41:* 391-403.

Young, Lewis. 1972. "American Blacks and the Arab-Israeli Conflict." Journal of *Palestine Studies* 2: 70-85.

Childbirth Customs in Orthodox Jewish Traditions

Karina Bodo
Nancy Gibson

Abstract: *The objective of the study was to describe cultural beliefs of Orthodox Jewish families regarding childbirth in order to help family physicians enhance the quality and sensitivity of their care. The findings were based on a review of the literature searched in* Medline *(1966 to present),* Healthstar *(1975 to present),* Embase *(1988 to present), and Social Science Abstracts (1984 to present). Interviews with several members of the Orthodox Jewish community in Edmonton, Alta, and Vancouver, BC, were conducted to determine the accuracy of the information presented and the relevance of the paper to the current state of health care delivery from the recipients' point of view. The main message of the study was that customs and practices surrounding childbirth in the Orthodox Jewish tradition differ in several practical respects from expectations and practices within the Canadian health care system. The information presented was deemed relevant and accurate by those interviewed, and the subject matter was considered to be important for improving communication between patients and physicians. Improved communication and recognition of these differences can improve the quality of health care provided to these patients. The conclusions drawn were that misunderstandings rooted in different cultural views of childbirth and the events surrounding it can adversely affect health care provided to women in the Orthodox Jewish community in Canada. A basic understanding of the cultural foundations of potential misunderstandings will help Canadian physicians provide effective health care to Orthodox Jewish women.*

A practical challenge faced by health care practitioners is that of providing effective health care to people from a variety of sociocultural backgrounds. In many cultures, health care and illness are perceived very differently from the conventional biomedical view. Arthur Kleinman[1,2] describes these perceptions and beliefs as explanatory models and suggests that conflicts between patients' and health care practitioners' explanatory models are the source of difficulty in treating patients from cultures other than the health care practitioner's.

The cultural context of childbirth influences the attitudes, values, and interpretations of individual women and gives them a basis to develop their own perspective on the meaning of childbirth.[3] Without an understanding of cultural backgrounds, important information can be missed easily. This article investigates customs surrounding childbirth in the traditions of Hasidic or Orthodox Jews and discusses the implications of these customs and practices for provision of effective health care to people of this group in Canada. It is important to note that customs and beliefs described in this paper are those of Orthodox Jews and do not apply to all other Jewish groups.

Members of the Jewish community are found throughout Canada; most reside in the central and western provinces and in metropolitan areas.[4] While many Orthodox Jewish women choose a physician within the Jewish community, there are likely to be instances where this is impossible. Therefore it is important to be aware of the potential sources of misunderstanding in the delivery of health care to these women.

Practices surrounding childbirth in most ethnic and religious groups are not restricted to the actual moment of birth. Consequently, related topics of conception and fertility, contraception and abortion, pregnancy, and the postpartum period will be discussed in addition to the birth event itself. Discussion of these issues will include recommendations for health professionals caring for women of this cultural group.

Quality Of Evidence

Information was acquired primarily from a literature search of several databases, including MEDLINE (1966 to present), HEALTHSTAR (1975 to present), EMBASE (1988 to present), and Social Science Abstracts (1984 to present). Articles were chosen based on their potential to contribute valuable information to the topic being researched, that is, the differences between the cultural beliefs of Orthodox Judaism and those of mainstream Canadian biomedicine with respect to the issues and events surrounding childbirth.

Texts that provided some insight into the cultural beliefs of Orthodox Judaism were investigated. Information extracted from these texts was verified in interviews or written communication with several members of the Orthodox Jewish community in Edmonton, Alta, and Vancouver, BC. A common theme running through the interactions with these representatives was the appropriateness of the information and the opinion that communicating these issues with the Canadian medical community would be beneficial in improving the quality and efficacy of health care.

Traditional Beliefs

Procreation is greatly encouraged in Orthodox Judaism. In fact, fertility and having a large family are a *mitzvah,* or good deed. Jewish practices are based primarily on the Old Testament of the Bible and the Talmud, a collection of laws and commentary on the five books of Moses. The *halacha* and *responsa* literature, which records individual decisions by rabbis over the centuries, was developed after the Talmud was codified and covers every aspect of daily life. Thus, the laws governing the life of Orthodox Jews were developed over 3000 years of debate, examination, and custom, and continue to develop in response to the changing times.[5,6] Reference will be made to these works throughout the paper, as they are the foundation of behaviour and practices for Orthodox Jewish women at all times of life, including pregnancy and childbirth.

Conception And Infertility

In Orthodox Judaism, the verse "Be fruitful and multiply and replenish the earth," from the Book of Genesis (1:28), is considered to be one of the most important commandments and responsibilities a Jew is expected to perform.[3,7] Many questions and concepts regarding childbirth have originated from this one statement. It is generally accepted that one male and one female child per couple is the minimum requirement for fulfilling this commandment.

The responsibility of procreation rests with the man, while it is a woman's right, but not her obligation, to bear children. Because the woman is the one who bears the risk for childbearing, she must not be obliged to do anything that threatens her life. According to the *halacha,* an investigation into the cause of infertility in a couple must begin with an investigation of potential sources of infertility in the woman first, before proceeding to the man. In vitro fertilization and embryo transfer are considered in the rabbinical literature. However, consultation with the couple's rabbi is necessary before performing any sort of therapy for infertility, as some issues have not been resolved in the Jewish laws.[7]

Sexual intercourse, apart from the purpose of procreation, is an important part of marriage. *Onah,* or "sexual visitation" for the woman's pleasure, is a woman's due in a marriage. However, the times during the month that sexual intercourse is allowed are strictly regulated according to the rules of *tahirat hamishpacha* or "family purity." For at least 12 days of the month (at least 5 days during the woman's menstrual flow and 7 "white" days after the last sign of bleeding), the woman is sexually unavailable or *niddah.* This means that the husband and wife do not touch, sleep in the same bed, or have sexual intercourse, and the man cannot receive anything directly from his wife's hands. At the end of the 12 days, the woman signals her return to a sexual phase by immersion in a ritual bath or *mikvah.*

This practice is thought to serve several purposes. It serves to maintain the sexual tension within a longrunning monogamous relationship and also ensures that increased sexual activity occurs at the most likely time of ovulation.[5,6] However, if a woman has a short menstrual cycle, this practice could actually ensure that she and her husband do not have sexual intercourse around the time of ovulation. A biomedical health care provider should be aware of this practice, as it could be a cause of perceived infertility. Consultation with the couple's rabbi and an explanation of the situation can provide rabbinical dispensation for shortening the time that the woman is *niddah.*

The rules of *tahirat hamishpacha* also cause distress for a woman who has intermenstrual spotting or if bleeding is caused by a pelvic examination. In addition, in order to enter the *mikvah,* one must be completely naked. Therefore, if a patient has a broken limb, she might appreciate a removable cast, as this will enable her to engage in sexual relations after her menses. Sensitivity to these situations will aid the health care professional's relationship with the patient and will assist the practitioner in providing the most appropriate treatment.

Contraception And Abortion

According to Orthodox Jewish law, the health of the mother, including her mental health, is always of primary concern. This law supersedes the *mitzvah* of childbearing and the ritual practices of holy days. Although the commandment is to "Be fruitful and multiply and replenish the earth," a woman may not be expected to "build the world by destroying herself."[8] Therefore, birth control is allowed in certain circumstances where a pregnancy would be harmful to the physical or mental health of the mother.

An exhaustive argument of whether birth control should be used and, if so, which type, is given in Feldman[8]; the ultimate conclusion is that the woman's sexual pleasure and her health supersede the *mitzvah* of childbearing. The contraceptive of choice is oral contraceptives, as they do not present a physical barrier to sperm and prevent the husband from committing onanism (coitus interruptus). They also impose no artificial barriers and allow the couple to "be of one flesh."[6] The rhythm method is not recommended because the rules of *tahirat hamishpacha* would mean almost total abstinence, which undermines the woman's right to sexual satisfaction.

Abortion may be considered if the mother's health is in danger. The fetus is considered a part of the mother's body with no separate soul of its own until its head or the greater part of its body has emerged. Therefore, if a choice must be made between the welfare of the mother and that of the fetus, the mother's welfare is paramount.

Generally, if abortion is to be considered, rabbinical dispensation is required to take what is perceived as a drastic course of action; in an emergency, physicians may act without prior consultation with a rabbi.[6] Most Jewish women will not wish to terminate an abnormal pregnancy unless completion of the pregnancy puts their lives at risk.[9] In the case of prenatal diagnosis of an abnormal fetus, an Orthodox rabbi is more likely to be in direct contact with the couple's physician than are rabbis of other branches of Judaism. He will also be very involved in helping the couple after the birth of a child with a hereditary condition or birth defect."[10]

Pregnancy

If a married Orthodox Jewish woman is seeing a male physician, certain rules apply. The door of the examining room must be unlocked and other people must be within hearing range. It must be possible for another health care professional to walk in unannounced. The woman must also be convinced that the male physician has a good moral character. In general, a female physician is requested, particularly for obstetric or gynecological care,[5] to avoid the risk of nudity in the presence of a man who is not the husband.

Orthodox Jews who follow the rules of *tahirat hamishpacha* may attend childbirth classes taught by women who understand their customs. It is common for pregnant women not to prepare for their babies in advance. The baby's name is not revealed before the official naming in case the Angel of Death decides to visit the nursery.[6]

Birth

Orthodox Jewish women entering labour are considered to be in mortal danger, and therefore any laws (including the rules of observing the Sabbath) may be set aside to care for her. The *mitzvah* of "saving a life" supersedes all others. The woman is considered to be in this state of risk for 3 days after the baby is born.[5]

The rules of *tahirat hamishpacha* apply as soon as there is bloody discharge from the vagina, and the husband is not allowed to physically comfort, support, or touch his wife at any time during labour or for 7 days after all discharge has stopped.[9] Therefore, hospital rules that allow more than one helper in the birthing room would be greatly appreciated by the mother, as a female friend or relative can then provide the physical support that, in Canada, is often expected from the husband.

The father may choose to participate actively by verbally communicating with his wife near her bedside, but he may not wipe her brow or hold her hand. The husband may also choose to participate spiritually by reciting from the Book of Psalms in a corner of the birthing room or in another room. The husband will not view the birth and will see the baby only after it has been lifted away from the mother, as he is not allowed to see his wife's genital area. Once he has seen the baby, he will lean over his wife, smile, and say *mazel tov,* or "good luck," being careful all the time not to touch her. Some mothers will give birth with a prayer book or a special prayer under their pillows as a talisman. Orthodox Jewish women will try to keep as much of their heads and bodies covered during labour as possible.[5, 6]

Postpartum Care

Breastfeeding is common among Orthodox Jewish women, and experienced mothers in the hospital often give calm and practical advice regarding breastfeeding to new mothers.[9] The diet of Orthodox Jewish mothers in Canadian hospitals is also a concern, and a proper kosher diet must be provided for the physical and mental well-being of mothers.

Orthodox Jewish mothers tend not to spend much time with their newborns in the hospital and are in no hurry to get home.[5] This is often because a woman with many children at home regards her few days at the hospital as a time of rest and relaxation. Her behavior should not be regarded as a lack of interest in the infant or her family.

Circumcision, or *brit milah,* is a sacred Jewish covenant. On the 8th day after birth, each male child is circumcised by the *mohel,* a religious functionary who has been formally trained to perform the circumcision. Immediately after the circumcision, the baby is given a drop of wine and his Hebrew name is bestowed. Staff in the hospital should not perform this task without the knowledge and consent of the parents. Sensitivity to this issue is of utmost importance to the parents, and the religious reasons for circumcision should not be overshadowed by the medical and hygienic reasons often cited in Canadian hospitals.[11] A female child is named in the synagogue on the first Saturday after her birth. Due to the traditional delay in naming the children and the couple's fear of a visitation by the Angel of Death, sensitive hospital staff will not pressure the couple to disclose the name of their child before the appointed time.

Conclusion

Traditional customs and practices of Orthodox Jews are very different from the expectations and practices surrounding childbirth in the Canadian health care system. It is important that practitioners be sensitive to variations in the beliefs of each patient. An open and receptive attitude is important at all times, but even more so when practitioners are interacting with patients of a different culture.

Acknowledgment

We thank the members of the Orthodox Jewish communities in Edmonton and Vancouver for their invaluable contributions. We also thank our colleagues for their advice and technical support.

References

1. Kleinman A. Concepts and a model for the comparison of medical systems as cultural systems. *Soc Sci Med 1958;12:83-93.*
2. Kleinman A. *Patients and healers in the context of culture: An exploration of the borderland between anthropology, medicine and psychiatry.* Berkeley, Calif: University of California Press; *1980.*
3. Callister L. Cultural meanings of childbirth. *J Obstet Gynecol Neonatal Nurs 1995; 24(4):327-31.*
4. Statistics Canada. *Population.* Ottawa, Ont: Statistics Canada; Cat. No. 93-313. 1993.
5. Feldman P. Sexuality, birth control, and childbirth in Orthodox Jewish tradition. *Can Med Assoc J 1992;144(1):29-33.*
6. Bash D. Jewish religious practices related to childbearing. *J Nurse Midwifery 1980; 23(3):39-42.*
7. Schenker J. Infertility evaluation and treatment according to Jewish law. Eur *J Obstet Gynecol Reprod Biol 1997;71(2):113-21.*
8. Feldman D. *Health and medicine in the jewish tradition.* New York, NY: The Crossroad Publishing Company; *1984. p. 34-44.*
9. Waterhouse C. Midwifery care for Orthodox Jewish women. *Mod Midwife 1994;4(9):11-4.*
10. Steiner-Grossman P, David K. Involvement of rabbis in counselling and referral for genetic conditions: results of a survey.
Am J Hum Genet 1993;53(6):1359-65.
11. Szasz T. Routine neonatal circumcision: symbol of the birth of the therapeutic state. *J Med Philos 1996;21(2):137-48.*

The Significance of Jewishness for Wittgenstein's Philosophy[1]

David G. Stern

Abstract: *Did Wittgenstein consider himself a Jew? Should we? Wittgenstein repeatedly wrote about Jews and Judaism in the 1930s, and biographical studies make it clear that this writing about Jewishness was a way in which he thought about the kind of person he was and the nature of his philosophical work. Those who have written about Wittgenstein on the Jews have drawn very different conclusions. But much of this debate is confused, because the notion of being a Jew, of Jewishness, is itself ambiguous and problematic. The paper provides a close reading of leading passages in which Wittgenstein discusses Jews and Jewishness, and argues that previous interpreters have been too quick to condemn or defend him. If we consider what it could mean to say that Wittgenstein was, or was not, a Jew, we will see that Wittgenstein's problems with 'Jewishness' arise out of the philosophically problematic nature of the concept, a philosophical problem he was unable to resolve.*

I. Was Wittgenstein a Jew?

Did Ludwig Wittgenstein consider himself a Jew? Should we? Wittgenstein repeatedly wrote about Jews and Judaism in the 1930s, and biographical studies make it clear that this writing about Jewishness was a way in which he thought about the kind of person he was and the nature of his philosophical work.[2] On the other hand, many philosophers regard Wittgenstein's thoughts about the Jews as relatively unimportant. Most studies of Wittgenstein do not even mention the matter, and those that do usually give it little attention. For instance, Joachim Schulte recognizes that 'Jewishness was an important theme for Wittgenstein'[3] but says very little more, except that the available evidence makes precise statements difficult. Rudolf Haller's approach in 'What do Wittgenstein and Weininger have in Common?' is probably more representative of the received wisdom among Wittgenstein experts. In the very first paragraph, he makes it clear that the sole concern of his paper is the question of 'deeper philosophical common ground' between Wittgenstein and Weininger, and not 'attitudes on femininity or Jewishness'.[4] Those who have written about Wittgenstein on the Jews have drawn very different conclusions. He has been lauded as a 'rabbinical' thinker [5] and a far-sighted critic of anti-Semitism,[6] characterized as a self-hating antisemite[7] and condemned for uncritically accepting the worst racist prejudices.[8]

But much of this debate is confused, because the notion of being a Jew, of Jewishness, is itself ambiguous and problematic. Instead, we need to consider what it could mean to say that Wittgenstein was, or was not, a Jew. Another way of putting this is to say that we should first consider different ways of seeing Wittgenstein as a Jew. Before rushing to judgment, we need to consider what it could mean to say that Wittgenstein was, or was not, a Jew, or an anti-Semite. This is not just a matter of tabulating various possible definitions of these expressions, but of considering the different contexts—cultural, social, personal—in which those terms can be used, and their significance in those contexts. In doing so, we need to give critical attention not only to the various criteria for being a Jew that Wittgenstein would have been acquainted with, and the presuppositions he might have taken for granted about Jews and Judaism, but also the ones that we use in our discussion of Wittgenstein as a Jew, and our motives for doing so. One of the great dangers in writing philosophical biography is the risk of turning the study of a philosopher's life and work into vicarious autobiography, wishful thinking, or worse.

Wittgenstein was certainly not, in any sense, a practicing Jew; he, his parents, and three of his grandparents were baptized by the Catholic Church. For instance, both Monk and McGuinness tell the story of how the young Wittgenstein wanted to lie about his Jewish background in order to join a Viennese gymnastic club, and had to be dissuaded by his brother Paul.[9] Both biographers make it clear that while the Wittgenstein family presented themselves in public as Christians, it was widely known that they were of Jewish descent. Wittgenstein did, on occasion, deny his Jewishness, and this was a charged matter for him. In 1935, the German government enacted the Nuremberg Laws, which specified that only those people with three or more Jewish grandparents were to be classified as Jews; those with one or two Jewish grandparents were classified as different grades of mixed race. In 1936 and 1937, while at work on what would become the first 180 sections of *Philosophical Investigations,* Wittgenstein confessed to friends and family that he had misrepresented the extent of his Jewish descent, claiming that one grandparent had been a Jew, when actually three of them were. In 1938, as a result of the *Anschluss* with Austria, the Nuremberg Laws became applicable to the Wittgenstein family. Wittgenstein, who was living in Britain at the time, took British citizenship. His brother Paul fled to Switzerland in July 1938. Meanwhile his sisters stayed in Austria, eventually making a deal with the Berlin authorities, under which they repatriated very substantial foreign assets in exchange for classifying them as non-Jewish, an arrangement Wittgenstein actively supported.[10] In a diary entry written after the German-Austrian *Anschluss,* he described the prospect of holding a German *Judenpass,* Jewish identity papers, as an 'extraordinarily difficult situation' and compared it to a 'hot iron' that would burn in his pocket.[11]

Readings of Wittgenstein's life are inevitably coloured by the interpreter's commitments, and often tell us more about the interpreter's imagination than Wittgenstein. In a diary written in 1931, he found himself drawn toward anticipating such a readership, and admonished himself to resist the temptation:

> In my mind's eye, I can already hear posterity talking about me, instead of listening to me, those, who if they knew me, would certainly be a much more ungrateful public.
> And I must do this: not hear the other in my imagination, but rather myself. I.e., not watch the other, as he watches me—for that is what I do—rather, watch myself. What a trick, and how unending the constant temptation to look to the other, and away from myself. [12]

Discussing the difficulties involved in writing a completely honest autobiography, Wittgenstein argued that the author's motives will always destabilize the autobiographical project of giving an accurate and consistent account of one's life.[13] Wittgenstein was not just suggesting that self-serving motives are ineliminable; he was also observing that whatever story one tells will be coloured by one's current concerns, which will, in turn, be affected by the telling of that story. Objectivity and impartiality, turn out, on closer inspection, to be particularly charged stances, precisely because of their claim to stand above the fray. Any attempt at a balanced and consistent account of the difficult questions about oneself will inevitably be marked by a certain instability and inconsistency, because no one can be indifferent about such matters. But anyone writing about Wittgenstein's life or thought—or, for that matter, anyone else's life and thought—must face the very issues that make autobiography particularly problematic. Why should the biographer be any more capable of Olympian impartiality than the autobiographer? Indeed, anyone who aims at a coherent account of the life of another faces two sources of potential conflict, two hermeneutic pitfalls.

Wittgenstein's favourite passage, which he quoted frequently, came from the introduction to Hertz's *Principles of Mechanics.* There, Hertz summed up his answer to debates over the meaning of terms such as 'force' or 'electricity': because the term has accumulated contradictory meanings, the only solution is to give some of them up. 'When these painful contradictions are removed, the question as to the nature of force will not have been answered; but our minds, no longer vexed, will cease to ask illegitimate questions'.[14] Wittgenstein thought of his philosophy as analogous: a matter of uncovering inconsistencies in our use of everyday terms that lead us to talk nonsense yet think we make sense. In a recent piece on Wittgenstein and Judaism, written in English, but published in German, 'Wittgenstein and Judentum,' [Wittgenstein and Jewishness] Brian McGuinness rightly observes that 'Jewishness' is just such a term. But instead of developing a Hertzian critique of 'Jewishness,' he tries to show that Jews and Jewishness in any sense were of very little significance for Wittgenstein. For instance, in the first paragraph of that paper, McGuinness insists that no one at the turn of the century would have thought of describing Wittgenstein's relatives as a Jewish family, passing over the point that their Jewish descent was known, and meant that they would be classified as converted Jews. Similarly, McGuinness reads Wittgenstein's writing about his Jewishness as an indirect way of talking about his philosophical method. Ultimately, he concludes that:

> In the end *[Letztlich]* Wittgenstein didn't consider himself Jewish, and we too don't need to do so. The concept is attractive, even though, or because, it is misleading: it is possible to think that it would have been good if all 'Jews' had felt solidarity, but also, that they should have—it is however just as possible to think something conflicting or even completely different. But in any case it is speculation—and not reality.[15]

Oddly, this is quite incompatible with his account in *Young Ludwig,* which stresses the importance of his Jewishness for Wittgenstein:

> Weininger had yet two important features in common with the young Ludwig. First he was Jewish. He suffered from the consciousness of that fact. He identified the Jewish with all that was (on his theory) feminine and negative. . . . The theme of the stamp put on a man's life and thought by his Jewishness often recurs in Ludwig's later notes, though, to be sure, he saw it more as an intellectual than as a moral limitation. Already in childhood he was preoccupied on a more practical level with dissociating himself for social and even moral reasons from all the different strata of Judaism in Austria. We shall see what remorse that cost him and can measure in that way how compelling the need for dissociation was.[16]

McGuinness does not say who he has in mind when he speaks of the 'attractions' of thinking of Wittgenstein as a Jew, but in a footnote he speaks disparagingly of others who have made this error, not his own earlier work. In that footnote, at the end of the paragraph quoted above, he writes:

> Here I have the impression, that the polemical part of what I have said, has already, essentially, been said before. It seems necessary to repeat it, even though, in talking about the topic, one risks furthering the very thing in question. That is part of the fascination of which I speak.[17]

However, he gives no references to his targets, and there are no references to those he is criticizing in his bibliography. This is, on the face of it, odd, for the scholarly literature on Wittgenstein's Jewishness is, for the most part, not well known. Perhaps this is because of McGuinness's concern about 'furthering the very thing in question,' an obscure object of fascination that he apparently considers best left unnamed. Cornish's speculative and imaginative account of Wittgenstein's Jewishness as the driving force behind Hitler's antisemitism is a good example of the dangers of applying the conspiracy theory approach to Wittgenstein, but it seems unlikely that it was the focus of McGuinness's attention.[18] Perhaps his principal target here is Ray Monk's biography of Wittgenstein, *Ludwig Wittgenstein: The Duty of Genius,* which takes the Weiningerian conception of the 'duty of genius' as its leading theme in interpreting Wittgenstein's life and work, even though Monk's excellent biography, which rightly gives Wittgenstein's Jewishness and his relationship to Weininger a central place, is never cited or mentioned in McGuinness's paper.

Comparing McGuinness's two accounts, one gets the impression that he has followed the path of dissociation from Jewishness that he originally saw in Wittgenstein; he begins by insisting on Wittgenstein's need to deny that he was a Jew, and ends up denying that Wittgenstein was a Jew. Contradictions between different conceptions of Jewishness are not so much the subject of McGuinness's discussion as enacted in its development. But if the concept of a 'Jew,' or 'Jewishness,' is so problematic, then questions about Wittgenstein's Jewishness need Hertzian treatment, not a direct answer. We can best begin by considering the connections between Wittgenstein and Weininger.

II. Wittgenstein and Weininger

In 1931, Wittgenstein included Otto Weininger on a short list of writers who had influenced him. Following the publication of Ray Monk's biography, with its emphasis on the Weiningerian theme of the 'duty of genius' as a key to understanding Wittgenstein's life and work, the question of how Weininger influenced Wittgenstein has received considerable attention. In *Sex and Character,* Weininger contrasted masculine originality with feminine reproductiveness, and held that Jews particularly exemplify the latter traits;

race, sexuality, and gender are all closely aligned in the Weiningerian economy.[19] Most of the Weininger literature is polarized, and constrained, by the dispute between those who find it necessary to condemn, or excuse, Weininger's use of such stereotypes.[20] Those who read Weininger sympathetically—Weininger's apologists—emphasize his observation that no one is entirely masculine, feminine, Jewish, or homosexual. Because these are ideal types, Weininger is not committed to racist, sexist, or homophobic views. Thus, according to Allan Janik: 'Weininger goes out of his way to insist that he does not identify the Jew as a member of a race. Judaism is a possibility for all men in his eyes'.[21] Those who read Weininger unsympathetically—Weininger's critics—argue that his writings implicitly invite and encourage such bigoted uses, even as they explicitly reject them.

There is a striking congruence between Wittgenstein's conception of Jewishness, genius and talent, and Weininger's. In a note written in 1931, Wittgenstein first distinguishes creative genius from mere talent, which is only reproductive, then continues:

> The saint is the only Jewish 'genius'. Even the greatest Jewish thinker is no more than talented. (Myself for instance.)
>
> I think there is some truth in my idea that I am really only reproductive in my thinking. I think I have never *invented* a line of thinking but that it was always provided for me by someone else & I have done no more than passionately take it up for my work of clarification. That is how Boltzmann, Hertz, Schopenhauer, Frege, Russell, Kraus, Loos, Weininger, Spengler, Sraffa have influenced me. Can one take Breuer & Freud as an example of Jewish reproductive thinking?—What I invent are new *comparisons*.[22]

On an apologetic reading, this talk of 'Jewishness' should be taken as a metaphorical discussion of creativity and originality, and the relationship between his temperament and philosophical method. McGuinness tries to minimize the role of Jewishness in the earlier passages by drawing on Kienzler's observation that in such places 'one can replace "Jew" by philosopher' without essentially changing the sense *[Sinn]*'.[23] Given a narrowly Fregean notion of sense, this may be strictly true, but it all depends on what one considers essential. Wittgenstein's talk of '*Jewish* reproductiveness' here contributes a significance to this passage that would be missing if he had spoken of 'philosophical reproductiveness'. Certainly, the paragraphs that follow explore Wittgenstein's conviction that he cannot produce anything fundamentally new, that his talent lies in making good use of others' work.

On a critical reading, what is most troubling is that Wittgenstein takes

Weininger's antisemitic ideas for granted. As Monk puts it, 'what is most shocking about Wittgenstein's remarks on Jewishness is his use of the language —indeed, the slogans—of racial anti-Semitism. The echo that really disturbs is not that of *Sex and Character,* but that of *Mein Kampf.*[24]

Around the same time, Wittgenstein recommended Weininger's book to several friends, including Moore. Responding to Moore's objections, Wittgenstein wrote:

> I can quite imagine that you don't admire Weininger very much, what with that beastly translation and the fact that W. must feel very foreign to you. It is true that he is fantastic but he is *great* and fantastic. It isn't necessary or rather not possible to agree with him but the greatness lies in that with which we disagree. It is his enormous mistake which is great. I.e., roughly speaking if you just add a '~' to the whole book it says an important truth.[25]

Unfortunately, Wittgenstein did not say what he meant by negating the whole book. Monk argues that while Wittgenstein rejected Weininger's idea of Woman, he adopted Weininger's valorization of the male genius, 'the duty of genius', contrasting it with most men's lives. Monk emphasizes the affinities between Wittgenstein's and Weininger's views about love and self-knowledge: Man can choose between the masculine and the feminine, love and sexuality; to find oneself is to find one's higher self and thus God, and escape the empirical self. Monk is right to stress that the later Wittgenstein rejected Weininger's view of Woman; on one occasion, Wittgenstein said of Weininger's views on this topic: 'How wrong he was, my God he was wrong.'[26]

Szabados finds it implausible that this is what Wittgenstein meant by negating Weininger, for it only changes the object of Weininger's prejudices.

> That the mature Wittgenstein would give the nod to stipulative, evaluatively loaded definitions of Man and Woman strains credulity. The suggestion is completely out of alignment with the resolute anti-essentialism of the late philosophy. So 'Man and masculinity are the sources of all evil' is not the important truth that we are supposed to get out of negating Weininger's book. For this is as much of an absurdity as his central theme, and between two absurdities there is nothing to choose. It rests on a kind of essentialism that the later Wittgenstein rejects simply in virtue of its prejudicial nature. The author of the *Investigations* is devoted to a method of *looking and seeing* how things are rather than saying and prejudging how things are. Both absurdities reveal a deep prejudice and distort the particularity and individuality of people.[27]

This reading of the text of the *Investigations is* attractive, but in the very sense McGuinness warns against. It would have been good if Wittgenstein had freed himself of Weininger's prejudices, but we should be wary of arguing from what we think our philosophical heroes should have believed to what they actually believed.

Both Monk and Szabados fail to see how much Wittgenstein identified with the complementary image of the abjectly feminine—both as Jew and homosexual.[28] Part of Weininger's achievement in Wittgenstein's eyes, I believe, was to clearly and honestly set out the prejudices of his age. In the late 1940s, Wittgenstein explained his admiration for Weininger by contrasting him with Kafka: Kafka, he said, 'gave himself a great deal of trouble *not* writing about his trouble', while Weininger, whatever his faults, was a man who really did write about his. Anscombe had lent Wittgenstein some of Kafka's novels; Wittgenstein, on returning them, compared Kafka unfavourably to Weininger, and recommended 'Weininger's *Sex and Character* and *The Four Last Things*'.[29] The latter is presumably a mistranslation, or misplaced memory of Weininger's *Über Die Letzte Dinge,* a posthumous miscellany of his other writings.[30] Weininger's pronouncements about Jews, gender, national character and sexuality are the kind of stereotypes about how people and culture 'must be' that Wittgenstein criticized in his attacks on 'dogmatism' and the use of 'prototypes' in the early 1930s. Another aspect of Wittgenstein's debt to Weininger was the central role Weininger accorded to what Freud called 'projection' in the construction of stereotypes: Weininger contends that the conception of women as either virgins or whores he sets out is a product of male needs, not of women's nature.

Monk and Szabados read Wittgenstein's image of negating Weininger's book as a matter of denying its odious components. But it is hard to avoid the conclusion that the negation we are discussing here is not the notion of Fregean logic, but rather the Freudian notion of denying what one cannot help identifying with. One can see this in the ambiguous reference to 'W.' in the first sentence of Wittgenstein's letter—'I can quite imagine that you don't admire Weininger very much, what with that beastly translation and the fact that W. must feel very foreign to you'—a 'W.' that both names and does not name its author. Wittgenstein saw in Weininger, and Weininger's anti-Semitism, a mirror of his own self-hatred, a way of figuring a relationship of identification and denial that he both had to and could not confront. In conversation, Monk has challenged this reading, pointing out that Wittgenstein explicitly used the Fregean negation sign. Certainly, there is no evidence that he intended to make use of the Freudian notion of denial; equally, there is good reason to think that Wittgenstein's fascination with Weininger arose out of an uneasy identification with that famously Jewish, homosexual philosopher who was himself deeply troubled by his own identity.

III. Wittgenstein's Strange Dreams

There is reason to think that Wittgenstein's uneasy relationship to his own racial identity, a relationship framed in terms of the prevalent anti-Semitic discourse of his times, also figures in his relationship to his sexuality. First, Weininger's racial and sexual theories are themselves mutually congruent, and both depend on drawing a binary contrast between a valorized and a denigrated term, a contrast that is drawn in strikingly similar ways in each case. Stepan's and Gilman's work on the anti-Semitism of this period has made clear the ways in which racial and gender theories draw on each other, so that the racial other, the feminine, and the homosexual are all constructed in terms of the same set of distinctions.[31] Second, the most troubling of Wittgenstein's remarks about the Jews were written in 1931, when he was considering marrying Marguerite Respinger, a friend of his family. Her visit to him in Norway in 1931 was conducted on strikingly Weiningerian lines. He found her a room of her own at a neighbour's house, and proposed that they prepare for a new spiritual life by reading the Bible together. Even Monk, who minimizes the links between Wittgenstein's attraction to the darker side of Weininger's thought and his own self-hatred, notes the connection between Wittgenstein's anti-Semitic writing in 1931 and his proposed marriage:

> Wittgenstein's remarks on Jewishness, like his projected autobiography, were essentially confessional, and both seem in some way linked to the 'sacred' union he planned for himself and Marguerite. They coincide with the year in which his intention to marry Marguerite was pursued with its greatest earnestness.[32]

The themes of race, gender, guilt and identity all converge in a 'strange dream' of Wittgenstein's, which he wrote down, in code, in one of his manuscript volumes, on December 1, 1929. The dream concerns a character named 'Vertsagt' or 'Vertsag'; the name is the only word *not* written in code.

> A peculiar dream. Today toward morning I dreamt: I see in an illustrated newspaper a photograph of Vertsagt, who is a much-discussed hero of the day. The picture shows him in his car. There is talk of his disgraceful deeds; Hansel is standing next to me and also someone else, similar to my brother Kurt. The latter says that Vertsag is a Jew but has enjoyed the upbringing of a rich Scottish lord; now he is a workers' leader. He has not changed his name

because it is not the custom there. It is new to me that Vertsagt, which
I pronounce with the stress on the first syllable, is a Jew, and I see
that his name simply means 'verzagt' [German for 'faint-hearted'.] It
doesn't strike me that it is written with 'ts' which I see printed a little
bolder than the other letters. I think: must there be a Jew behind every
indecency? Now Hansel and I are on the terrace of a house, perhaps
the big log-cabin on the Hochreit, and along the street comes Vertsag
in his motor-car; he has an angry face, slightly reddish fair hair and a
similar moustache (he does not look Jewish.) He opens fire with a
machine-gun at a cyclist behind him who writhes with pain and is
mercilessly gunned to death with many shots. Vertsag has driven past,
and now comes a young poor-looking girl on a cycle and she too
receives Vertsag's fire as he drives on. And these shots, when they hit
her breast make a bubbling sound like an almost-empty kettle over a
flame. I felt sympathy for the girl and thought: only in Austria could
it happen that this girl would find no helpful sympathy and people
watch as she suffers and is killed. I myself am afraid to help her
because I fear Vertsag's shots. I go towards her, but look for cover
behind a plant. Then I wake up. I must add that in the conversation
with Hansel, first in the presence of the other person and then after he
had left us, I am embarrassed and do not want to say that I myself am
descended from Jews or that Vertsag's case is my own case too. . . .
I wrote the dream down immediately after waking up.[33]

Hänsel was a close friend, the first person he wrote to in 1936 to confess he had
concealed his Jewishness, asking Hänsel to pass on his confession to his
family.[34] In his notes on the dream, Wittgenstein tries, three times, to interpret
the significance of Vertsagt's name. In the dream, he thought he saw 'that his
name simply means "verzagt",' which is German for 'faint-hearted'. After
waking, he came to think that it was really written 'Pferzagt', which means
nothing at all. His closing attempt suggests that 'the name as I pronounced it in
the dream, "Vèrt-sagt" is Hungarian. The name had for me something evil,
spiteful and very masculine about it'.

   Clearly, the dream is connected with Wittgenstein's pervasive sense of
guilt and its connection with his discomfort with his sexuality and racial
origins. Monk takes the dream to be about Wittgenstein's sense that he was
'hiding something . . . allowing people to think of him as an aristocrat when in
fact he was a Jew'. Consequently, he treats the trail of associations as a
distraction from the manifest content of the dream, and the initial thought that
the case of Vertsagt is his own case, the case of a man who hides his origins,
and is too faint-hearted to admit it.[35] It is surely right to take Wittgenstein's
attempts to make sense of the name as themselves faint-hearted and a
distraction from thinking about the fact that the predicament of the protagonist

is his predicament. But the search for the meaning of the name is not just a screen: looked at one way, the names are nonsensical; looked at in another way, they all have similar and connected sounds and meanings. Christoph Nyiri has pointed out that despite Wittgenstein's repeated attempts to decode the name, he fails to consider a striking alternative: that the word is *'versagt'*, from *versagen,* the German word not only for 'failed', 'denied',—an obvious construal under the circumstances—but also 'betrothed'. The usage in the sense of 'betrothed' is no longer common—it is not in the current *Duden*—but it is in the 1969 *Langenscheidt,* and it would have been familiar to Wittgenstein.[36]

Nyiri's piece, written before he had seen Monk's biography, takes it for granted that Wittgenstein was not betrothed. Monk's account, presumably based on his conversations with Marguerite Respinger—specific sources for such matters are not given in his biography—gives the impression that while Wittgenstein might have desired a celibate marriage with her, this was never a realistic possibility. Wittgenstein's diary from this period presents a rather different picture, which is that Marguerite needed him at a time of personal crisis, but that this could not be a permanent relationship. Wittgenstein interprets another complicated dream, from late 1931, as being about how he imagines he is bound to Marguerite by a thousand ties, but as a matter of fact, it is easy for him to walk away from her.[37] In any case, it seems fair to say that the Vertsagt dream epitomizes Wittgenstein's sense of failure at the time, and particularly the failure of their proposed 'union'.

The theme of struggling to make sense of nonsense, and in particular of a name containing consonants with similar sounds, recurs in another dream that Wittgenstein wrote down early in 1932.

> Today I dreamt the following strange dream. Someone (was it Lettice? [Ramsey]) said to me that someone was called Hobbson 'with mixed b'; which meant, that one pronounced it 'Hobpson'. I woke and remembered that Gilbert [Pattison] once told me about the pronunciation of a word that it was 'pronounced with mixed b,' which I had understood as 'mixed beef' [in English] and didn't know what he meant, but it sounded as if he meant that one would have to have a dish called 'mixed beef' in one's mouth when saying the word, and I had understood Gilbert to have said it as a joke. I remembered all that immediately on waking. Then it sounded less and less plausible to me, and by the time I'd got dressed it seemed obvious nonsense. (By the way, if one went into this dream, it leads to thoughts about racial mixing, and what that means to me.)[38]

Lettice Ramsey was a close friend and confidante of Wittgenstein's, with whom he could discuss his feelings for Marguerite; Pattison a friend with whom he joked and played with nonsensical language. Wittgenstein does not explain the connection he sees between this dream and his thoughts about mixed race. But both dreams give great significance to almost imperceptible differences in pronouncing a name that is difficult to say correctly, a name whose meaning seems clear during the dream, then elusive, and ultimately nonsensical. In each dream racial difference, and differences in meaning between nonsense words, play a central part. A name takes on a racially charged significance, but the significance resists his analytic efforts. One further connection here is that both nonsense and racial mixing arise out of combinations that are not permitted; both are offences against the normal ways of going on. Both seem to make sense within Wittgenstein's 'strange' (1.12.29) and 'peculiar' (28.1.32) dreams, but turn into nonsense when he tries to reconstruct their meaning. Wittgenstein's unsuccessful struggle to make sense of the nonsense names in the Vertsagt and Hobbson dreams is an uncanny parody of the traditional philosophical quest to explain a name's meaning in terms of what it stands for.

One can see the same tension between identification and denial in a passage where Wittgenstein explores the idea of comparing the Jews to a disease:

'Look on this wart//swelling// *[Warze//Beule//]* as a regular limb of your body!' Can one do that, to order?

Do I have the power to decide *at will* to have, or not to have, a certain ideal conception of my body?

Within the history of the peoples of Europe the history of the Jews is not treated so circumstantially as their intervention in European affairs would actually merit, because within this history they are experienced as a sort of disease, anomaly, & nobody wants to put a disease on the same level as normal life & nobody wants to speak of a disease as though it had the same rights as healthy bodily processes (even painful ones.)

We may say: this bump *[Beule]* can be regarded as a limb of one's body only if our whole feeling for the body changes (if the whole national feeling for the body changes.) Otherwise the best we can do is *put up* with it.

You may expect an individual to display this sort of tolerance or even to disregard such things; but you cannot expect this of a nation since it is only a nation by virtue of not disregarding such things. I.e., there is a contradiction in expecting someone to retain the original aesthetic feeling for his body & also to make the swelling *[Beule]* welcome.[39]

Peter Winch's 1980 translation for the German *Beule* was 'tumour'. Presumably the change was made because 'tumour' is not supported by current German dictionaries or usage: in contemporary German, a *Beule* is a bump or swelling, with no implication of malignancy. But there is a clear etymological connection with the English 'boil'—a 'hard inflamed suppurating tumour'.[40] Jacob and Wilhelm Grimm's historic dictionary makes it clear that the principal senses of the term in the nineteenth century were far from benign: their two leading definitions of the term both characterize it as a tumour.[41] That sense was still alive in the 1960s, although by then it was no longer the leading meaning. The entry for *'Beule'* in a German-English dictionary first published in 1964 begins as follows: 'bump, lump, swelling; *(Geschwür)* boil, tumo(u)r; . . .'[42] This strongly suggests that Wittgenstein must have been aware of the negative connotations of the term, and that 'tumour' is the correct translation. The context in which Wittgenstein used the word does provide additional support for the original translation: he first wrote 'wart', an unhealthy growth, and compares the *Beule* with a disease.

This passage has attracted attention in the secondary literature, and several English readers have been quick to condemn it for its noxious racist similes. Monk calls it 'anti-Semitic paranoia in its most undiluted form'.[43] Isaac Nevo reads this passage as primarily self-directed anti-Semitism, but also as intolerant nationalism:

> The genocidal fantasy with respect to the Jewish tumour, which in the period this was written was being acted out on the European scene, is articulated by Wittgenstein from within. The analogies and judgements here are his own. The Jewish anomaly could, after all, be portrayed as a curable, rather than incurable, disease . . . But the nationalism Wittgenstein displays in this passage is defined by intolerance.[44]

Szabados, however, emphasizes Wittgenstein's use of distancing devices in setting out these dangerous ideas. The opening sentence is an instruction to see things in a certain way, placed within quotation marks; the second asks us whether it is possible to carry out the instruction. This is followed by a further question, an outline of a way of looking at European history that is about to be rejected, then a 'we may say' and a 'you may expect'. He reads Wittgenstein as bringing up racist ideas to help us see their dangers, and offering philosophical therapy:

> What we have here is an attempt at a precise description and diagnosis of the conceptual and political roots of the problem the liberal democracies found themselves in, in the wake of the

Holocaust: how to restructure and reinscribe the nation-state and what it is to belong to it, so that the conditions leading to intolerance of difference and subsequent genocide do not recur.[45]

Szabados is right that Wittgenstein does not straightforwardly endorse the antisemitic ideas he explores in this passage, and Wittgenstein's critics have been far too ready to assume that he accepted the prejudicial views he discusses. Also, one must remember that these were private notes, never prepared for publication. However, while Wittgenstein might have expanded the proposals and questions just quoted with the sensitive exploration of nationalism and racism Szabados sketches, there is no evidence he did so. Instead, what follows are Weiningerian reflections on how Jews supposedly are only interested in money as a form of power:

> Power & possession are not the same thing. Even though possession also gives us power. If Jews are said not to have any sense for possession that is presumably compatible with their liking to be rich; for money is for them a particular sort of power not possession. (I should for instance not like my people to be poor, since I wish them to have a certain power. Naturally I wish them to use this power properly too.)[46]

'People' here translates the German *Leute*, and so refers to Wittgenstein's family, not the Jews. Thus this is not only a reflection on his conception of Jewishness, power, and possession, but also concerns his extraordinarily wealthy family. As we have already seen, seven years later his sense of the proper use of power would lead him to side with his sisters in their dispute with his brother over how best to respond to the German annexation of Austria, in favour of his sisters' paying for non-Jewish identity papers.

Another passage about the Jews, also from 1931, makes it clear how little Wittgenstein was able to transcend the stereotypes about Jews and nation that were current at the time.

> 'Fatherlandless rabble' (applied to the Jews) is on the same level as 'crooked-nosed rabble,' for giving yourself a fatherland is just as little in your power, as it is to give yourself a particular nose.[47]

This passage takes certain prevalent negative stereotypes about the Jews—that they are a rabble, lack a fatherland, are crooked-nosed—as a point of departure, and does nothing to challenge them. These are hardly the words one would expect of the critic of 'intolerance of difference' Szabados describes. A critique of intolerance of difference may well draw on Wittgenstein's writings, but that critique is not articulated there.

IV. The Significance of Jewishness for Wittgenstein's Philosophy

Is there a connection between Wittgenstein's writing on Jews and his philosophy? What did he mean when he spoke of himself as a 'Jewish thinker' in 1931? Monk interprets these ideas as self-directed antisemitism, humbling himself by describing his work as merely reproductive, reminding himself of 'his limitations, of his "Jewishness".'[48]

> It is as though, for a brief time (after 1931 there are, thankfully, no more remarks about Jewishness in his notebooks), he was attracted to using the then current language of anti-Semitism as a kind of metaphor for himself. . . . So long as he lived, Wittgenstein never ceased to struggle against his own pride, and to express doubts about his philosophical achievement and his own moral decency. After 1931, however, he dropped the language of anti-Semitism as a means of expressing those doubts.[49]

Yuval Lurie sees a direct connection between developments in Wittgenstein's views about meaning and his giving up this talk of Jewishness. For it was around this time that Wittgenstein began to talk about family resemblances, the similarities that things of certain kinds have in common with each other without sharing a common essence. 'Is this simultaneity coincidental? I think not. It seems to me that he found he could no longer hide behind the claim that he was merely conducting a metaphysical discussion about the ideal Jew when he spoke of Jews as he did.'[50] Lurie, like Szabados, supports this reading by connecting Wittgenstein's particular use of the concept of Jewishness with the Weiningerian notion of a prototype, a conception of an idealized instance of the concept in question, a notion that Wittgenstein rejected shortly after these discussions of the Jews in 1931. Lurie also observes that Wittgenstein's subsequent discussions of talent and genius, creativity and originality, make use of other metaphors, such as talk of how seeds grown in different soils will grow differently.

Strictly speaking, Monk is correct in saying that there are no more remarks about Jewishness, per se, after 1931 in Wittgenstein's surviving notebooks, and Lurie is right that Wittgenstein did develop other ways of thinking about reproductiveness and originality. But there are remarks about Jews and the Bible, from 1939 or 1940, where the antisemitic metaphors and connections of the early 1930s recur. Wittgenstein once again asks how courage and character distinguish genius from talent. On the first page of *Culture and Value*, Mendelssohn is introduced as an exemplar of Wittgenstein's idea of Jewishness, and connected with Wittgenstein's own ideals. Wittgenstein compares the Jew to a tree that avoids tragedy by bending, rather than breaking: 'Tragedy is something unjewish. Mendelssohn is perhaps the most untragic of composers.'[51] Wittgenstein takes it for granted that the Jew lacks the courage, or resistance, required for tragedy. Indeed, he identifies his own ideal in these terms, for the passage continues: 'Tragically holding on, defiantly holding on to a tragic situation in love always seems quite alien to my ideal. Does that mean my ideal is feeble? I cannot & *should not judge.* '[52] In 1939-1940, Wittgenstein returns to the question 'What is lacking in Mendelssohn' s music? A 'courageous' melody?'[53]

The following passages were written at the same time:

> The Old Testament seen as the body without its head; the New T[estament]: the head; the Epistles of the Apostles: the crown on the head.

> If I think of the Jewish Bible, the Old Testament on its own, I should like to say: the head is *(still)* missing from this body The solution to these problems is missing. The fulfillment of these hopes is missing. But I do not necessarily think of a head as having a *crown*. . . .

> The measure of genius is character,—even if character on its own does *not* amount to genius.

> Genius is not 'talent *and* character', but character manifesting itself in the form of a special talent. Where one man will show courage by jumping into the water, another will show courage by writing a symphony. (This is a weak example.) . . .

> There is no more light in a genius than in any other honest human being—but the genius concentrates this light into a burning point by means of a particular lens. [54]

Although Wittgenstein does not explicitly make any of the claims about 'the Jews' that one finds in the earlier remarks, he still takes those ideas for granted. Wittgenstein is still using the Jews to think about his identity: his Bible, the Jew's and the Catholic's are compared to a body, a headless body, and a crowned body. Apparently, it is integral to Wittgenstein's conception of his Christianity that it be contrasted with the supposed shortcomings of Judaism. Isaac Nevo reads this as a figure of the Jewish faith as 'a living death'

> [T]he essential point is that variation, or even schism within Christianity does not constitute an anomaly, or a disturbance. . . . The 'Jewish Bible,' on the other hand, constitutes a real disturbance: a (living?) body without a head.[55]

While it is not as strikingly antisemitic as the earlier material, Wittgenstein is still discussing genius and talent in the context of a Biblical analogy that evokes the Jews who lost their heads, and worse, in the Shoah.

Wittgenstein's later philosophy, with its far-reaching criticism of essentialism and platonism about meaning, certainly lends itself to a critique of antisemitism. On the other hand, his continued uncritical use of Jewish stereotypes shows that he was far from being fully successful in applying his own methods. Indeed, his final recorded reflection on antisemitism, from 1948, begins by comparing antisemitism to a knot he could not untie:

> If you cannot unravel a tangle, the most sensible thing you can do is to recognize this; & the most decent thing, to admit it. [Antisemitism.]
>
> What you should do to cure the evil is *not* clear. What is *not* permissible is clear from one case to another.[56]

It is hard to know what to make of this passage. Nevo reads it as Wittgenstein's confession that he was still entangled in antisemitism, and contemplating suicide, the 'honourable' Weiningerian way out.[57] But this is extremely speculative. Wittgenstein neither says what unraveling the tangle would be, nor specifies what one 'must *not* do'. The reference to a tangle does evoke an image Wittgenstein repeatedly used for the nature of philosophy. In the final, postwar, version of a passage first drafted in 1930, he writes:

> How does it come about that philosophy is so complicated a structure? It surely ought to be completely simple, if it is the ultimate thing, independent of all experience, that you make it out to be. Philosophy unties the knots in our thinking; hence its result must be simple, but philosophizing has to be as complicated as the knots it unties.[58]

This suggests that his talk of a tangle one cannot unravel was a way of acknowledging that antisemitism was a philosophical problem that Wittgenstein was not able to resolve, or cure. Wittgenstein's confidence that it was clear what *not* to do in particular cases is hardly reassuring, in view of what we have seen of his own actions. Antisemitism is strikingly akin to a Wittgensteinian philosophical problem: it arises from taken-for-granted prejudices and the misuse of language, and can only be dissolved by changing people's lives. The philosophical significance of Jewishness for Wittgenstein is not primarily that he thought of his philosophy as Jewish, but that Jewishness was not a problem that he was able to write about philosophically.

Finally, we can briefly return to the question: was Wittgenstein a Jew?

My Hertzian answer is that we would be better off distinguishing different senses of the term, and reflecting on their role in his life and in our own. Wittgenstein's problematic Jewishness is as much a product of our problematic concerns as his. There is no doubt that Wittgenstein was of Jewish descent; it is equally clear that he was not a practicing Jew. But insofar as he thought of himself as Jewish, he did so in terms of the antisemitic prejudices of his time. It would have been good if he could have untangled those prejudices, but he did not do so.

Notes

1   This paper, on the place of Jewishness in Wittgenstein's philosophy, is an abridgement of a longer paper, 'Was Wittgenstein a Jew?', which includes an extended discussion of the problematic relationship between a philosopher's life and work. It was written for a conference on Wittgenstein, philosophy and biography held at Virginia Polytechnic & State University, Blacksburg, VA, in March 1999, and will be included in a book edited by James Klagge, *Wittgenstein: Biography and Philosophy* (Cambridge University Press, 2001). The other contributors to the book are Ray Monk, James Conant, Kelly Hamilton, Louis Sass, Alfred Nordmann, Joachim Schulte, Hans-Johann Glock and Brian McGuinness.

      Earlier versions of this paper were presented to the 6th North American Lesbian, Gay and Bisexual Studies Conference; a conference on 'Body Matters' at the University of Hull, North Humberside, England; the Society for Lesbian and Gay Philosophy; the History of Science and Technology program, UC Berkeley; the Iowa Philosophical Society; a conference on Russell and Wittgenstein at American University; and the Canadian Philosophical Association meeting in Edmonton, Alberta. I particularly want to thank Geeta Patel, who got me to write a four-page paper on Wittgenstein and Weininger, the many people whose constructive comments led me to keep on rewriting that paper until it turned into this one, and the University of Iowa, the Alexander von Humboldt Foundation, and the Department of Philosophy at the University of Bielefeld for fellowship support during which this paper was completed.

2   The principal published primary sources are Ludwig Wittgenstein, *Denkbewegungen: Tagebücher* [Movements of Thought: Diaries] *1930-1932, 1936-1937 (MS 183)*, ed. Ilse Somavilla (Innsbruck, Austria: Haymon Verlag, 1997) and *Culture and Value,* revised second edition, trans. P. Winch (Oxford: Blackwell, 1998). The principal biographies are Brian McGuinness, *Wittgenstein: A Life. Young Ludwig (1889-1921)* (London: Duckworth, 1988) and Ray Monk, *Ludwig Wittgenstein: the Duty of Genius* (New York: The Free Press, 1990).

3   Joachim Schulte, *Wittgenstein: an Introduction,* trans. William Brenner and John Foley (Albany, NY: SUNY Press, 1992), pp. 16-17.

4   Rudolf Haller, *Questions on Wittgenstein* (Lincoln, NE: University of Nebraska Press, 1988), p. 90.

5   Russell Nieli, *Wittgenstein: From Mysticism to Ordinary Language* (Albany, NY: SUNY Press, 1987).

6   Béla Szabados, 'Was Wittgenstein an Anti-Semite? The Significance of Anti-Semitism for Wittgenstein's Philosophy', *Canadian Journal of Philosophy* 29 (1999), pp. 1-28. See also 'Autobiography after Wittgenstein', *The Journal of Aesthetics and Art Criticism* 50 (1992), pp. 1-12; 'Autobiography and Philosophy: Variations on a Theme of Wittgenstein', *Metaphilosophy* 26 (1995), pp. 63-80; 'Wittgenstein's Women: The Philosophical Significance of Wittgenstein's Misogyny', *Journal of Philosophical Research* 22 (1997), pp. 483-508.

7   Yuval Lurie, 'Jews as a Metaphysical Species', *Philosophy* 64 (1989), pp. 323-47. See also 'Wittgenstein on Culture and Civilization', *Inquiry* 32 (1989), pp. 375-97 and *Ludwig Wittgenstein: the Duty of Genius, p.* 317.

8   Gerhard Wassermann, 'Wittgenstein on Jews: Some Counter-examples' , *Philosophy* 65 (1990), pp. 355-65.

9   *Wittgenstein: A Life, op.* cit., p. 49; *Ludwig Wittgenstein: the Duty of Genius, op.* cit., p. 14.

10   *Ludwig Wittgenstein: The Duty of Genius,* ibid., pp. 396-400; Brian McGuinness, 'Wittgenstein und Judentum', in Ursula A. Schneider (ed.), *Paul Engelmann (1891-965) Architektur Judentum Wiener Moderne* (Vienna: Folio Verlag, 1999), pp. 74-75. The English text of this paper will be published in James Klagge (ed.), *Wittgenstein: Biography and Philosophy* (Cambridge University Press, 2001).

11   Ludwig Wittgenstein, *Bergen Edition* MS 120, 123r (Oxford: Oxford University Press, 1998-). 14.3.1938.

12   *Denkbewegungen: Tagebücher, pp.* 64-65. November/December, 1931. My translation.

13   Oets Bouwsma, *Wittgenstein: Conversations, 1949-1951* (Indianapolis, IN: Hackett, 1986), p. 70.

14   Heinrich Hertz, *The Principles of Mechanics,* trans. D. Jones and J. Walley (London, 1899), p. 8.

15   'Wittgenstein and Judentum', op. cit., p. 76; all translations from the German are my own.

16   *Wittgenstein: A Life,* op. cit., p. 42.

17   'Wittgenstein und Judentum', op. cit., p. 76; n. 40.

18   Kimberly Cornish, *The Jew of Linz: Wittgenstein, Hitler and Their Secret Battle for the Mind* (London: Century Books, 1998).

19   Otto Weininger, *Sex and Character,* anonymous 'authorized translation from the sixth German edition', but omitting all footnotes (New York: Heinemann, 1906). First edition, *Geschlecht und Charakter, 1903.*

20   See Barbara Hyams and Nancy A. Harrowitz, 'A Critical Introduction to the History of Weininger Reception', in Nancy A. Harrowitz and Barbara Hyams (eds), *Jews and Gender: Responses to Otto Weininger, pp.* 3-20 (Philadelphia: Temple University Press, 1995), pp. 3-20.

21   Allen Janik, *Essays on Wittgenstein and Weininger, p.* 101; cf. pp. 87 ff., 98 ff. (Amsterdam: Rodolpi, 1985). See also Janik, 'How did Weininger Influence Wittgenstein?' in *Jews and Gender,* op. cit., pp. 61-72.

22   *Culture and Value,* op. cit., p. 16. 1931.

23   'Wittgenstein und Judentum', op. cit., p. 71; Wolfgang Kienzler, *Wittgenstein's Wende zu seiner Spätphilosophie 1930-1932: Eine historische und systematische Darstellung, p.* 43 (Frankfurt am Main, Germany: Suhrkamp, 1997).

24   *Ludwig Wittgenstein: The Duty of Genius,* op. cit., p. 313.

25   Ludwig Wittgenstein, *Cambridge Letters: Correspondence with Russell, Keynes, Moore, Ramsey and Sraffa.* Edited by Brian McGuinness and G. H. von Wright (Oxford: Blackwell, 1995), p. 250. 23 August 1931.

26   Drury, in *Recollections of Wittgenstein,* in R. Rhees (ed.) (New York: Oxford University Press, 1984), p. 91.

27   'Wittgenstein's Women', op. cit., pp. 492-3. The closely parallel passage in 'Was Wittgenstein an Anti-Semite?' pp. 16-17, which begins 'That the mature Wittgenstein would give the nod to stipulative, evaluatively loaded definitions of race, sex and nationality strains credulity', indicates how important this claim is for his reading.

28   See Stanley Cavell, 'Postscript (1989): To Whom It May Concern', *Critical Inquiry* 16 (1990), pp. 248-90.

29   *Ludwig Wittgenstein: The Duty of Genius,* op. cit., p. 498.

30   Otto Weininger, *Über Die Letzte Dinge* [On the Last Things] (Vienna & Leipzig: W. Braumuller, 1904).

31   Nancy Stepan, 'Race and Gender: The Role of Analogy in Science', *Isis* 77 (1986). Sander Gilman, *Jewish Self-Hatred: Anti-Semitism and the Hidden Language of the Jews* (Baltimore, MD: Johns Hopkins University Press, 1986); *Freud Race and Gender* (Princeton, NJ: Princeton University Press, 1993).

32   *Ludwig Wittgenstein: The Duty of Genius,* op. cit., pp. 317-18.

33   Ludwig Wittgenstein, *Wiener Ausgabe* [Vienna Edition], Michael Nedo (ed.) (Vienna: Springer Verlag, 1993-), MS 107, pp. 219-222. 1.12.1929.

34   Ilse Somavilla (ed.) *Ludwig Hänsel—Ludwig Wittgenstein. Ein Freundschaft,* (Innsbruck: Brenner Studien, vol. 14, 1994).

35   *Ludwig Wittgenstein: The Duty of Genius,* op. cit., pp. 279, 280.

36   J. C. Nyiri, 'Wittgenstein 1929-31: Conservatism and Jewishness', p. 22. In Nyiri, *Tradition and Individuality* (Dordrecht: Kluwer, 1992). The unpublished Bergen transcription of the dream spells the fifth occurrence of the name as 'Verlag'.

37   *Denkbewegungen: Tagebücher,* op. cit., pp. 63-64.

38   Ibid., p. 67. 28.1.32.

39   *Culture and Value,* op. cit., p. 18. 1931.

40   *Shorter Oxford English Dictionary,* vol. I, 212 (Oxford, 1973).

41   Jacob and Wilhelm Grimm, *Deutches Wörterbuch 1745-6* (Leipzig: Hirzel, 1854).

42   Heinz Messinger and Werner Rüdenberg, *Langenscheidt Concise German Dictionary English-German* p. 114 (Langenscheidt, 1964; McGraw-Hill, 1969).

43   *Ludwig Wittgenstein: The Duty of Genius,* op. cit., p. 314; see also p. 315.

44   Isaac Nevo, 'Religious Belief and Jewish Identity in Wittgenstein's Philosophy', *Philosophy Research Archives* 13 (1987-8), p. 238.

45   'Was Wittgenstein an Anti-Semite?' pp. 7-8.

46   *Culture and Value,* op. cit., p. 18. 1931.

47   *Denkbewegungen: Tagebücher,* op. cit., p. 59. 2.11.31.

48   *Ludwig Wittgenstein: The Duty of Genius,* op. cit., p. 317.

49   Ibid., pp. 316, 317.

50   'Jews as a Metaphysical Species', ibid., p. 340.

51   *Culture and Value,* op. cit., p. 3. 1929.

52   Ibid., pp. 3-4. 1929; not in previous editions.

53   Ibid., p. 40. 1939-1940.

54   Ibid., pp. 40-41. 1939-1940.

55   'Religious Belief and Jewish Identity in Wittgenstein's Philosophy', op. cit., p. 236.

56   *Culture and Value,* op. cit., p. 95. 4.11.1948.

57   'Religious Belief and Jewish Identity in Wittgenstein's Philosophy', op. cit., p. 242.

58   Ludwig Wittgenstein, *Zettel,* trans. G. E. M. Anscombe, §452 (Oxford: Blackwell, 1967). Earlier versions include *Philosophical Remarks* §2, 1930; Big Typescript §90, p. 422, 1933-4.

The Economics of Religion, Jewish Survival, And Jewish Attitudes Toward Competition In Torah Education

Dennis W. Carlton
Avi Weiss

Abstract: *This article examines the attitude of Jewish law to competition in light of the economist's understanding of the benefits of competition and the beneficiaries from intervention in the competitive process. The punchline of this paper is simple. Although Judaism has used a whole host of restrictions on competition and has had its share of legislation to promote private interests, there has been one area that has generally been a consistent exception to impediments to competition—the teaching of Torah. This exception is all the more remarkable because those who were in a position to influence the legislation often stood to benefit from such restrictions. From this stress on teaching, we show that the foundation was laid for the survival and perpetuation of Judaism.*

1. Introduction

This paper examines the attitude of Jewish law to competition in light of the economist's understanding of the benefits of competition and the beneficiaries from intervention in the competitive process. There are at least two reasons to use economics to understand Jewish law, and we will illustrate both. First, the straightforward application of economics to *halacha* (Jewish law) can be of historical interest-figuring out how certain laws impeded or accelerated economic developments and which groups were harmed and which were helped. This type of analysis is akin to a study of current-day antitrust policy or regulation in which one figures out which group benefited from the government intervention and whether the intervention was based on an uninformed understanding of economics (though the failure to understand economics is a more serious criticism today than hundreds or even thousands of years before economics was developed as a science). The second reason is to investigate not the consequences of a particular decision but the underlying value system that can be inferred from the decision.

The punchline of this paper is simple. Although Judaism has used a whole host of restrictions on competition and has had its share of legislation to promote private interests, there has been one area that has generally been a consistent exception to impediments to competition—the teaching of Torah. This exception is all the more remarkable because those who were in a position to influence the legislation often stood to benefit from such restrictions. From this stress on teaching, the foundation was laid for the strategy that Judaism followed to insure its survival and perpetuation. We also show that the teaching was designed to influence both ritual and ethical behavior by influencing beliefs. The stress on both ritual and belief is important in light of the recent innovative and insightful work on religion by Lawrence Iannaccone.[1] In that work, the emphasis has been on explaining how groups can succeed in avoiding free-rider problems by adopting behaviors that are costly. By sorting out free riders, the group can succeed in attracting and keeping active members who provide each other with collective goods (for example, attendance at services, active participation, friendly environment, social interaction). Iannaccone put less emphasis on understanding how the cult or religion creates values or affects beliefs. Indeed, in that literature, it is difficult to distinguish a bowling club from a religion. It is perhaps more accurate to describe this recent work as deepening our understanding of community formation in small groups. It provides insights into how a religion should internally organize for success. In this article, we wish to bring to the forefront the desire of a religion—Judaism in particular—to alter beliefs and thereby alter actions and at the same time to perpetuate itself.

Economists are trained to resist the notion that preferences are manipulable and focus instead on using prices as incentive devices. That is why, in part, religion has been regarded as an area outside of economics. But religion is a powerful incentive device that is used in regulating social and economic interactions. Unless economists wish to avoid what is one of the most powerful incentive mechanisms shaping history, they must face squarely the issue of the creation of values.[2] Moreover, the emerging fields of entrepreneurship and leadership now taught in business schools and elsewhere are closely related to the study of how religions can create values. We begin in Section II with a simple model of religion focusing on altering beliefs and actions. We then take some initial steps in Sections II and III to understand how a religion can create and perpetuate its values and, in the Appendix, develop a model to illustrate our points. In Section IV we turn to a description and analysis of the role of priests and prophets during the time of the First Temple and show that, although the priests were given exclusivity in carrying out sacrifices, and although, given their position, they had the ability and possibly even the moral right to corner the teaching market, they left open the teaching of Torah to all. We explain how this dichotomy established a precedent that was to influence subsequent generations and was a key force in explaining how Judaism has survived. In Section V we discuss in some detail the attitudes toward competition in Jewish law since the Mishnah and show the remarkable consistency in the preservation of competition among Torah teachers. Given the huge differences in economic circumstances among Jews over time and space, this consistency reveals the high value that Judaism placed on teaching Torah, with the ultimate result that Judaism has survived.

II. A Simple Model of Religion

Religion can have a powerful effect on behavior. Many religions attempt to shape the beliefs of their adherents, with the result that their adherents alter their behavior. By making interpersonal behavior subject to divine scrutiny, a religion can induce desirable interpersonal behavior; in this way religion provides a low-cost enforcement mechanism for inducing such behavior. For example, by making the rule requiring honest weights and measures a divine commandment, the transaction costs of engaging in trade fall. The customer does not have to expend resources to verify the quantity of his purchase, and the state can spend less on enforcing honest behavior. Religion can therefore be a valuable mechanism for a state to use to help enforce its laws.

Let R be the rules (or more accurately their interpretation) of the religion, a_i be the actions of individual i, c_i be the consumption of individual i, and $u_i(c_i)$ be the utility of individual i. Let $P(R, a_i)$ be the divine penalty associated with actions a_i (which might include consumption) given rules R, and let λ_i be the individual's probability of belief in the existence of a divine authority. The typical utility function for individual i depends only on that individual's consumption. We allow the penalty function to depend on more than consumption. In particular, it depends on the "distance" between the person's actions and the actions specified by the "rules" laid down by the religion. So, for example, how one acquires income (honestly or not) could influence the penalty if the religion specifies that honesty is required.[3] The penalty function could also depend upon the characteristics or actions of others, so that individual i could incur a penalty if others are hungry while individual i consumes plenty of food. Thus, if, as in Judaism, the giving of charity *(tzdaka)* is required, the failure to do so implies a penalty and thereby negatively affects the individual's utility. This means that, as a special case, there can be a penalty if the actions chosen by individual i deviate from the actions that would be chosen if individual i had a particular utility function—such as one that specifies altruism wherein the utility of others matters to individual i. So, for example, if the religion wants to encourage individuals to care about others, there would be a divine penalty any time the chosen actions differ from those that the interdependent utility function would specify.[4] Of course, the religion may also not want its followers to "overdo" it and may place limits on the amount of "good" an individual may do in order to save one from himself. Thus, for example, in Judaism there is a maximum amount (20 percent) of one's assets that one is permitted to donate to charity.

A religion must supply answers to two basic sets of questions. First, how should the rules be chosen? In modern parlance, what are the religion's mission statement and contents? Second, once the rules are chosen, how does the religion cause people to believe that λ_i is sufficiently near one so that they will adhere to the rules? The two tasks are obviously related in that the rules are likely to affect λ_i. For example, a new religion advocating child sacrifice would today have a difficult time gaining acceptance in most parts of the United States, and such a religion would have a low λ_i. Similarly, the actions of others could influence an individual's assessment of λ_i. Hence, λ_i can depend on both R and Z_i, where Z_i stands for conditions outside of individual i's immediate control, including, but not limited to, the actions of others as well as the individual's past actions.

Individual i's expected utility is given by

$$U[c_i, a_i; Z_i] = u(c_i; Z_i) - \lambda_i(R, a_i, -; Z_i)\, P(R, a_i, Z_i),$$

where Z_i includes the individual's past actions, and where we have now explicitly incorporated the dependence of each relevant function on Z_i. The individual's budget constraint is given by $\Sigma p_i c_i \leq I(a_i, Z_i)$, where I is the individual's income, which depends on a_i and Z_i. Note, in particular, that one's actions affect one's income and also one's utility. Treating a_i as a continuous variable, in equilibrium we have

$$- \lambda_i \frac{\partial P}{\partial a_i} = \mu \frac{\partial I}{\partial a_i},$$

where μ is the Lagrangian multiplier. This equality says that the marginal utility cost of one's actions is weighed against their monetary benefit. Note in particular that there is a feedback from actions into consumption. One may choose actions that would yield less than the maximal income, so consumption is altered by one's belief structure. The term Z_i appears in the income function since others' behavior can affect the opportunities that are available to the consumer. The term R does not appear directly in the income function; rather, the rules affect income through one's actions. In the absence of a belief in divine authority ($\lambda_i = 0$), individual i faces the usual consumer maximization problem. As λ_i rises, the individual alters his behavior to conform to the religion's rules. The same effect occurs as the penalty rises. Therefore, belief and the penalty for actions that deviate from the rules are substitutes for each other in terms of affecting actions.

Assuming a Nash equilibrium, each individual chooses a_i and c_i to maximize his own utility, taking the actions and consumption of others as given. One immediate consequence is that it is quite possible in equilibrium for both $U(c_i, a_i; Z_i)$ and $u(c_i; Z_i)$ to be strictly greater when individuals believe in divine authority than when they do not.[5] The reason is that the actions of others are altered by religion, and this can benefit individual i, as occurs, for example, when religion causes individuals to act so that transaction costs fall. To take a simple example, if religion forbids fraud at the time of sale, then to the extent that religion decreases fraud, it reduces the resources that firms would otherwise have to spend to detect fraud, causing trade to be less costly to engage in. Not only can believers ($\lambda_i = 1$) be better off than they would otherwise be, but so can nonbelievers.[6] The nonbelievers can obtain benefits from the actions of believers. Indeed, religion can cause nonbelievers to behave differently than they would otherwise because of the actions of the believers. If the actions taken by the nonbelievers cause them to prosper at the expense of believers, we would suspect that effect would reduce the number of believers. In such a case, we would expect the religious authorities, if they have the power to do so, to impose taxes or restrictions on the nonbelievers in order to reduce the incentive to become a nonbeliever.[7]

Religions will therefore have effects on the actions of both nonbelievers and believers. Although it is possible for a religion to make the actions of both believers and nonbelievers more in accord with its rules, the converse can also be true.[8] For example, if the religion demands that sellers always accept the first offer of a buyer and that buyers must offer a price no lower than market price, a nonbelieving buyer would be able to offer a price of zero and obtain the product from a believing seller. That is why the way in which the religion's rules affect interactions with nonbelievers may be critical in explaining its survival and why in many religions, including Judaism, behavior toward insiders is sometimes different from behavior toward outsiders. This reasoning suggests that successful religions will choose rules where the gains to believers exceed those to nonbelievers and that such an outcome is likely to occur in a situation where the actions of believers and nonbelievers are strategic complements (an increase in a_i leads to an increase in a_j).

After choosing a set of rules the adherence to which will generate benefits, how does a religion create a group of believers? The behavior of others will matter in the formation of beliefs. There are at least two mechanisms at work. First, many psychological experiments show that people adapt their beliefs about probabilities in order to justify their actions and minimize the dissonance between their beliefs and actions (cognitive dissonance). Therefore, if one is constantly required to take observable actions, such as those associated with ritual, which make sense only if God exists, then one will revise upward one's probability of belief in God. Communal prayer, as is required in Judaism, is therefore one way of reinforcing or creating beliefs. Participating in ritual acts may be required if one is to avoid being ostracized from society. Individuals may dislike admitting they are engaging in ritual actions just for the sake of keeping their friends from jettisoning them and so "adjust" λ_i upward in order to justify their actions. That is why requirements not to deal with nonbelievers on the same terms as believers are potent tools to foster belief, especially when the relative number of believers is large. The notion that actions can affect belief (or preferences) is captured by the principle in Judaism that actions done without the proper intent will lead to them being done with the proper intent *(mitoch shelo lishma ba lishma). So,* for example, a selfish individual, forced continually to donate to the poor, will eventually donate willingly. This is the reason that we believe that λ_i is a function of one's past actions.[9]

Second, suppose that individual *i* cares about his parents' (or friends') utility, which depends on how he behaves.[10] If his parents are believers, then the interdependence in utility will cause individual *i* to act as if he is a believer.[11] At this point, whether it is God or parents that one is trying to keep happy is irrelevant for understanding behavior.[12] Indeed, the extraordinary benefit one receives in Judaism for honoring parents highlights the importance of others in fostering belief. (The only one of the Ten Commandments for which there is a reward given in the commandment is the one about honoring parents—the reward is so that "you" shall long endure. The "you" can be interpreted as the Jewish nation.).[13] By stressing honor due parents, Judaism reinforces the taking of actions that the parents approve of and, by the preceding argument, will lead to a change in λ_i—or equivalently to the transmission of beliefs and values from one generation to the next.[14] This is another way in which λ_i is a function of outside influences (Z_i).

III. Transmission of Values

Once a religion is created, it will survive only if it can transmit its central principles to succeeding generations while at the same time being adaptive enough to adjust to changed circumstances. Inflexible rules could create distortions that would impose, especially in changed circumstances, such huge costs that the net benefits of belonging to this group diminish. The recent studies of addiction[15] and religion[16] teach us that institutions or social capital have to be created and enhanced so that the costs of staying in the group remain small. Exactly what constitutes successful survival strategies for a religion will depend on a whole host of factors, such as wealth, political power, and geographic dispersion of the population. A comprehensive theory of survival is a rich research question that we examine only in its relation to Judaism.

We discuss three factors that we believe are important in understanding Judaism's survival: its ability to reconcile its religion with hardship; its lack of political power that led to the accumulation of human, not physical, capital; and its reliance on debate and decentralized teaching.

First, a religion that teaches that times will always be prosperous is unlikely to survive in the face of contradictory evidence. But when a group loses power and is, for example, subjugated and impoverished, why would they not join another group? Why should they not believe that they bet on the wrong God and should switch? Although that undoubtedly occurred, sometimes in large numbers, Judaism introduced a crucial innovation relative to surrounding ancient pagan religions. That innovation was the lesson that even when times are bad (and at least early on Judaism taught that times are bad because people have done wrong—a position that has adherents to this day), God will never abandon the Jews and eventually prosperity will return provided the Jews return and follow the Torah.[17] Such an optimistic belief guarantees not only that the necessary economic investments for prosperity will be made but also that the necessary investments in human capital, specifically, the study of the Torah, will be made.[18]

Second, for most of their history, Jews have not had centralized political power. More typically they lived in foreign countries where, for the most part, their rights to own valuable physical property and amass wealth were at the often unpredictable discretion of foreign powers. This suggests that physical institutions were unlikely to provide any necessary infrastructure. Hence, after the destruction of the Second Temple (70 C.E.), investments shifted almost exclusively to investments in human capital.[19] The development of Rabbinic Judaism (the Judaism of today)—including the codification of the Mishnah, the debates that formed the basis for the Talmud, together with the continuing Torah commentaries and development of Jewish law—represent this enormous investment in a body of knowledge that forms a historical inheritance for future generations. This body of knowledge continues to accumulate and provides a rich and portable form of social capital. If this knowledge is considered relevant, it represents an asset whose value is increasing over time.[20] In terms of Iannoconne's model, it explains how the odds of surviving can grow over time. But we must turn to the third feature of Judaism, its reliance on debate and decentralized teaching, to understand why this body of knowledge should remain relevant and valuable.

The dispersion of Jews across the world meant that the circumstances faced by Jews varied enormously.[21] As is well known from the economics of franchising, the optimal response to widely varying conditions is to significantly decentralize decision making. The trick, of course, is to do so without undermining the central body of rules and beliefs so as to cause the religion to splinter.[22] One mechanism Judaism used to allow decentralization without splintering was to elevate the role of scholars who make decentralized decisions but, at the same time, to give greater precedential weight to older scholars and commentators. In this manner, *poskim* (scholars who set the law) can be divided into four groups according to chronological order—Tana'im, Amora'im, Rishonim, and Acharonim. The Tana'im are those scholars who lived during the time the Mishnah was composed (until about 200 C.E.)—they are the rabbis cited in the Mishnayot. The Amora'im were the rabbis during the period of the Gemara (until about 500 C.E.), the Rishonim were the early commentators (until about 1550 C.E.), and the Acharonim are rabbis from then until today. It is clear from the Talmud that an Amora never disagreed on a point of law with a Tana unless there was another Tana to back up his opinion. Similarly, in later *responsa,* commentaries, and codifications, Rishonim never set law in disagreement with Amora'im, and Acharonim never disagreed on a point of law with Rishonim. Such a hierarchy also appears within categories, strictly based on chronology.[23] This technique demands that even radical reformers must have a thorough knowledge of the historical tradition.

The model Judaism followed was to discuss and debate from a common text.[24] This model creates at once a connection to tradition and a built-in adaptive mechanism. The power of this approach is that, even though separate communities can pursue different paths and interpretations, they can remain identified as the same religion. Consequently, despite the existence of some quite different laws and customs across communities, the study of Torah has remained central in all Jewish communities.[25] ("The study of Torah is as important as all the mitzvot combined.").[26] Perhaps the most striking current example is that of Ethiopian Jews, whose isolation from other Jews for at least a thousand years did not prevent them from being recognized as Jews and being reabsorbed (but not without significant difficulties) into Israel. The knowledge of Torah and the adherence to *halacha* (Jewish law) immediately linked a population isolated in a primitive economy to their modern coreligionists.

The only way to transmit the knowledge of a religion's rules from one generation to another is to teach it to the younger generation. And, presumably, the best teachers will be highly prized for playing a key role in perpetuating knowledge (or, alternatively, in interpreting the rules in a way that is both engaging and sensible in light of the circumstances). In Judaism, the Torah teaches that the parent has the responsibility to teach his children Torah .[27] To the extent that parents do try to teach Torah, this creates an incentive for parents to become better informed about the Torah than they would otherwise be. As every teacher knows, the best way to learn material is to be required to teach it. No teacher wants to be embarrassed by lack of knowledge before one's students, especially when the students are one's own children. Interestingly, the placing of the responsibility of teaching Torah on the parents makes both the parents and the children more knowledgeable about Torah. However, specialization produces gains, so there is a trade-off between having a parent (who may be ignorant) try to teach instead of a trained teacher. The obligation of a parent can be discharged by hiring a teacher, but even here the parents' duty would be to remain involved with the teaching. The value of specialized teachers was recognized early in Judaism, and, as we report in Section IV, public education was instituted around the first century B.C.E.

Competition among Torah teachers fosters the goal of creating high-quality decentralized education. It also is a surefire way to simultaneously transmit a common heritage and allow adaptation to changed circumstances.[28] We now turn to a more detailed discussion of the rules aimed at competition among teachers.

IV. The Early Period: Until the Destruction Of the First Temple

The teaching of Torah was not the central religious activity of the early Hebrews; instead, animal sacrifice was. The priests were assigned the exclusive right to perform these sacrifices, which were used in part to support the priests. Perhaps because sacrifice was so important to the early Israelite religion, severe restrictions and fights on who could perform religious rites (and how) proliferated (for example, the story of Korach, the story of Aaron's two sons, the conflict between the Aaronite priests centered in Jerusalem and the Levitical priests elsewhere).[29] Although the priests were the exclusive agents to perform animal sacrifice, it would appear that the priests were not the exclusive agents to disseminate or interpret the Torah. Indeed, quite the opposite appears true. Each father is charged with the responsibility to teach his sons the Torah,[30] and the Torah emphasizes that it should not be regarded as esoteric laws known to only a select few. As the Torah explicitly states, "For this Instruction [namely, the Torah] which I command you today is not hidden from you nor distant from you. It is not up in the heavens to say 'who will go up to the heavens and take it down for us and tell it to us so we can do it.' Nor is it across the sea to say 'who will cross the sea for us to take it and tell us so we can do it'. For it is very close to you, in your mouths and hearts to do it."[31] This passage from Deuteronomy could reflect the decision by Josiah to centralize the economically important sacrifices in the Temple in Jerusalem and decentralize the (then) less important function of teaching. Moreover, it is clear that the prophets play an important role in disseminating God's commandments, and the prophets are not drawn exclusively from the class of priests or from any other closed social group. In short, in the time of the First Temple, performing sacrifices, not teaching, was the service with exclusivity.

And yet, the Kohanim had the right to demand such exclusivity in teaching.[32] The Levites were not given a part of the land of Israel—instead their portion was in the service of the Lord, and each tribe supported the Kohanim and Levites in their midst. Part of this job of servicing the Lord was in the dissemination of the Torah, as written in Malachi:[33] "For the lips of the Kohen will keep thought and the Torah will be requested from his mouth, for he is the Angel of the Lord," with the meaning of the first section being that this is one of the jobs given to the Kohanim.

Why is it that the priests did not seek exclusivity in teaching, despite already having such exclusivity in the giving of sacrifices? Possibly someone may have recognized the benefits that competition brings and realized that restricting competition in teaching would be undesirable for belief and knowledge transmission. Or possibly the initial economic value of cartelizing teaching may have been small, especially in comparison with the economic value of controlling sacrifices, upon which early Judaism was based. By the time centralized animal sacrifice temporarily ceased, after the destruction of the First Temple (586 B.C.E.) and during the subsequent Babylonian exile, the precedent that teaching was not restricted to the Kohanim may have been firmly established and become too difficult to change, especially in light of the loss of power of Israel to Nebuchadnezzar. Whether motivated by altruism, miscalculation, historical accident, divine intervention, or dumb luck, the decentralization of Torah teaching beginning at the period of the First Temple set an important precedent that, as we will see, was followed by later generations.

Our analysis about the role of priests in teaching and sacrifice differs from the insightful analysis of A. Raskovich,[34] who uses the theory of vertical restrictions involving price and territory to understand the role of priests. He argues that the priests were assigned exclusive territories and were required to charge fixed prices (the Torah specifies the in-kind payment that the priest can retain from the sacrifice), thereby creating incentives for the priests to compete with each other through the provision of religious services—such as the teaching of Torah.[35] However, Raskovich's hypothesis that priests did not compete on price is undermined by his own analysis, which recognizes that Levites raised animals that were likely sold for sacrifice. Price competition could occur through lowering the prices for the priest's animals. With price competition occurring, the incentive to provide services, such as teaching, vanishes. Moreover, we note that there is some uncertainty among historians regarding the importance of the in-kind sacrifice payment to priests, who were also supported by the wealth of the Temple. If priests were supported primarily by the wealth of the Temple and not by the in-kind payments, then there would not be the incentives that Raskovich discusses to provide services such as the teaching of Torah. We therefore disagree with the preeminent role that Raskovich suggests that the priests had in teaching.[36]

Aside from their role in teaching, the prophets, and not just the exclusive class of priests, play an important role in belief transmission. Recall our earlier discussion about how beliefs could be created in an environment in which everyone is encouraged to engage in rituals in order to avoid ostracism by the existing believing community. The prophets urged the Israelites to follow all the Torah's teachings, both those involving ritual and those involving ethics. (The Torah makes no distinction between the two, and in some instances one can debate which category a particular law fits into.) The prophets also railed against performing only the rituals (for example, sacrifices) unless one also acted in accordance with a belief in God.[37] The prophets wanted to raise λ_i, which would then affect both interpersonal actions and sacrifice. On the other hand, given their exclusivity in the performing of sacrifice, the priests should have cared only about increasing the demand for sacrifice regardless of whether other actions were affected. Accordingly, the prophets, not the exclusive tribe of priests, were critical in transmitting Torah and beliefs that translated into actions.[38]

V. Rabbinic Judaism: Attitudes Toward Competition[39]

The Talmud followed by the subsequent codifications of Jewish law together with the *responsa* literature provide a rich source of information regarding restrictions on competition over the last 2,000 years. Because the conditions under which Jews have lived over the centuries have varied so much, and because restrictions in one set of circumstances may not make sense under another, one should be wary about leaping to any general principles that would apply under most or all economic conditions from an observation of the laws prevailing in one particular place or time. However, we find a remarkable consistency in the lack of restrictions on teaching across a wide variety of circumstances. This allows us to infer a general conclusion regarding the value that Judaism places on education.[40]

Although Judaism is generally described as having a favorable view toward competition,[41] Judaism has restricted competition on many occasions. We will discuss what have probably turned out to be the two most important general restrictions on competition, *hasagat g'vul (yored le'omanut chavero)* and *herem hayishuv*. In both cases, there is a strong general exception to impeding competition for Torah teachers, a position that would not be consistent with the self-interest of Torah teachers, who would desire to restrict entry.[42] As we shall see, this lack of self-interest contrasts with other instances of restrictions on competition that were designed to protect select groups. This lack of self-interested legislation protecting teachers is noteworthy because the rabbis who had the ability to promulgate such rules and would have benefited from such rules chose not to do so.[43] This does not mean that scholars never had self-interested rules promulgated in their favor. Quite the contrary, scholars received many special rulings and, in general, were held in high esteem. For example, scholars were exempt from paying taxes in walled cities, were exempt from the entry restriction on setting up shops selling cosmetics,[44] and were given priority in bidding for certain property.[45] It is only in the competition to teach that scholars generally get no respite.[46]

The general restrictions on entry often come under the category *hasagat g'vul*—the removal of a neighbor's landmark. The rabbis extended the concept of *hasagat g'vul* to cover encroachment on another's business. We begin our analysis of entry restrictions with Bava Batra 21b, in which R. Huna rules that the resident of an alley with a business in that alley can prevent a resident of another alley in the same town from opening a competing business. In contrast, R. Huna ben R. Joshua argues that entry cannot be prevented if the entrant is a resident of another town and pays taxes to this one. Moreover, if the entrant is a resident of the same alley, he cannot be prevented from competing. The opinion of R. Huna ben R. Joshua prevails. What remains unresolved is whether the entry into one alley by a resident of another alley in the same town is allowed. Despite this disagreement, there is a long discussion in Bava Batra 21a of how one cannot block entry related to the teaching of children. R. Huna concedes[47] that even his protectionist views would not apply to those who teach Torah.

The discussion in the Talmud makes clear that each teacher is fearful that a rival will outperform him, and this fear spurs extra effort, with the consequence that more knowledge is disseminated. The thrust of this discussion is the clear recognition of the benefits of competition and the paramount importance of teaching as a central value of Judaism. Indeed, this high regard for education explains why teachers were one of the five groups who could be dismissed without notice if they commit a grievous error. (The other groups are professional tree planters, butchers, bloodletters, and town scribes.)[48] This high regard for Torah education also explains why Torah teachers are exempt from certain "zoning" rules. For example, the Mishna states that if a shop is set up in a residential area, the residents can shut the shop down if they find that the noise of people coming into the shop disturbs their sleep. This rule, however, does not apply if the noise comes from students attending Torah classes.[49] In our view, the emphasis placed on free competition in teaching reflects the strategy that Judaism chose to follow to survive—decentralized teaching.

In subsequent decisions on general restrictions on competition, the free-entry view of R. Huna ben Joshua was not always followed. R. Moses Isserles (b. 1525) indicates in an approving discussion of a protectionist ruling by R. Eliezer ben Joel ha-Levi (b. 1140) of Bonn that deprivation from an incumbent of his livelihood can justify entry restrictions. Elsewhere, however, R. Isserles appears to reject a protectionist view. R. Moses Sofer (b. 1762) similarly adopts the view that financial ruin can justify entry restrictions. R. Moshe Feinstein (b. 1895) agrees and goes further to add that the reduction in the incumbent's earnings below the average of his peer group can justify entry restrictions. Under the protectionist's view, these general entry restrictions do not apply if the financial ruin is due to the incumbent's unwillingness to become more efficient. However, if the incumbent lacks the ability to become more efficient, then protection is accorded. In other words, under the protectionist rulings, a firm with a superior technology can be prevented from entering and competing if the result would be the financial ruin of the incumbent.

We find the protectionist rulings to be in accord with many entry restrictions in modern times—often supported by special interest groups. However, we note that the primary concern expressed in these protectionist opinions has been with the financial ruin of the incumbent. One plausible interpretation is that the financial ruin of a resident creates a hardship to that community. The resident may need to be supported or could otherwise cause problems to the community from idleness.[50] We simply note that these concerns should be of less relevance in a modern economy in which there is both labor mobility and a social welfare net. In such cases, restrictions on competition are exactly what they seem— special interest legislation. There would seem to be only a weak basis in even the protectionist view of Jewish law for such legislation.

These protectionist rulings would appear to leave open the possibility that a teacher could be prevented from entering into competition if the financial ruin of the incumbent was likely. However, we note that the authoritative code of Jewish law, the Shulchan Aruch (mid-1500s), states, "If there is a teacher of children and another comes who is better, the better teacher must replace the incumbent."[51] Moreover, according to R. Joseph Saul Nathanson of Lemburg (b. 1810), the freedom of movement that Torah teachers of children possessed must also apply to teachers of Talmud on the Talmudic grounds (Bava Batra 2lb) already discussed as well as on the legal fiction that there can be no financial deprivation because the income that such teachers earn should not be regarded as direct wages.[52] R. Moses Sofer (b. 1762) (who we just discussed as supporting a protectionist view on entry in the case of financial deprivation) is opposed to entry restrictions on any religious ministrant to the extent that the person would produce rivalry in Torah teaching.[53] To the extent that there remained any uncertainty about the application of protectionist rulings to education, some recent cases have resolved the issue. The highest rabbinical tribunal in Israel has stated that it would not prevent competition from a rival religious teacher, and in another case it refused to restrict entry for the publication of the Talmud without regard to the possibility of financial deprivation.[54] These views are in accord with the high value placed on teaching and dissemination of knowledge in Judaism.

The other major doctrine used to prevent entry is *herem hayishuv*.[55] The doctrine was used to prevent outsiders from settling in a town and thereby starting to compete with residents. Unlike the case of *hasagat g'vul*, where the tax payment of outsiders allowed them to enter and compete, no such principle applied here. The doctrine was used commonly throughout medieval times, in parts of Western Europe (France, Germany, Italy, and England) and Eastern Europe. The doctrine was not applied in Muslim countries, where Jews were often under less severe economic restrictions than in Christian Europe regarding the activities that the ruling authorities allowed Jews to do. Despite the view in major codes (for example, Mishnah Torah, Shulchan Aruch) endorsing the free-entry philosophy of R. Huna ben Yehoshua, these *herems* were widespread and would appear to be of much greater significance in restricting entry than the doctrine of *hasagat g'vul*. However, religious teachers were one of the notable exceptions (another was refugees).[56] That is, even when economic circumstances were so dire as to cause (with rabbinic approval) general entry restrictions to be promulgated in clear violation of Talmudic principles (specifically, free entry of out-of-town residents who agreed to pay taxes), such entry restrictions on teachers were uncommon.

There undoubtedly were some cases under both the *hasagat g'vul* and *herem hayishuv* doctrines where interest groups may have succeeded in placing entry restrictions on teachers (though, other than the cases noted in notes 43 and *56 supra,* our search of the *responsa* literature failed to reveal any such cases). Our point is that there was generally a distinction between teachers and other occupations in the placing of entry restrictions and that generally teachers were free of such entry restrictions.

VI. Conclusion

A religion consists of a belief in God combined with rules that God wants adherents to follow. Each religion must follow some strategy to survive. Judaism wound up following the strategy of the decentralized teaching of Torah. From its very beginnings, the teaching of Torah became a familial obligation and then later a communal one. Unlike sacrifice, teaching was not the realm of a select few. This failure of any interest group to relegate Torah teaching to itself carried through to Talmudic times and later. While restrictions on general competition arose, Torah teachers typically were free of any such restrictions. It is particularly remarkable that the scholars—who were in large part in control of Jewish law—generally chose not to close their profession or enact restrictions on entry but instead chose to keep competition thriving in their profession. As the Talmud recognizes, there are benefits to such competition: "Jealousy among scholars increases wisdom."[57]

Acknowledgment

We thank Barry Chiswick, Deborah Dobrusin, Steven Katz, Aaron Levine, Gregory Pelnar, Eric Posner, Alex Raskovich, Jacob Rosenberg, Rabbi Gershon Seif, Robert Stillman, an anonymous referee, and participants at the International Conference on Law, Jewish Law and Economics, held at Bar-Ilan University in December 1998, for helpful comments.

Notes

1. See, for example, Lawrence R. Iannaccone, Sacrifice and Stigma: Reducing Free-Riding in Cults, Communes, and Other Collectives, 100 J. Pol. Econ. 271 (1992); Lawrence R. Iannaccone, Why Strict Churches Are Strong, 99 Am. J. Soc. 1180 (1994); Lawrence R. Iannaccone, Introduction to the Economics of Religion, 36 J. Econ. Literature 1465 (1998).

2. There are at least two approaches to the topic "creation of values." The typical one is to assume that preferences are determined exogenously and to treat religion and culture as exogenous determinants of those preferences. An alternative approach is to treat the rules of the religion and culture as incentives designed to influence behavior; hence, at any instant, they can be described as a system designed to cause an individual to behave "as if" the individual possessed certain values. If an individual behaves "as if" he has certain values, he may make economic (or psychological) investments so that his subsequent behavior will be well predicted by the "as if" values, even when the initial incentives change. We take the second approach.

3. Although not usual, it would be possible to have a enter the utility function.

4. The penalty function could also include community sanctions when actions are observable.

5. Of course the effect on $u(c_i; Z_i)$ could well go in the opposite direction, as the loss in personal freedom of choice (for example, in Judaism, forbidden foods, limitations on activities permissible on the Sabbath, and so on) would tend to lower direct utility from consumption.

6. Nonbelievers could be worse off if the religious impose negative externalities on them. Thus,

for example, the closing of streets on the Sabbath, restrictions on entertainment on the Sabbath, and restrictions on the availability of nonkosher foods negatively affect the nonreligious.

7. See the Appendix for simple examples of the principles laid down in this section of the paper in a game theory context, including an evolutionary analysis.

8. Using the language of Jeremy I. Bulow, John D. Geanakoplos, & Paul D. Klemperer (Multimarket Oligopoly: Strategic Substitutes and Complements, 93 J. Pol. Econ. 488 (1985)), the issue is whether the actions of the two groups are strategic substitutes or complements.

9. Notice that belief in God is simply an intermediary step in creating "desirable" preferences. If an atheist develops these preferences, the religion has accomplished its goal. Cognitive dissonance could therefore work either through altering belief in God or by directly altering preferences.

10. See Gary S. Becker, A Theory of Social Interactions, 82 J. Pol. Econ. 1063 (1974), for an analysis of interdependent utility functions within the family.

11. If parents care about their children's utility and independence of beliefs, then there could be a reverse effect. However, since parents tend to raise children to have beliefs similar to themselves, we would expect this reverse effect to be weaker than the one discussed in the text.

12. What happens when parents die? Does their effect vanish? Not necessarily, for at least three reasons. First, λ_i may have become large by the first mechanism (cognitive dissonance) and then remain high because a high λ_i is needed to justify past acts if one is reluctant to admit that their prior behavior was not a reflection of their own preferences. Second, the utility of individual i can depend on what his parents would have thought of his actions. Third, during his parents' lifetime, the individual may have made irreversible investments that create gains from continuing to be (or act as) a believer.

13. R. Saada Gaon Exodus 20:11.

14. As parents of children whose ages range from 6 to 23, we are also well aware of the limitations parents sometimes have over their children's actions and beliefs.

15. Gary S. Becker & Kevin M. Murphy, A Theory of Rational Addiction, 96 J. Pol. Econ. 675 (1988).

16. Iannaccone, Sacrifice and Stigma, supra note 1.

17. For example, Leviticus 26:3-13; Deuteronomy 28:1-14.

18. The Torah speaks of the collectivity of Jews following the rules. Because it is unclear what percentage must do so to avoid collective punishment, there could be a free-rider problem even for a believer if the divine punishment to him were based solely on collective action and not on any of his individual actions.

19. Indeed, these investments in human capital began during the Babylonian Exile after the destruction of the First Temple (586 B.C.E.). Many scholars believe that during this time the Torah was codified and brought back to Israel by Ezra and Nehemiah when they led the return from Babylon to Israel. A large Jewish community was likely left in Babylon, where centralized animal sacrifice was not being practiced.

20. No doubt one response can be utter rejection of the relevance of the inherited wisdom. This did sometimes occur as, for example, in Western Europe during the 1800s and in Russia during the late 1800s and early 1900s.

21. The Dalai Lama has studied Judaism to learn lessons for how his religion can survive now that he and many of his followers are separated because the hostile policies of the Chinese have forced him into exile in India. See Rodger Kamenetz, The Jew in the Lotus (1994).

22. The content of the rules together with economic conditions will influence the incentive to take actions that deviate from the rules. As economic conditions change, the rules of a successful religion will have to adapt, otherwise the cost of remaining a believer may be too high. This reasoning would explain why in a cross section of the population one should expect a negative correlation between wealth and the level of adherence to the religious rules (those most able to prosper economically will find it in their interest to be least constrained by rules), but that over

time in the face of economic growth, the rules of the successful religion should change (for example, to conserve time as labor increases in value) so that the overall religiosity of the society need not.

23.   The Midrash says that there is a continual lessening of understanding of the Torah as we move further away chronologically from receipt of the Torah at Sinai.

24.   Much of Jewish study, especially Talmudic study, is not about rules but about interpretation and debate. The Talmud poses far more questions than it answers and, in sometimes excruciating detail, reports various sides of an argument.

25.   For example, among Ashkenazi Jews polygamy was banned about 1,000 years ago, but this ban did not apply to Sephardic Jews until recently.

26.   Shabbat 127a.

27.   See, for example, Deuteronomy 6:5-9. This passage ("Take to heart these commandments . . . Teach them to your children. Recite them when you are at home and when you are away, when you lie down and when you arise . . . inscribe them on the doorposts of your house") is said three times each day by observant Jews, and both Orthodox and nonOrthodox Jews commonly affix this prayer to their doorpost *(mezuzah)*.

28.   Although the discussion in this section has focused on Judaism, the underlying ideas are applicable to any religion. So, for example, it is a general principle that a benefit of de-centralization of authority is its greater ability to adapt over time and over space to disparate conditions. One would therefore expect religions (for example, Catholicism) with a very central hierarchy to change slowly, to have difficulty in countries where its central hierarchy is not politically supported, and to work best when applied to relatively homogeneous groups. In contrast, religions (for example, Protestantism) with less hierarchical structure should be able to change faster and be better suited for turbulent times and heterogeneous populations.

29.   See Geoffrey P. Miller, Ritual and Regulation: A Legal-Economic Interpretation of Selected Biblical Texts, 32 J. Legal Stud. 477 (1993).

30.   Deuteronomy 6:5-9.

31.   Deuteronomy 30:11-14.

32.   The Levites (one of the tribes) comprise the priestly class. The Kohanim are members of the tribe of Levi and are descendants of Aaron.

33.   Malachi 2:7.

34.   A. Raskovich, You Shall Have No Other Gods Besides Me: A Legal Economic Analysis of the Rise of Yahweh. 152 J. Institutional & Theoretical Econ. 449 (1996).

35.   In the usual theory of vertical restrictions (see, for example, Dennis W. Carlton & Jeffrey M. Perloff, Modern Industrial Organization, ch. 13 (3d ed. 2000)) the territorial and price restrictions channel a firm's competitive incentives into the provision of services to attract customers. It also follows that with restrictions on competition, priests would benefit from prophets whose exhortations should have increased demand for the priests' services. However, we are unaware of any suggestions that priests paid prophets. (See Y. Kaufman, Israel in Canaan and the Age of Classical Prophecy, in Great Ages and Ideas of the Jewish People 59 (Leo W. Schwartz ed. 1956).)

36.   Despite these differences with Raskovich, we recommend his paper and thought-provoking arguments.

37.   See, for example, Isaiah 58.

38.   In the language of agency theory, the priests received a reward (they kept a portion of the sacrifice) when the population understood rules specifying sacrifice, but not when the population understood the rules specifying interpersonal conduct (with the exception of sin offerings). Because of their skewed incentives, priests should be expected to have promoted sacrifice over ethical interpersonal conduct.

39.   We draw on the excellent discussions in Aaron Levine, Free Enterprise and Jewish Law: Aspects of Jewish Business Ethics (1980), and Meir Tamari, With All Your Possessions: Jewish

Ethics and Economic Life (1987). We are especially grateful to Aaron Levine and Rabbi Gershon Seif for helpful conversations. We have skipped much of the period of the Second Temple. In brief, the exile of the Jews to Babylon forced them to develop the religion without the central reliance on animal sacrifice. The leadership of Ezra and Nehemiah in instituting regular readings of the Torah on market days (Mondays and Thursdays—a custom followed to this day) when they returned from Babylon to Israel (around 400 B.C.E.) established a systematic attempt to teach Torah regularly. The reforms, promulgated by Yehoshua ben Gamla (Bava Barra 21a) somewhere around the first century B.C.E., instituted education supported by a community tax for all over the age of 6 or 7. Until Yehoshua ben Gamla (a high priest during the time of the Second Temple), Torah was taught only by fathers to their sons, and teaching by scholars was done only for those over the age of 16 or 17. Those without fathers, and those whose fathers were unable to teach, did not learn Torah. It is stated (Bava Barra 21a) that but for the decree by Yehoshua ben Gamla, Torah would have been forgotten from Israel. The drawback of this reform is that the parents' incentive to learn Torah was lessened. The advantage is the gains from specialization in teaching.

40.   In speaking of "the value that Judaism places on education," we are not propagating the view that there is one central decision maker in Judaism whose preferences we are uncovering. Rather, we have taken the view that the result of any decision is the consequence of various conflicting political and economic interests among different groups. The outcomes of those conflicts are observable; one can then talk of those outcomes reflecting "underlying values," but such talk is imprecise. The analyst observes the outcomes of an equilibrium, not the underlying demand (or supply) curve for, say, education.

41.   For example, Tamari, supra note 39, at 86.

42.   If teachers are not paid, then all this discussion about free entry is quite beside the point. In fact, although there are clear sentiments in the Talmud expressing disapproval of payment (for example, Nedarim 36b-37a, Pirke Avot 4:5, and later codifications (for example, Rambarn (b. 1135 C.E.), Mishna Torah, Laws of Talmud Torah 1:7)), the practicalities clearly prevailed requiring teachers to be paid. As just discussed in note 39 supra, during the Hasmonean period, communities were required to tax themselves to insure that teachers would be provided. The Talmud explains that teachers could also be considered "babysitters" and so could be paid, or, alternatively they could be paid to teach the punctuation of the Torah (which is not considered part of the Torah since Torah scrolls are written without punctuation) (Nedarim 37a). Rambam explains that if a father could not fulfill his responsibility to teach his son, he is required to hire a teacher. R. Moshe Feinstein (b. 1895) cites R. Moses Isserles for the opinion that being paid for teaching is necessary for practical purposes—"in order to push along Torah, push it [in reference to a hostile attitude regarding payment in the Shulchan Aruch] aside." The bottom line is that compensation for teaching Torah was and is common.

43.   We have tried to come up with explanations based on self-interest for this behavior, but we do not find our possible explanations particularly convincing. Two possible explanations are as follows. First, the rabbis who set the rules *(poskim)* are not necessarily those who teach children. Suppose that the populations of *poskim* and "ordinary" teachers are distinct, with the *poskim* serving only as the teachers of advanced students who become either *poskim* or ordinary teachers. Suppose further that the supplies of *poskim* and teachers are not linked. For example, suppose that *poskim* and ordinary teachers have separate training programs so that it is possible to restrict one program without affecting the other. The *poskim* would then want to restrict their own supply, but would oppose a restriction in the number of ordinary teachers because that would reduce the demand for *poskim* services as teachers of ordinary teachers. We are not convinced that the bulk of the historical evidence is consistent with this proposed explanation, based on self-interest, for the lack of restrictions on ordinary teachers for several reasons. First, it is not clear that the poskim and ordinary teachers were always completely separate groups. Second, although there is some evidence that occasionally one yeshiva (a center for advanced study often run by a *posek)*

was able to prevent the entry of a rival (see, for example, Piskei Din Yerushalayim, Dinei Mamonot U'viurei Yahadut 5:165, apparently in accord with Maharsham 5:15 & 6:210), there is strong support for the opposing view that no such entry restriction is justified (see, for example, Kol Mevaser 1:8, Hazon Ish 3:1, Minchat Yitzchak 4:75, Piskei Din Rabaniyim 8:129 & 6:90, and especially Shoel U'meshiv 1:13). Finally it is likely that, contrary to our above supposition, the supply of *poskim* and ordinary teachers was linked in the sense that they were both students in the same class so that a restriction on the number of ordinary teachers (achieved by a restriction on the size of advanced classes) would also restrict the number of *poskim*—eventually raising the wages of *poskim*. Hence, it is not at all clear whether the self-interest of the poskim is advanced by opposing a restriction on the number of ordinary teachers. A second possible explanation, based on teacher self-interest, for the opposition to entry restrictions is that teachers value mobility highly (for example, to be close to centers of learning) and would therefore prefer to be unencumbered by any restrictions on where they could work.

44.   Bava Batra 22a.

45.   Shulchan Aruch.

46.   It is useful to distinguish entry restrictions from content restrictions. We speak only of the former in this paper. Excommunication was used to ban individuals with heretical ideas.

47.   Bava Batra 21b.

48.   Bava Batra 21a.

49.   Bava Batra 20b.

50.   Hence, it may be more efficient to allow an interference in competition than not. In the case of teaching, the externality that teaching creates (survivability) generally trumps any concern with financial distress, as we discuss below.

51.   Yorah Deah 245:18.

52.   See Levine, supra note 39, at 17.

53.   Id. at 18.

54.   Id. at 32. A possible exception to this generally favorable view of competition among scholars is R. Moshe Feinstein's (b. 1895) ruling preventing the establishment of a synagogue near another (Igrot Moshe Responsa Choshen Mishpat 1:38). However, Feinstein makes clear that this ruling applies not to teachers but only to the nonteaching functions of the synagogue. One interesting feature in this ruling is the notion that if a competing synagogue is established for nonlivelihood reasons (for example, altruistic reasons) and, for example, the rabbi takes no pay, then that competition can be prevented by an incumbent who does derive a livelihood.

55.   See, for example, Louis I. Rabinowitz, The Herem Hayishub: A Contribution to the Medieval Economic History of the Jews (1945); and Tamari, *supra* note 39, at 113.

56.   Tamari, supra note 39, at 115. Rabbis were one of the categories of exception. However, toward the end of the 700-year period during which the *herem* operated, in some locations rabbis were able to prevent entry of other rabbis apparently on the grounds that rabbis performed some functions that were noneducational. We are unaware of a systematic use of a *herem* against teachers. However, we are aware of one case where a *herem* was used in Italy against a religious teacher in the late 1400s. Interestingly, Italy also has a case where it applied the *herem* to prevent entry of refugees, another of the usual categories of exception to the *herem*. (See Rabinowitz, *supra* note 55, ch. 10.)

57.   Bava Batra 21a.

58.   We could alter this assumption slightly to say that the player deciding how to act receives greater benefit from dealing with one of his own, so that d > c and a > b. This will not change the conclusions at all.

Appendix

Strategic Behavior I: A Two-Person Game

Assume there are two individuals—one with a high value of λ and one with a low value of)λ. Each can decide to act religiously (R) or nonreligiously (NR). The payoff table might look something like Figure A1. The high-λ player prefers that both act religiously. If, however, the low-λ player acts nonreligiously, the high-λ player may still be better off if he acts religiously (cases d, e, and f) than if he does not. This would depend on the magnitude of the "penalty" discussed in the text. For the low- λ player, the worst-case scenario is when he acts religiously and the high-λ player does not. However, when the high-λ player acts religiously, the low-λ player may be better off (cases a and d) or worse off (cases b, c, e, and f) from also acting religiously. In fact, as in cases c and f, he may be better off when the high-λ player acts religiously than when he acts nonreligiously (as per the externality discussed in the text).
The Nash equilibria are as follows:

     1. In case a there are two pure strategy equilibria, R-R and NR-NR. Similarity is important, and it is unclear whose beliefs will prevail.

     2. In cases b and c, the equilibrium is NR-NR. In this case the negative externality on being different is great, and since NR dominates for the low-λ player, it is also chosen by the high-λ player.

     3. In case d, the equilibrium is R-R. Again there is an externality, but in this case there is a dominant strategy for the high-λ player, so his desires prevail.

     4. In cases e and f, the equilibrium is NR-R. Only in this case do we get heterogeneity in actions.

Strategic Behavior II: Evolutionary Considerations

Assume for simplicity that there are two types of players—those for whom $\lambda = 0$ and those for whom $\lambda = 1$. Each player in the economy interacts with each other player in the economy an equal number of times. Players for whom $\lambda = 1$ will always act in a religious manner (R), since the penalty for not doing so outweighs other considerations. However, those for whom $\lambda = 0$ can act as if $\lambda = 1$ (R). Assume that in the initial equilibrium all those for whom $\lambda = 0$ act nonreligiously (NR) and that the share of $\lambda = 1$ people in the population equals α. The payoff table for the $\lambda = 0$ individual would look something like Figure A2.

     The player has to decide whether to remain true to his beliefs and act NR or to act R. We assume that each person prefers to deal with his own kind. Hence, the reward one person will receive if the other person who is dealing with him believes they are alike is greater than if that other person believes they are different. This assumption amounts to assuming that $a > c$ and $d > b$.[58]

     When α is small, there are two equilibria—(1) all $\lambda = 1$ people act R and all $\lambda = 0$ people act NR and (2) all people act R. Assume that the first equilibrium holds initially. If α grows sufficiently large, the $\lambda = 0$ player will prefer to act R rather than NR, even if all other NR people act NR. At this point all $\lambda = 0$ people will act R. To be precise, this will occur when $\alpha > (d - b)/[(d - b) + (a - c)]$. (Note that under the assumptions above regarding the relative sizes of these parameters, $0 < \alpha < 1$.)

High-λ Player

	R	NR
R	4,5	1,3
Low-λ Player	a) 3, 1	6,2
NR	b) 5, 1	
	c) 7, 1	
	d) 3, 3	
	e) 5, 3	
	f) 7, 3	

FIGURE A1.—Payoff table for interactions between the low-λ and high-λ individuals

Group

	R (α)	NR ($1 - \alpha$)
Nonreligious Player — Act R	a	b
Act NR	c	d

FIGURE A2.—Payoff table for the $\lambda = 0$ individual

Group

	R (α)	SR (β)	NR ($1 - \alpha - \beta$)
Any Player Except R — Act R	9	7	5
Act SR	7	9	7
Act NR	5	7	9

FIGURE A3.—Payoff table for all but the religious individual

Group

		R (α)	SR (β)	NR $(1 - \alpha - \beta)$
	Act R	8	6	4
Semireligious Player	Act SR	7	9	7
	Act NR	4	6	8

FIGURE A4.—Payoff table for the semireligious individual

Other assumptions are, of course, possible. If, for instance, the honesty argument given in the text prevails, it is possible that $b > d$ since one always does better dealing with an R person than with an NR person. In this case, acting R dominates.

We expand this analysis to include a third person, for whom $0 < \lambda < 1$. We will denote this person SR (for semireligious). We now assign a payoff table based on these assumptions:

1. The proportion of SR players in the population is β.

2. The more similar the player to the person he is dealing with, the greater the payoff.

These assumptions lead to the payoff table in Figure A3 for all but the religious person (whom, we recall, always acts R).

We now add the following assumption:

3. There is a cost to acting differently from what you are, and this cost grows as you change your behavior more.

This yields the payoff table for the SR player (Figure A4). Solving the resulting inequalities, the SR player will act R if $\alpha > 3/4$ and will act NR if $1 - \alpha - \beta > 3/4$. The table for an NR player is different given the penalty associated with deviant behavior and looks like Figure A5. The NR person will also act R if $\alpha > 3/4$ and will act SR if $\alpha + \beta > 3/4$ and $\alpha < 3/4$.

The above examples may help in understanding a fairly recent trend in religious observance. There is a feeling that the level of observance in religious communities has been increasing. This could be understood in our model by noting the markedly higher birthrates among the religious than among the nonreligious. Since these higher birthrates lead to higher values for α (and possibly β), greater portions of the population will decide to act semireligiously (as $\alpha + \beta$ increases) and then religiously (as α increases). Moreover, as stated in the text, *mitoch shelo lishma ba lisha*—cognitive dissonance can lead people who behave in a religious manner to increase their values of λ—further reinforcing the trend toward greater religious observance.

Group

		R (α)	SR (β)	NR $(1 - \alpha - \beta)$
	Act R	7	5	3
Nonreligious Player	Act SR	6	8	6
	Act NR	5	7	9

FIGURE A5.—Payoff table for the nonreligious individual

Cultural Sensitivity Training in Mental Health: Treatment of Orthodox Jewish Psychiatric Inpatients

Elizabeth Sublette
Brian Trappler

Abstract: *The authors describe some of the cultural/religious issues which arose in the treatment of major psychiatric disorders among Orthodox Jewish inpatients at SUNY Health Science Center's University Hospital (SUH) in Brooklyn, New York. The distinct ways in which cultural and religious factors impacted on presentation, therapeutic interventions, and transference-countertransference reactions are noted. Specific reference is made to the use of religion by patients and families as a means of defense, rationalization or power-brokering. Via case vignettes, the authors explore ways of distinguishing between culturally appropriate vs. maladaptive behaviors in the Orthodox population. Practical solutions are suggested for sensitive ways to surmount culture-based barriers to effective inpatient therapy in this group.*

Introduction

Over the last 50 years, the importance of ethnocultural factors in the psychotherapeutic process has been increasingly studied (Devereux, 1953; Ticho, 1971; Griffith, 1977; Comas-Diaz & Jacobsen, 1991). Although some authors have described culture-specific aspects of psychiatric treatment of Orthodox Jews (Bilu & Witztum, 1993; Witztum *et al.* 1990; Mintz, 1992, Ostrov, 1978; Paradis *et al.*, 1997), little has been published concerning issues of inpatient treatment of this population (Trappler *et al.*, 1995). While the term "Orthodox" embraces a range of religious practices, with a number of ethnic and idealogic sub-groups, for the purposes of this article the term "Orthodox" will refer to those Jews whose Eastern European cultural background and strict interpretations of Torah law have led to the greatest separation from the values of secular society. This group includes both Hasidic and non-Hasidic Jews. For more information concerning Orthodox sub-groups, see Mintz (1992). For such patients, issues of cultural sensitivity would presumably have the largest impact.

During the period 1994-1998, we treated 15 Orthodox patients from the nearby Brooklyn community on the psychiatric inpatient unit at SUH, a 30-bed voluntary unit, with an average length of stay of about 30 days. The patients consisted of 11 males and 4 females; mean age was 36.7 years. They had the following diagnoses: schizophrenia, 6 patients; schizoaffective disorder, 3 patients; bipolar disorder, 4 patients; major depressive disorder, 2 patients. Diagnosis was made by structured interview using DSM-IV criteria (American Psychiatric Association, 1994).

Staffing consisted of 3 full-time psychiatrists (one of whom [B.T.] is Orthodox), 3 part-time psychologists, 2 psychology fellows, 5 psychiatric residents, 2 social workers, a full-time family therapist, nursing staff and 3 full-time activity therapists. In addition, a variety of trainees worked on site, such as medical students, activity therapists, and psychology interns. On the unit, emphasis was placed on combined therapies, including pharmacotherapy; psychodynamically-oriented individual, group, and family therapies; and a variety of therapeutic activities such as arts and crafts, music and cooking. All staff and patients also attended large community meetings three times a week. The other inpatients were of widely diverse cultural, racial and socioeconomic backgrounds, reflecting the multi-ethnic population found in Brooklyn, NY. Case histories have been altered in non-essential details to protect the privacy of the patients.

Integrating Orthodox Patients into the Milieu Therapy

The practice of Orthodox Judaism is extremely structured and regulates all activities of daily life. For example, each day contains mandatory periods for prayer. Adult Jewish men are also required, during morning prayers, to put on phylacteries ("tefillin"), ritual objects consisting of two leather boxes containing Biblical verses, which are affixed to the forehead and one hand by means of long leather straps. Ritual pervades even mundane activities such as meals, which must be kosher, and which are preceded and followed by ritual washing of the hands and blessings.

Our unit is a treatment setting where scheduled groups and activities are considered important in providing structure for disorganized patients. Patients meet with occupational therapy staff each morning to assign officer positions for community meetings, to discuss privilege levels, and to receive their schedules for activity and group therapy meetings. Those with privileges can participate in walks and gym activities twice a week. Under these conditions, the schedule may run counter to the religiously-determined daily activities of the Orthodox patient. In such cases, the inability to pray at accustomed times with phylacteries could exacerbate the anxiety of the religious patient. The objective of providing structure through community activities may thus potentially become counterproductive for the Orthodox patient, as a result of the clash of milieu and religious cultures. On the other hand, the need for adherence to prayer schedules can potentially become a way for patients to distance themselves, avoid social interactions, or feel stigmatized as different from their peers. Furthermore, it may be difficult for non-Orthodox hospital staff to determine the true extent of normal ritual versus hyperreligiosity or pathologic prolongation of ritual functions.

Our major cross-cultural therapeutic goals, therefore, included integrating the Orthodox patients into the milieu environment and allowing legitimate religious practices while setting limits on maladaptive ritual. Where possible, religious rituals were honored. For instance, the Orthodox patients were provided with kosher meals but were expected to eat in the main dining room with the other patients; male patients were allowed to bring in their phylacteries to be used under supervision, provided they were not too disorganized or on suicide precautions; and particular times for study and prayer were allowed, as long as they did not conflict with the unit's schedule. Patients were given time for prayer but were expected to show some flexibility where this conflicted with unit schedules, which would take precedence; they could pray before or after, but not during, community meetings.

Six out of our group of fifteen patients displayed involvement with ritual which conflicted with milieu activities. These included ritual hand washing, study, and prayer. Two very regressed schizophrenic patients were frequently involved in compulsive rituals which shielded them against the threat of social stimulation.

> A. was a 35-year-old schizophrenic man with a long history of hospitalizations at acute and long-stay facilities; he had never completed high school. The patient was disorganized, poorly groomed, and his room was in a state of disarray. He would easily become overwhelmed and overstimulated in community meetings. During these times, he immersed himself in prayer and stated that his religious needs did not allow him to attend the meeting, or that he could not attend because he was "studying to be a rabbi". As his neuroleptics were titrated, he gradually tolerated longer periods of exposure to community meeting, accompanied by a trusted staff member, and eventually made relevant verbal contributions.

The Jewish Sabbath begins Friday night just before sundown and extends until Saturday evening. During this time period, Orthodox Jews are not permitted to engage in many of the recreational activities that take place on an inpatient unit, including watching television, listening to radio, turning on electric lights, writing, cooking, or creative arts. Similar prohibitions pertain to Jewish holidays, many of which last two days. During these times, patients' families cannot visit if they live farther than walking distance from the hospital, due to the prohibition against any form of motorized travel.

Just as non-Jewish patients can be expected to experience difficulty in being away from their families over major holidays, so too Jewish patients find it depriving to be hospitalized during Sabbath and holiday times. Although observing the various Sabbath prohibitions may be possible on an inpatient unit, the patient will miss most of the positive aspects of the Sabbath day, which at home is spent with communal immersion in study, prayer, and festive meals.

Cultural sensitivity with regard to the Sabbath included permission for patients to light Sabbath candles in the activities room, under supervision, and granting of relative-accompanied passes for Sabbath and holidays whenever possible, even when they conflicted with unit schedules:

> *B.* was a 40-year-old single woman, schizophrenic, whose mother had also been schizophrenic and had died 8 years previously. The patient had the responsibility of being the homemaker for her father, who is a prominent rabbi in the community. On arrival on the unit, *B.* was diagnosed and required frequent observation. Her father would visit on the Sabbath. By the time the Jewish holidays arrived, she had been on the unit for 3 weeks. Her father was able to escort her on 4-hour pass to have the holiday festival meal at the home of the patient's aunt, who lived 20 minutes' walking distance from the hospital.

Modesty and Sexuality

Social contacts between men and women in the Orthodox communities, especially among Hasidim, are conducted in a highly structured and protected way. Children are educated in single-sex schools, and religious and social events usually have separate seating for men and women. Casual communication between Orthodox adolescents of the opposite sex is discouraged. Dating is time-limited and carried out with the distinct purpose of marriage, between young people whose suitability has been established in advance by the respective families. For more information on arranged marriages among the Orthodox, see Rockman (1994). Safeguards against improper sexual behavior are stringent: other than husband and wife, two people of opposite sex are not permitted to be alone together in a potentially intimate situation. Even casual touching or hand shaking (as taken for granted in Western culture), is prohibited between men and women. For more information on religious law and customs regarding sexual conduct among the Orthodox, see Rockman (1993). Moreover, Orthodox men are forbidden to have exposure to potential sources of erotic stimulation. including suggestive TV ads, movies or reading material. These prohibitions protect the male from the temptation to masturbate and from even accidental nocturnal emission, both considered sinful according to Jewish law. Within the community, women's dress and behavior are therefore carefully regulated to conform to rabbinically-established standards of modesty, which include covered arms, legs and, for married women, hair. Moreover, women will not dance or sing in public where they could be observed by men.

Given this religious/cultural background, the expectation that Orthodox patients will fully interact therapeutically in a milieu-type of environment might be unrealistic. For this reason, some patients have been shown to be more comfortably treated on combined medical/psychiatric units which function more like a conventional hospital setting (Trappler *et al.*, 1995). In this group of 15 patients, however, our experience was that most were able to participate in community meetings and therapeutic groups: male patients sat next to female patients and participated in discussions. Although this is a small cohort, our observation was that the relevance of a given patient's contribution and the degree of involvement, like the rest of the patient community, appeared to depend more on diagnosis and severity of illness than on cultural factors. For example, the bipolar manic patients were able to engage most easily, while the most regressed schizophrenic patients showed the greatest degree of withdrawal. In most cases, however, casual peer interaction on the unit appeared to be limited to patients of the same sex.

Although our Orthodox patients were expected to engage in milieu therapy groups, objections to certain activities were respected as being culturally appropriate. For example, in a music/movement group, the activities were conducted in a way that interpersonal distance was maintained, and female patients were not expected to dance in front of a male audience. We also have a "no-touch" policy on the unit, which is strictly enforced; the philosophy behind this is to discourage any form of erotic or romantic involvements, as this could exacerbate conflicts and symptoms and thereby hinder therapy. This policy was found to be useful in neutralizing anxieties about expectations for undue intimacy and allowed Orthodox patients to retain a certain interpersonal distance without feeling stigmatized.

Patients were randomly assigned to primary therapists, according to unit policy. Establishing a therapeutic alliance between a non-Jewish female therapist and an Orthodox male patient presented a particular challenge. Staff members were counselled to recognize that a variety of culturally-appropriate defense behaviors would likely be evident on the part of patients, including avoidance of physical contact (hand-shaking) and eye contact. Patients' wishes to have doors kept unlocked or ajar during individual therapy were respected as being culturally appropriate rather than treatment resistant.

Two male patients, one schizophrenic, the other schizoaffective, developed powerful erotic transference relationships toward their non-Jewish female therapists. While attempting to negate such feelings, they struggled to maintain their attachments. One was able to work through some of his conflict over the erotic material in therapy; the other was not:

> C., a 26-year-old male with schizoaffective disorder, told his therapist in a later period of recovery that earlier mutism in sessions was associated with intrusive erotic thoughts. The therapist had been careful not to stimulate such fantasies through "immodest" dress or sessions in closed rooms but allowed the patient to express his fantasies, without distancing herself within the therapeutic relationship.

> Upon admission, A. (see above) was severely regressed. He would call his therapist "mommy" but at other times would express erotic wishes: "Can I marry you?" He never acted on his fantasies within the therapeutic relationship but often appeared overwhelmed by sexual fantasies and primitive affects in this regard. His utterances in therapy groups and intrusions in the corridor were disruptive of the milieu, and his therapist frequently had to set limits on these behaviors. When this failed, the patient needed to be restricted to his room. Although high doses of clozapine and valproic acid reduced the intensity of these behaviors over time, he never gained sufficient coherence of thought to "work through"his fantasies.

In hindsight we questioned whether it was therapeutically appropriate to place the most regressed patients with opposite-sex therapists. Since the cultural/religious prohibitions appear so powerful, it may be unreasonable to expect such patients not to regress or to be overwhelmed by unacceptable fantasies and impulses.

Issues of Identity

The religious Jew has a highly-developed sense of separateness from the surrounding culture, stemming from an extremely different life style and from desire to preserve the purity of the Torah religion. This sense of separateness may deepen into mistrust of outsiders, fueled by a history replete with persecutions, pogroms, and the Nazi Holocaust. Thus isolation from neighboring cultures nurtures a forced intimacy within the community, and in particular within the Orthodox family. This wary attitude toward secular encounters impacts profoundly on the therapeutic relationship, in which Orthodox patients may be mistrustful of the secular therapist's ability to comprehend their world view.

Divergent attitudes toward birth control exemplified this transcultural gap. The practice of having many children is universal among the very Orthodox; it is a legal obligation deriving from the commandment to "be fruitful and multiply" and is powerfully reinforced by cultural practice. In order to practice birth control, an Orthodox couple must seek an individually-tendered Rabbinical decision ("heter") based on the application of religious law to their individual circumstances. Although experiencing multiple pregnancies and raising a number of children adds stress to patients already burdened by mental illness, suggesting birth control may heighten patients' anxiety and even result in termination of treatment.

> This was the first hospitalization for D., a 36-year-old Orthodox married woman with bipolar disorder. Her husband was a salesman who struggled to support their 7 children. The patient had been repeatedly manic over the previous 10 years, and her involvement in Jewish "outreach" activities led to neglect of the household. Her husband was angry about her poor care of children; moreover, he felt he could no longer support a family of this size. He had obtained a rabbinical ruling that the couple practice birth control. The patient. however, refused to comply, experiencing the inability to bear more children as a reflection of personal failure; she repeatedly tried discontinuing her lithium in order to conceive. Her powerful identification with the cultural ideal of having many children was reinforced by her grandiosity and poor insight. Finally, her husband moved out of the house.

This patient expressed initial suspicion of her secular female Jewish therapist, whom she believed was in collusion with her husband in an attempt to control and disempower her. Limit setting on the patient's unrealistic goals were thus hampered by her distrust of the therapist's value system, which she used as a resistance to engagement in psychotherapy. In approaching this patient, the therapist was careful to support the patient's religious ideals, validating her lofty goals. This required recognition of the patient's feelings of loss and disappointment at relinquishing the role of childbearing. With lithium treatment, individual supportive psychotherapy, and marital counseling, the patient's grandiosity diminished, her trust in the therapist improved, and it eventually became possible to negotiate the husband's reentry into the family.

In another case, the patient's loyalty to her husband led to displacement of anger toward her male therapist:

E., a 49-year-old female bipolar patient, had been very angry and demeaning toward her therapist, claiming that he was disrespectful of her religious sensitivities. After establishing more therapeutic trust, it emerged that the patient was angry at her husband, who was draining their financial resources by keeping his own private apartment, to which he would escape whenever she relapsed.

This issue was resolved in individual as well as marital therapy. Thereafter the patient no longer complained about her therapist's "disrespect"; ironically, the therapist was himself Orthodox.

On occasion, attempts were made to exploit an Orthodox therapist as an ally against the non-religious hospital staff. In each of the following three vignettes, either the patient or family attempted to induce the therapist into collusion, which served partly as a barrier against engaging in the milieu environment:

F. was a 19-year-old schizophrenic who was noncompliant with medications at home and was admitted following violent and aggressive behavior toward his parents and younger siblings. While on the unit, on more than one occasion, he attempted to assault other patients and was placed in seclusion by nursing staff. Whenever this happened (day or night), the patient's father called the Orthodox psychiatrist at home, insisting that his child be taken out of seclusion.

Patient C. (see above) was diagnosed with schizoaffective disorder. He lived with his grandfather. The patient had been constantly thought-disordered and unable to perform basic tasks on the unit. His grandfather was told by the primary therapist not to pressure the boy to return to work in a bank. The grandfather sought out the team leader, an Orthodox psychiatrist, for reassurance that the boy would be cured. He felt that the team was being overly pessimistic because "they don't believe in God, but you believe and you understand that he will be cured." The grandfather thwarted attempts at referral for day treatment. He would attempt to manipulate the family sessions by appealing to the psychiatrist to negate the decisions of the treatment team.

The treatment team was attempting to have patient B. (see above) referred to the day treatment program prior to discharge from the hospital. The team believed this was important for autonomy and socialization of the patient. Her father expressed concern that the program would expose his daughter to the influences of secular culture. The father acted out his objection by insisting that he escort his daughter to her screening appointment. Although the request was denied, the father arrived in the hospital five minutes before the scheduled appointment, insisted on meeting with the Orthodox psychiatrist on the team—bypassing the primary therapist—and attempted to convince him that the patient would "fail the interview" if he were not present. Ultimately, the patient attended the appointment accompanied by the activities therapist alone and expressed relief at this outcome. She was accepted into the program and, one year after discharge, continued to attend.

Culture-Specific Expression of Dependency Issues

The latter vignette exemplifies co-dependency between psychiatric patient and caregiver within the framework of the Orthodox family. In this case, the father was counseled concerning his daughter's frustration and shame about being unmarried, at age 40, in the Orthodox community. The acceptance of his daughter's need for autonomy was facilitated by cultural sensitivity on the part of the therapist, whose interpretation showed recognition of the father's right to receive respect from his daughter and his embarrassment at his daughter's poor grooming and eccentric behavior, especially considering his prominent role in the community. The father was also given support in dealing with issues of separation and unresolved bereavement over loss of his wife. After several sessions, he no longer used religious rationalizations for his separation anxieties, and he freely allowed his daughter to attend the outpatient program.

Communication

Among Orthodox Jews, communication is governed by religious precepts and customs attesting to the deep belief in the power of speech, including the "danger of an unguarded tongue." Particularly relevant to psychiatric treatment are the following: 1) the commandment to honor one's parents: 2) the prohibition against gossiping or speaking badly of others; 3) the fear of bringing evil fortune on oneself by drawing attention to an illness or even human weakness or frailty.

Strict adherence to these precepts concerning speech can be detrimental in the therapeutic setting, where, for example, the inhibition of the free exchange of information can hinder efforts to obtain a complete psychosocial history. During psychotherapy, patients may be reluctant to discuss problematic relationships, especially with parents, whom they are duty-bound to honor. This overriding sense of loyalty on the part of the patient may extend to other family members or even the community at large.

In addressing issues of communication, one successful approach employed by us has been to explain that feelings of resentment and hatred for a parent often result from unresolved conflicts, which need to be addressed in order to bring the relationship to a higher level of honor and respect. Conjoint sessions with the authority figures, occasionally held in the presence of a rabbi, sometimes led to shifts in attitude and behavior on the part of both patient and codependent figure.

> F. (see above) had his first psychotic break 3 years previously, following the death of a sibling. Six months prior to this, he had donated a kidney to that sibling. The sibling had initially responded to therapy but died after several months from other medical complications. The family had come in for several family sessions and questioned whether there could be a relationship between the patient's symptoms, his closeness to the sibling, and the sibling's death. The family informed staff about the history; the patient himself had never divulged this information, because, as he later told her therapist, he did not want it to sound as if his parents had forced him to perform the organ donation, which could have reflected negatively on them.

Once the information was out in the open, the patient was able to discuss these traumatic life events with his therapist; he was able to question whether the sibling's death might have been his fault, as a result of the failure of the transplant. At the conclusion of therapy, he expressed feeling unburdened by this disclosure.

Confidentiality

In the Orthodox community, there is a powerful emphasis placed on confidentiality. For example, mental illness in a family member is often kept secret even from other close members of the nuclear family. One powerful force against disclosure is the fear that community knowledge of mental illness in the family might prevent marriage of other family members. This fear ("shidduch anxiety") is not necessarily unrealistic, given the close scrutiny applied to a family in the marriage arrangement process. Families might therefore seek mental health services in remote centers, or seek non-Jewish therapists, to prevent exposure within the community.

> As part of the treatment plan for patient D. (see above), the therapist proposed family sessions which would include some of the older children; the patient believed this would help them to understand her difficulties in coping with the stresses of daily life. Her husband,

however, refused to sanction this plan, as he preferred to have the children, as well as other people in the community, believe his wife was hospitalized for "dehydration".

The therapist had some success in exploring the use of stigma as a rationalization, as part of the systemic denial used by this family. The husband had never confronted his feelings about his wife's illness. Nor had he attempted to set limits on her maladaptive behaviors. Cultural sensitivity required acknowledging the family's fear of the stigma of mental illness as a real social concern, while also addressing the husband's use of denial as a defense. This process led to a more adaptive approach to his wife's disability.

Discussion

Cultural Factors in the Initial Interview with Orthodox Patients

The experience of being an inpatient on a psychiatric unit can be a distressing experience for a patient of any culture, entailing loss of liberty; removal from normal pursuits and environment; exposure to patients who may be intrusive or violent; experiencing the side-effects associated with neuroleptics; and coming to terms with the nature of one's illness. For the Orthodox patient, emerging from a subculture so highly defended against the values of a secular environment, this sense of alienation is heightened. Hospitalization creates a forced engagement with a new environment, which may devalue the patient's sacred reality. Activities of daily living become subject to social and medical scrutiny challenging his beliefs and religious practices, causing the patient to feel naked and exposed, stripped of cultural symbols. Within the individual therapeutic relationship, the secular therapist may react with ignorance, perplexity, or even repugnance toward certain aspects of Orthodox culture. One relatively successful approach used in the past to avoid this cultural alienation has been hospitalization of Orthodox psychiatric patients on the combined medical-psychiatric unit (Trappler *et al.*, 1995). Such patients receive the benefits of psychopharmacologic intervention and close observation; however, in bypassing the challenges of the milieu environment, they also lose its benefits. With this group of patients, we chose an alternate approach, striving to cushion some of the alienation by modifying certain ward policies and fostering culturally sensitive attitudes among staff, as described above. In our case, the presence of an Orthodox psychiatrist on the unit was the catalyst for such sensitivity training. We found that many Orthodox patients among our population adapted well to the milieu setting once the above-mentioned courtesies were observed.

In Israel, some mental health care providers have sought to increase the familiarity of the (outpatient) environment in other ways: 1) enlarging the therapeutic encounter to include "chaperons", i.e., family members or friends, not as subjects for therapy but as "cultural bridges" to assist the patient in overcoming discomfiture (Heilman & Witztum, 1994); 2) familiarizing themselves with the writings of certain charismatic Hasidic rabbis to establish a common universe of discourse with patients from a particular sect (Bilu & Witztum, 1993); and even 3) incorporating mystical kabbalistic incantations as an ancillary treatment modality (Heilman & Witztum, 1994).

Our approach did not utilize the "chaperon" model, although we found that engaging other family members in treatment was often successful in fostering bonding of the patient with the primary therapist. Religious delusions held by Orthodox patients were treated in the standard way; we did not find it necessary to enter into a different cultural reality by invoking ritual practices. Indeed, we question the approach used by Heilman and Witztum (1994) of using mystical incantations as a treatment modality. Two significant differences should be noted, however, between the Israeli and American cultural environments: 1) Although the American Orthodox Jewish community is insular, its members still experience a much greater secular exposure, with a concomitantly higher level of cross-cultural desensitization, than their Israeli counterparts. 2) Powerful political and religious tensions exist between secular and Orthodox Jews in Israel, which may create a significant cultural barrier between therapist and patient. Additional use of chaperons, role playing, or quotation of mystical texts may be a necessary compensation required uniquely in that setting. On the other hand, the use of such non-traditional techniques may represent a countertransference overcompensation by therapists "going native" as a means of coping with their own feelings of cultural alienation from their co-religionists.

Transference and Countertransference

Our particular population of patients and therapists generated several notable types of transference/countertransference problems, which varied somewhat according to the cultural characteristics of the dyad: non-Orthodox Jewish therapist with Orthodox patient; non-Jewish therapist with Orthodox patient; Orthodox therapist with Orthodox patient. Superimposed upon these permutations were the conditions of same- or mixed-sex dyad, the diagnosis of the patient, and the severity of illness.

The relationship between Orthodox patient and non-Orthodox therapist tended to be fraught with certain inherent tensions. Treatment ideals held by the therapist, such as developing the patient's autonomy and exploration of fantasy (e.g., anger toward parents, erotic thoughts) may be considered by the patient as antithetical to the precepts of the Torah. Conversely, issues of belief and faith regarded by the Orthodox patient as a form of enlightenment may be interpreted by a secular therapist as a form of defense or even a denial of reality. In cases where the therapeutic dyad included an Orthodox psychiatrist, the therapist was forced to struggle with his own conflicts involving authority, especially when interacting with senior community members perceived as wise or saintly.

Our work thus extends that of Comas-Diaz and Jacobsen (1991), who have noted that cross-cultural psychotherapy "provides more opportunities for empathic and dynamic stumbling blocks, in what might be termed 'ethnocultural disorientation'." They describe a number of general transference/countertransference reactions to which the interethnic therapeutic dyad may be vulnerable, including overcompliance and friendliness; denial of ethnicity and culture; mistrust, suspicion and hostility; and ambivalence.

Certain forms of countertransference reactions manifested themselves most frequently in our setting:

1) Non-Orthodox Jewish therapists were particularly vulnerable to feelings of embarassment and anger at being identified with their "primitive" co-religionists. Both patient and therapist were likely to consider many aspects of the other's way of life to be misguided. It was essential to the establishment of a matrix of trust that the therapist be aware of potential types of cross-cultural countertransference hostilities. For example, in dealing with female patients with large families committed to having even more children, some therapists had to struggle with their more "modern" views on appropriate family size and life quality vs. the normative Orthodox cultural expectation. Therapeutic interventions targeting limitation of family size were most likely to succeed when approached from exploration of both the patient's defenses and the culturally-acceptable (i.e., rabbinically sanctioned) options for implementing limitation of family size. Another example of countertransference hostility was noted in therapists who were targeted by patients as objects for religious conversion or enlightenment. Manic patients, in particular, tended to proselytize, evoking avoidance or emotional coldness by therapists.

2) A reaction most frequently observed with non-Jewish therapists was overdeference to religious intrusions. Such therapists tended to overcompensate as a defense against their own anxiety about being religiously insensitive. In some patients, ritual was clearly used as a defense against fragmentation, such as with disorganized patients whose refusals to attend meetings were rationalized as religious obligations for prayer or study. In such cases, the task

for the therapist was to discern which patient reactions constituted culturally-appropriate attitudes as opposed to treatment resistance masquerading as religiosity.

Culture-Specific Behaviors

A notable culture-specific behavior seen in the Orthodox Jewish patient and family was that of power-brokering, centering around their relationship with the authority figure of the doctor. Deference to authority is pivotal in the dynamics of the Orthodox culture: throughout religious texts respect and obedience to parents, teachers and rabbis are emphasized. In addition, the impulse to align with authority exemplifies the worldview common in Eastern Europe, the origin of most of the Orthodox patients in our population. In those societies, normative interactions with authority was often determined by "connections" with those in power ("*protektsiya*"). In such a system, reciprocity of favors based on personal loyalty was the accepted way of circumventing an unwieldy bureaucracy. (For an example in another context, see Simic, 1974).

This operational strategy was often invoked by Orthodox family members, challenging the boundaries of milieu and the authority of the interdisciplinary team, in a kind of culture-specific form of "splitting." In particular, such families would not acknowledge the authority of our paramedical staff; when recommendations by the team were not popular with the patient or family, team members would simply be bypassed while collusion was sought with the attending psychiatrist, unit chief, or even the hospital director. When the Orthodox psychiatrist resisted such collusion in favor of supporting team decisions, he experienced countertransference feelings of resentment toward the manipulative family members, guilt for betraying their expectations, and embarassment in front of colleagues about coreligionists' exploitative behaviors. In each case. these conflicts were brought up during team meetings, in which the psychiatrist benefited from the therapeutic team discussion in terms of reality testing, team support, and strategizing.

In contrast to the relatively culture-specific behavior of power-brokering, co-dependency is a more universal issue which manifested itself in our population in culture-specific ways, e.g., the reluctance of caregivers to allow patient relatives to attend day programs, using religious rationalizations. Of the Orthodox patients who were treated on our unit, 7 out of 15 had co-dependent relationships with family members, who included parents, siblings, grandparents, and children; another 2 patients had more purely dependent relationships. All co-dependent and dependent patients were schizophrenic except one, who was diagnosed as schizoaffective, with predominant schizophrenic symptoms. In 5 our of 7 co-dependent relationships, patients continued to act in dependent and submissive ways to their authority co-dependent figures. In all instances of co-dependence among our patients, the caregiver was single, socially isolated and emotionally dependent on the patient. Rules of loyalty and honor toward parents dominated Orthodox patients' resistance to confronting these conflicts in individual therapy or allowing resolution of such conflicts in family therapy.

Conclusions

Cultural sensitivity training at SUH with respect to the Orthodox Jewish population evolved as a result of recurring issues encountered in milieu treatment and transference analysis of psychotherapy sessions under supervision by the Orthodox attending psychiatrist. In some instances, tensions arose within the milieu setting that led staff to adjust unit policies in order to achieve greater sensitivity to the cultural/religious concerns of the Orthodox patients. This training is part of a larger effort at our institution to foster sensitivity toward the multi-ethnic population we serve. For example, the Department of Psychiatry provides an 8-week course in transcultural psychiatry for first-year psychiatry residents, as well as a workshop entitled "Spirituality and Psychiatry". It would seem that similar programs should be *de rigeur* for clinical teaching centers in urban areas with culturally diverse populations or for enclaves of a particular ethnic subgroup, e.g. Orthodox Jews in Brooklyn; Hmong in California (see Fadiman, 1997).

Based on our experiences, we offer the following practical recommendations for psychiatric staff dealing with Orthodox Jewish inpatients:

1. Adjustments in unit policy may allow the patient to maintain a connection to normative Orthodox life by allowing essential religious practices, provided such rituals do not disrupt the therapeutic community or treatment of the individual patient.

2. In order to forge a therapeutic alliance, sensitivity to religious values should include respect for attitudes, dress codes and sexual sensitivities that diverge from the prevailing culture. In the case of very regressed patients, assigning a therapist of the same sex may be optional to reduce patient anxiety.

3. The therapist should exercise vigilance concerning transference/counter-transference reactions triggered by feelings of cultural alienation. Awareness of specific variants of transcultural anxiety as described above may help supervisors to recognize and contain acting out both on the part of the patient and therapist. Conflicts which center around religiously—or culturally—sensitive material should be discussed in a neutral fashion seeking

to reconcile religious and therapeutic values. However, the therapist must endeavor to avoid extending cultural sensitivity to the point of collusion with patients or families when counterproductive to treatment goals.

4. Any hospital providing inpatient psychiatric treatment to distinct cultural groups should endeavor to liaise with community representatives. For example, an Orthodox rabbi might serve not only as a spiritual mentor for patients, but also as a valuable cultural resource for clinicians, and may function as a transcultural bridge, much as a translator would be utilized in the case of language barriers. (See Trappler, *et al.*, 1995 for an instance in which a rabbinic ruling allowed psychiatrists to define the parameters of culturally reasonable ritual behavior by Orthodox OCD patients.)

In the absence of formal outcome measurements, we have so far been limited to anecdotal impressions of the effects of our interventions. Our definition of successful culturally sensitive intercessions often consisted of the resolution of individual crises in treatment that occurred around religious issues. As interventions were made in a natural clinical setting, it was not feasible to compare the results of applying cultural sensitivity to the potentially deleterious effects of withholding it. On the basis of our ongoing work in this area, however, we hope to explore the possibility of developing instruments to appraise both the effectiveness of culturally-sensitive interventions (including the outcomes of various permutations of the therapist/patient dyad) and the acquisition by trainees of competence in cultural sensitivity.

In summary, our findings suggest that modest modifications of unit policies, in conjunction with cultural sensitivity training for staff, served to render our milieu inpatient unit more conducive to effective treatment of the Orthodox Jewish patient. Although our patients were treated on a unit with abundant staff and the presence of an Orthodox psychiatrist, we believe that conscientious clinicians in other settings could apply the principles we have outlined to achieve a greater cultural sensitivity and thereby an improved therapeutic rapport with this population.

References

AMERICAN PSYCHIATRIC ASSOCIATION (1994) *Diagnostic and Statistical Manual of Mental Disorders, 4th Ed.* Washington, D.C. American Psychiatric Press.

BILU, Y. & WITZTUM, E. (1993) Working with Jewish ultra-orthodox patients: Guidelines for a culturally sensitive therapy. *Culture, Medicine & Psychiatry, 17(2)*, 197-233.

COMAS-DIAZ, L. & JACOBSEN, F.M. (1991) Ethnocultural transference and countertransference in the therapeutic dyad. *American Journal of Orthopsychiatry, 61(3)*, 392-401.

DEVEREUX, G. (1953) Cultural factors in psychoanalytic therapy. *Journal of the American Psychoanalytic Association, 1*, 629-655.

FADIMAN, A. (1997) *The Spirit Catches You and You Fall Down: A Hmong Child, Her American Doctors, & The Collision Of Two Cultures.* New York, Straus & Giroux.

GRIFFITH, M.W. (1977) The influences of race on the psychotherapeutic relationship. *Psychiatry, 40,* 2-40.

HEILMAN, S.C. & WITZTUM, E. (1994) Patients, chaperons and healers: Enlarging the therapeutic encounter. *Social Science and Medicine, 39(1),* 133-43.

MINTZ, J.R. (1992) *Hasidic People: A Place in the New World.* Cambridge. MA: Harvard University Press.

OSTROV, S. (1978) Sex therapy with Orthodox Jewish couples. *Journal of Sex and Marital Therapy, 4,* 266-278.

PARADIS, C.M., FRIEDMAN, S., HATCH, M. & ACKERMAN, R. (1997) Orthodox Jews. In *Cultural Issues in the Treatment of Anxiety* (ed. S. Friedman). New York: the Guilford Press.

ROCKMAN, H. (1993) Sex shmex—as long as you love your wife: A review of the laws and guidelines regarding sexual behavior among orthodox Jews. *Sexual and Marital Therapy, 8(3),* 255-267.

ROCKMAN, H. (1994) Matchmaker matchmaker make me a match: The art and conventions of Jewish arranged marriages. *Sexual and Marital Therapy, 9(3),* 277-284.

SIMIC, A. (1974) The best of two worlds: Serbian peasants in the city. In *Anthropologists in Cities* (eds. G.M. Foster & R. V. Kemper). Boston: Little, Brown & Co.

TICHO, G. (1971) Cultural aspects of transference and countertransference. *Bulletin of the Menninger Clinic. 35.* 313-334.

TRAPPLER, B., GREENBERG, S. & FRIEDMAN, S. (1995) Treatment of Hassidic Jewish patients in a general hospital medical-psychiatric unit. *Hospital and Community Psychiatry, 46,* 833-835.

WITZTUM, E., GREENBERG, D. & BUCHBINDER, J.T. (1990) "A very narrow bridge": Diagnosis and management of mental illness among Bratslav Hasidim. *Psychotherapy, 27(1),* 124-131.

Understanding and Treating Perfectionism In Religious Adolescents

Ben Sorotzkin

Abstract: *This article discusses issues related to understanding and treating perfectionism in religious adolescents. The author discusses the distinction between the quest for perfection and the pursuit of excellence, some of the disorders associated with perfectionism and grandiosity (e.g., narcissism, obsessive-compulsive disorders), and the underlying affects (shame, guilt). The impact of parenting on perfectionistic tendencies is discussed at length as is the influence of adolescence and of religious beliefs. The unique challenges of treating religious perfectionists and the question of the advisability of a religiously similar therapist are explored. A case example drawn from the author's clinical experience with an Orthodox-Jewish population is presented.*

This article will examine issues unique to the treatment of religious adolescents, with a focus on a problem prevalent among Orthodox-Jewish adolescents, namely perfectionism, which often leads to severe depression and other emotional disorders (Blatt, 1995). Perfectionism is also associated with obsessive-compulsive individuals who seek perfection with regard to self-control and self-restraint, and with narcissistic individuals who need to see themselves as perfect (Miller, 1996). Chronic back pain and other somatic conditions have also been attributed to the stress associated with perfectionistic tendencies (Sarno, 1998).

Perfection vs. Excellence

A perfectionist can be defined as someone who is driven by fear of failure to strive compulsively toward goals beyond reach and reason. This can be contrasted with someone who is motivated by a desire for success to strive for excellence (Hamachek, 1978). One of the characteristics that distinguishes the pathological form of perfectionism from the nonpathological striving for excellence is how the person reacts to a less-than-perfect performance.

Perfectionists not only derive no satisfaction from a less-than-perfect performance, they even experience a sense of humiliating defeat (Sorotzkin, 1985). In contrast, people who strive for excellence take pride in their effort, and derive a sense of pleasure from their superior performance even if it is less than perfect, because they accept both personal and environmental limitations (Pacht, 1984).

Parental Influence

Disapproving and Critical Parents

Parents of perfectionists tend to be nonapproving or inconsistently approving. Their love is conditional on their child's performance. In general they are overly critical and demanding. In contrast, striving for high standards and excellence is associated with parents who are positive, supportive, and encouraging and who set high standards for themselves (Blatt, 1995; Hamachek, 1978), and not just for their children.

Unrelenting overcriticalness can result in a child with deep-seated feelings of inferiority that he or she feels can only be ameliorated by feelings of grandiosity and perfection (Rothstein, 1991). The narcissistic injuries resulting from the inevitable, less-than-perfect performances and failures of grandiosity further feed the flames of inferiority feelings.

Shame

Pervasive feelings of shame often underlie the need for perfection (Sorotzkin, 1985). Miller (1996), in her insightful book on shame, invokes Broucek's (1991) concept of "objectifying," where the child is treated by the parent as an object rather than a subject. Broucek (1991) sees shame as "a response to having one's status as a subject ignored, disregarded, denied, or negated" (p. 8). He gives an example of a small child who "approaches his mother excitedly wanting to tell her about something he has just experienced. Mother looks at him and says with a frown, `Your shirttail is hanging out'" (p. 47). Miller (1996) suggests that an "objectifying" upbringing could result in an obsessive-compulsive person where "[t]he self is viewed as a collection of functions that are adequately or improperly executed and is viewed without regard for inner life as something to be recognized and valued" (p. 47).

Parents who are not attuned to their children's emotional needs (and certainly if they criticize those needs) will induce a feeling that having emotional needs is in itself shameful (Orange, Atwood, & Stolorow, 1997). This often happens in two phases. In the first, the parent hurts the child's feelings in some way. Then when the child reacts with negative emotions, he or she is criticized for the reaction (Stolorow, 1997). This can result in children who focus on their performance at the expense of their feelings (a major feature of perfectionism) and/or create a need for perfect control over feelings. It should be noted that it is the parents' general, overall attitude toward affect, coined the "parental metaemotion" by Gottman, Katz, and Hooven (1996) that is the focus of our concern rather than specific parenting styles.

What Will the Neighbors Say?

Parents of perfectionists are more likely to stress extrinsic motivations for behavior and the fear of the disapproval of others. They see themselves through the eyes of others rather than measure themselves by the yardstick of their own values and standards. Miller (1996) describes a child from such a family as one who "continually judges himself and others with a critical, outsider's eye, as if he is a thing, not a center of experiences. He seldom suspends such activity and seldom feels alive in the world. Every moment of sensation, analysis, or emotion is heavily overlaid with judgments about performance and appearances" (p. 122). This causes the individual's sense of self to be heavily dependent on the reaction of others (over which the person has little control), rather than on the person's own internal standards and values. As a result, there is a deep sense of emotional vulnerability that can induce a need for perfection as a means of avoiding this danger.

The emphasis of form over substance exhibited by parents of perfectionists was recently illustrated by a patient whose relationship with his mother had deteriorated to the point where they had not spoken to each other in weeks. As a result, he did not send her a Mother's Day card. His parents were outraged. When he tried to explain that it did not make sense to send such a card when the relationship was so negative, they could not understand his reasoning. His father kept saying, "But you know how important this is to your mother!" The message the patient got was that his parents were more concerned with the superficial appearances of the relationship than with its true nature.

Seeing Pathology Where There Is None

The perfectionistic need to have total control over feelings and behaviors often reflects viewing them out of context, thereby experiencing them as much more negative and pathological than they really are. This can also reflect early parental influences, as described by Kohut (1997):

> Parents who are not able to establish empathic contact with the developing child will . . . tend to see the constituents of the child's oedipal aspirations in isolation . . . [as] alarming sexuality and alarming hostility in the child instead of larger configurations of assertive affection and assertive competition. . . . (p. 235)

This insight has recently been confirmed by a study that found that mothers of aggressive boys were more likely to judge normal reactions of children as "noncompliance," and even more significantly, attribute defiant intent for this "noncompliance" (Strassberg, 1997).

Parental Expectations for Perfection

At times, the parental expectation for perfection is directly expressed, either by constant criticism of imperfect performance or by overt verbalizations by the parents that less than perfect is unacceptable. These children quickly learn that only by being perfect can they hope to escape the unbearable feeling of being a disappointment to their parents. There is no such thing as "that was good enough." In contrast, there are other situations when there is no overt rejection, but rather a sense of emotional neglect, perhaps as a result of the parents being wrapped up in their own emotional needs. Children from such homes will often strive for perfection in the hope that they will thus merit the interest and approval of their parents. The need for perfection, in such cases, is often experienced as internally imposed.

A less-common variation was recently illustrated by a perfectionistic religious youngster who recalled that his father was constantly praising him throughout his childhood, but for some reason it always made him uncomfortable. It was only after exploring these events and feelings in therapy that he understood that his father needed the patient's accomplishments to "feed" his own undernourished sense of self (i.e., the praise reflected the need of the parent rather than the need of the child). The patient's perfectionism was a result of his dread of being responsible for his father's psychic devastation if his son was less than perfect.

Some parents attribute their children's perfectionism to the highly competitive schools they attend. Yet, clearly, not all the students who attend these schools suffer from perfectionism. It seems more likely that highly competitive schools exacerbate perfectionistic tendencies in students from the types of homes described above.

Perfectionism And Adolescence

Research indicates (see Blatt, 1995) that perfectionism is more prevalent among adolescents because of their tendency toward idealism, and a tendency toward dichotomous thinking—black or white, saint or sinner—and that perfectionism is frequently a factor in adolescent suicide attempts. The association between perfectionism and suicide seems to be especially strong in regard to gifted adolescents. There seems to be several reasons for this. Gifted children are in fact superior to their peers in intelligence and often superior in academic achievement and other areas. This makes them more vulnerable to perfectionistic and grandiose fantasies, especially since they are often encouraged in their perfectionism by their parents and teachers. Their superior intelligence also makes it easier for them to cover up their emotional distress, since they do better academically than most of the other students even when they are unable to function at top form. The adults in their lives are often too impressed by their intelligence to pay attention to their emotional life.

The evaporation of the grandiose fantasy is likely to happen during adolescence for a number of reasons. This is often the time when youngsters begin to realize (often subconsciously) that they are living someone else's dream rather than their own life. This makes the effort to maintain their progress and accomplishments, already made difficult by the need for perfection, an unbearable burden rather than a natural process (see Omer, 1997 for an interesting case illustration). This is also the time when youngsters begin to make more of their own decisions. Perfectionistic adolescents have great difficulty with this task. There is the realistic fear that it will not be a perfect decision, since few decisions are. Likewise, many decisions are based, to a significant degree, on feelings, and perfectionistic youngsters are not sufficiently in touch with their feelings and thus are lacking an essential tool for the task of decision making.

The Impact Of Religion

Religious youngsters are encouraged to be idealistic (at least in their religious studies, if not at home), and the idealized role models whom they are taught to emulate are often presented as having always been perfect in all aspects of their lives, while the struggles and failures that they had to endure before reaching their eventual exalted level of spirituality are not acknowledged.[1] It is not surprising therefore, that, in the author's experience, perfectionism seems to be more prevalent among this segment of the population.

Religions such as Orthodox Judaism that emphasize performance and behavior over belief and attitude could be seen as providing legitimization—for those emotionally predisposed to neurotic religiosity (Spero, 1985b)—to overvalue superficial performance at the expense of emotionality, affection, and relationships. The impact of the traditional, arranged process of finding a suitable marriage partner can further overemphasize the importance of superficial and external qualities for those with such an emotional predisposition. This emphasis on superficial behavior can be distorted to the point of feeling sinful for having "normal" emotions.

As indicated above, parents of perfectionists tend to stress extrinsic motivations for behavior. In their recent comprehensive review of the literature on religion and psychotherapy, Worthington, Kurusu, McCullough, and Sandage (1996) distinguish between "intrinsically religious people" who view religion as an end in itself, and "extrinsically religious people" who view religion as a means to achieve other ends (e.g., social status, security, acceptance). Intrinsically religious people are more open to change and derive positive mental health benefits from religion, unlike extrinsically religious people who may experience negative mental health consequences from religion. Worthington et al. (1996) also cite a study by Bergin that compared religious students who develop emotional disorders with those who do not. The healthy students were likely to have benevolent parents, nonconflictual childhoods, a smooth religious developmental history, and real, nondramatic religious sentiments. In contrast, the more troubled students had conflict-laden childhoods and discontinuous religious commitment. Many experienced depression, anxiety, and rigid perfectionism. Not surprisingly then, the author's experience indicates that the parents of Orthodox-Jewish perfectionists tend to fall under the category of "extrinsically religious people."

Religious perfectionistic adolescents will often intensify their religious devotion as a reaction to emotional distress. As noted by Spero (1985b), however, "[w]hen religious belief is adopted to disguise or even resolve deeper psychological disorder, the disguise is generally transparent or the resolution only apparent and mediocre" (p. 8).

The religiously required capacity for guilt that reflects a realization that one has violated an internalized standard, and where the object of negative evaluation is the person's behavior, is often expressed as shame that reflects a negative evaluation of the self (Lewis, 1971; Tangney, 1995).[2] Such people often try to "overcome" their "defect" via perfectionism (i.e., total control over their thoughts, feelings, and behaviors).

Saint or Sinner (or Saint *and* Sinner)

The need for grandiosity and perfection prompts many perfectionists to split off or disavow those parts of themselves that they perceive as being bad or evil. These "evil" elements may, in fact, be normal feelings and reactions (e.g., jealousy) but which they have been influenced to feel are reflective of inherent inner badness. This disavowal refers to the dissociative process Kohut (1971) terms a "vertical split," where different sectors of self-experience are defensively segregated from each other as a means of avoiding intolerable conflict. The split is vertical because the dissociation is achieved via disavowal, where different, unintegrated perspectives alternate with each other, rather than by repression (a horizontal split), where a relatively permanent perspective excludes certain aspects of awareness from becoming conscious (Orange et al., 1997).

This dissociation actually helps perfectionists come closer to achieving their goal of grandiosity, since the positive aspects of their personality can operate (temporarily, of course) without the hindrance of the negative aspects. The flip side of this is that when the infantile and regressive forces do inevitably assert themselves, they do so without the moderating influence of the sequestered positive forces in their personality, resulting in more serious and extreme forms of acting out.

Since the personality is not adequately integrated, emotional growth is stunted and the infantile, shameful self can never grow up. On the other hand, since the disavowal can never be totally effective, the "good" part continues to strive for perfection and grandiosity as proof the "bad" part is "not really me."

Similarly, Broucek (1991) describes a "dissociative type" of narcissist, where the "idealized self exists in a split-off dissociative form and is often detectable in the form of a subtle air of superiority and entitlement that exists side by side with a more consciously articulated self-devaluation" (p. 60). This is why perfectionists can describe themselves, in the same sentence, as both better than everyone else and worse than everyone else (a saint and a sinner).

There is another factor that prevents the positive elements of the perfectionist's personality from moderating his or her infantile impulses. Since parents of perfectionists often react with harsh criticism to the most minor of infractions, the child is unable to distinguish between different levels of "badness." (This recalls the objections raised by some to calling every injustice a "holocaust," as it fails to distinguish between various levels of evil.) This encourages the attitude that "if I cannot be perfect I might just as well do the worst thing." I have found that those patients with obsessive-compulsive or narcissistic personality disorders, who feel compelled to be perfectly religious, are the ones who are also likely to commit what they consider the most grievous sins whenever they are no longer able to sustain their self-defined exalted status (e.g., if they cannot stop themselves from violating a "minor" sin). In their minds there is no gradation in levels of "badness."

Psychotherapy with Perfectionists

Deflated Grandiosity

Perfectionistic adolescents typically come to therapy after a breakdown in the split, usually after a blow to their feelings of grandiosity or even just a lack of mirroring (Garland & Zigler, 1993). Some patients report that the strain of maintaining perfection becomes so burdensome that they feel compelled to act out in a most negative manner as a means of jettisoning the burden. Their agenda for therapy is to turn back the clock to the time when they were able to maintain the illusion of perfection. Initially, they have little interest in emotional growth or integration of affect since they had long ago been compelled to abandon natural emotional responsiveness in favor of desirable behaviors. They are really striving to look perfect more than to be perfect since they "know" how bad they really are. But, consistent with their early life experience, how they look to others is what really counts. The need for therapy is experienced as a disgraceful narcissistic injury and the antithesis of perfection and grandiosity. Miller (1996) relates this feeling to the following imaginary childhood situation:

> [A] child . . . asks his mother, "Mom, will you go to the park with me?" and the mother's response is, "What's the matter with you? You can't go by yourself?" In other words, the wish for human com-panionship inherent in the request is not recognized and valued . . . but is reinterpreted as a deficiency with regard to autonomy. (pp. 79-80)

The author agrees with Miller (1996) who is "uncomfortable with the notion that an essential therapeutic function is the mirroring of infantile grandiosity and perfection" (p. 129). Orange et al. (1997) are also critical of the notion of mirroring defensive grandiosity. They recommend neither mirroring nor puncturing the grandiosity. Rather they suggest waiting for "opportunities to make contact with the painful affect walled off on the other side of the vertical split" (p. 82).

     While the therapist clearly has to be empathic in regard to the patient's need for perfection and infantile grandiosity,[3] the goal of therapy is to find satisfaction and meaning in the process of growth and in the everyday activities of the self. This is more difficult than it sounds since it is very painful for someone with a poor self-image to give up the dream of glory inherent in perfection for the, as yet never experienced, joy of gradual emotional growth. A crucial ingredient of successful therapy is recognizing and taking pride in every small step of progress. The difficulty this entails for the perfectionist was expressed by one youngster: "You don't understand, how can I be proud of a step toward solving my problem when I'm not yet ready to admit that I have a problem!"[4]

Perfectionistic, religious youngsters will often claim that they enjoy their religious studies and other religious activities. They are therefore mystified as to why they experience so many emotional roadblocks in these very same activities. Closer analysis, however, reveals that what they are enjoying is only the escape from feeling the shame they would have felt if they did not perform their religious duties, rather than intrinsic enjoyment from the activity itself.

Often, at the same time the therapist is encouraging the patient to feel pride in his or her small steps, the teacher or parent is making it clear that he or she is not at all impressed since the patient is so far from where he or she should be.

Performance Without the "Burden" of Emotions

The resistance to giving up grandiose goals is exacerbated by the fact that perfectionism can have a positive impact on performance (Flett, Hewitt, Blankstein, & Mosher, 1991), albeit at a high cost to emotional health (that in turn, eventually impacts negatively on performance). As religious perfectionistic patients become emotionally healthier they may seem, at least superficially, to be less religiously observant. The patients themselves may be troubled by this and their families may likewise react negatively to the therapy and therapist as a result. It is difficult for many people to see that, qualitatively, their religious observance is becoming more meaningful.

Another problem is the feeling of loss when perfectionists realize that many of the accomplishments they have been so proud of (e.g., religious activity) were the result of unhealthy, "neurotic" needs. As they become more knowledgeable about psychological issues, they may also become perfectionistic in the process of therapy, by trying to become the perfect emotional specimen (i.e., by not having any anxieties, conflicts, or fears). (Of course, therapists are also susceptible to perfectionistic tendencies that impact on the therapy [Garcia-Lawson & Lane, 1997].)

The Need for External Validation

Another goal of therapy is to develop the ability to measure oneself with internalized standards and values (religious, moral, and so on), rather than through the eyes of others. There are many difficulties to overcome in achieving this goal. The perfectionist needs the adoration of others to fill the "black hole" left by lack of early mirroring. Unlike early mirroring that encourages positive feelings about the self which is still a "blank slate," the later adoration needs to counteract an intensely experienced negative self-image. For this reason, being proud of one's own normal achievements is not enough for the perfectionist, especially since the person knows the "truth" about himself or herself. With others, in contrast, there is the hope of impressing them with a grandiose, perfect performance. The problem here, of course, is that the fix is short-lived, as the person thinks, "if they only knew the truth about me they would not be so impressed." In his comprehensive review of the literature, Blatt (1995) reports, "brief treatment, both pharmacologic or psychologic, appears to be relatively ineffective with self-critical, perfectionistic individuals . . ." (p. 1014).

Religious Therapist vs. Nonreligious Therapist

Religious patients often use their religious beliefs as a resistance (e.g., "my religion requires that I strive for perfection"). In order to deal with this resistance, therapists of the same religious background as the patient would have an obvious advantage. They would find it easier to distinguish between neurotic versus healthy religiosity (Spero, 1985b), and are more willing than secular therapists to question and explore clearly "erroneous" beliefs (Worthington et al., 1996). They are also less likely to imply that the patient's religious beliefs have only psychological meaning, an implication that religious patients are likely to experience as a narcissistic injury (Spero, 1985a). While religious people will sometimes request a nonreligious therapist because they fear being condemned by a religious therapist for what they perceive as sinful behavior, the nonjudgmental and empathic attitude of the therapist will lack the full therapeutic impact if the patient is thinking to himself or herself, "Of course the therapist accepts me, he does not even understand what's wrong with this behavior."

Perfectionistic patients, who tend to have internalized a superficial perspective, will often attribute their emotional difficulties to the restrictions imposed by their religious beliefs since many of their daily conflicts involve these restrictions. This allows them to deny the impact or even the existence of family conflict or other underlying dynamics (just as parents may blame "bad friends" and/or a "naturally overactive evil inclination" as a means of denying family problems). A religiously similar therapist who is aware of many emotionally healthy people who live with the same religious restrictions is more likely to detect the underlying dynamic issues.

But there are also distinct dangers in a religious patient being treated by a religiously similar therapist. While highly religious patients usually prefer religiously similar therapists (Wikler, 1989; Worthington et al., 1996), this preference can mask a patient's defense against full engagement in the psychotherapy process (Spero, 1990; see also Worthington et al., 1996). Transference and countertransference issues may also become exacerbated (Peteet, 1994) as the therapist hears his or her own religious beliefs being presented in a distorted manner or being attacked as the cause of the patient's emotional difficulties. There is also a risk that a therapist will so closely identify with a patient's beliefs and experiences that they are not recognized as containing psychologically significant material (see Atwood & Stolorow, 1984).

It is interesting to note that according to the research literature, even when religious patients request religiously similar therapists, they do not want the therapy to focus on religion (Worthington et al., 1996). Still, the issue of religion and religious conflict will inevitably come up with religious patients especially if they are in treatment with a religiously similar therapist. Peteet (1994) discusses four levels at which the therapist can approach religious issues, ranging from acknowledging the religious issues but focusing exclusively on their psychological dimensions, to addressing the religious problems directly within the treatment through the use of a shared religious dimension. In choosing the approach to take, Peteet emphasizes the importance of determining the need represented by the patient's presentation of a religious problem in therapy.

Discussing religious doctrine with a patient carries the danger of assuming the role of pastoral counselor and can induce strong countertransference reactions (Peteet, 1994). Yet, it also holds the opportunity to explore psychological factors contributing to idiosyncratic religious beliefs and experiences.

Case Illustration

Psychotherapy with Samuel, an 18-year-old Orthodox-Jewish youngster, underscored some of the unique issues involved in treating perfectionists in general, and religious perfectionists in particular.

Samuel was a senior at a religious residential high school who was truly living a double life. On the one hand, he excelled in all areas of school life. He possessed a superior intelligence and was a star student in both religious and secular studies. His religious teachers told him many times that they saw him as a future religious leader. In spite of the intensity of his religious studies, he was also a popular student and a successful athlete.

And yet, there was a darker side to his life. After hours of intense religious studies, he would suddenly feel compelled to go to a topless bar and act out sexually in a variety of ways. He would then feel consumed by shame and humiliation, feelings that he would try to banish by intensifying his religious studies even further. He felt like he was two people rolled into one. The fact that his public persona was at such odds with his self-image created unbearable tension and inner turmoil.

All his achievements were experienced by Samuel as meaningful only as a way of maintaining his external facade. While his successes did feed his grandiose, perfectionistic fantasies, they had no impact on his core self-concept.

The tension between the grandiose fantasies and the underlying self-devaluation was felt from the very first session. Samuel kept oscillating between convincing me how superior he was in his religious and secular studies (with the focus mostly on how highly he is held in other people's esteem) and recounting to what levels of depravity his behavior has sunk to.

As is common with perfectionists, who are not likely to view emotions as an important factor in influencing their behavior, he saw his problem as reflecting an incidental aberration in an otherwise perfect being (i.e., a naturally high level of testosterone) rather than reflecting emotional distress. His initial agenda for therapy was to get help in "controlling" his sexual impulses.

An exploration of his early years revealed a childhood growing up in a cold and loveless house. "I felt like I was a border renting a room, not like a child living with his parents." His mother was cold and distant, while his father was very critical, controlling, and often physically abusive. Being of superior intelligence, he found some measure of self-esteem by superior academic performance. He always felt that if he performed perfectly, maybe his mother would show more interest and his critical father would not have anything to criticize.

Eventually, the drive for perfection became so powerful, that an intense fear of failure (defined as anything less than perfect) developed. This fear intensified to the point of lying about his grades. If he got 90% on his test, he would tell everyone that he got 98%. As graduation time approached, he became panicky that everyone would wonder why he was not chosen to be valedictorian if he had the highest average.

The dynamics of his sexual acting out also reflected his

perfectionistic attitude. When he found that he could not control his urges to masturbate (that in part, reflected his need to escape his state of chronic tension) he felt that he "might as well" visit a prostitute ("saint or sinner" syndrome).

Samuel's need to seem perfect also affected his athletic life. While he was superior in most sports, for some reason he had never learned to play tennis. And so he lived in terror that someone would discover this terrible "deficiency." Whenever his friends wanted to play tennis he would come up with various excuses in order to avoid playing without revealing this "deep dark secret."

As the gap between his public and private image widened, Samuel became increasingly despondent and was close to suicide on a number of occasions. Yet, he remained careful not to show any signs of depression in school. When he could no longer cover up his feelings he would say that he was not feeling well and would go home for a few weeks where he would stay in bed in a severe depression. At one point he was too frightened to stay in his own room and so he slept with his parents in their bed (at the age of 17) for a few days. In spite of these obvious symptoms of depression, his parents never sought professional help for Samuel, until he took the initiative.

In therapy, Samuel was highly motivated and exhibited a capacity for psychological insights, and a therapeutic alliance was established fairly quickly.

Samuel at first found it difficult to relate to his feelings as a serious area of concern, or to relate to affect from an internal perspective. At one point he explained that the way he knows that he is not happy, is "when I realize that my face is frowning" (i.e., how he looks to others).

As he became more attuned to his feelings he came to understand how early faulty mirroring created an emotional "black hole" that could only be filled with grandiose, perfectionistic accomplishments. He also came to the conclusion that his image of God as harsh, punitive, and rejecting was more a transference from his paternal image than a reflection of his religious belief.

He began to understand the connection between emotional distress and acting out, so that he got a deeper understanding of his own behavior. In the past, he viewed his acting out simply as evil impulses that had to be overcome with sheer force. Now it was "fight smarter (i.e., to recognize the events and feeling states that precipitate his acting out), not harder."

At first, Samuel felt a profound sense of loss realizing that many of his religious accomplishments were motivated by immature emotional needs, rather than by "pure" spiritual aspirations. Fortunately, he was able to accept that emotional growth was a worthwhile goal and so he could feel a sense of accomplishment in this arena.

Initially, Samuel responded positively to my nonjudgmental attitude and unconditional positive regard, especially as I was religiously similar to him. But at some point he began to feel that, at his age, and especially from the perspective of his religious training, positive regard cannot truly be totally unconditional. I suggested that having standards and goals (religious or otherwise) could actually promote self-esteem, providing the major emphasis was internal (and not to impress others) and the goals were reasonable for his particular situation.

He came to the conclusion that emotional health was a prerequisite for healthy religiosity and this further motivated him in his therapeutic endeavors. His initial inclination, not surprising for a perfectionist, was to demand of himself to instantly become a perfect emotional specimen. He would feel humiliated if his reaction revealed any remnants of pathological needs. But as therapy progressed, he became more accepting of his humanness and so he became more reasonable with his expectations.

As his depression lifted and he became less perfectionistic, the intensity of his religious commitment, at the behavioral level, receded. This troubled him, both because this had been his sole source of positive feelings and because of his concern that he was shirking his religious duties. But here too, he began to see that while it was true that the external manifestations of his religiosity were receding, he was also acting out much less (i.e., the "split" was healing).

Another area of concern was his relations with his parents. At fast he was very hesitant to label their behavior toward him as abusive. While this is a common reaction of abused children, and a major factor in the abused becoming abusers (Briggs & Hawkins, 1996), it can be especially difficult for religious children who worry that they are violating their religious duty of honoring parents. This concern also caused Samuel to resist the thought of becoming more assertive in dealing with his parents. At his own initiative, he discussed this issue with his Rabbi who was initially very restrictive in what he felt the patient could say to his parents. When I reviewed with the patient what he told the Rabbi, it became clear (as is often the case in these situations) that Samuel had not been open as to how unreasonable his parents were toward him. When, with my encouragement, he gave his Rabbi a more honest and detailed description of his interactions with his parents, the Rabbi was very supportive of his efforts to be more assertive toward his parents.

The patient was pleasantly surprised to find that he was able to influence his parents to treat him more reasonably and their relationship improved significantly.

He became more involved in satisfying interpersonal relationships and took pride in asking friends to teach him to play tennis. He felt a sense of freedom and an unloading of a burden in not needing to project a perfectionistic image; "I can just be a plain, normal person." He decided not to pursue full-time religious studies because it was associated in his mind with grandiosity. Instead, he is continuing with parttime religious studies and volunteer work that he is finding to be more gratifying than the burden of perfectionism.

Conclusion

In recent years, clinicians have reported an increased readiness among religious people to avail themselves of psychological services (e.g., Manevitz & Barnhill, 1993). In the Orthodox-Jewish community, the change has been dramatic. Adolescents have confided to troubled friends that they themselves were in psychotherapy as a means of convincing their friends to go also, something unheard of even 10 years ago.

This has given clinicians and researchers more opportunities to understand and study the issues unique to this population and the therapeutic approaches most effective in treating religious patients. Further research is needed to ascertain if perfectionism is in fact more prevalent in the religious community, and the differences among various religious groups in this regard. Since the author's clinical experience with religious adolescents is primarily with members of the Orthodox-Jewish community, generalization to other religious groups cannot be assumed.

In treating religious perfectionists, the challenge is seen as helping them recognize and resolve the psychological issues underlying the perfectionism they exhibit in their religious life, without causing them to feel compelled to abandon the religious beliefs so central to their personal world. This can best be done by replacing the illusory grandiosity of perfection with the gratification from real, albeit modest, achievements.

Acknowledgments

The author wishes to acknowledge the encouragement and support of the members of his peer supervision group; Drs. G. Bessler, L. Bryskin, R. Shapiro, E. Weinstein, and M. Wikler—and the helpful comments of three anonymous reviewers.

Notes

1.   While biblical figures are frequently presented as flawed, the Talmudic literature emphasizes that they were considered flawed only in contrast to their exalted spiritual level. More recent religious heroes, with whom contemporary youngsters may more readily identify, are more often portrayed in perfectionistic terms.

2.   While traditional Jewish sources speak approvingly of the capacity for shame, that seems to refer to what Broucek (1991) terms "anticipatory shame" or a sense of shame that inhibits us from doing or saying something that would cause this emotion. This is contrasted with shame as an affective reaction to something already present that leads to repression and concealment, and eventually to various emotional disorders. Broucek (1991) sees the sense of shame as "vital . . . to the individual and collective, emotional, moral, and spiritual welfare" (p. 5).

3.   Most often perfectionistic patients will not spontaneously reveal their grandiose fantasies and the associated perfectionistic self-demands, both because they have never reflected on the connection between these fantasies and their symptoms ("prereftectively unconscious" [Atwood & Stolorow, 1984]), and because of the shame involved in revealing their grandiosity to others (Kohut, 1971). The grandiosity is usually uncovered in the process of trying to understand their symptoms. The severe anxiety of the social phobic, for example, is more understandable when it is realized that he or she experiences a less-than-perfect performance as a humiliating defeat.

4.   It is interesting to note that Worthington et al. (1996) discuss another category of religious motivation—"quest oriented" (that seems to be related to, and share the advantages of, the "intrinsic motivation" category), where one values the process of religious pursuit more than finding religious truth.

References

Atwood, G., & Stolorow, R. (1984). *Structures of subjectivity: Explorations in psychoanalytic phenomenology.* Hillsdale, NJ: Analytic Press.

Blatt, S. (1995). The destructiveness of perfection: Implications for the treatment of depression. *American Psychologist, 50,* 1003-1020.

Briggs, F., & Hawkins, R. M. F. (1996). A comparison of the childhood experiences of convicted male child molesters and men who were sexually abused in childhood and claimed to be nonoffenders. *Child Abuse and Neglect, 20,* 221-233.

Broucek, F. (1991). *Shame and the self.* New York: Guilford.

Flett, G., Hewitt, P., Blankstein, K., & Mosher, S. (1991). Perfectionism, self-actualization, and personal adjustment. *Journal of Social Behavior and Personality, 6,* 147-160.

Garcia-Lawson, K. A., & Lane, R. C. (1997). Thoughts on termination: Practical considerations. *Psychoanalytic Psychology, 14,* 239-257.

Garland, A. F., & Zigler, E. (1993). Adolescent suicide prevention: Current research and social policy implications. *American Psychologist, 48,* 169-182.

Gottman, J. M., Katz, L. F., & Hooven, C. (1996). Parental metaemotion philosophy and the emotional life of families: Theoretical models and preliminary data. *Journal of Family Psychology, 10,* 243-268.

Hamachek, D. E. (1978). Psychodynamics of normal and neurotic perfectionism. *Psychology, 15,* 27-33.

Kohut, H. (1971). *The analysis of the self.* New York: International Universities Press.

Kohut, H. (1997). *The restoration of the self.* New York: International Universities Press.

Lewis, H. B. (1971). *Shame and guilt in neurosis.* New York: International Universities Press.

Manevitz, A., & Barnhill, J. (1993). Treating a 38-year-old Chassidic man with delusional depression. *The Journal of Psychotherapy Practice and Research, 2,* 258-267.

Miller, S. B. (1996). *Shame in context.* Hillsdale, NJ: Analytic Press.

Omer, H. (1997). Narrative empathy. *Psychotherapy, 34,* 19-27.

Orange, D., Atwood, G., & Stolorow, R. (1997). *Working intersubjectively: Contextualism in psychoanalytic practice.* Hillsdale, NJ: Analytic Press.

Pacht, A. R. (1984). Reflections on perfection. *American Psychologist, 39,* 386-390.

Peteet, J. R. (1994). Approaching spiritual problems in psychotherapy: A conceptual framework. *The Journal of Psychotherapy Practice and Research, 3,* 237-245.

Rothstein, A. (1991). On some relationships of fantasies of perfection to the calamities of childhood. *International Journal of Psychoanalysis, 72,* 313-323.

Sarno, J. (1998). *The mindbody prescription: Healing the body, healing the pain.* New York: Warner.

Sorotzkin, B. (1985). The quest for perfection: Avoiding guilt or avoiding shame? *Psychotherapy, 22,* 564-571.

Spero, M. H. (1985a). The reality and the image of God in psychotherapy. *American Journal of Psychotherapy, 39,* 75-85.

Spero, M. H. (1985b). Selected metaclinical problems in the psychotherapeutic treatment of the disordered, religious personality. In M. H. Spero (Ed.), *Psychotherapy of the religious patient* (pp. 5-15). Springfield, IL: Charles C. Thomas.

Spero, M. H. (1990). Parallel dimensions of experience in psychoanalytic psychotherapy of the religious patient. *Psychotherapy, 27,* 53-71.

Stolorow, R. (1997). Dynamic, dyadic, intersubjective systems: An evolving paradigm for psychoanalysis. *Psychoanalytic Psychology, 14,* 337-346.

Strassberg, Z. (1997). Levels of analysis in cognitive bases of maternal disciplinary dysfunction. *Journal of Abnormal Child Psychology, 25,* 209-215.

Tangney, J. P. (1995). Recent advances in the empirical study of shame and guilt. *American Behavioral Scientist, 38,* 1132-1145.

Winkler, M. (1989). The religion of the therapist: Its meaning to Orthodox-Jewish clients. *Hillside Journal of Clinical Psychiatry, 11,* 131-146.

Worthington, E. L. Jr., Kurusu, T. A., McCullough, M. E., & Sandage, S. G. (1996). Empirical research on religion and psychotherapeutic processes and outcome: A 10-year review and research prospectus. *Psychological Bulletin, 119,* 448-487.

Of Mongrels and Jews: The Deconstruction Of Racialised Identities in White Supremacist Discourse

Abby L. Ferber

Abstract: *This research explores the construction of race and mixed race identities in a wide variety of white supremacist newsletters and periodicals published between 1969 and 1993. While traditional accounts of the white supremacist movement treat it as a movement concerned with race relations, the author reads this discourse as a site of the construction of race. In white supremacist discourse, interracial sexuality is defined as the ultimate abomination, and mixed race people pose a particularly strong threat. This paper explores ways that mixed race people, and Jews in particular, threaten the construction of a supposedly pure white racial identity. Drawing upon the insights of poststructuralism, this analysis will explore the role of boundary maintenance and the threat of border crossings in the process of constructing racial identities.*

Traditional studies of the white supremacist movement approach it as a far right movement representing white, and specifically white male, interests. The movement is defined as both racist and anti-Semitic, and viewed from a race relations approach. Journalists, historians and sociologists have attempted to explain who the members of this movement are, and what factors explain why they join, as well as documenting the activities of the movement and accounting for its increasing or decreasing power and popularity at various historical junctures and in various social contexts. It is usually taken for granted that the movement represents the interests of a segment of the white population, and espouses hatred and advocates violence against blacks, Jews, and other non-white racial groups. Racial identities are assumed and accepted as given. This research, in contrast, explores white supremacist discourse as actively constructing racial identities.

This research is part of a larger project which explores the construction of racialised, gendered identities in contemporary white supremacist discourse. Producing the illusion of racially pure identities is at the heart of the white supremacist project. I have reviewed the publications of a wide variety of white supremacist organisations published between 1969 and 1993 (for a complete list of primary sources, see reference list). While white supremacist discourses are diverse and varied, and have changed over the past thirty years responding to changes throughout society, there are certain constants within the discourse. Because white supremacist discourse is primarily concerned with constructing white identity and maintaining white privilege, the variety of white supremacist publications share an obsession with interracial relationships, perceived as the ultimate threat to that identity. This obsession has remained pervasive throughout the history of the white supremacist movement in the US and Europe, and this paper will explore precisely why this issue presents such a constant threat. I read white supremacist discourse here as ideological narratives which produce racialised identities and subjects. Not simply *about* race, this discourse *constructs* race.

Constructing Racial Essence

While white supremacist discourse adamantly supports the notion that race is a biological and/or god-given essence, a review of the discourse reveals the social construction of that essence. As Diana Fuss points out, 'there is no essence to essentialism . . . essence as irreducible has been constructed to be irreducible' (Fuss, 1989, p. 4).

Throughout white supremacist discourse, whiteness is constructed in terms of visible, physical differences in appearance. According to one article, true whites are Nordics, 'the thin, fair and symmetric race originating in Northern Europe' *(Instauration,* February 1980, p. 13). In another article, Nordics are described as

> the only cleanly chiselled faces around. And there are other ways they stand out. The world's finest hair and finest skin texture are in Scandinavia. Some of the world's tallest statures, largest body size and most massive heads are also found in Northern European regions. *(Instauration,* January 1980, p. 15)

Jews similarly are constructed as a race in this discourse, made identifiable by physical markers such as 'long kinky curls and typical hooked nose, thick fleshy lips, slant eyes and other typical Jew features' *(Thunderbolt,* no. 301, p. 6).

According to Christian Identity theology, difference is destiny—it is god-given. Non-whites, and especially blacks, are not simply different biologically or genetically from whites, they are also not considered God's children. They are defined as pre-Adamic mud people, not the offspring of Adam. As a *Thunderbolt* article claims, 'the coloured and mongrelised races do not have God's Spirit and cannot be accepted . . . [we] cannot change God's laws' *(Thunderbolt,* January 1974, p. 10).

Eschewing religion, other publications provide an evolutionary perspective. An article in *Instauration* entitled 'Evolution vs Integration' emphasises this, explaining,

> the Negro brain is only 10.6 per cent smaller than a white's. But in regard to the more recently attained capacity for abstract and rational thought, the gap is much larger . . . There is no underlying unity upon which to build or maintain a functioning social matrix. Despite all attempts to integrate them, the five races of mankind are still following Coon's separate lines of biological and historical evolution. *(Instauration,* January 1980, p. 21)

This article suggests that any attempt to integrate the races runs counter to the natural course of evolution, and is bound to fail. Genetic difference, and evolution as the path of increasing differentiation, are constructed as rooted in nature, thereby also reifying inequality as a natural, permanent fact of life.

A great deal of effort is put into physically distinguishing races from one another. Both the book and film that go by the name *Blood in the Face* take their name from some white supremacists' supposition that Jews cannot blush and only true whites show 'blood in the face' (Ridgeway, 1992). Rather than revealing race as a biological essence, this discourse reveals the continued effort required to construct racial differences. Judith Butler suggests that identities are constructed through 'the reiterative and citational practice by which discourse produces the effects that it names' (Butler, 1993, p. 2). The construction of identity is not a singular act or gesture, but rather, a process which must be continually repeated 'in order to establish the illusion of its own uniformity and identity' (Butler, 1991, p. 24).

Ironically, this process of reiteration which constructs racial difference also reveals the construction of these identities, thereby putting this

> identity permanently at risk . . . That there is a need for repetition at all is a sign that identity is not self-identical. It requires to be instituted again and again, which is to say that it runs the risk of becoming *de*-instituted at every interval. (Butler, 1991, p. 24)

As we find in white supremacist discourse, even though racial identity is posited as a biological or god-given fact of nature, a tremendous amount of effort is put into defining them.

While a great amount of written space is devoted to delineating physical racial differences, these physical differences are always interpreted as signifying deeper, underlying differences. Physical differences produce the illusion of an inner racial essence. This racial essence is represented as immutable. As an *NSV Report* article about Jews claims,

> We fight for things that they cannot understand because of their nature; and because of their nature, they can never understand because they are aliens. Even if they changed their religion, they will not be a part of our Folk. They can never be a part of our Folk for they are aliens. They might as well be from another planet because they are not of our world. *(NSV Report* October/ December 1987, p. 1)

Constructing the illusion of a racially pure white identity is central to the white supremacist project. It is not surprising, then, that mixed-race people serve as a powerful threat to the maintenance of racial purity. Interracial sexuality is referred to as the 'ultimate abomination' (Ridgeway, 1990, p. 90) and white supremacist discourse is obsessed with miscegenation. In *Bodies That Matter*, Judith Butler contends that this threat is central to the construction of subjects. Butler suggests that the central point of deconstruction, often missed in social constructivist analyses, is that the construction of subjects simultaneously produces abjected identities.

> Hence, it is not enough to claim that human subjects are constructed, for the construction of the human is a differential operation that produces the more and the less 'human', the inhuman, the humanly unthinkable. These excluded sites come to bound the 'human' as its constitutive outside, and to haunt those boundaries as the persistent possibility of their disruption and rearticulation. (Butler, 1993, p. 8)

Gender and race are not identities imposed upon bodies, but, rather, bodies only become culturally intelligible as they become gendered and racialised. The heterosexual imperative produces as subjects those who conform to the gendered norms of cultural intelligibility. At the same time, this regulation produces a domain of abjection, a realm of the culturally unintelligible. As Butler points out, it is

> important to recognise that oppression works not merely through acts of overt prohibition, but covertly, through the constitution of viable subjects and through the corollary constitution of a domain of unviable (un)subjects—abjects, we might call them . . . Here oppression works through the production of a domain of unthinkability and unnameability. (Butler, 1991, p. 20)

The assumption of properly gendered identities occurs in relation to this realm of the abject. The regulation of heterosexuality constructs gendered subjects, and identification always takes place against a corresponding threat of punishment, yet the production of subjects is frequently constrained not only by the regulation of heterosexuality, but by other regulatory regimes as well. Exploring white supremacist discourse, the regulation of interracial sexuality emerges as central.

While Butler demonstrates the production of culturally intelligible gender identities, and the simultaneous production of a realm of abjection, Omi and Winant suggest that there is a similar process at work in the production of coherent racial identities. They point out that

> one of the first things we notice about people when we meet them ... is their race. We utilise race to provide clues about who a person is. This fact is made painfully obvious when we encounter someone whom we cannot conveniently racially categorise—someone who is, for example, racially 'mixed' or of an ethnic/racial group with which we are not familiar. Such an encounter becomes a source of discomfort and momentarily a crisis of racial meaning. Without a racial identity, one is in danger of having no identity. (Omi and Winant, 1986, p. 62)

Racialised identities govern our notions of culturally intelligible humans. As Omi and Winant here suggests, the production of coherent racial identities, like the production of coherent gender identities, requires the simultaneous production of 'unviable (un)subjects' (Butler, 1991, p. 20). Informed by this theory, my research explores the regulation of heterosexual and 'racially pure' sexuality in white supremacist discourse, where the production of culturally intelligible racialised identities at the same time relegates mongrels and Jews to the realm of the inhuman.

Mongrels: Border Crossings

The production of racialised subjects requires the corresponding threat of punishment, and throughout this discourse that threat plays a central role as it is reiterated over and over. The subject must repeatedly disassociate itself from the abject to construct itself as a subject.

> It is this repeated repudiation by which the subject installs its boundary and constructs the claim to its 'integrity' . . . This is not a buried identification that is left behind in a forgotten past, but an identification that must be levelled and buried again and again, the

compulsive repudiation by which the subject incessantly sustains
his/her boundary . . . subject-positions are produced in and through a
logic of repudiation and abjection. (Butler, 1993, p. 114)

The figures of abjection, then, are essential to the production of racialised subjects. The construction of stable racial identities can only occur in relation to the production and regulation of the 'impure'.

It is through the construction and maintenance of racial boundaries and the demarcation of 'whiteness' as a racially pure identity that the white subject is constructed. For white supremacists, the construction of racial purity requires a policing of the racial borders. The construction of distinct races requires border maintenance and interracial sexuality is the greatest threat to this maintenance.

Poststructuralism has highlighted the importance of paying attention to boundaries and the role of borders in constructing coherent conceptual categories. The meaning of any identity is derived from its relationship with its binary opposite. However, binary oppositions conceal the interdependence of the two terms; the two terms depend upon each other for meaning. Additionally, as Jacques Derrida points out, this relationship is hierarchical, one side of the opposition is always constructed as more important, primary or originary than the other (Derrida, 1976; Scott, 1988). Blackness, for example, as long as it is carefully separated and subordinated to whiteness, poses no threat to the existence of a white identity; in fact, blackness is necessary to the definition of whiteness. While blacks are the focus of a tremendous amount of attention in white supremacist discourse, they are primarily constructed as a threat to white identity, privilege and safety. White supremacist discourse argues that blackness must be carefully bounded and controlled; the threat must be neutralised. The discourse presents the possibility of white and black co-existence as long as the races are geographically separated. Separation and the maintenance of racial boundaries are the key. It is precisely for this reason that mixed race people pose such a great threat. Those who are mixed race threaten the white/black binary; they signify the instability of that opposition. While those who are discovered to be mixed race are actually legally defined as black in the US, they nevertheless represent a particularly strong threat to the construction of racial identity based on the illusion of white racial purity. Mixed race people signal the instability and permeability of racial boundaries, and threaten the construction of racial identity as a natural, inherent essence.

If subjects only become culturally intelligible in this discourse as they become racialised, mixed race people cannot be granted subject status; they symbolise the realm of the unlivable. It is in relation to this realm of the unlivable, and through the maintenance of racial boundaries, that white subjects are produced and their identity is secured. They become visible, racialised subjects through the abjection of the impure. The realm of the abject, however, haunts the subject 'as the spectre of its own impossibility, the very limit to intelligibility, its constitutive outside' (Butler, 1993, pp. xi-xii).

Throughout this discourse, mixed race individuals serve as figures of racial punishment, figures of abjection. 'Mongrels' do not meet the racialised norms of cultural intelligibility 'which qualifies a body for life within the domain of cultural intelligibility' (Butler, 1993, p. 2). For example, in *The Turner Diaries,* a widely read white supremacist utopian novel which served as a model for the Oklahoma City bombing, readers are warned,

> The enemy we are fighting fully intends to destroy the racial basis of our existence. No excuse for our failure will have any meaning, for there will be only a swarming horde of indifferent, mulatto zombies to hear it. There will be no White men to remember us. (Macdonald, 1978, p. 2)

Not only is race at stake then, but what it means to be human, as well. As Omi and Winant and Butler have suggested, the construction of human subjects occurs through the construction and regulation of intelligible racial and gender identities. Macdonald suggests that there will be no humans left, only what are referred to as 'mulatto zombies'. Without a stable racial identity, one can have no human identity in this discourse. As Butler explains,

> the 'coherence' and 'continuity' of 'the person' are not logical or analytic features of personhood, but, rather, socially instituted and maintained norms of intelligibility . . . the very notion of 'the person' is called into question by the cultural emergence of those 'incoherent' . . . beings who appear to be persons but who fail to conform to the gendered [and racialised] norms of cultural intelligibility by which persons are defined. (Butler, 1990, p. 17)

An article in the *New Order* describes mixed race individuals as:

> Malformed pieces of humanity sporting a combination of woolly negroid hair, white complexion and slanted mongol eyes. They call themselves 'black people', but they are neither black, white or yellow, but all and none of these races. These are the children of integration. They have no culture, no common heritage, no identity and no pride. What would you call them? Half-castes? Hybrids? Monsters? *(New Order,* September 1979, p. 7)

They are defined as defective, degenerate, monster-like; once again their humanity is put in question. Similarly, articles in *White Power* refer to them as 'mongrel monstrosities' *(White Power,* February 1973, p. 3). Interracial sexuality is constructed as a threat to both racial and human identity, producing instead *incoherent* beings, 'brown zombies'.

As we saw earlier, racial identity not only is posited as determining physical characteristics, but personality, behaviour, culture and national identity. Mixed race people, then, are not only distinguished by physical characteristics, but are defined as 'negroidal mongrels who on their own could not build a pyramid or modern city' *(Thunderbolt,* August 1979, p. 9). Elsewhere we are told that 'a mulatto or mongrel race is a shiftless, lazy, mindless, leaderless and slave-like race which must have a racial superior 'boss-man' to tell them what to do' *(Thunderbolt,* no. 297, p. 3). In stark contrast to the repeated celebrations of the accomplishments of the white race, white supremacist discourse suggests that mixed race people are inhuman, incapable of surviving on their own, incapable of creating anything worthwhile.

In order to exist as a culturally intelligible being, one must be racialised. To have no pure race makes living impossible—'mongrels' occupy the site of impossibility and unlivability. As *New Order* articles warn, interracial sexuality will result in a 'race-mixed and totally dead America' *(New Order,* March 1979, p. 8), 'a fate worse than death . . . is what mongrelisation is all about. It is a living death' *(New Order* Spring, 1982, p. 2).

Mixed race individuals are denied subject-status in this discourse, and they are perceived as a particularly strong threat to the racial identity of whites. The realm of the abject, to which mixed race people have been relegated, 'bound[s] the 'human' as its constitutive outside, and . . . haunt[s] those boundaries as the persistent possibility of their disruption and rearticulation' (Butler, 1993, p. 8). If white identity is dependent upon racially pure reproduction, and its place on one side of the binary opposition of white/black, it is essential for white supremacists to be able to recognise who is white and who is not. *Their own identity depends upon it.* While race is constructed through the reiteration of physical differences which are visible and knowable, the existence of mixed race individuals is represented as a threat to this surety. In a *National Vanguard* article entitled 'Beware the Almost Whites!' readers are warned that interracial sexuality produces

> a continuous range of mongrels between the two racial extremes. Near the White end of the spectrum there will be some who . . . will be almost indistinguishable from the true Aryans. Drawing the line between what is Aryan and what is not becomes more and more difficult. *(National Vanguard,* August 1979, p. 5)

As a *New Order* article explains, 'The 'murder by miscegenation' device works all too well when 'almost Whites' can gain acceptance when a nigger cannot'

(New Order, March 1979, p. 2). The existence of 'almost whites' poses a threat to the constructed surety of racial identity and symbolises the insecurity and permeability of racial boundaries, threatening the possibility of racially pure reproduction and racially pure identities.

In white supremacist discourse, mongrelisation is depicted as leading to the genocide of the white race. A typical article describes it as 'the genocide of the White race by irreversible downbreeding with a hopelessly inferior race' *(White Power,* March 1972, p. 4). A *National Socialist White People's Party* recruitment flyer warns, 'race-mixing and integration mean White genocide'. Mongrelisation is equated with genocide, the extermination of a race of people, because it means the loss of the illusion of white racial purity. As an article in the *Thunderbolt* explains,

> Mongrelisation is the worst form of 'genocide'. If you kill 99 per cent of a race, but leave the other 1 per cent pureblooded, they will in time restore the race; but when you mongrelise them, you have destroyed that race eternally. Once mixed with the Black or Yellow Races, the White Race would be totally and forever destroyed. *(Thunderbolt,* 25 April 1975, p. 10)

Another article asserts,

> any large scale intermarriage . . . would mean the . . . abolition of the White Race. We would simply cease to exist in the world of the future . . . A race once polluted with the decadent genes of the lower, backward, and underdeveloped races of the world is lost forever. *(Thunderbolt, 30* May 1975, p. 8).

Intermarriage is considered even deadlier than outright war because

> even a global war in which the Jews were victorious, would leave a few Whites to breed back the race. Their final solution is MONGRELISATION. A mongrel can only breed more mongrels. *(Thunderbolt,* January 1974, p. 10)

Similarly, a *New Order* article asserts, 'there is one sure way of killing a nation —to destroy or to fatally dilute the blood of its creators' *(New Order* March 1979, p. 2).

Mongrelisation becomes synonymous with genocide in this discourse. If subjects only become living, viable subjects as they become racialised, mongrelisation, then, is death—the destruction of life. Interracial sexuality is depicted as threatening to erase racial differences and identity and the actual continued existence of the white race and humanity. Regulations prohibiting interracial sexuality actually serve to consolidate racial identities, and any transgression of the boundaries threatens to destroy this identity.

The Jew: Boundary Mediator and Destroyer

White supremacist discourse presents a range of racial enemies: blacks are constructed as a threat if not thoroughly separated from whites. Mixed race people, the product of racial intermixture between whites and non-whites, but blacks especially, are a threat because they symbolise the breakdown of the borders separating whites from non-whites. Jews, however, are constructed as the ultimate enemy, the very source of the breakdown of these racial borders. According to the *New Order,*

> The single serious enemy facing the White man is the Jew. The Jews are not a religion, they are an Asiatic *race,* locked in mortal conflict with Aryan man which has lasted for millennia, and which will continue until one of the two combat peoples is extinct. *(The New Order,* March 1979, p. 3)

As the *Thunderbolt* proclaims, it is a 'WAR of EXTERMINATION—God's seed against Satan's seed. ONLY ONE WILL SURVIVE' *(Thunderbolt,* January 1974, p. 10). Jews are racialised in this discourse, and defined as a biologically distinct race. However, according to Christian Identity theology, subscribed to by a number of the publications reviewed here, Jews are not simply different genetically and biologically, but are depicted as the children of Satan rather than God.

The Identity Church movement was first recognised as a strong presence within the white supremacist movement in the 1970s and early 1980s. The racist and anti-Semitic Identity doctrine provides the theological underpinnings for a variety of white supremacist organisations, and links various groups together.

Identity doctrine has its foundations in British Israelism, with origins in Great Britain in the mid-1800s (Zeskind, 1986). Based on an 'idiosyncratic reading' of the Bible, British Israelism holds that the people of Israel settled in Northern Europe before the Christian era. According to the Bible, ancient Israel was divided into two kingdoms: the Northern portion consisted of ten of the twelve tribes descended from Jacob, and when the area was conquered the ten tribes were lost. The Jews of today are supposedly descendants of the Southern kingdom, but according to Identity belief:

characteristics of the racial type we recognise as that of the Jews today were the result of intermarriages in the days of Ezra and Nehemiah. At that time a mutation of the blood stream occurred . . . (which was) . . . a defection from God's will. (Zeskind, 1986, p. 196)

This racialisation of biblical beliefs recasts the ancient Hebrews as a race, whose descendants today are the Aryans, and recasts Jews as the product of race mixing.

Theologians in the US have contributed to Identity doctrine, adding the 'two seed' theory (Ridgeway, 1990, p. 54). US Identity doctrine holds that there were two creations: the first was the male and female created in Genesis 1: 26-27, and the second was the creation of Adam and Eve in Genesis 2: 2-6. These two accounts supposedly produced two separate races. Adam is the ancestor of the Caucasian race today, and the other male and female produced the pre-Adamic 'mud people', people without souls, defined as today's blacks and other non-Jewish non-whites. According to Identity doctrine, Satan seduced Eve, and then Eve introduced sexual intercourse to Adam. So Eve was impregnated with two seeds, Satan's evil seed, producing Cain, and God's, producing Abel. When Cain, the evil one, was cast out of Eden, he supposedly married a pre-Adamic woman, producing the Jewish race. According to this account, Jews are not only the children of Satan, but once again the product of racial intermixture (Aho, 1990; Anti-Defamation League, 1988b).

As explained in an article in the *Thunderbolt* entitled 'Satan's Children vs God's Children', when Cain was cast out of Eden he married an Asiatic woman.

His offspring continued mixing with Asiatics, many of whom had previously mongrelised with Negroes, and they continued this miscegenation down through the years. This Cainite line had Satan's spirit, not God's . . . The genetic function of their existence is to do the works of their father (Satan) by destroying the White Adamic Race . . . This Cainite race (if you can call mongrels a race) became the people, who today, are known as JEWS . . . over 80 per cent of today's Jews are descendants of the Khazars, who were . . . of Turk-Mongol blood mixed with White Europeans. *(Thunderbolt,* January 1974, p. 10)

As these accounts demonstrate, Christian Identity theology defines Jews not merely as a separate race, but an impure race, the product of mongrelisation.

Jews, then, occupy the abject site of mongrelisation and symbolise all that goes along with that designation. The position of Jews is ambiguous throughout this discourse because while Jews are defined as mongrels, they are also produced discursively as a distinctive race in a way that mongrels more generally are not. Mixed race people pose a threat because they symbolise racelessness and the breakdown of racial identity, and hence, humanity. Jews, however, are defined as mixed race, and so raceless. This state of racelessness becomes their racial essence. It is their essence to attack and destroy pure racial identities. Additionally, it is often emphasised that Jews today do not allow intermarriage for themselves. For example, a *Thunderbolt* article explains that

> they are advocating [interracial sexuality] for White Christians and members of the colored races but not for members of the Jew race . . . They have long realised that the fusion of all the other races (while maintaining the purity of the Jew race) will produce a race of mongrels more subservient to their domination. *(Thunderbolt,* no. 297, p. 3)

Curiously, then, Jews are defined as simultaneously mongrels and a pure race. Jews are produced as a race whose central racial identity is impurity, mongrelisation, mixture. The pure essence or racial core of the Jew represents all that is antithetical to the meaning of a healthy race. Racial identity is predicated upon an imagined purity, and the existence of Jews is a threat because their racial identity represents impurity, chaos, boundary transgressions. It is for this reason that geographical segregation is acceptable for all other races, but Jews must be exterminated. The existence of Jews is a threat, and so every last Jew must be exterminated to secure white existence.

In *Modernity and the Holocaust,* Zygmunt Bauman suggests that Jews have traditionally been assigned the role of transgressors:

> The conceptual Jew was a semantically overloaded entity, comprising and blending meanings which ought to be kept apart, and for this reason a natural adversary of any force concerned with drawing borderlines and keeping them watertight. The conceptual Jew was *visquex* (in Sartrean terms), slimy (in Mary Douglas's terms)—an image construed as compromising and defying the order of things, as the very epitome and embodiment of such defiance. (Bauman, 1989, p. 39)

While the essence and core of the Jew is constructed as symbolising this site of impossibility and chaos, the behaviour of Jews is described as an extension of that position. Race-mixing and interracial sexuality, the severest threat to the existence of a white racial identity, is posited as a result of Jews. Almost every discussion of race-mixing, whether it is school bussing, or intermarriage, attributes it to Jews. A multitude of articles found throughout all of the various periodicals attempts to demonstrate that Jews are responsible for integration and race-mixing. For example, *Thunderbolt* has published articles with titles like 'Jewish Leaders Supporting Race-Mixing', 'Jews Finance Race-Mixing Case', 'Jewish Organisations Back Interracial Marriage', and 'Why Do Jews Support Race-Mixing?' *(Thunderbolt,* no. 297, pp. 1, 3). According to the *NSV Report,* Aryans are facing 'organised mutiny of biologically inferior people, led by the Jews against the White race' *(NSV Report,* April/June 1983, p. 5).

Mongrels and Jews, then, are constructed differently as threats. While mongrels represent the possibility of racelessness and inhumanity, it is the Jews who are depicted as encouraging and speeding along the process of mongrelisation between whites and blacks. The essence of the Jew is produced as an inherent threat to racial purity. Separation of the races is the end goal for the wide range of white supremacist groups. Geographical apartheid is presented as the only way to guarantee racial purity and prevent the threat of racial mixing. For example, an *Instauration* article warns,

> It is not black power that we need to fear. We should fear black coexistence in the same living space . . . once our race is gone because of integration with blacks, we are done. *(Instauration,* April 1980, pp. 13-14)

Because Jews come to embody impurity and border crossings, throughout this discourse the presence of the Jew is defined as the roadblock to racial segregation. For example, a *White Power* article demonstrates the role attributed to Jews consistently throughout this discourse:

> Now that the busses are rolling on their genocidal journey of bringing White and Negro children forcibly together in the schools, our Jew-dominated government is moving relentlessly on to the next step: forced mixing of the races in housing . . . to carry out the lunatic program of interbreeding. *(White Power,* March 1972, p. 3)

While whites fear mixing with blacks, it is assumed that if Jews were out of the picture, separation of blacks and whites would be assured. Blacks are frequently depicted as stupid and animal-like, merely following the lead of the Jews, and without the Jews it is believed that blacks would no longer demand equality and integration. For example, a *New Order* article suggests that without the prodding of Jews and white liberals,

> what happens to the negro? [He] clumsily shuffles off, scratching his woolly head, to search for shoebrush and mop. In the final debate, an ape will always be an ape. *(New Order,* September 1979, p. 14)

Instauration articles explain that the Jew serves as the mediator between non-Jewish groups. A book entitled *The Mediator,* by Richard Swartzbaugh, is published by the press which publishes *Instauration,* and *Instauration* articles frequently discuss this book, referred to as an 'underground classic'. Swartzbaugh

> shows how this mediating role becomes a necessity in cases where mutually antagonistic groups are to be found within the same living space and where some sort of accommodation is desired. That is why the Jews have always done their best artificially to create such situations (i.e., by breaking down American and British immigration bars). *(Instauration* April 1979, p. 28)

This work suggests that Jews encourage, benefit from, and thrive on the breakdown of racial boundaries. Once again, this is seen as rooted in Jewish nature—it is part of their racial essence. As an NSV *Report* article explains,

> It is the Jews who are the purveyors of death! Jews are a very negative people. They cannot help it. It is their racial personality. They will destroy your nation, race, culture, civilisation, family and whatever you value. *(NSV Report,* January/March 1989, p. 1)

Jews are constructed as a race which by nature disrupts and destroys.

This discourse suggests that racial boundaries and the separation of races are natural, but the Jew, who symbolises and embodies the unnatural, the chaotic, disrupts the natural order of separation and white superiority. As a *Thunderbolt* article explains, 'When misled liberals and Jews constantly tell negroes that they are equal to (or better) than Whites, hatred and violence erupts when they are unable to compete' *(Thunderbolt,* August 1979, p. 8).

Jews are depicted as controlling many facets of US society, ranging from the media to the banking and finance industries, and they are depicted as using their position to increase interracial sexuality. For example, a *White Power* article entitled 'Race-Mixing in the Movies' asserts that Hollywood and the motion picture industry were created by, and are controlled by, Jews who

> have taken a leading position as a promoter of race-mixing and miscegenation . . . This medium is now being systematically used to undermine our Aryan values and destroy our White identity. *(White Power,* June/July 1969, p. 3)

Another article suggests that the 'Jew controlled media' are brainwashing children and teenagers into accepting interracial sexuality and homosexuality so that

> White kids see miscegenation and homosexuality portrayed as the 'in' thing, and anyone who opposes this sort of filth is castigated as a 'racist' or a 'prude'. *(White Power,* February 1973, p. 3)

The feminist movement is also considered part of the Jewish plan to divide and mongrelise the white race. Jews are considered the driving force behind feminism, 'never less than a third of the leadership of feminist organisations' *(National Vanguard,* January 1983, p. 17). Similarly, a *White Power* article confirms that

> the 'Women's Movement' which evolved out of the social turmoil of the 1960s had a distinctly Jewish approach and leadership . . . . they seem to be less interested in securing equal rights for women than in turning men and women into unnatural rivals, each struggling against the other for supremacy instead of working together. *(White Power,* no. 105, p. 4)

Jews are assumed to be behind all equality movements, whether for racial or gender equality, because it is defined as inherent in Jewish nature to disrupt and threaten difference. The Jew represents the destruction of borders, threatening the very existence of racial identities. As Bauman suggests,

> the conceptual Jew performed a function of prime importance; he visualised the horrifying consequences of boundary-transgression . . . *The conceptual Jew carried a message; alternative to this order here and now is not another order, but chaos and devastation.* (Bauman, 1989, p. 39)

The breakdown of natural racial boundaries is depicted as leading inevitably to interracial sexuality, part of the Jewish plan to exterminate the white race. If interracial sexuality is depicted as a form of genocide, then it must be Jews who are behind it. According to the *NSV Report,* 'Jewish parasites . . . race-mix our people into oblivion' *(NSV Report,* October /December 1988, p. 2). The end goal of what is constructed as the Jewish plan of promoting interracial sexuality is white genocide and world domination. A *Thunderbolt* article proclaims

> They hope that our seed will vanish into the Jewish contrived 'melting pot' with the negroes, Puerto Ricans, Asians and Mexicans in order to create a brown skinned non-White world of the future. The Jews are waging a fierce battle to stop intermarriage within their own race. If the Jews are the last race able to retain their own racial identity they will be able to use their money power to control any mentally dulled race of mongrelised zombies that might eventually be the majority. *(Thunderbolt,* January 1974, p. 7)

According to a *White Power* article entitled 'Jews Planning White Genocide', 'world Jewry's chilling Final Solution [is] the physical and spiritual genocide of the White race they despise' *(White Power,* February 1973, p. 3).

Conclusion

The construction of white racial identity, and the maintenance of white privilege, is the central project of the contemporary white supremacist movement. The construction and maintenance of racial boundaries is essential to the production of white identity in white supremacist discourse. Purity is central to the definition of racial identity, and the construction of racially pure identities simultaneously produces the threat of miscegenation. Within this discourse, mongrels and Jews pose a threat to the construction of white racial identity because they symbolise the permeability of racial boundaries and the threat of boundary transgressions. Mongrels and Jews become the embodiment of this threat and serve as images of boundary confusion and chaos. The production of racialised subjects occurs through the maintenance of racial boundaries, and each of these figures in some way disrupts, threatens, or transgresses the boundaries which are essential to the production of the white subject.

The production of intelligible racial subjects simultaneously produces a range of unintelligible un-subjects. Within contemporary white supremacist discourse, mongrels and Jews are defined as inhuman monsters. They form the constitutive outside against which the coherent subject is constructed. The regulation of interracial sexuality, then, is a continuous effort at boundary maintenance, producing racialised subjects as well as improper non-subjects: Mongrels and Jews serve as figures of racial punishment: the threat of impurity. They are accordingly denied subject status. As Butler has asserted, it is essential that we explore not only the construction of human subjects, but those simultaneously *not* constructed as human. The racialised subject is produced in white supremacist discourse over and against the improperly racialised, the inhuman, the culturally unintelligible.

More than merely a discourse about race relations, this article demonstrates the active production of racial identity within the discourse. If, as contemporary theory asserts, race is a social construction, we cannot take racial classifications for granted in our analyses. Instead, we must explore the varied processes and sites of its ongoing construction.

Acknowledgments

This research has been supported by grants from the Center for the Study of Women in Society and the Humanities Center at the University of Oregon, Eugene, Oregon. 1 thank Linda Fuller, Miriam Johnson, Sandra Morgen, Forrest Pyle, Joel Pollack, David Theo Goldberg and the anonymous reviewers for their insights and encouragement.

References

Aho, J.A. (1990) *The Politics of Righteousness: Idaho Christian Patriotism*, Seattle: University of Washington Press.

The Anti-Defamation League of B'nai B'rith (1988a) *Extremism on the Right: A Handbook*, New York.

— (1988b) *Hate Groups in America: A Record of Bigotry and Violence*, New York.

Bauman, Z. (1989) *Modernity and the Holocaust*, Ithaca: Cornell University Press.

Butler, J. (1990) *Gender Trouble: Feminism and the Subversion of Identity*, New York: Routledge.

— (1993) *Bodies That Matter: On the Discursive Limits of Sex*, New York: Routledge.

Derrida, J. (1974) *Of Grammatology*, translated by G.C. Spivak, Baltimore: Johns Hopkins University Press.

— (1982) *Margins of Philosophy*, translated by A. Bass. Chicago: University of Chicago Press.

Ferber, A.L. (1995a) 'Exploring the Social Construction of Race: Social Science Research and the Study of Interracial Relationships', in N. Zack (ed.), *American Mixed Race: Exploring 'Microdiversity'*, Rowman and Littlefield Press.

— (1995b) ''Shame of White Men': Interracial Sexuality and the Construction of White Masculinity in Contemporary White Supremacist Discourse', *Masculinities*, Summer.

Fuss, D. (1989) *Essentially Speaking: Feminism, Nature and Difference*, New York: Routledge.

Macdonald, A. (1978) *The Turner Diaries*, Hillsboro, Virginia: National Vanguard Books.

Morrison, T. (1992) *Playing in the Dark: Whiteness and the Literary Imagination*, New York: Vintage Books.

Omi, M. (1991) 'Shifting the Blame: Racial Ideology and Politics in the Post-Civil Rights Era', *Critical Sociology* 18 (3): 77- 98.

Omi, M. and H. Winant (1986) *Racial Formation in the United States: From the 1960s to the 1980s*, New York: Routledge.

Ridgeway, J. (1990) *Blood in the Face*, New York: Thunder's Mouth Press.

Scott, J. (1988) 'Deconstructing Equality-Versus-Difference: Or, the Uses of Poststructuralist Theory for Feminism', *Feminist Studies*, 14 (1, Spring): 33-50.

Young, I.M. (1990) 'The Ideal of Community and the Politics of Difference', in L. J. Nicholson (ed.), *Feminism/Postmodernism*, New York: Routledge.

Zeskind, L. (1986) *The 'Christian Identity' Movement*, Atlanta: Center for Democratic Renewal, Published by the Division of Church and Society of the National Council of the Churches of Christ in the USA.

Primary Sources

The following periodicals were reviewed for the years listed:

1. *Instauration* (1976-83): 'seemingly intellectual', racist and anti-Semitic magazine published by Howard Allen Enterprises, Inc., in Cape Canaveral, FL. *Instauration is* edited by Wilmot Robertson but little is known about this corporation. John Tyndall, leader of Great Britain's neo-fascist National Front, has called *Instauration* 'a highly articulate and stimulating monthly ... enjoying growing popularity among ... the National Front' (Anti-Defamation League, 1988a: 152).

2. *The National Alliance Bulletin* (1978-80), and

3. *National Vanguard* (1978-84): both periodicals are published by the National Alliance, in Mill Point, WV, a Neo-Nazi group headed by William Pierce and founded in 1970. The National Alliance originated from the Youth for Wallace campaign in 1968, run by Willis A. Carto, but split from Carto in 1970 and became the National Alliance, run by former members of George Lincoln Rockwell's American Nazi Party.

4. *The New Order* (1979-83): published by Gerhard Lauck, in Lincoln, NE. Lauck heads the neo-Nazi National Socialist German Workers Party (known overseas as NSDAP-AO). 'The NSDAP-AO's circulation is so widespread that it allegedly is recognised by the West German government as the primary source of propaganda materials to [their] underground' (Klanwatch Intelligence Report, 1993: 8). *The New Order* is widely read and distributed by various white supremacist groups because 'membership and distribution materials are easy to obtain' (Klanwatch Intelligence Report, 1993: 9).

5. *N S Bulletin* (1974-83), and

6. *White Power* (1969-78): both periodicals are published by the National Socialist White People's Party, which changed its name to the New Order in 1982. This organisation is headed by Matt Koehl, with headquarters in Arlington, VA, and later New Berlin, WI. This organisation is the direct descendant of the original neo-Nazi organisation in the US, the American Nazi Party.

7. *The NSV Report* (1983-93): quarterly newsletter of the National Socialist Vanguard, started in 1983, and headed by neo-Nazi Rick Cooper and Dan Stewart, former National Socialist White People's Party member. This group has closely aligned itself with the Church of Jesus Christ Christian Aryan Nations, a Christian Identity church, in Coeur d'Alene, Idaho.

8. *The Thunderbolt* (1974-84): published by the National States Rights Party (NSRP), founded in 1958, and edited by J.B. Stoner and Edward Fields, 'among the most extreme anti-black, anti-semitic hatemongers in the US' (Anti-Defamation League, 1988a: 29). The ADL describes the NSRP as 'ideologically hybrid ... a bridge between the Ku Klux Klan and the American Nazi groups. The *Thunderbolt* had long been the most widely read publication among the Klans and other hate groups' (Anti-Defamation League, 1988a: 44).

9. *The Torch* (1977-79): published by The White People's Committee to Restore God's Laws, a division of the Church of Jesus Christ, a Christian Identity church, and

10. *White Patriot* (1979-84): Newsletter of the Knights of the Ku Klux Klan, the second largest Klan group in the US, are both edited by Thomas Robb. Robb is national KKK 'chaplain' as well as minister of the Church of Jesus Christ, a Christian Identity church in Arkansas. Robb has close ties to David Duke's National Association for the Advancement of White People, as well as with neo-Nazis in the US and West Germany.

The collection contained sporadic issues of the following periodicals which I chose to include in order to insure that I reviewed as wide a range of publications as possible:

11. *Crusader* (no dates): published by the Knights of the Ku Klux Klan, out of Metairie, LA.

12. *The Fiery Cross* (1979): published in Swartz, Louisiana, official organ of The United Klans of America, in Tuscaloosa, AL.

13. *The National Socialist* (1982-83): published by The World Union of National Socialists.

14. *The Northlander* (1978): no information available.

15. *NS KAMPFRUF / NS Mobilizer* (1974-83): published by the National Socialist League.

16. *The Spotlight* (1986): published by the Liberty Lobby.

17. *Voice of German Americans* (1977-80): no information available.

18. *The Western Guardian* (1980): Christian Identity periodical published by Western Guard America.

The Matrices of Malevolent Ideologies: Blacks and Jews

Laurence Mordekhai Thomas

Abstract: *This essay aims to shed some light on the perennial tensions between Blacks and Jews in the United States. Beginning with a brief account of both racism and anti-semitism, the author argues that both groups have embraced, if only unwittingly, negative stereotypes concerning the other. He then suggests an innocent confusion that came about during the Civil Rights movement. Finally, the author stresses the fact that each group must recognize that its suffering, however egregious, does not thereby give it such substantial insight regarding the suffering of the other group that each can understand the other without listening to the other.*

Just as society must have a scapegoat, so hatred must have a symbol. Georgia has the Negro and Harlem has the Jew.

James Baldwin (1948)

There is no better evidence that a set of beliefs about a group amount to nothing other than the raging winds of malevolent ideology (anti-semitism, racism, sexism, and so forth) than that, in the face of countervailing factual evidence and conceptual considerations, the very preposterousness of the beliefs is no barrier at all to their being held as indisputable truth. Indeed, in some instances the beliefs are so preposterous that they might as well be a formal contradiction: p and –p.[1] What is more, it turns out far too often that people will resonate emotionally with the beliefs in question, although at an intellectual level they recognize the absurdity of the beliefs.

While it is true that throughout history all sorts of groups have been the object of malevolent ideology, I want to focus upon Jews and Blacks. The malevolent ideology of anti-semitism has a very long history and, to varying degrees, has been found in every society where Jews have made up a minority of the population. As for the malevolent ideology of racism against Blacks, I shall focus upon the black experience in the United States; for American racism against Blacks is astonishing for both its persistence and viciousness in a country that prides itself on having taken the political rhetoric of equality to heights of eloquence yet unparalleled by any other country in the world. In no other country do we find one of the most sustained and vigorous defences of the inferiority of Blacks and, at very same time, an equally sustained and vigorous defence, heralded before all the world, of equality for all.

Specifically, I should like in this essay to consider the ways in which, for better or worse, the perception which Blacks and Jews have of one another has been influenced by the malevolent ideology of the other. My guiding principle in this essay can be expressed as follows: I have met very few Jews who would deny the existence of anti-semitism in America; and I have met very few Blacks who would deny the existence of racism in America. Most Jews and Blacks will allow that even among well-meaning people such attitudes can surface, albeit in rather muted and ever so subtle ways. I merely maintain there is simply no reason to suppose that either Blacks or Jews could have entirely escaped the subtle ways in which the malevolent ideology of the other manifested itself in American society. I write not with maliciousness, but with the conviction that no small amount of moral progress begins with the understanding that our own suffering, however horrible, does not put us beyond the pale of malevolent ideologies. I conclude Section 4 with some remarks concerning the influence of Farrakhan. For this purpose, there are two reasons why the United States is particularly suitable for this analysis. The obvious and main one is that substantial numbers of each group live in the United States. Another reason, however, is that the media influence of the United States is second to none. Thus, America's images of people—its own denizen and others —find their way around the world. What is more, it is generally acknowledged throughout the world that a major commercial success in film and popular music, for instance, generally requires success in the American market. The Beatles, for instance, are undoubtedly immortalized because of their success in the United States. Thus, those outside America who seek such success deliberately tailor their productions accordingly.

Any satisfactory discussion of these matters should shed some light on the mounting tension between Blacks and Jews after the Civil Rights Movement, which seemed to be a most remarkable moment of cooperation between the two peoples. I say a word about this at the end of Section 4, suggesting that we would do well to distinguish between political allies and social neighbours. A natural question, though, is: why Blacks and Jews rather than Jews and some other group or Blacks and some other group? One can say because of the magnitude of the suffering of these two, but this obviously comes too close for comfort to inviting invidious comparisons. There is a better answer. America is very much a Christian nation, and among conservative Christians Judaism plays a central role in the fulfilment of prophecy. With Blacks, by contrast, there are the institution of American slavery and Jim Crow laws. Thus, for reasons that are quite independent of one another, Jews and Blacks are a deep, deep part of the landscape of the American psyche.

Starting in the order of the historical inception of each malevolent ideology, and so with Jews first, I begin with a sketch of the malevolent ideology of each group. As the reader shall discover, it is a most striking fact about the oppression of both Blacks and Jews that the invocation of Christianity plays a central role. One should not deny that in the name of Christianity much good has been done. Abolitionists were often Christians, as were many rescuers of Jews during the Holocaust. Still, the amount of evil done in Christianity's name is morally chilling.

1. The Malevolent Ideology of Anti-Semitism

I have remarked that malevolent ideologies constitute an efficient way of containing those targeted. What reason could there be, or have been, for a group of people wanting to contain the Jews? This is an especially interesting question, since the number of Jews in the world have always been comparatively small. I would imagine that most of us have to be reminded that early Christianity was actually a part of Judaism and, moreover, that the ascendancy of Christianity (which until Martin Luther's Protestant Reformation was synonymous with the Catholic Church) did not happen all at once, but that it took around nine centuries for the doctrine to achieve the predominant place that it has gained in Western culture—an outcome that required some serious political manoeuvring. One of the linchpins of the Christian doctrine is, of course, the Second Coming; and the early Christians believed that the occurrence of that eschatological event was most imminent.[2] Needless to say, its occurrence would have settled religious matters resoundingly in their favour, more so than any argument could ever hope to do. The early Christians realized this, and were eagerly awaiting its occurrence. During that wait, the Jews, with their belief that Jesus was not the messiah, were just a nuisance at best and at worst a bunch of stubborn disbelievers in Christ, who would soon have indubitable evidence that they were wrong. But as time passed without the occurrence of this eschatological event, Jews became an embarrassment to Christianity in that from the outset they had denied that Jesus was the messiah.[3] Were the Jews right?

Of course, other religious groups denied that Jesus was the messiah, but the historical origins of Christianity gave the denial on the part of Jews a formidable potency. After all, Jesus was a Jew and, according to Christianity's rendering of the texts, Judaism just is the spiritual precursor to Christianity. Besides, as I noted in the preceding paragraph, early Christianity was a part of

Judaism. Thus, *a fortiori*, this denial by Jews had a formidable potency. Blaise Pascal wrote, 'If all the Jews had been converted by Jesus Christ, we would no longer have any suspicious testimony from them. And if they had all been exterminated, we would not have any such testimony at all' *(Pensées,* Serie XXIV, p. 592; my translation in the text). Had Pascal, who was born in 1623, made a like claim regarding other religions, his audience would have been utterly puzzling, wondering what point he was trying to make. Not with the Jews, however. Only the Jews could have produced 'suspicious' testimony against Christ.[4]

There was an internecine struggle between Jews and the early Christians, regarding the relation of each to the other, that simply excluded other religions. On the one hand, the Christians were claiming that Jesus was the messiah that the Jews had been waiting for and that had been prophesied in the various texts that Jews held so dear to them; on the other, Jews were insisting that nothing of the sort was true and that, after all, they were in an authoritative position to know, since by the admission of Christians themselves it is the texts of Judaism that tell the story of the messiah and the traditions implied therein from which he is to come. This was not the sort of debate that allowed for religious arbitration, if you will, by other religious groups. The stakes were far too high. And matters were exacerbated by the failure of the Second Coming to occur early on.

Clearly, if Christianity was to succeed, then the denial by Jews that Jesus was the messiah had to be stripped of any credibility, even as the occurrence of the Second Coming had to be conceded to the indefinite future.[5] It is easy to miss how formidable a task this was if we read prevailing religious attitudes of Western culture back into the time of the early Christians.

For instance, it is of no small consequence that Christianity is no longer threatened by the postponement into the indefinite future of the Second Coming. Whereas the very non-occurrence of this eschatological event once gave substantial weight to the claim made by Jews that Jesus was not the messiah, that is no longer true. Some of the words of Jesus are now so central a part of Western culture that they often serve as reference points for everyone, Christian and non-Christian alike. Consider such expressions as 'love thy neighbour', 'turn the other cheek', or the Golden Rule, 'do unto others as you would have them do unto you'. In fact, not only has the Golden Rule come to be such a part of Western culture that its religious reference is slowly receding out of sight, but what is generally lost on people is the Judaic origins of both this rule and the saying 'love thy neighbour'. Yet again, none of this was true during the time of the early Christians. As for the miracles attributed to Christ, what must be remembered is that magic was part of the cultural scene in a way that is virtually inconceivable nowadays, at least in much of Western culture.

It would not occur to most individuals today that there is someone in society with powers who could affect the chances of its raining, whereas during the time of the early Christians it was commonly enough thought that there were such individuals.[6] So what had to be established is not just that Jesus performed extraordinary feats, or that he had special powers, since that sort of thing was said of others, but that what he did transcended the category of magic commonly attributed to others. Obviously, the greatest miracle attributed to Jesus is that he rose from the dead. Suffice it to say that, during the time of the early Christians, people were not immediately inclined to believe that such a thing occurred, which brings us back to the idea of the Second Coming. As a matter of doctrinal veracity for the early Christians, the claim that Jesus rose from the dead was compounded by the fact that his rising from the dead and returning again to establish the kingdom of heaven on earth were doctrinally coupled. To the early Christians, it was obvious that the non-occurrence of the latter cast a long shadow of doubt upon the former. This, in turn, cast doubt upon their claim that he was the messiah, which reminds us what the Jews had been claiming all along. So as I remarked, if Christianity was to succeed, then the denial by Jews that Jesus was the messiah had to be stripped of any credibility, in view of the authoritative position that Jews were in *vis-à-vis* the texts and traditions of Judaism.

Well, there is no better way to ensure that the words of a people are decisively discounted by others than to paint a picture of them as evil in the mind of others. Indeed, the Jew turns out not just to be contingently evil, but inherently so, as their being associated with the devil makes abundantly clear. It is this turn towards the view that Jews are inherently evil that reveals that we have a malevolent ideology in the case of the Jews. After all, Christian doctrine insists that all individuals are sinners, owing to the fall of Adam and Eve. So to make Jews evil in a most despicable way, it became necessary to find horrendous things that Jews did that Christians generally did not do. And indeed we find attributed to Jews the very fulsome practice of using gentile blood for Jewish rituals. This is quite ironic, of course. For given Talmudic laws concerning kashrut and ritual cleanliness, few things could be more antithetical to Jewish life, at any level, than the use of human blood for any kind of ritualistic purposes. The ritual of circumcision results in the loss of some blood; it does not call for the use of blood. No doubt the Exodus story from Egypt, involving sheep blood on the door posts of Jewish homes whereby the first-born male was spared, is what allowed the attribution that Jews used blood for ritualistic purposes to gain credibility. In any case, this attribution was most damning because, as in the case of witches, evil had already been associated with the use of human blood.

From a completely different direction, I dare say that another factor that allowed this attribution to take hold is the relatively inexorable Jewish commitment to non-assimilation. The idea here is not to blame the victim.[7] Quite the contrary, it is to point to the unfortunate truth that people are generally suspicious of those who do not conform and that when things go wrong it is very easy for people to lay blame at the door of those whose ways they do not understand and find mysterious. Jews are an instance of, rather than an exception to, a quite universal behaviour. Over the centuries, Jewish life has undoubtedly struck many as difficult to make sense of, as it does many today. In a rhetorical way, I briefly take just three issues.

• What exactly is the point of kashrut laws? For the non-Jew, it can be difficult to see why a Jew would not eat a well-prepared meal of the right sorts of foods in the home of a non-Jew off plates that are unquestionably clean. Surely the Jew could make an exception just this once. From time to time, it is likely that non-Jews suspected that they were somehow being indicted by kashrut observances, 'Am I not clean enough for you to eat at my house?'

• How on earth can a single instance of work on the Sabbath harm anything? I mean, is it not just plain stupid to inconvenience oneself so, or to take such a loss? Certainly there is no harm in jotting down a few words with a pen.

• And what exactly is wrong with carrying things outside the home? This question becomes even more troubling when one learns that the home can be understood in an extended way to embrace an entire neighbourhood. How can otherwise smart people be such sticklers for such bizarre rules unless they are morally demented in some way.

From this, the next step is not that Jews must be evil. But at a time in history when superstition was rampant, I trust that one can see how this inexplicable behaviour on the part of Jews made it relatively easy for an undesirable attribution against them to take hold. None is a better target for suspicion than those who do not conform by way of practices and rituals that others cannot fathom. So it is even today.

I want to bring this part of the discussion to a close with one last observation. As with myself, I am sure that a great many Jews were taught that the winds of anti-semitism first began blowing with the charge that the Jews killed Christ.[8] I suggest, however, that things had to be the other way around: The winds of anti-semitism were already blowing, and the charge of killing Christ ensured that they would continue to do so. Christianity needed to have ascended to dominance in Western culture or to be evidently on its way to doing so before that charge against Jews could have the force that the Church wanted it to have. In Christianity's nascent stage, when it was competing for dominance with not only Judaism but other religions, the charge of killing Christ would probably have been counterproductive. Aside from the fact that in the early years Jesus simply did not have the stature that would have given this charge against the Jews any real leverage against them, what would it mean to accuse a few Jews of killing an all-powerful being? So the origins of anti-semitism against Jews needed to have a different source, a sketch of which I have provided. A mysterious people are easy grist for the mill of ill-will and hate; and during troubled times, a mysterious people are easily seen as porters of evil itself. Along with witches, this is how Jews came to be seen. With that stigma in place or at least clearly gaining a foothold in the minds of individuals, the Church's charge that the Jews killed Christ had a credibility among Christians that it could not otherwise have had, and it is seen as indisputable evidence of a morally bankrupt character already attributed to Jews.

Perhaps textual support for this is to be found in the Gospel of John. Notice that although John does not hold back at all in associating the Jews with the devil (in fact, the claim is that the devil is the father of the Jews, John 8: 42-47), the author does not rail against Jews as killers of Christ. Had this been the prevailing view of Jews when John wrote, then, in light of the extremely harsh characterization of the Jews that he does give, John would have incorporated that view in the text. But his account of the role which Jews played in the crucifixion of Jesus is no more harsh than the accounts found in the other gospels, though we do not find in them the vituperative characterization of the Jews (having the devil as their father) that we find in the Gospel of John.

The ideology of anti-semitism targets Jews as morally inferior, not just in the sense that they lack moral refinement, as a person can lack moral refinement but have quite salutary motivations. Rather, Jews are said to be morally inferior in that they are morally bankrupt in terms of their motivations and desires. They are inescapably moved to do things, including engaging in unjust, self-serving economic practices, that no morally decent person is ever moved to do, except perhaps—and only perhaps—under the most trying of circumstances. In *Vessels of Evil,* the term I use is 'irredeemably evil'. The Holocaust, of course, represents a most virulent expression of the conception of the Jew as irredeemably evil. But the stereotype of the Jew remains that of one who is given to vice.

2. The Malevolent Ideology of Racism
Against American Blacks

I turn now to Blacks in the United States. As we all know, slavery was not instituted by America. Indeed, many centuries earlier we find that Aristotle thought it obvious that there should be slaves, since he thought it obvious that some individuals were inferior to others: slaves and women, for example, were inferior to men. It is not likely, though, that he thought that slaves should be black. More poignantly, the alleged inferiority of women to men in all quarters of the earth makes it abundantly clear that humankind was rather used to the idea that an entire category of people could be inferior to others. The suggestion here is not that sexism is on the same continuum as slavery. By contrast, nothing occurs in a vacuum; and, plausibly, a world without sexism would have been far less receptive to slavery as America conceived of it. Of course, the world has had its share of hostilities independent of gender. But whereas this theme was generally played out in terms of nationality or religious background, it is America which so relentlessly played the theme of group inferiority in terms of physical features alone: skin colour, hair texture, and facial morphology.

Now, as the number of slaves rose dramatically, the issue of containing slaves obviously became a problem. It is no doubt tempting to think that the problem's solution was brute force and the threat of death. But not so. It is revealing to look quickly at the difference between American slavery and apartheid in South Africa, which came about a century after slavery had ended in the various provinces that now comprise the nation of South Africa.[9]

In South Africa, the solution to the containment of more than twenty million Blacks by approximately five million Whites was by way of a police state. It was understood that Blacks were simply a labour force. Apartheid allowed Blacks to be around Whites solely for the purposes of labour. Interpersonal relationships between Blacks and Whites, as in the case of black servants in white homes, were highly constrained. The majority of Blacks who laboured for Whites went back to their shanty towns to live among themselves. It cannot be argued that South African Whites came as close as they could to slavery without actually having to endure the stigma of slavery. For apartheid was horrendous enough, and for the longest of time the so-called developed nations of the world did not seem much bothered by its existence. Accordingly, it is hard to imagine that from the very start a system of slavery itself would have occasioned moral outrage among the very nations that were so unphased by the moral ugliness of apartheid. What seems much more likely is that South African Whites wanted to keep to a very minimum all interpersonal relationships between Blacks and Whites. Nor did South African Whites seem much to care if South African Blacks took any delight in labouring for Whites, just so long as Blacks laboured for them. The police state model served white South Africa well.

From an economic standpoint this model would have served America much better. Surprisingly, perhaps, the thing that got in the way of the implementation of this model is that in America slaves were the property of individuals, and not the state. South Africa's past demonstrated that a small minority can quite successfully control a sizable majority, when the majority is being controlled in a manner that is characteristic of a police state. In America, that kind of control at the level of each individual slaveowner was extremely difficult, if not impossible, to sustain in most cases. A corollary to this point is that there simply could not have been uniformity of control among slaveowners, such as was maintained in South Africa; and the differentials in control would have been another problem. Two other considerations are most relevant here. One is that whereas five million white South Africans could effectively control more than twenty million Black South Africans by killing ten or twenty or a hundred or even a thousand Blacks whenever a sufficient threat was needed, this was not an option for American slaveowners, since they would soon be out of the very slaves they owned. For South Africa, there was indeed an indefinite supply of Blacks to draw upon at no additional costs. Not so for slaveowners, since each new slave had to be purchased. Besides, the Blacks killed in South Africa belonged to no one but the state, if that; whereas to kill a slave in America was to destroy another's property. The other consideration is that, because slaveowners could not be indifferent to whether their slaves survived physically, the physical proximity of white slaveowners and black slaves which, again, stemmed from the private ownership of slaves, was simply not conducive to a police state approach.

So slave owners needed to contain their slaves, but a police state approach was not an option, owing primarily to the very factor that probably made slavery seem so attractive, namely, private ownership. Of course, there was much physical harm, including death, done to slaves, but there can be no doubt that something other than mere physical threat was needed to contain the slaves. As a complementary means of control, a normative story was told according to which Blacks are rightly subordinate to Whites and according to which Blacks would place their trust in their white owners. This story was to be embraced by all—Blacks and Whites (whether slaveowner or non-slaveowner), slaves and non-slaves. The effective telling of this story of inferiority was facilitated by both the utter dislocation and the natal alienation of Blacks that occurred as a result of the practice of slavery existing for approximately ten generations (counting twenty years as a generation).[10] As a result, Blacks were deprived of their narratives—that is, a set of stories and ennobling rituals that are relatively isomorphic to the group in question. I suggest that when a people are surrounded by an ideology that targets them as inferior, there is nothing that renders them more vulnerable to precisely those feelings of inferiority than the absence of a narrative in their lives. A well defined narrative is a psychological buffer in a hostile environment. Without a buffer, a pervasive ideology has to take its toll. (Thus, it is clear that I am using the word 'narrative' in a positive sense.)

The telling of this story of black inferiority was also facilitated by the doctrine of Christianity. Emphasizing that the righteous would be rewarded in heaven, that material possessions were generally an impediment to salvation, and that meekness and forgiveness were fundamental virtues, a religion could not be more suited to the conditions of American slavery without actually condoning it than Christianity.[11] For black slaves, Christianity was an extraordinary psychological salve in the midst of a most devastating psychological environment. To be sure, black slaves gave their own imprimatur to Christian worship, an imprimatur that is admired the world over. There was not, however, a substantive change in the doctrine of Christianity. There are many styles of Christian worship, as is shown by the difference between the Catholic and Protestant denominations. In fact, because of the place of the Pope in Catholicism, the doctrinal divide between Catholicism and Protestantism is as a matter of principle far greater than the divide between white and black Protestants in America. The richness of black Christian worship in America has been in the style of worship rather than in a unique reading of Christianity.

The ideology of racism against Blacks defined Blacks as intellectually deficient. The term I use in *Vessels of Evil* is 'moral simpleton'. According to this ideology, neither intellectual, cultural, nor moral excellences were within the reach of Blacks. Now, social arrangements very nearly insured that this would be a self-fulfilling prophecy, both in the eyes of Whites and in the eyes of Blacks. Regarding the first, suffice it to say that to an unsympathetic eye nothing makes for a quicker judgment that a person is incapable of achieving things than merely the absence of success, as if the capable succeed regardless of the circumstances. Regarding the latter, there is the psychological reality that nothing plagues self-confidence like the systematic absence of success, no matter how *bona fide* the explanation for its absence might be. This is so if only because success is generally incremental. Given equal natural talent and the same age, the experienced practitioner will invariably perform better than the novice. Slavery ensured that for years to come black slaves and then free Blacks in general would be novices in matters of intellect and culture. And it will not do to point to accomplished people like Harriot Jacobs, Frederic Douglass, or Booker T. Washington, all of whom were former slaves; for these were exceptional people by any reasonable standards.

On the moral front, of course, there was no shortage of experiences which called for moral deliberation on the part of Blacks. But composite pictures matter; and it is very difficult to attach considerable weight to the moral opinions one regarded as intellectually and culturally incapable.

I am well aware that an increasing number of Blacks rejects the thesis that slavery gave rise to feelings of inferiority on the part of Blacks. Clearly, Blacks suffered from physical brutality (including unjust death) and the absence of freedom. But the idea that the only things that Blacks suffered from during 200 years of slavery were physical brutality and the absence of freedom is just so much nonsense. There is simply no theory of human psychology that would support the view that slavery did not give rise to feelings of inferiority; for we know the damage that ten years of abuse can do to a child's self-esteem. The response generally made here is that slave parents loved rather than abused their children. True enough. And arguably, slave children were not besieged by feelings of inferiority.[12] But self-esteem is a dynamic rather than static phenomenon; accordingly, it stays in place only if reinforced. By the time a slave child reached teenage years, there was little in society that would reinforce her or his self-esteem from then on. In any case, those who would deny the inferiority thesis owing to slavery leave themselves open to the very charge they wish to deny. For if the only harm of slavery were the denial of freedom, then one might have expected that by now the black American experience would have been quite different. A cursory look at the post-slavery history of Blacks in America reveals a most painful absence of cooperation among Blacks in the face of on-going racism. The black church, the most powerful and independent black institution in America for years, has never been a pervasive cooperative force among Blacks.[13] As an explanation here, racism will not do. But feelings of inferiority will, especially when one bears in mind that success is incremental. Much of black behaviour, as found in the ghetto, can be explained by the desire for immediate affirmation—a desire that is common enough given sustained feelings of inferiority.

I have not claimed that American slavery resulted in Blacks being intellectually inferior. As with W.E.B. DuBois, I believe no such thing.[14] The claim, rather, is that owing to the experience of slavery a great many Blacks have been plagued by feelings of inferiority. As DuBois was painfully aware: over generations, nothing sustains an ideology that a people are inferior than the general absence of success on their part. This is so even when the absence of success is caused by the very category of individuals who make the judgment.

A final comment: it is possible to believe that something is inferior and yet cherish it dearly, as is sometimes the case with pets. Regarding Blacks in America, not only were they thought to be intellectually inferior but they were thought to have less moral standing than Whites, which is the philosopher's way of saying that a black life was worth less than a white life. No account of slavery would be complete that failed to draw attention to this moral reality. In the absence of a narrative to buffer Blacks, one cannot begin to fathom the damage that this did to the self-respect of Blacks, bearing in mind the importance of distinguishing between black children and black adults. There is a pain that Black adults experienced against which black children were undoubtedly shielded, albeit to varying degrees.

3. Being Ideologically Configured

We are almost in a position to consider the ways in which, for better or worse, the lives of Blacks and Jews have been influenced by the malevolent ideology of the other. But a little ground work is first in order regarding the ways in which malevolent ideologies generally operate.

A great many people will insist that they do not have a prejudiced bone in their body. To be sure, there are those who without hesitation or embarrassment will make it clear that they cannot stand certain kinds of people. But I think it is fair to say that if all those who claimed not to be prejudiced towards anyone were not, then the world would truly be a different place, even allowing for those who are unabashedly prejudiced. What is surprising is not just that some people are prejudiced contrary to what they say, but that some otherwise very decent people fall into this category. That the wicked should be blind to their ways is somewhat understandable. How is it, though, that very decent people fail to see their own prejudices? Part of the answer has to do with the fact that most people are commendable in that they sincerely subscribe to the idea of equality for all. And it is perhaps natural for people to reason as follows regarding themselves:

• if I sincerely subscribe to the idea of equality for all, and so to the idea that prejudice against anyone is a bad thing,

• then there are no prejudices that operate in my life.

Unfortunately, this is a fallacious inference, as sincerity of belief does not entail truth. People have sincerely and deeply held all sorts of beliefs about which they have been quite mistaken. The other part of the problem is that people suppose that their prejudices will manifest themselves in a very straightforward, tell-tale fashion. In other words, it is erroneously held that prejudices involve a kind of readily detectable cognitive dissonance. Not so, however. Prejudice can be ever so subtle—sometimes masquerading as reasonable caution;

sometimes as inquisitiveness; sometimes as hard objectivity. And so on.

People are emotionally configured by the prevailing patterns of social behaviour to which they are continually exposed. As a result some forms of behaviour just 'feel' right and other forms do not, and therein lies the normative force of the emotional configuration. The demanding female professor does not come across as nurturing and to numerous students that does not 'feel' right; hence, they respond with a hostile interpretation of her non-nurturing behaviour. To say that things do not 'feel' right in this instance is just to say that things do not resonate—that there is affective dissonance—with how the students have been emotionally configured. As our example shows, how things 'feel' can be normatively biased against someone in a most substantial way.

Yet, how things 'feel' constitutes a guiding force in our lives—a kind of primitive from which we start. Time and time again, substantial judgments are made just on the basis of how things feel, where no attempt is made to explicate or understand the basis for one's feelings. In some instances, there is a straightforward sense in which the explication is actually deemed somewhat irrelevant; for even if it is true that one morally ought to feel comfortable working with such-and-such a kind of person, the fact that one does not does not bode well for having that person as a colleague, in any case. Thus, an admittedly immoral feeling can actually seem to have an acceptable place in the moral justification of behaviour. This, however, is already quite explicit. In most cases there are simply 'feelings' on the basis of which an individual is judged reprehensible or frowned upon, where the basis for those feelings is none other than that the individual's appearance or mode of self-presentation generates considerable affective dissonance owing to an emotional configuration on the part of that person's audience that embodies deep, deep prejudices. For instance, the so-called 'cheap Jew' and 'arrogant Black' often turn out to be doing precisely whatever anyone might reasonably be expected to do, except in their case things 'feel' differently. For instance, at a flea market bargaining is part of the dynamics and in philosophy both quickness of mind and self-confidence are very prized goods. But the Jew who bargains at the flea market, just like any non-Jew would, is somehow being untoward, and the quick thinking, self-confident American Black in philosophy, whose mode of self-presentation accords with any non-black in philosophy who is so characterized, will almost certainly be seen as displaying unwarranted arrogance. This is hardly surprising when one views the image of the Jew and the Black that, even to this very day, is so pervasive in the media, for instance. And one can be utterly confident that any prejudiced view of a group that is pervasive in the media abounds in society at large; and that any such prejudiced view has emotionally configured those not belonging to the group in question.

To be sure, such emotionally prejudiced configuration takes place to varying degrees; and some people manage to counteract in large measure the forces that give rise to prejudiced emotional configurations regarding various groups. None of this I have denied, though. In any case, no one succeeds in such counteraction without a conscious effort. And while that effort may begin with a sincere desire not to be biased, it simply cannot end there.

To avoid any misunderstanding, let me point out that the account of emotionally configured prejudices offered is compatible with the reality that things can be overdetermined or improperly labelled. A person who feels uneasy interacting with an X (Jew or Black) need not, on that account alone, be harbouring X-ist sentiments. Nor is every offence which an X might experience at the hands of a non-X rightly construed as an instance of X-ism. Suppose that the occasion for social interaction occurs between a strikingly handsome male X and a female non-X, say Jane. The male X, however, does not act in the way that Jane expects a most handsome man to behave. He is shy, demure, and so forth, which is precisely what makes her feel uncomfortable. Given just this information, we should certainly not suppose that she harbours X-ist sentiments. Now, she may even offend male X by questioning his manhood for not acting like other guys; and feeling terribly spurned, she specifically points out the truth that any other male of kind X would have been besotted by her sexual interest in him. With this latter remark, especially, should we label Jane's behaviour X-ist? This is far from obvious. Jane need not have been thinking 'You, an X, are lucky to have the likes of me taking an interest in you'. Although she expected the male X in question to behave like other Xs, this expectation is purely statistical, and not based on any normative view that Xs are comparatively inferior, animal like, or whatever. Jane need only have been operating with a statistical generalization in the way that we (in the United States) tend to do with males of enormous height, supposing at the very least that such males (used to) have an interest in basketball.

The discussion allows us to be a bit more precise. Statistical generalizations coupled with an unfounded, unwarranted normative view of inferiority or depravity is the mark of an emotionally prejudiced configuration. And for all of life's complexities and overdeterminations there can be powerfully good reasons for thinking that precisely such a coupling is in place. (The claim of complexity can be made of flirting behaviour, too; yet no one denies that in general such behaviour is readily recognized.) Finally, a fundamental premise of this essay is that it would be a grave mistake for either Jews or Blacks to suppose that their respective sufferings have given them an immunity to acquiring an emotionally prejudiced configuration against the other. As I have said, while no one need be racist or anti-semitic, sincerity of belief, alone, does not deliver that outcome.

4. In the Grips of Malevolent Ideology

We are now in the position to consider the ways in which, for better or worse, Blacks and Jews have been influenced by one another's malevolent ideology. Alas, I must say that the influence has been for the worse. In view of the reality that both Blacks and Jews have endured extraordinary evil, there is a temptation to think that if any two people on American soil ought to understand one another it ought to be Blacks and Jews. But this is an instance where the vision of hindsight is somewhat blurred. For the thought that Blacks and Jews ought to understand one another ignores the circumstances under which their encounter began, as if they simply met with their respective moral wounds on neutral ground void of any ideological backdrop. Nothing could be further from the truth.[15]

Because the Holocaust had so demolished Jewish populations and culture throughout Europe, the United States—New York City, in particular—came to have one of the largest concentrations of Jews in the world. And by the 1900s, the glow of the Reconstruction era was completely gone. Without slavery, we nonetheless have America at its rawest. Is it not astonishing that the Jim Crow era comes after Reconstruction?[16] Finally, the Second World War added a certain surrealism and consciousness to it all, as Blacks and Jews alike found themselves the object of derision in America's armed forces. So the 1930s and 1940s mark an excellent time period for examining the ways in which Blacks and Jews have been influenced by the malevolent ideologies of one another.

David S. Wyman (1984) reports that the first mention by the *New York Times* of Jews in concentration camps occurred on page 8. Even allowing that America was in one of its isolationist phases then, if anything should have been front page news surely the concentration camps should have been. So the fact that what should have been front page news was relegated to page 8 tells us reams about the level of anti-semitism in America. And, of course, we know that Ivy League schools during this era had a ceiling on the number of Jews they would admit. After all, it was the role of these schools to produce good Christian gentlemen; anyway, no one really thought that there were good gentlemen besides Christian ones, or non-Christians who affected Christian mannerism. But Jews did flourish in New York City. Indeed, the Ivy League quota system had the unanticipated consequence of turning City College into one of the most esteemed institutions of the CUNY system—indeed, among American colleges and universities in general. But these happy coincidences should not blind us to the reality of anti-semitism in America: Jews were not just non-Christians, they were non-Christians as a matter of principle. This, coupled with their supposedly idiosyncratic ritualistic practices, could not have given American society much more of a reason to be wary of Jews.

On the other hand, during the first half of the twentieth century, the idea that Blacks were intellectually inferior to Whites and had less moral standing than Whites could not have been any more prevalent than it was then—short of slavery itself, that is (see Franklin, 1989). The Jim Crow era made an utter mockery out of the idea that Blacks were no longer slaves, revealing how empty the notion of freedom could be this side of slavery. Essentially, the practices of every public and private institution that required some form of state regulation and accreditation implied that Blacks were inferior. At all levels, public education at predominantly black institutions was inferior in quality to white schools, which is no less true today. And while some private black schools did fare better than most publicly supported black schools—Tuskegee Institute and Fisk University being two of the more notable exceptions—even the better private institutions were inferior to most white institutions, private or public. The only haven in this regard was the black church. To be sure, Whites generally regarded black forms of worship as lacking in proper religious decorum, to put it mildly; however, the church (along with the synagogue) was the one public institution (at least in the sense of being tax-exempt) that did not require state accreditation, and there was very little regulation to speak of. In any case, black and white worship operated so independently of one another that neither was seen as getting in the way of the other. Yet, the majesty of the black church could not overshadow the stamp of intellectual inferiority that otherwise marked nearly every aspect of black life.

It does not take much thought to see that the way in which Blacks and Jews were situated in American society around the 1930s did not really lend itself to mutual understanding of one another's plight. Although each group was concerned with the injustice of exclusion, the concern was from quite distinct vantage points. More poignantly, the malevolent ideology of racism hardly made Blacks inviting to Jews; and the relevant ideology of anti-semitism hardly made Jews inviting to Blacks. Moreover, each group's own sense of identity did not help matters. Besides, there was very little casual social interaction between Blacks and Jews, such Jews being infrequent guests in the homes of Blacks and conversely.

Blacks approached Christianity with a certain fervour. This is no doubt understandable given the salutary role which the church has played, and continues to play, in black life. Still, a literal interpretation of the Gospel of John regarding the character of Jews, according to which the devil is the father of the Jews, could not possibly have put Jews in a favourable light in the eyes of Blacks. This is especially so, since by the 1930s the idea that the Jews, spoken with an atemporal sweep, were responsible for the death of Jesus was well in place. After all, this would account for the morally questionable economic practices of Jews in black urban ghettoes. Respectfully, let me state with a certain rhetorical force the line of reasoning that must have prevailed, 'why but for Christianity, which Jesus gave to the world, life would have been intolerable for Blacks in America, both during and after slavery; and not only did the Jews have him killed, which was bad enough. Worse still, they are yet unable to see the error of their ways'. So clearly there were limits to just how responsive Blacks were going to be to Jews, and Jews certainly had to be aware of this. After all, it will be remembered that John F. Kennedy's Catholicism was a major public concern that he had to address in his successful bid for the presidency of the United States; for Catholics were not the right kind of Christians. Clearly, then, public sentiment regarding Jews was even less favourable. Drawing upon Section 3, the idea here is not that Blacks self-consciously embraced the negative view of Jews put forth in the Gospel of John, or that Blacks were constantly reminding themselves of the myth that the Jews had killed Christ. Instead, the idea is that a literal reading and acceptance of the New Testament, coupled with prevailing anti-semitic thought in American society, yields a certain emotional configuration, which significantly disfavours trusting Jews completely. And few aspects of social interaction are ineluctably tied to feelings, pure and simple, than trust itself.

By contrast, Jews admittedly have a most remarkable record for sur-viving persecution, as even the most ardent enemies of Jews will concede. Accordingly, the toll that the past of slavery was obviously taking upon Blacks could not possibly have put Blacks in a favourable light in the eyes of Jews. And this judgment was surely sealed by the very idea that Jews who were victims of the Shoah might be flourishing afterwards in America. For it is com-monly held among Jews that for all of its nefariousness, the evil of American slavery is indisputably surpassed by the evil of the Shoah, because death, and so the attempt to exterminate the Jews, is surely the ultimate evil.[17] So Jews looked askance, as did others, at a people who seemed to be floundering by the 'mere' tragedy of American slavery itself. How could that evil have so derailed the lives of Blacks, when the greatest of evils had not had a like effect upon the lives of Jews? Invariably, that ever so haunting question was asked: 'how is that they cannot just stick together like we do?' Needless to say, this general line of thought was most in keeping with the idea that Blacks were intellectually inferior. Non-Jews, too, asked the question, 'how is that Blacks cannot just stick together like Jews do?' And the absence of a satisfactory answer made it difficult not to entertain the idea that Blacks were intellectually inferior. Once again, the idea here is not that Jews self-consciously embraced the view that Blacks were inferior, but that, against the backdrop of a racist ideology, the absence of success among Blacks and the success among Jews, yielded an emotional configuration that resonated with the idea that Blacks are inferior.

I have tried to offer a satisfactory answer to that haunting question, with the account of a narrative that I have offered, arguing that Jews have had a narrative well in place but that black Americans have not, distinguishing sharply between a narrative and a culture.[18] I do not wish to repeat those arguments here. Rather, I wish to draw attention to a certain fallacy of reasoning that involves comparative discussions of the Shoah and American slavery. Even if one accepts the thesis that the Shoah was a significantly worse evil than American slavery, what does not follow is that understanding regarding the former yields specific insight into the latter. For evil is not impoverished. Evil admits of such divergence that it is certainly possible for Event$_1$, to be more evil than Event$_2$, and yet for the two events to be radically unlike one another. Suppose that one person loses both of her feet and arms owing to the malicious antics of a gang, and another loses only one eye. Not unreasonably, one would say that the former has been made worse off than the latter. She certainly knows what it is like to be physically impaired. All the same, the former does not quite know what it is like to be without an eye; and it would be wrong for her to think that she could grasp the other's suffering by simply extrapolating from her own experiences, though she is worse off than he is. Our understanding of evil is not transitive, even when there is an experiential vector that allows us to say that the suffering of one (person or group) is greater than another's.

The Shoah and American slavery were two morally atrocious institutions, but in radically different ways. The telos of the Shoah was extermination; the telos of American Slavery was natal alienation through utter subordination in the face of the demand for trust. Aside from the general category of being profoundly unjust, one cannot begin to fathom, to comprehend the experiences of one institution by simply extrapolating from the experiences of the other. The deaths of slavery, during the infamous Middle Passage, were not about the extermination of Blacks; and the slavery of the concentration camps was not about natal alienation. Now, without relying simply upon the idea of Jews being self-absorbed, there can be little doubt that Jews generally regarded the Shoah as a greater atrocity than American slavery;[19] there can also be little doubt that Jews felt compassion for the plight of Blacks in America. Likewise, the Holocaust drew compassion from American Blacks. But things quickly become considerably more complicated, which brings us back to the malevolent ideologies of racism against Blacks and anti-semitism.

Anti-semitism is one thing; the Holocaust, though a most virulent manifestation of anti-semitism, is quite another. A person could embrace some (considerably weaker) form of anti-semitism without ever coming even close to endorsing an evil like the Shoah. Thus, and this is of enormous importance, a hard moral stance against the Holocaust is not *ipso facto* a hard moral stance against anti-semitism generally. Accordingly, compassion for the suffering that Jews endured during the Holocaust does not necessarily mean compassion for the suffering that Jews might endure owing to less virulent forms of anti-semitism. And so the thesis that Blacks had compassion for Jews in Nazi Germany does not entail anything like the complete absence of anti-semitism on the part of Blacks. On the other hand, compassion is compatible with vast inequalities. Kings can have compassion for their inferiors, without meaning to diminish the social distance between them. Holocaust survivors testified that Dr Ernst B. (see Lifton, 1986) had compassion of Jews, though years later he remained a committed Nazi, and so a committed anti-semite. Alas, feelings of compassion are compatible with the belief that the other is deeply inferior to one.

No doubt the line of thought that I am about to develop can be easily enough anticipated. If I am right, the good will of Blacks and Jews towards one another generally did not in important ways reach fruition; and this is owing for the most part to the malevolent ideologies that each had embraced about the other. Blacks never fully rejected the anti-semitic message that Jews are avaricious by nature; Jews never fully rejected the message that Blacks are in fact intellectually inferior. Most significantly, each group's sense of its own identity was a formidable obstacle to its rejecting the malevolent ideology of the other: with Blacks fervently embracing Christianity and Jews showing a remarkable ability to survive in spite of it all. None of this detracts from the truth that Blacks and Jews felt genuine compassion for one another. On the contrary, that each did is no doubt part of the explanation for each group being blind to the reality that it was still very much in the throes of the malevolent ideology that stigmatized the other.

Finally, although both groups were indeed victims of the injustice of exclusion, each group wanted that injustice to cease in ways that were importantly different. In a never realized quest, culminating in the Civil Rights Movement and expressed most eloquently by Martin Luther King in his speech 'I Have a Dream', Blacks wanted America to make good the democratic ideal that a person should be judged by the character of his deeds rather than the colour of his skin. For all practical purposes, skin colour would cease to have any relevance in society. Jews, by contrast, did not want an analogous form of inclusion for themselves. True, all agreed that a person should be judged by the character of her deeds rather than the colour of her skin. Being Jewish, though, was not to cease having any relevance in society; accordingly, being a Jew, unlike being a Black, was not to cease having any relevance in society. Observe that regardless of the religious commitments a Jew might be thought to have the category of secular Jew was and remains a very meaningful one, and that an analogous category for Blacks did not emerge from the Civil Rights Movement. Nor did it occur to anyone that such a category ought to have emerged. Religion aside, equality was not supposed to render the category of Jew irrelevant in the way that it was supposed to render the category of Black. This shows that Jews and Blacks cannot be taken as functionally equivalent categories.

There is a way in which both Black and Jew could miss the difference between them. For the ideal of democracy certainly represented the end of both racism and anti-semitism. So understood, democracy represented a good for both Black and Jew. But things are seriously underdescribed here; for as Sartre clearly saw, the democratic ideal of times past, at least, resolves the problem of malevolent ideologies, by insisting that the set of features which anchors the ideology, skin colour or religious/ethnic background, is itself irrelevant. Regarding the champion of democracy, Sartre eloquently wrote:

> He does not recognize the category of Jew, neither the category of Arab, nor Negro, nor bourgeoisie, nor worker: there is only man, who throughout time and in all places appears the same to 'the democrat (Sartre 1954, p. 65; my translation).

E Pluribus Unum

The failure to attend to democracy's solution to the problem of difference sheds some light on how the Black and the Jew could each miss the difference between them. The failure to do so also sheds some light on the tension between them, and in a way that brings us to the present.

There can be no doubt that during the Civil Rights Movement, Jews gave mightily of themselves to help Blacks in the struggle for equality. No other people have a comparable record. In light of that fact, Jews have been deeply pained by the tumultuous rise of anti-semitism among Blacks, finding its increase quite incomprehensible—as evidence of base ingratitude. The heightened anti-semitism is hard to make sense of even if one supposes—just for the sake of argument—that (some) Jews were patronizing towards Blacks during the Civil Rights Movement. For that supposition will not detract one iota from the truth that Jews gave mightily of themselves, without thought of personal gain. So how is that anti-semitism has seemingly raged like a wild fire across the black community?

No one answer will be entirely satisfactory. In fact, part of the problem is that not all hostility on the part of Blacks towards Jews is rightly regarded as anti-semitism. Still, it is indisputable that anti-semitism has risen among Blacks; and part of the answer, I suggest, has to do with Sartre's insight regarding democracy. To offer any explanation in this regard is to tread very treacherous waters. The reader is asked to bear with me to the end of the explanation. Throughout the explanation, I shall talk about how things might have appeared, proceeding very self-consciously.

I begin with the general observation that it is problematic in social interaction when two parties appear to embrace the same ideal equally, but differ substantially in how they interpret that ideal. This is so even when (i) neither party has misled the other or is otherwise culpable or (ii) there has been no history of mistrust or ill-will between either party. But from the outset, owing to the influence of racism and anti-semitism, the second of these two conditions did not, in the first place, hold between Blacks and Jews either prior to or during the Civil Rights Movement. It is in this context that one should factor in that they were not after the same thing. While both wanted an end to the injustice of exclusion, each had a different conception of the good of inclusion. Jews wanted to be respected in America while being just that—Jews. Thus, the democracy of inclusion that Jews sought—identity-acceptance inclusion, let us call it—was not one that eradicated the fact of their difference but one which accommodated it. By contrast, the democracy of inclusion that Jews admirably pressed for on behalf of Blacks, and that Blacks themselves seem to have wanted, during the Civil Rights Movement—identity-fashioning inclusion, let us call it—is one that appeared to eradicate the fact of difference between Blacks and Whites, in favour of the so-called melting pot idea: *E Pluribus Unum.* And there was the rub. Therein lies the appearance of patronization: the melting-pot was good enough for Blacks, but not for Jews. In the language of respect, it appeared in retrospect that Jews were insisting that Blacks accept a less robust measure of respect than Jews themselves were prepared to accept. Recall, again, the category of secular Jew. In most cases, Jews who gave of themselves so gallantly in the Civil Rights Movement embraced the category of Jew, even if it was that of secular Jew. This much can be conceded without denying the existence of Jewish self-hatred. Needless to say, though, one should want to resist at all costs the idea that a secular Jew is but a self-hating Jew.

Without ignoring other differences between Blacks and Jews, it is the aforementioned difference that in the eyes of some Blacks rendered the good will of Jews during the Civil Rights Movement rather suspect, and in a quite disconcerting way. Bearing in mind that the ideology of anti-semitism entails that Jews characteristically have morally bankrupt motives, then the very appearances of things made it possible to give a most unsavoury interpretation of the role of Jews in the Civil Rights Movement. In a most painful way, the malevolent ideologies of both racism and anti-semitism took its toll in what should have been unmarred as a triumph of social cooperation between Blacks and Jews as political allies.

For all their help, the truth of the matter is that in the minds of Jews (or other non-blacks, for that matter) Blacks did not seem to display the unity of peoplehood that was so characteristic of Jews, where this unity is explicated not in terms of suffering only. Without an explanation for the absence of the unity of peoplehood among Blacks, who were phenotypically demarcated to begin with, the myth of black inferiority was simply underscored. Identity-fashioning inclusion, *á la* Sartre, thus seemed to be just the solution for a people so diminished. Being a people, Jews needed only identity-acceptance inclusion; not being a people, Blacks needed identity-fashioning inclusion. And this is where the influence of racism enters the picture. American slavery had been radically underdescribed. In particular, the profound pain of natal alienation occasioned by American slavery had been roundly ignored by American society. Indeed, this slavery was not like any other practice of slavery. On the other side, Jews remained a mysterious people to Blacks. And as I have noted, the motives of anyone who is mysterious easily become suspect when things go wrong. Needless to say, the prevalence of anti-semitism did not help matters, nor did the fervour with which Blacks embraced Christianity. The Civil Rights Movement, then, far from making these differences irrelevant, served only to accentuate them. Allowing that this movement stands as one of the greatest moments of good will in American history, there is the painful reality that good will between two peoples—perhaps good will at its very best—was so easily marred by the prism of malevolent ideologies through which each was viewing the other.

Looking in retrospect, we can state the tension quite succinctly: Jews came as a people, united by more than the scars of suffering, to help a people who lacked precisely that unity. That differential was, and remains, very real, indeed. Neither skin colour nor geographical origins as such suffice to show that we have a people thousands of years later. Nor, *a fortiori*, does commonality of suffering. But that very real difference void of understanding, owing in large measure to the prevalence of anti-semitism and racism, resulted in the good will of Jews being roundly misunderstood.

Failing to understand the power of a narrative, it has been generally supposed among Blacks that it has been the ability of Jews to pass for white that explains their success in America. In fact, this idea has infected the thinking of many Jews as well. But formal game-theoretical considerations reveal this line of reasoning to be flawed. For if Jews could so readily pass for white, precisely what becomes a mystery is their relative unity. By contrast, since Blacks cannot readily pass for white, precisely what becomes a mystery is their lack of unity. And so witness the power of malevolent ideologies: not only has racism and anti-semitism been an obstacle to two peoples having untainted good will towards one another, but even worse, these two ideologies have been a barrier to each group's own self-understanding.

No explanation of the rise of anti-semitism among Blacks would be complete without some reference to Louis Farrakhan and the Nation of Islam. My explanation, quite simply, is that his appeal among Blacks is owing to two things. One is his recognition that in a hostile society like America Blacks need a narrative, in the technical sense in which I am using this word, if they are ever to achieve equality, indeed, if they are ever to take themselves seriously. If I am right, then skin colour alone cannot be the basis for peoplehood. With Blacks the idea is a silly one to begin with, given the colour-range of people travelling under the banner 'black' or 'African-American'. The second reason is that in portraying Jews as devils, the Nation of Islam (not to be confused with the religion of Islam) plays masterfully upon the ways in which Blacks, by way of Christianity, have been emotionally configured in a prejudicial way with respect to Jews. For as I have indicated in this essay and have argued quite pointedly in *Vessels of Evil,* the Christian texts, especially the Gospel of John (8th chapter), paints a rather horrific picture of the Jews. Farrakhan's demonization of the Jews is a veritable lightning rod among black audiences, generating extraordinary depths of hostility. The truth of the matter, though, is that Jews have often been a target of virulent hostility among those in society who have felt passed over or profoundly threatened, as with members of Christian groups of the far-right whose members are white (see Barkun, 1994). There is no reason to suppose that Blacks have any special immunity in this regard. What has changed, then, is not the pattern as such, but simply the colour of those instantiating the pattern. And this pattern is born of a prejudiced emotional configuration informed by Christianity's negative conception of the Jew. Of course, none of this excuses Blacks, any more than it excuses Christian groups of the far-right.

A final observation is worth making here. The enormous cooperation between Blacks and Jews that took place during the Civil Rights Movement made Blacks and Jews political allies. But people can be political allies without being social neighbours, where the latter is a matter of interacting on a regular basis regarding matters pertaining to daily living as they effect one's home life. Social neighbours have insight, if only through exposure, into one another's lives that cannot be gained from afar. And Blacks and Jews have never really been social neighbours. This consideration harkens back to the idea noted in Section 1 that a mysterious people is easy grist for the mill of ill-will and hate. At the time of the Civil Rights Movement, most people, including Blacks, did not have a grasp of Jewish traditions as they played themselves out in the lives of Blacks. Arguably, most people, including Blacks, do not now. These traditions have never really been a part of the public life of America in the way that Black gospel singing is, for instance. One can know that a *bris* is a religious ceremony where a Jewish male is circumcised and yet not appreciate just how important it is even for secular Jews to have their sons participate in this ritual.

Likewise for the Passover celebration. I suggest that in many ways Jews have remained a mysterious people to Blacks, and that Farrakhan has been able to exploit this reality.

I want to conclude this section with one simple comment upon the issue of Jews and black slavery. Whether or not some Jews were involved in American slavery, and there is no need to deny the fact that some were, it is manifestly clear that most Jews could not have been slave owners; for if most had been, then surely most Blacks would have been Jewish and not Christian. However, we learn from the testimonies of slaves themselves that they took on the religion of their masters, namely Christianity. Anti-semitism back then was too rampant for Jews to have even thought of mingling with Christians enough to produce the grip which Christianity came to have upon black slaves.

5. Conclusion: A Lesson to Learn

To repeat: I have met very few Jews who would deny the existence of anti-semitism in America. Similarly, I have met very few Blacks who would deny the existence of racism in America. Most Jews and Blacks will allow that even among well-meaning people such attitudes can surface, albeit in rather muted and ever so subtle ways. The surprise—if, indeed, that is the word for it—is the extent to which Jews and Blacks generally regard themselves as non-racist and non-anti-semitic, respectively. In fact, one might ask how it is possible for anyone to concede that just about any-and-everyone manages to be infected to at least to some extent by the prejudices against its group, but that she or he is not at all infected by the prejudices against other groups. Part of the answer, of course, has to be that people are naturally inclined to view themselves in a favourable moral light. But this can only be part of the answer, and certainly not one with which the Black or the Jew can be content, since from the outset each maintains that prejudices against their own group can operate even among very well-meaning people.

The other part of the answer, I believe, draws upon the discussion of emotional configuration developed in Section 3 of this essay. There is a tendency to believe that precisely because one has been a victim of extreme bias in a systematic and sustained way, one thereby acquires an immunity to the emotional configuration that is characteristic of persons who are biased towards others or, in any case, one would detect very early on the formation of such an emotional configuration in one's life. One can perhaps see how the line of reasoning might go, with the Black or the Jew thinking that insofar as he is masterful at detecting even biases against his own group when such biases manifested themselves in subtle ways at the level of emotional configuration, then he would be masterful at detecting biases manifested in this way against others, whether in his own person or in others. One can actually imagine this line of reasoning being given a very high rhetorical flourish, 'if from my own struggle with malevolent ideologies, I have not learned to recognize the subtle problems that other peoples might encounter, then what have I learned? My own suffering will, indeed, have been in vain'.

This rhetorical flourish perhaps explains the tendency to suppose that precisely because one has been a victim of extreme bias one thereby acquires an immunity to the emotional configuration characteristic of such biases. This tendency may very well be borne of the desire to wrestle a moral victory from the pain of suffering. Alas, if there is anything to be learnt from the history of Blacks and Jews in the United States it is the truth that this sort of moral victory is a very elusive one. This truth indicts no one, though. Rather, it teaches us a very hard moral lesson, namely, that unless we are prepared to earn the trust of others by listening to them speak about their suffering, we cannot understand their suffering, though we have suffered mightily ourselves—it being understood that the concern of those who speak is not to blame but to enlighten. Thus, the key to understanding the suffering of others is not our own suffering, as horrendous as that may be or have been, but the courage to engage in the act of moral deference (see Thomas, 1992-93, 1993). And sometimes, so it would appear, that takes more courage than risking physical harm itself.

Acknowledgments

In writing this essay, I am deeply grateful to a number of people in Paris, France: to Edward De Sa Pereira with whom I had numerous discussions regarding this essay, and whose forceful criticisms necessitated my starting anew; to Giles Rougemont for his enormous knowledge of French literature on both Jews and the Middle Ages, and for bringing to my attention the magnificent work of Bernard Blumenkranz (see Note 2 below); and to Charlotte De Sa Pereira and Carole Heidsieck who both graciously secured salubrious working conditions for me. Thanks are also owed to Susan Shapiro and Jennifer Parkhurt, to Carole Kessner whose important work on Blacks and Jews has meant much to me, and to Rabbi Shimon Brand whose vision inspired this essay. David Theo Goldberg has graciously commented upon the penultimate draft of this essay. The argument developed here draws upon, but goes very much beyond, my thought in *Vessels of Evil: American Slavery and the Holocaust* (1993).

This essay is a revised version of my essay delivered to the conference 'The 'Other' as Threat: Demonization and Anti-semitism', sponsored by the Vidal Sassoon International Centre for the Study of Anti-semitism, Hebrew University. A version of this essay was presented in 1994 as the 5th Meyer Warren Tenenbaum and LaBelle Tenenbaum Lecture, The University of South Carolina.

Notes

1.   For a lovely discussion of these matters, see David Theo Goldberg, *Racist Culture* (1993, ch. 6). Goldberg cogently argues that racisms are not necessarily irrational in any formal sense (pp. 130-33); for as he observes, one may consistently believe that Xs are lazy when it comes to work, but pushy when it comes to their rights (p. 132). My remarks are consistent with this thought; for I claim that malevolent ideologies can be highly preposterous—not that they are, in fact, formal contradictions.

2.   On this, see the work of E.P. Sanders (1993, pp. 179-180). Jesus' followers generally thought that he would return while they were all still alive, which became while some were still alive, which became while at least one was still alive. Sanders then notes that by the time we get to the New Testament Book 11 Peter, sceptics are being told that 'with the Lord one day is a thousand years, and a thousand years as one day' (II Peter 3: 3-4).

3.   1 am much indebted here to Bernard Blumenkranz, *Juifs et Chretiens dans Le Monde Occidental: 430-1096,* 1960. 'Le Messie nest pas encore venu; Jesus n'a pas ete le Messie promis, disent les Juifs' (p. 251). In the absence of the Second Coming, the expansion of Christianity was taken as evidence of its veracity. The following discussions reveals just how seriously early Christians took the universality of Christianity: 'En effet, les auteurs chretiens rapppellent volontiers la preuve de la verite du Christianisme qui se trouverait dans le fait qu'il est repandue sur toute la terre. L'existence de l'Etat juif en Orient se trouvait etre une flagrante contradiction a cette affirmation et les Juifs n'ont pas manque de la signaler. Chretien de Stavelot repond a cette objection . . . que [le royaume juif des] Khazars qui sont une peuplade de Huns se sont convertis au Judaisme; mais, qu'en meme temps, les Bulgares qui, eux aussi sont une peuplade de Huns, se sont convertis de leur tote au Christianisme. De ce fait . . . l'Eglise se trouve presente parmi les Huns et garde ainsi son caractere universel' (p. 237).

4.   Gavin I. Langmuir writes the following: 'For Christians, however, Jews and Judaism remained crucially important. Although Jews posed no serious or enduring physical threat to the survival of Pauline Christianity, the very existence of Jewish religiosity and Judaic religions posed a fundamental problem for Christians and the new Christian religions, for it was an internal problem, a birth trauma. Christians could never escape their awareness of competing with Judaism. Even before there was a distinctive Christian religion, the early followers of Jesus and Paul had challenged the legitimacy of the authorities of the dominant Judaic religion and tried to attract others to their beliefs about Jesus'. See Langmuir's *History, Religion, and Anti-semitism* (1990, p. 282).

    Most significantly, Langmuir distinguishes between anti-Judaism and anti-semitism, writing: 'If anti-semitism is defined as chimerical beliefs or fantasies about 'Jews', as irrational beliefs that attribute to all those symbolized as 'Jews' menacing characteristics or conduct that no Jews have been observed to possess or engage in, then anti-semitism first appeared in medieval Europe in the twelfth century (p. 297). For Langmuir, the early struggles between Jews and Christians as the latter sought dominance over the former were anti-Judaic and not anti-semitic.

5.   As Michael Barkun observed in *Religion and the Racist Right* (1994), nothing was more devastating to the credibility of a group of Christians than a prediction of the messiah that failed to come true; and nothing lent itself more readily to such devastation to credibility than precise claims about when the messiah would return.

6.   My understanding here owes much to E.P. Sanders' (1993) extremely illuminating chapter 'Miracles'. What counted as miracles were common enough then. His assessment is that 'in the first century Jesus' miracles were not decisive in deciding whether or not to accept his message and also that they did not 'prove' to his contemporaries that he was superhuman' (p. 134). And he later writes that 'the miracles attributed to Jesus are not greatly different from those attributed to other Jews in the same period' (p. 163). Magic was common among Jews who were

thought to have inherited the wisdom of Solomon (p. 138)—and Jesus was a Jew.

7.   See Jean-Paul Sartre, *Reflexions sur la question juive* (1954). He writes, 'L'antisemite reproche au Juif d'etre Juif' (p. *69*). It might seem to some that Sartre is blaming the victim. I think not. Rather, he is drawing to attention the unwillingness of gentiles to be accepting of nothing more than the nonconformity of the Jew. On the other hand, Sartre does seem to hold that the Jew is awash in self-hatred and shame for being a Jew, thus writing, 'Ce n'est pas l'homme mais le Juif que les Juifs cherchent a connaitre en eux par l'introspection; et ils veulent le connaitre pour le nier' (p. 117).

8.   Michael Krausz (1993) writes 'Whatever the historical facts of the matter, a significant portion of the Christian world assumes as part of its organizing narrative that the Jews killed their Messiah Christ' (p. 266*)*. Noting that 'the range of legal dispute between Jesus and others [that is, other Jews] was well within the parameters of normal debate' and so not matters of life and death, E.P. Sanders (1993, p. 269) maintains that the Jew Caiaphas—whose job as a high priest was to maintain order in Judea and, especially, Jerusalem—undoubtedly had Jesus arrested and killed for being a political agitator, especially for Jesus's highly provocative behaviour at the Temple; and that the accounts that we find in the Gospels reflect the eagerness of early Christians to find favour with the Romans. Accordingly, Sanders further suggests that Pilate did not succumb to any pressure from any Jewish crowd, as depicted in all of the Gospels, but had Jesus summarily executed as per Caiaphas's recommendation. The sentiments of Sanders are echoed by John Dominic Crosson (1994, 1995). As Crosson (1994) observes in the first work, the idea that Pilate was a meek ruler who spinelessly acquiesced to the demands of Jews is utterly preposterous. 'Brutal crowd control was [Pilate's] specialty', Crosson writes (p. 141).

9.   I am indebted here to conversations with David Theo Goldberg (regarding South Africa) and Mark David Wood (regarding Christianity and slavery). The state of South Africa was formed in 1910. The institution of apartheid was formulated in the 1930s and 1940s, and formalized into law after assumption of political power by the Nationalist Party in 1948.

10.   The term 'natal alienation' is taken from Orlando Patterson, *Slavery and Social Death* (1982). The idea is put to great use in ch. 6 of *Vessels of Evil*.

11.   Only until very recently was the idea still prevalent in black Christian thought that what happens to one on earth was irrelevant, just so long as one made it to heaven. See Samuel G. Freedman's wonderful book, *Upon this Rock: the Miracles of a Black Church* (1993). An analysis of 'sermons from black churches in the 1930s . . . [revealed that] . . . three-quarters dealt with other-wordly topics', making God's greatest influence being in the world beyond. In response to a voter-registration drive in the 1940s, one black clergyman explained 'All we preachers supposed to do is preach the Lord and Saviour Jesus Christ and Him crucified and that's all" (pp. 171-72). I am deeply grateful to Norman Oder for bringing this work to my attention.

        As to the hold that Christianity had upon the lives of slaves, perhaps nothing reveals this more than the testimony of slaves themselves. See John W. Blassingame (ed.), *Slave Testimony: Two Centuries of Letters, Speeches, Interviews, and Autobiographies* (1977). To be sure, some slaves were persuaded by Christianity that slavery was wrong, but few took slavery to be an indictment of Christianity. See, e.g., p. 225.

12.   In his work *Conceiving the Self* (1979), Morris Rosenberg notes that black children in impoverished schools did not suffer from low self-esteem, contrary to what might have been supposed. This is because they did not see themselves in comparison with white children in well-supported schools. Upon reflection, this is surely right. My point in the text is that as children edge toward adulthood, their comparison class naturally broadens; and therein lies the problem for black children who start out with high self-esteem, but who are dealt a very harsh hand by the world of racism. Frederick Douglass's observations about his own life in his *Life as a Slave* underscores my point. He writes, 'it was a long time before I knew myself to be a slave. I knew many other things before I knew that . . . . [K]nowing no higher authority over me or the other children than the authority of grandmamma for a time there was nothing to disturb me; but,

as I grew larger and older, I learned by degrees the sad fact, that the 'little hut', and the lot on which it stood, belonged not to my dear old grandparents, but to some person who lived a great distance off, and who was called, by grandmother, 'Old Master" (pp. 142-43). Of course, Douglass was a genius whose awareness of slavery surely had less of a deleterious effect upon him than it did upon many a slave.

13.   But see Cornel West, *Prophesy Deliverance* (1982), who argues that Christianity can play a vital role in black flourishing. The evidence, however, would not seem to support this. I am grateful here to Mark Wood's Ph.D dissertation (1994).

14.   See the words of W.E.B. DuBois in *Dusk of Dawn*, 'It is true, as I have argued, that Negroes are not inherently ugly nor congenitally stupid. They are not naturally criminal and their poverty and ignorance today have clear and well-known remediable causes. All this is true; and yet what every coloured man living today knows is that by practical measurement Negroes today are inferior to whites' (p. 1 of ch. 7). 1 believe that this difference is part of the explanation for the self-hate among Blacks that Julius Lester draws attention to in his 'The Lives People Live' (1994).

15.   In writing this section, I am indebted to several essays in Paul Berman, *Blacks and Jews: Alliances and Arguments* (1994); Paul Berman, 'The Other and the Almost the Same'; Julius Lester, 'The Lives People Live'; Henry Louis Gates, Jr 'The Uses of Anti-semitism, with 'Memoirs of an Anti-Anti-Semite'; and, especially, Clayborne Carson 'The Politics of relations between African-Americans and Jews'. By way of Sartre, I try to capture some of Berman's thought regarding Jewish identification with Blacks via 'abstract political reflection' (p. 11). And I accept the point—expressed by Lester and Gates—that despair among Blacks is a major factor in the hostility that we are seeing among Blacks, a point that I draw upon in the conclusion of Section 4.

16.   For a poignant description of Jim Crow, see Lerone Bennett, Jr, *Before the Mayflower: a History of Black America* (1988). He writes (p. 256): 'by 1901 Jim Crow was a part of the marrow of America. But he was no longer singing. The song-and-dance man had turned mean: he had become a wall, a system, a way of separating people from people. Demagogue by demagogue, mania by mania, brick by brick, the wall was built; and by the 1890s America was two nations—one white, one black, separate and unequal'.

17.   Richard Rubenstein, The Cunning of History (1975, ch. 3), advances what I call the continuum hypothesis regarding the view that the Shoah was worse than American Slavery. Recently, the most sustained defense of this view comes from Steven J. Katz, *The Holocaust in Historical Context, Vol. II* (forthcoming). See, also, Vol. I, Katz (1994).

18.   In *Vessels of Evil*. However, the distinction between culture and narrative is drawn in Thomas (1994).

19.   For as I remarked at the beginning of Section 2, slavery was not new with American slavery. What is more, supposed intellectual inferiority has been thought by many to be a quite natural justification for social inferiority. By contrast, going to great lengths and expense to gather a people from various parts of the earth in order to exterminate them has never been thought to be justified merely in virtue of the differences attributed to those people being inferior in some way or the other. Thus, by history's own reading of itself, the validity of which need not be assessed here, the Holocaust stands as an evil quite unlike other evils. For a discussion of social attitudes concerning differences, see Goldberg's (1993, pp. 28-34) discussion of Locke, Hume, and Kant. For two other recent philosophical discussions that bear upon the topic of race, see Bernard Boxill, *Blacks and Social Justice* (1984) and Howard McGary and Bill E. Lawson, *Between Slavery and Freedom* (1992).

References

Baldwin, J. (1948) *The Harlem Ghetto.*

Barkun, M. (1994) *Religion and the Racist Right,* Chapel Hill, NC: University of North Carolina Press.

Bennett, L., Jr (1988) *Before the Mayflower: a History of Black America,* New York: Penguin Books.

Berman, P. (1994) 'The Other and Almost the Same' in P. Berman (ed.) *Blacks and Jews: Alliances and Arguments,* New York: Delacorte Press.

— (1994) *Blacks and Jews: Alliances and Arguments,* New York: Delacorte Press.

Blassingame, J.W. (ed.) (1977) *Slave Testimony: Two Centuries of Letters, Speeches, Interviews, and Autobiographies,* Baton Rouge, LA: Louisiana State University Press.

Blumenkranz, B. (1960) *Juifs et Chretiens dans Le Monde Occidental, 430-1096,* Paris: Imprimatur National.

Boxill, B. (1984) *Blacks and Social Justice,* Totowa, NJ: Rowman and Allanheld.

Carson, C. (1994) 'The Politics of Relations between African-Americans and Jews' in P. Berman (ed.) *Blacks and Jews: Alliances and Arguments,* New York: Delacorte Press.

Crosson, J.D. (1994) *Jesus: a Revolutionary Biography,* New York: Harper San Francisco.

— (1995) *Who Killed Jesus? Exposing the Roots of Anti-Semitism in the Gospel Story of the Death of Jesus,* New York: Harper San Francisco.

Douglass, F. (1994) *Life as a Slave,* New York: Library of America.

DuBois, W.E.B. (1986) *Dusk of Dawn,* New York: Library of America.

Franklin, J.H. (1989) 'The Two Worlds of Race: a Historical View' in J.H. Franklin (ed.) *Race and History: Selected Essays 1938-1988,* Baton Rouge, LA: Louisiana State University Press.

Freedman, S.G. (1993) *Upon this Rock: the Miracles of a Black Church,* New York: Harper Perennial.

Gates, H.L., Jr (1994) 'Memoirs of an Anti-Anti-semite' in P. Berman (ed.) *Blacks and Jews: Alliances and Arguments,* New York: Delacorte Press.

— (1994) 'The Uses of Anti-semitism' in P. Berman (ed.) *Blacks and Jews: Alliances and Arguments,* New York: Delacorte Press.

Goldberg, D.T. (1993) *Racist Culture: Philosophy and the Politics of Meaning,* Cambridge, MA: Basil Blackwell.

Katz, S.J. (1994) *The Holocaust in Historical Context, vol. II: The Holocaust and Mass Death Before the Modern Age,* New York: Oxford University Press.

Krausz, M. (1993) 'On Being Jewish' in D.T. Goldberg and M. Krausa (eds) *Jewish Identity,* Philadelphia, PA: Temple University Press.

Langmuir, G.I. (1990) *History, Religion, and Anti-semitism,* Los Angeles: University of California Press.

Lester, J. (1994) 'The Lives People Live', in P. Berman (ed.) *Blacks and Jews: Alliances and Arguments,* New York: Delacorte Press.

Lifton, R.J. (1986) *The Nazi Doctors: Medical Killing and the Psychology of Genocide,* New York: Basic Books.

McGary, H. and B.E. Lawson (1992) *Between Slavery and Freedom,* Bloomington, IN: Indiana University Press.

Patterson, O. (1982) *Slavery and Social Death,* Cambridge, MA: Harvard University Press.

Rosenberg, M. (1979) *Conceiving the Self,* New York: Basic Books.

Rubenstein, R. (1975) *The Cunning of History,* New York: Harper and Row.

Sanders, E.P. (1993) *The Historical Figure of Jesus,* New York: Penguin Books.

Sartre, J.-P. (1954) *Reflexions sur la question juive,* Paris: Editions Gallimard.

Thomas, L. (1992-93) 'Moral Deference', *Philosophical Forum, XXIV, (1-3,* Fall-Spring): 233-31.

— (1993) 'Moral Flourishing in an Unjust World', *Journal of Moral Education,* 22.

— (1994) 'Narrative Autonomy and Group Identity: Blacks and Jews', in P. Berman (ed.) *Blacks and Jews: Alliances and Arguments,* New York: Delacorte Press.

Thomas, L.M. (1993) *Vessels of Evil,* Philadelphia, PA: Temple University Press.

West, C. (1982) *Prophesy Deliverance: an Afro-American Revolutionary Christianity,* Philadelphia, PA: Westminster Press.

Wood, M.D. (1994) 'The Politics and Theology of Prophetic Pragmatism: a Contribution to the Critique of Radical Political Philosophy', Ph.D. Dissertation, Syracuse University.

Wyman D.S. (1984) *The Abandonment of the Jews: America and the Holocaust,* 1941-45, New York: Pantheon Books.

The Public Debate on Life and Death Choices: A Response from a Jewish Hospital Chaplain

Phyllis Toback

Abstract: *This article addresses the issue of life and death choices from the perspectives of a Jewish chaplain. The author explores the tension between the law (Halachah) and experience or story (Aggadah), and the impact of that tension on lives and decisions; cites persons and situations from biblical material, oral tradition, and modern times that illustrate the human struggle with these disputed issues; explores different levels of pain and our understanding of and response to suffering; invites reflection on the range of humanly possible responses to pain; illustrates how meaning in life nurtures the desire to live; focuses on the role of chaplains in listening and responding to persons and helping to activate the impulse of hope; and suggests how chaplains can be patient advocates and prophetic voices within communities and institutions.*

As a Jewish hospital chaplain working in a large church-affiliated medical center I feel the challenge to respond to increasing discussions about active euthanasia and assisted suicide. I hear from patients, families, staff members and chaplains a growing concern that we pay more attention to the desires of patients to be spared unnecessary pain, and that death be viewed as an acceptable alternative to what appears to be irrevocable emotional and physical suffering.

In the last few years the government and the hospital community have moved a great deal toward addressing self-determination rights of patients and families. I have seen a significant impact on the way the needs and rights of patients have been addressed. I've also seen a significant increase in the number of patients and families wanting to have louder and clearer voices in decision-making.

As a chaplain, I am often positioned between doctors and patients and their families. I am asked to interpret and facilitate decision-making when wishes of patients and/or families present challenges to traditional approaches to treatment and the efforts of physicians to preserve and sustain life. I have heard numerous wishes for death for self or loved ones.

As a Clinical Pastoral Educator I am involved in the training of seminarians, clergy, and laity to do pastoral care and possibly enter the profession of hospital chaplaincy. Several important dimensions of this training include developing an awareness of specific values and beliefs we bring to our experiences from our faith traditions and personal histories, how to journey with people whose beliefs, values and life situations differ from our own, and how we are affected and influenced by these experiences. What follows reflects some of my personal journey with respect to the particular issue of suicide as an option for the hopelessly and terminally ill.

I see myself as somewhat to the left of, yet needing to be in constructive dialogue with, the clearly stated traditional Jewish voices insisting on prohibitions against suicide. I bring my tradition to my personal and professional experiences with pain, suffering, physical debilitation, and dying. As I encounter people, I am pressed with questions, from others and myself, about what meaning life has in the face of suffering. I am challenged to articulate ways I can journey pastorally with people confronted with these difficulties. And I am led to the question of how I can be an advocate for the suffering and dying in relation to health care institutions and faith communities.

Voices from the Jewish Tradition

As a chaplain and pastoral educator, I experience the tension between claims of principle or tradition, on the one hand, and those of experience, on the other. This tension is inherent in my religious experience as well. As a Jew who is associated both with the Conservative and Jewish Renewal Movements, I acknowledge the challenges of modernity to traditional practice, and attempt to remain in organic relationship with the tradition, while addressing new issues creatively.

I see two strands in Judaism, a clear, straight thread of Halachah (Law) and a more meandering thread of Aggadah (Story). Halachah is the code of norms, laws, teachings, and principles that have bound Jews together for thousands of years. Halachah holds us to the concept that people are created in the image of God. Life is sacred. Only God can create it and only God can take it away. Sanctity is a higher principle than autonomy and comfort. Suicide and voluntary euthanasia are not acceptable paths. This position is embraced by all four major branches of Judaism.

Aggadah is "that which is told." It is a heterogeneous body of materials that includes narratives, legends, tales, homilies. It communicates truths derived from human experience. It can be in tension with Halachah, and is often neither systematic nor orderly.

The question of how suicide had been addressed in the Jewish tradition led me not only to the Halachah, but also to narratives about suicide. Examples in biblical material are numerous. Abimelech, son of Gideon (Judges 9:54) and Saul (1 Samuel 31:4) committed suicide to avoid being taunted by their enemies. Samson's act of heroism (Judges 16:25-30) was also in part a response, to end being taunted. Jonah asked to be thrown overboard, partly in remorse for the suffering inflicted on others by his flight from God. In none of these cases does Scripture appear to condemn their drastic actions.[1]

But the voices of Scripture do not end in ancient history. Judaism has an Oral Tradition, seamed together with the Biblical one. The voices of rabbis throughout the ages are recorded and stand as authority for their own time. Their Responsa preserve the replies to questions about disputed issues. Even modern narratives, legends, and stories, such as the tales of the Hasidim, recorded by Martin Buber, are taking their place as part of our Scripture.

Another significant association for me is to think about assisted suicide and active euthanasia in the context of the extreme situations Jews were placed in during the Holocaust. What do the voices of fifty years ago have to add to the litany of thousands of years of Jewish response to suffering?

In much of contemporary conversation about suicide, distinctions have been made between suffering that has a physical origin and that which is psychological or spiritual. We seem to have more clarity, for example, about people who are in intractable physical pain from cancer, than about people who are in agony about the loss of autonomy, such as from diminished physical or mental capacity which is not necessarily physically painful (e.g., paralysis), or from loss of significant external resources (such as a spouse, financial resources, dependable social structures) which give meaning to their lives. It is not simply the existence of a physical condition, but also the emotional and spiritual responses to that condition that result in the experience of despair and the desire for death. That which is tolerable for one person may not be for another. I think these are connected in complex ways. What happens to the inside of a person's body and spirit may be the result and/or cause of what is happening externally.

Contemporary conversation also makes much of the distinction between "rational" and "irrational" in the discussion of suicide. What is claimed to be "rational" may really be a matter of the absence of overt emotions, or a consistency of self-presentation, or the ability to communicate effectively with another. These are not necessarily a good measure of the extremity of the situation. On the other hand, "irrational" behavior may spring from some deep place that is beyond our understanding or ability to respond to, but that nevertheless makes a powerful claim for itself. This is most striking to me in the cases where people make courageous and difficult choices in favor of remaining alive. They "irrationally" choose functioning as fully as possible in the face of what for most people would be unbearable suffering and difficulty.

In the material from the Holocaust there are numerous examples of the intermingling of the physical and spiritual and emotional suffering, and of the rational and irrational responses to it. There are many anecdotes about suicides. It is known that "many Jews had suicide pills in case they should be caught by the

Gestapo and be unable to withstand torture. This particularly applied to those who had to work at the Gestapo building."[2]

There are records of dozens of suicides, often by courageous people in positions of communal responsibility who felt profound hopelessness for the plight of others.[3] Perhaps the most poignant case brings together the Aggadah and the Halachah.

Rabbi Oshry in the Kovno ghetto was approached in October 1941 by the head of a distinguished Jewish family. Ten thousand men, women and children had already been taken away for slaughter. The man told Rabbi Oshry he was convinced from what he had heard that the "sadistic SS troopers would not simply kill him when he was taken, but would first torture and slay his wife, children, and grandchildren before his eyes. He did not believe he would be able to withstand such torture."

He asked if it was "permissible to hasten his end, to set his own hand against himself, even though it not be lawful? This, so that his own eyes not see the destruction of his family. And so that he himself not die a violent death after unspeakable tortures . . . and that he might have a proper Jewish burial."[4]

In Rabbi Oshry's thorough and careful deliberation of the case, he leaned heavily on a thirteenth century authority who referred to King Saul's death, and who thought that "in any case of suicide because of a multiplicity of troubles, worries, pain, or utter poverty, there is not the slightest reason to deny mourning rites" (Rosenbaum 1976:37).

Oshry concluded that the Kovno case was parallel to Saul's and that suicide would be permissible. He cautioned that it applied "if the person who kills himself out of fear of affliction and pain is a God-fearing man. In his case especially one may judge his intentions favorably. Not so in the case of those . . . who commit suicide because of trivial matters and who do not believe in a God who nourishes and sustains all. . . . Therefore, in our present case, where certainly he will be horribly tortured as King Saul would have been, it appears that it would be permissible for him to commit suicide" (Rosenbaum 1976:38).

Rabbi Oshry indicated that "while he permitted suicide in this case, he prohibited his decision from being widely publicized at the time [because] it would have given aid and encouragement to the Nazis" (Rosenbaum 1976:39).

Several things are striking to me in this case. One is that this man felt it necessary and important to consult with his revered Rabbi, and to address suicide on a moral and religious level. The question and answer exchanged included a serious consideration of the context of the decision, personally, communally, and in the light of the religious tradition.

The fact that Rabbi Oshry not only made the decision he did but also preserved this decision as a *responsum* also seems extremely important. Not only do we have anecdotal material but we also have a legal ruling. Clearly this is an extreme case and it does not alter the stand on suicide in general that is held in the tradition, but it points to the fact that sometimes we must acknowledge that we are out there on the edge of what is possible and tolerable, and that such extreme situations demand unprecedented responses. I don't think any one of us can predict when we will be in a situation that asks us to stretch beyond all that we have traditionally held as firm ground. Hopefully we will have the courage to remain in dialogue with values we hold dear, and yet also speak out of the truth that we find in this new situation.

The Meaning of Life

Having moved out to the terrible edge with this excruciating case, I want to move back to consider another position which is perhaps not being sufficiently addressed in the dialogue about suicide. It is that in the face of overwhelming difficulties many people waver in their thoughts of death, and often do in fact focus on living rather than dying. In his classic account, *Man's Search for Meaning*, psychiatrist Viktor Frankl, a Holocaust survivor who spent three years in Auschwitz, reports:

> I remember two cases of would-be suicide, which bore a striking similarity to each other. Both men had talked of their intentions to commit suicide. Both used the typical argument—they had nothing more to expect from life. In both cases it was a question of getting them to realize that life was still expecting something from them; something in the future was expected of them. We found, in fact, that for the one it was his child whom he adored and who was waiting for him in a foreign country. For the other it was a thing, not a person. This man was a scientist and had written a series of books which still needed to be finished. His work could not be done by anyone else, any more than another person could ever take the place of the father in his child's affections. [A person who] knows the "why' for his existence . . . will be able to bear almost any "how."[5]

Rabbi Abraham Joshua Heschel speaks about the nature of humans in *Who is Man*? He describes the differences between what people are and what can be expected of them,[6] between the human nature that is a biological given, a "thing," and the "who" that people can be, with "boundless unpredictable capacity for development" (Heschel 1965:39). In front of a restaurant that I frequent, I often see a beggar with one leg, crutches, and a styrofoam cup, which he rattles loudly at all the passersby. Every time I see him I am reminded of a chaplain colleague of mine who also has one leg. The difference between them was that I knew her for months before I learned, from her, that she had one leg missing from the hip down! She had an artificial limb, with which she negotiated imperceptibly, through the many corridors of the hospital where she worked as an oncology chaplain. After months of seeing this man, I consulted with the Chairman of a Rehabilitation Center, who offered the resources that would provide this man with an artificial limb, and occupational therapy. When I provided the information to him, he thanked me and blessed me. But years later, he remains on that streetcorner. How different are the responses people make to their difficulties!

Several other people who challenge my understanding of suffering come to mind. Some have been profoundly disabled and have had good reason to consider wanting to die, much more so than some of the people that Dr. Kevorkian has assisted with suicide.

Steven Hawkings, the eminent physicist, was stricken with ALS in his early twenties at the beginning of his career. He made a choice for a particular professional path based on the knowledge that he had only several years to live. But it was a choice in favor of accumulating skills and making a contribution to science. Now, many years beyond his original life expectancy he continues to be productive, writing books, lecturing, travelling world wide, educating students. He has been almost totally paralyzed for years, and communicates with his only available physical resource, a finger or two that push a button that operates a computer that writes, letter by letter, and generates an artificial voice.

Another person afflicted with ALS was the distinguished Jewish theologian Franz Rosenzweig (1886-1929). In his final years, when he had lost all speech and mobility, he nevertheless, with the aid of a specially constructed device, and a devoted wife, sustained numerous relationships and correspondences, and produced important translations and theological reflections.

I have had personal acquaintance with a scientist and physician afflicted with multiple sclerosis. In his final years he was confined to a wheel chair. Eventually he could barely move, breathe, or speak, but he worked in his laboratory every day until just before his death, supervising a large number of graduate students and assistants, and successfully winning important grants and carrying through numerous scientific projects.

These people focussed on living while they were dying. For them pain and debility were subordinated to productivity and creativity. They stretched my understanding of the limits of endurance and meaningfulness of life. I don't want to glorify suffering, but I want to stand in awe of the range of responses that are humanly possible.

Journey with People

When I work professionally with persons who are in pain, suffering, and dying, I am reminded of people, including patients in the hospital, who leave me with a sense of awe about how they live. But my task with patients is to not bring my own expectations, but to be a listener. They need to be listened to, to be respected, to be journeyed with, to have their concerns and struggles taken seriously.

In the book of Job, the so-called comforters fail sorely, except at the very beginning of their visit: "Now when Job's three friends heard of all this evil that was come upon him, they came every one from his own place . . . and they made an appointment together to moan him and to comfort him. . . . So they sat down with him upon the ground seven days and seven nights, and none spoke a word unto him; for they saw that his grief was very great" (Job 2.11-13).

Some of the principles illustrated here are that 1) people need to respond. They need to come from their "own place" to the place of the sufferer. 2) They need to sit "on the ground" with the person—literally try to get down to their level and be with them where they are. 3) Sometimes it means being willing to invest a lot of time ("seven days and seven nights"). 4) Not saying anything can sometimes be the most helpful thing that is done—to be silent and listen.

When people are filled with their suffering they need to empty from that vessel of pain. My job is to listen. When a person presents me with a desire to commit suicide, I want to be respectful and patient enough to hear them out, to hear all the pain that is needing to be shared, before I begin to be in dialogue with them. But sometimes people present me with their emptiness. In these cases they may be totally bereft of all resources and strength. Then my role becomes more active.

I'd like to describe a recent experience with a patient who attempted suicide. Although this man's difficulties are not on the same scale as others in the literature, it nevertheless reflects both the same kind of language, and also a model of pastoral responses to him. I discovered him quite by accident. I was doing routine pre-op visits and he was on the list because he needed surgery to his wrist, which he had slit, badly damaging the nerves in his fingers. He was in the psychiatric ward. When I asked him how he was doing, he communicated his despair about his injury because he was a house painter and might be losing his ability to use his hand for work.

He told me that he had tried to kill himself because of his hopelessness about his alcoholism and drug addiction, which had led to his loss of wife and children and alienation from family of origin. He had no place to live, no job, and no visible future employability. He literally had nowhere to go. But the very fact of my being there evoked in him a memory of how he had been "born again" years ago, and how he had attended a church that meant a lot to him. He had drifted away from that church, although a glimmer of connectedness remained.

Together we began to explore some possibilities. I was able to provide him with referrals to some spiritual communities and half-way houses. I began to see a light in his eyes that had not been there when I first arrived.

This was not a man who was terminally ill physically, but his physical addiction, physical injury, and absence of social and spiritual resources were all conspiring to encourage him on a path of self-destruction. The hospital was not going to keep him beyond his physical convalescence, and the nurse who cared for him thought it likely that he would soon try another suicide attempt if he were just left to be out on the streets. But somewhere in him was an impulse to hope.

The Jewish tradition speaks of the *Yetzer Tov* (the good impulse) and the *Yetzer Harah* (evil impulse) that exists in every person. My experience is that these impulses exist in all of us in varying degrees. We have impulses toward death and impulses toward life and love. We have feelings of despair and feelings of connectedness to values and traditions we hold dear. I believe the task of the chaplain is to create a safe space where all of these feelings may be expressed.

I have been at hundreds of deathbeds in the last nineteen years. Many times the scenes are terribly painful. Often there is a need to lament about the suffering, the meaninglessness of it all. People often speak about wanting death to come soon. Sometimes they wonder what can be done to change the situation, to make it come out differently. But rarely do people raise the question of active euthanasia.

My sense is that for the vast majority of people the desire for death is communicated the way it is by the Biblical character Job. Death is wished for, but the outcome belongs to a Power greater than themselves. Some say they feel this is in God's hands to decide.

Others might point to more impersonal Forces such as Nature or Random Chance. But for many of these people there is an underlying acceptance, I believe, of moral, ethical and physical order in the Universe.

I think that the increasing interest in Advance Directives comes from the sense that machines are impeding the natural order of things and getting in the way of "God's will." When people use the word Euthanasia, I think they mostly mean withdrawal of death-delaying treatments.

In any event, when people wish to address their relationship to illness and/or dying, and talk about what has been important to them, chaplains can offer special resources. We may be invited to help persons explore what have been the values and meanings in their lives, which persons, institutions, activities, faith relationships have been important to them, and to what extent is continuity with any of these relevant at this time.

In my own family I had occasion to be involved with an 83 year old uncle who was dying. This man was in much pain from his terminal cancer, which affected numerous parts of his body. A respirator made it difficult for him to communicate.

In his final weeks there were times when he made a choice to emotionally detach from contact with those who were visiting with him. But he also drew comfort and meaning from the presence of his children and grandchildren, who had travelled from a distance to be with him.

Several days before he died, additional relatives and friends gathered with him to celebrate his birthday, and brought a cake. His nurse took a fingerful of butter cream icing and put it to his lips. He tasted it with pleasure and then made the "OK" sign with his hand. It was a powerful moment of celebration for this whole family.

This was a man who had lived his life with zest and energy, and communal meals had been one of his ongoing pleasures. One of his daughters subsequently reported that the final weeks with her father were the "best time they had ever had together." For those days to have been shortened would have meant a loss of all of them. Clearly this was not a pleasurable time. But there is a mystery about the process of dying that sometimes involves the mingling of the terrible and the wonderful.

Those of us who have the opportunity can encourage the recognition and enhancement of these possibilities with those we are called to accompany. Nevertheless, when I am called to be present in a situation where joy does not mitigate the suffering, and where all the possibilities and resources for making some sense of this suffering have been exhausted, then I try to be present as Job's comforters initially were, or as the Lamenter in the Psalms, so that persons in excruciating pain need not feel abandoned.

I do not believe that it would be helpful to change the current legal policy about voluntary assisted euthanasia, and I would not want to be in the position of being asked to assist someone in suicide. But I humbly acknowledge that I do not know the extent to which my principles would be tested and changed by my experience with a person. I believe that what happened to Rabbi Oshry could happen to me.

Advocacy

Having said that I do not have an interest in pressing for changes in current policies, I do nevertheless want to say some things about ways I think I, and other chaplains, can be advocates for patients in extremis, can be prophetic voices in the community and in institutions, so that their situations and needs are not ignored.

I think that one of the ways I can help in this area is by seeing to it that there is as much understanding as possible around the issues of self-determination with respect to withdrawal of treatment.

I want to take advantage of all the opportunities I have to assist patients and their families in understanding these rights, to speak in public situations where ethical issues can be clarified, and to encourage increased education by all medical, institutional, and clergy professionals.

One of the ways that this work needs to be advanced is in inviting people to be more deliberate in their pursuit of good communication with one another. Filling out forms, or agreeing to abide by forms are not substitutes for ongoing dialogue between the concerned parties about the implications of a patient's wishes.

I would like to see more support for families. They often need encourage-ment and advice on how to be present and available and honest with the people they love who are suffering.

As a chaplain in a medical center that has a large number of support groups, I personally see the positive impact of these groups on families and patients. It is tremendously helpful to have a place to go to speak about the pain of this situation, to practice being honest with oneself and others, to get feedback about ways to manage that have worked, and to be directed to helpful resources.

I'd like to see support for families from our government. I think we need legislative changes that will enable people to have the necessary resources of money, supportive services, housing options, and equipment that enhances the quality of life.

Patients should not have to look toward death because they see their lives as intolerable physical and financial burdens on those they love. I'd like to see the religious communities take on more responsibility for the support and care of those who are without resources—be they family, finances, or spiritual.

Our mobile, fragmented society has lost the advantages of extended families that previous generations have had. Laity as well as professionals in congregations need to be encouraged to take on some of this role. Many people in congregations would like to help be supportive of the suffering and dying, but lack skills or encouragement. This is a lack that I and my colleagues in chaplaincy can increasingly address.

I am reminded of a man I met who was suicidal because of AIDS, but whose desire to live and be connected with people was substantially improved by being given a chance to live in a caring community that reached out to him. The effect of his finding this community and of being open to receive what they offered was that his life had taken on new meaning. He reached beyond his own personal concerns to others who shared his suffering or who could benefit from his self-understanding and ability to articulate his situation.

Our knowledge of pain control needs to be increased. Practice continues to linger behind available resources. Recent studies indicate that patients are often significantly under-medicated, because of some inappropriate concerns about addiction. There needs to be more encouragement of alternative approaches to pain.

As a person committed to holistic care, and who believes in the impact of emotions and spirituality on physical well-being, I think we need to move beyond technological approaches and expand our understanding of the phenomenon of pain. For example, the *Chicago Tribune* of February 11, 1993 described a Hindu festival in Singapore called Thaipusam where hundreds of people felt no pain from being skewered and pierced by steel.

In sum, I would like to see chaplains involved in the debate around voluntary assisted euthanasia by raising questions about how society and various institutions and communal structures can be responsive to the needs of those who suffer. I think this can best be done, not by legislating the right to commit suicide, but by thinking of ways to be increasingly supportive and respectful of the living as they live out their dying. On the one hand, we need to be more willing to claim the gifts and skills we have to communicate what we have seen, and what we know and understand about people and their needs. This is a prophetic role that can be expressed by reaching out into the communities and structures where others may want and need to hear from us. On the other hand, we need also to be humble about the limits of our energies and powers, and to see that we are only a small part of the Whole. There is a vast untapped resource of "ordinary people" who have tremendous capacities for caring and support for one another, who need to be valued and affirmed, and guided to use the skills they have. We can help design, organize and facilitate various educational and training programs directed toward these people, both from within the institutional settings where we work, and out in the communities we live in and visit. We can provide ongoing support and affirmation for those who take on this work of care. There are already numerous models available to us of self-directed self-help groups and grass roots social activism. Applying these models to the support of those who feel helpless and hopeless can have an increasingly broad impact on society. We can respond to the concerns about dehumanization, by helping to increase the number of human beings who feel empowered to help those who wish to face their dying with a living that has connectedness to a caring community and the sources of meaning and strength in their lives. In this way we will all acknowledge and live out of both our common humanity and our divinely-given potential for *Tikkun Olam*—Perfecting the Universe.

Notes

1. For a fuller discussion of these stories, see Arthur J. Droge and James D. Tabor, 1992. *A Noble Death: Suicide and Martyrdom Among Christians and Jews in Antiquity*, HarperCollins, New York.
2. Tory, Avraham, 1990. *Surviving the Holocaust: The Kovno Ghetto Diary*, edited, with an introduction by Martin Gilbert, textual and historical notes by Dina Porat, translated by Jerzy Michalowicz. Harvard University Press, Cambridge, Mass, 167 fn 4.
3. Robinson, Jacob. 5725-1965. *And the Crooked Shall be Made Straight: The Eichmann Trial, the Jewish Catastrophe, and Hanna Arendt's Narrative*. Jewish Publication Society of America, Philadelphia 186-187.
4. Rosenbaum, Irving J. 1976. *The Holocaust and Halakhah*, KTAV, New York, 35-36. Rosenbaum cites the most important source for his work as Rabbi Ephraim Oshry's 3 volume collection, *Teshuvot Mi-Maamakim* ("*Responsa from the Depths*") and notes that Rabbi Oshry is one of the few rabbinical scholars surviving the Holocaust, and that he occupied a distinguished New York pulpit and the presidency of the Rabbinical Board of New York. (Rosenbaum 1976:vi.)
5. Frankl, Viktor E. 1976. *Man's Search for Meaning*, Pocket Books, New York, 126-27.
6. Heschel, Abraham J. 1965. *Who is Man?*, Stanford: Stanford University Press.

Body Image and Eating Behaviors in Orthodox and Secular Jewish Women

Marci E. Gluck
Allan Geliebter

Abstract: Objective: *To explore the impact of religion on the development of disturbances in body image and eating behaviors.* Participants: *78 Orthodox Jewish women were compared with 48 secular Jewish women.* Design: *Participants completed the Body Shape Questionnaire (BSQ), the Eating Disorder Examination–Questionnaire Version (EDE-Q), and the Figure Rating Scale (FRS).* Results: *Despite a similar body mass index of 22.2 ± 2.8 SDs, the secular women scored significantly higher on the BSQ (P = .005) and the EDE-Q (P = .004) than the Orthodox women. Secular women also had greater eating disorder symptomatology: more laxative use(P = .02) and a trend toward more vomiting (P = .06) and diuretic use (P = .06), although not more binge eating. They were twice as likely to have a fear of becoming fat (P = .05) and were four times as likely to be influenced by their shape and weight (P = .001). Also, despite increased media exposure, the secular group chose an ideal body size on the FRS similar to that of the Orthodox group, suggesting their greater body dissatisfaction on the BSQ was related to greater cultural pressure for thinness (P = .007) and more shame about appearance (P = .04).* Conclusion: *Our findings show that membership in a strict, insulated religious group such as Orthodox Judaism may protect women, to some extent, from developing body dissatisfaction and eating pathology.*

An estimated five million Americans suffer from eating disorders.[1] About 90-95% of these disorders occur in females,[2] although the incidence appears to be increasing in both genders.[3] There is considerable cultural pressure for women to be thin[4] and for males to be muscular.[5] Magazine centerfold models have become increasingly thin for females[4] and increasingly muscular for males.[5] Exposure to these values may increase the risk of disordered eating and excessive weight control in women,[6] and may lead to lower self-esteem[7] and anabolic steroid use in men.[8]

Women may be more likely to develop eating disorders than men[2] because women report more body image disturbance,[9] with a greater misperception of being overweight.[3] Approximately 95% of women over-estimate their body size—nearly two times the percentage of men who do so.[10]

According to the sociocultural model for the development of eating disorders, there is great cultural pressure on women to be thin, especially in those countries or cultures that have a food surplus.[3] In westernized, more affluent cultures, women prefer a thin body type,[11-14] and for most, the current standard of female beauty is unattainable.[15] Eating disorders are considered culture-bound syndromes because of their relative rarity in nonwesternized countries.[4,10,12,16]

The role of religion has been largely neglected in this sociocultural model.[17] Religion, in general, is related positively to mental health,[18] and religious women are better adjusted psychologically.[19] Several investigators have proposed a relationship between Judaism and eating disorders.[17,20,21] Although Jews, who are mostly secular, make up approximately 2% of the U.S. population, they were overrepresented (13%) in one eating disorders treatment facility's inpatient clientele.[22] In the Jewish culture, food, which is commonly associated with love,[1] is emphasized in large family meals on the Sabbath and during many religious holidays.

Orthodox Jews, who constitute 10% of American Jewry,[23] maintain a social solidarity among themselves. They retain a cultural distance from the larger secular society by their appearance and way of dress, by eating kosher foods, and often by language. They observe the Sabbath,[23] forgoing daily work activities for time allotted to family[24] and reflection on spiritual matters.[23]

Many Orthodox Jews live in segregated neighborhoods, and their children attend private Jewish schools. The sexes are kept separate during the schooling process, free selection of dates is discouraged, and sexual relations are restricted. Women wear modest clothing that covers most of their bodies, and after marriage they wear head coverings such as kerchiefs or wigs.[25] Mass media, especially television, are distrusted as promoting an irreligious secular outlook.[26] Men study the Torah for as long as financially possible, often postponing careers even after being married. Women are expected to be married, rear children, and support their husband's pursuit of the Torah.

Evidence that eating disorders occur in religious Jewish communities is limited. A 1996 study found that one in 19 girls from Orthodox and Syrain Jewish communities in Brooklyn, NY, had an eating disorder—surprisingly, a rate 50% higher than in the general population.[27] Anecdotal evidence indicates that Orthodox Jewish women are frequently treated in both inpatient (I. Sacker, MD, oral communication, 1997) and outpatient (J. Hirschmann, CSW, oral communication, 1997; A.K. Kohl, MSW, oral communication, 1997) settings.

Although secular and Orthodox Jews often live in the same communities, they embody different cultural values.[28] We predicted that secular women—because of greater cultural pressure to be thin—would report more body dissatisfaction and more disturbed eating behaviors and attitudes than Orthodox women.

Participants

Participants included 225 students from several different universities and colleges in the Northeast. Those included in the data analysis were female undergraduates, less than 27 years old, born in the United States, who reported Judaism as their religious affiliation and Caucasian as their ethnic identification. Fifty-one students were excluded because they were either male or not Jewish. The remaining 174 Jewish respondents were asked to specify their denomination and complete an Orthodox traditions scale. Respondents were coded as Orthodox if they reported either "Jewish," "Orthodox," or "Modern Orthodox" and answered "always" to each of the three Orthodox traditions (1) "keep kosher in my home;" (2) "observe kosher laws while dining out;"(3) "observe the Sabbath"—and if they answered "never" to the phrase "conduct business on Saturday." Participants were coded as secular if they reported either "Jewish," "Conservative,"or "Reform," and answered "never," "rarely,"or "sometimes" to the above questions. Seventy-eight participants (45%) were classified as Orthodox, and 48 (28%) as secular (Table). Forty-eight participants were excluded from the data analysis because they fell in between the secular and Orthodox criteria.

Qualified respondents were 126 females, ages 18-26 years (20.0 ± 1.0 SD). Based on their reported current height and weight, body mass index (BMI) was 16.7-40.9 (22.2 ± 3.0 SD) and did not differ between groups (frequency [F; 1,118] = .53; P = not significant [n.s.]). The secular women were less likely to be married than the Orthodox women (chi-square [χ^2; 1,126] = 5.0; P = .03). Their characteristics are shown in the Table.

Procedures

Candidates were invited to participate during one of their classroom sessions or weekly sorority meetings. The study investigator made a brief announcement and assured anonymity. About 20 (8%) of the 250 students in attendance did not complete the survey. Procedures and questionnaires were approved by various institutional review boards of the colleges.

Instruments

Students completed several questionnaires. Body dissatisfaction was assessed with the Body Shape Questionnaire (BSQ),[29] and eating behavior was assessed with the Eating Disorders Examination–Questionnaire Version (EDE-Q).[30]

Table
Demographics by Religious Group (M ± SD)

Characteristic	Orthodox	Secular
N	78	48
Age	20 ± 1.5	20 ± 1.4
Marital Status*		
Single	86%	98%
Married	14%	2%
Year of College	2.3 ± 1.0	2.5 ± 1.2
SES*†	3.8% ± 1.0	4.3% ± .93
Low	1%	2%
Mid-Low	9%	2%
Moderate	23%	10%
Mid-High	33%	37%
Highest	24%	43%
BMI	22.0% ± 3.3	22.4% ± 2.3

M = mean; SD = standard deviation; SES = socioeconomic status; BMI = body mass index

*The secular women were less likely to be married and were from higher SES families than the Orthodox women (P < .05).

*† SES was assessed using the Hollingshead scale, ranging from 1-5; 1= low, 5 = highest.

None of the participants met the full criteria for anorexia nervosa, bulimia nervosa, or binge eating disorder. Individual diagnostic items on the EDE-Q were examined further for eating disorder pathology. Respondents were dummy-coded as having a "fear of fat" if they scored a 4 or higher on both item #13 ("Have you had a definite fear that you might gain weight or become fat?") and item #14 ("Have you ever felt fat?"). Participants were dummy-coded as overvaluing the importance of shape and weight if they scored a 4 or higher on both item #30 ("Has your shape influenced how you think about yourself as a person?") and item #31 ("Has your weight influenced how you think about yourself as a person?"). They were coded as binge eaters if they had at least one episode of eating a large amount of food with a sense of loss of control.

The Sociocultural Attitudes Towards Appearance Questionnaire (SATAQ)[31] was used to assess women's recognition and acceptance of societal standards of appearance. The Rosenberg Self-Esteem (RSE) Inventory,[32] as well as the Figure Rating Scale (FRS),[33] which has nine female silhouettes ranging from very thin to overweight, were also completed. On the FRS, participants indicated by number (10-90) their current body size and their ideal figure. The difference between current and ideal was considered a measure of body image discrepancy.

Lastly, participants completed the Religious Identification Question-naire,[32] which assessed the strength of their religious identity. They also completed a scale assessing observance of Orthodox traditions and media exposure, including watching television and reading fashion magazines.

Socioeconomic status (SES) was assessed with the Hollingshead scale, which delineates five levels of status, based on parental occupation and education.[34] Secular participants had a significantly higher SES than Orthodox participants ($F[1,115] = 6.5$; $P = .012$; Table).

Factor analyses did not support construct validity for the subscales for the EDE-Q or the cultural attitudes measure (SATAQ); therefore, total scores were used for each. Three items (#6, #10, and #12) were omitted from the total score on the SATAQ because they did not load on the construct. Two SATAQ items that measured the construct of "cultural importance" were summed: item # 8 ("Attractiveness is very important if you want to get ahead in our culture") and item # 9 ("It is important for people to work hard on their figures/physiques if they want to succeed in today's culture"). Also, a shame index was formed by summing three items from the BSQ: item # 7 ("Have you felt so bad about your shape that you have cried?"), item # 20 ("Have you felt ashamed of your body?"), and item # 29 ("Has seeing your reflection made you feel bad about your shape?").

Data Analysis

Analysis of covariancewas used to compare parametric data between religious groups, and χ^2 and logistic regression were used to compare categorical data. Results are presented as mean ± SD. Multiple linear regression (MLR) was utilized to determine significant predictors of body dissatisfaction (BSQ) and eating pathology (EDE-Q). Predictors were entered into the equation if they explained additional variance (.05 cutoff). Two-tailed $P < .05$ was required for statistical significance. Data were analyzed with the Statistical Package for the Social Sciences, version 7.5.1 (1996; Chicago, IL).

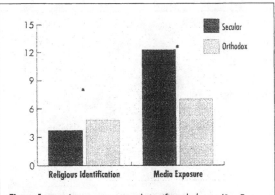

Figure 1. *Secular women scored significantly lower (* = P < .001) on religious identification and significantly higher on media exposure than the Orthodox group.*

Results

As expected, secular women scored lower than Orthodox women on the religious identification questionnaire (F[1,125] = 51.7; P < .0001), and secular women scored higher on the subscale of media exposure (F[1,125] = 62.1; P < .0001; Figure 1).

Secular women also scored higher on the BSQ (F[1,125]=8.0; P = .005) and on the total EDE-Q score (F[1,125] = 8.5; P = .004; Figure 2). Secular women were also significantly more likely to use laxatives (χ^2 [1,123] = 5.8; P = .02), with a trend toward more vomiting (χ^2 [1,123] = 3.4; P = .06) and diuretic use (χ^2 [1,123] = 3.4; P = .06). There were no group differences in binge eating (χ^2 [1,100] = .21; P = n.s).

Logistic regression revealed that secular students were twice as likely as Orthodox students to have a fear of becoming fat (odds ratio [Exp (B)] = 2.3, P = .05), and four times more likely to be greatly influenced by their shape and weight (Exp [B] = 3.8; P = .001). These findings held even when controlling for SES and media exposure. Marital status was not a significant covariate and was therefore not used in the analyses.

Secular women showed a trend toward scoring higher on the SATAQ (F[1,125] = 3.7; P = .056). They also scored higher on the items measuring cultural importance (F[1,124] = 7.4; P = .007) and felt significantly more shame (F[1,123] = 4.2; P = .04) than the Orthodox group. After controlling for SES and media exposure, these differences lost significance, but there was substantial collinearity between SATAQ, SES, cultural importance, and shame.

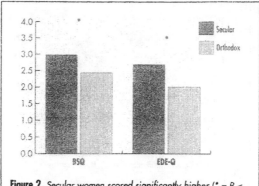

Figure 2. *Secular women scored significantly higher (* = P < .001) on the Body Shape Questionnaire (BSQ) and the Eating Disorders Examination (EDE-Q) than the Orthodox group.*

On the FRS, there were no significant group differences in current appearance ($F[1,122] = .92$; P = n.s), ideal appearance ($F[1,122] = 1.3$; P = n.s), or body discrepancy ($F[1,121] = .11$; P = n.s). There were also no group differences on the RSE ($F[1,125] = 0.6$; P = n.s).

We further investigated predictors of body dissatisfaction (BSQ) and eating pathology (EDE-Q) by conducting an MLR with the religious groups (secular vs Orthodox), SES, and media exposure entered into the equation. For BSQ, only religious group was significant, accounting for 6% of the variance in BSQ scores ($R2 = .06$; $P < .03$). For EDE-Q, both SES and religious group significantly accounted for 11% of the variance ($R^2 = .11$; $P = .001$).

Discussion

The results of this study confirm that secular women have greater body dissatisfaction and more overall eating disorders than Orthodox women. The unexpected similarity in rates of binge eating among secular and Orthodox women might be due in part to the weekly Sabbath meal, when a large amount of food is eaten, perhaps, at times, with some loss of control.

Surprisingly, the groups did not differ on the perceptual measures of body image (FRS). These findings are similar to our recent study[35] that did not find differences on perceived current or ideal body size on the FRS among African-Americans, Asians, and Caucasians, despite less body dissatisfaction and eating pathology in the African-American group. In the current study,[36] the secular women had increased media exposure and were therefore expected to have a smaller ideal, yet their ideal body size on the FRS did not differ from the Orthodox women. Thus, exposure to media and endorsement of the "thin ideal" alone cannot explain differences in body dissatisfaction and eating pathology. However, it has been shown that internalization of sociocultural attitudes contributes to pressure for thinness more than simple media exposure,[37] and is associated with a sense of shame when a woman's actual self fails to match up to her ideal self.[38] The women in the secular group experienced more shame about their body appearance. Although the findings on cultural importance and shame did not hold up when covarying for media and SES, they should not be discounted. The SATAQ items themselves concern the media and are related to SES, and the high collinearity suggests they are measuring similar constructs.

Previous studies have found that increased pressure for success and a competitive environment can promote eating disorders,[4,39] as well as increased confusion about the current role of women in today's society.[20,40] Our study suggests that Orthodox Judaism might, to some extent, protect women against developing body dissatisfaction and eating pathology. In Orthodox Judaism, there is less emphasis on the physical attractiveness of women, and less pressure for success and achievement for women outside the home.[25] The Sabbath may also be protective by emphasizing social support, and providing perceptions of rigid lifestyle control[41] as an alternative outlet for control of shape and weight.

These protective aspects of the Orthodox Jewish religion might also generalize to other religious groups. One recent study[42] of both men and women in the Old Order Amish found less body weight dissatisfaction and less inaccuracy of perception of body size among young persons. However, older obese persons of both genders had body dissatisfaction, and older obese men and nonobese women overestimated their body size. The authors speculated that perhaps the group's "separateness" guarded the youth from the pressures for desiring a thinner body or overestimating size. The young Amish women did not exhibit greater body dissatisfaction than men, as observed in most studies of nonreligious groups. Similarly, a recent study[43] of obese individuals found that males had more body image disturbance and overestimated their body size to a greater degree than their female counterparts. There has been a recent rise in eating disorders among men[3] as the ideal body size for males has become increasingly muscular.[5] However, compared to men, women are still much more likely to be diagnosed with an eating disorder.[3]

Our study revealed less psychopathology concerning eating behavior and body image in an insulated religious group of Orthodox Jewish women. By comparison, the secular Jewish women had significantly more body dissatisfaction and eating pathology, which may be mediated by greater cultural pressure to be thin and more shame about appearance.

References

1. Strasser T. The Jewish psyche becomes ripe field for eating disorders. *Jewish Bulletin of Northern California*; November 22, 1996. Available at: http://www.shamash.org/jb/bk961122/1aeat.htm. Accessed October 4, 2001.

2. Walsh BT. Eating disorders. In: Tasman A, Kay J, Lieberman JA, eds. *Psychiatry*. Philadelphia, PA: WB Saunders Co; 1996: 1202-1216.

3. Andersen, AE. Gender-related aspects of eating disorders: A guide to practice. *J Gend Specif Med* 1999; 2(1):47-54.

4. Garner DM, Garfinkel PE, Schwartz D, Thompson M. Cultural expectations of thinness in women. *Psychol Rep* 1980;47(2):483-491.

5. Leit RA, Pope HG Jr, Gray JJ. Cultural expectations of muscularity in men: The evolution of *Playgirl* centerfolds. *Int J Eat Disord* 2001;29(1):90-93.

6. French SA, Story M, Neumark-Sztainer D, et al. Ethnic differences in psychosocial and health behavior correlates of dieting, purging, and binge eating in a population-based sample of adolescent females. *Int J Eat Disord* 1997;22(3):315-322.

7. Blouin AG, Goldfield GS. Body image and steroid use in male bodybuilders. *Int J Eat Disord* 1995;18(2):159-165.

8. Pope HG Jr, Katz DL. Psychiatric and medical effects of anabolic-androgenic steroid use: A controlled study of 160 athletes. *Arch Gen Psychiatry* 1994;51(5):375-382.

9. Cash TF, Winstead BA, Janda LH. The great American shape-up. *Psychology Today* 1986;20:30-37.

10. Thompson JK, Thompson CM. Body size distortion and self-esteem in asymptomatic normal weight males and females. *Int J Eat Disord* 1986;5(6):1061-1068.

11. Furnham A, Baguma P. Cross-cultural differences in the evaluation of male and female body shapes. *Int J Eat Disord* 1994;15(1):81-89.

12. McCarthy M. The thin ideal, depression and eating disorders in women. *Behavior Research* 1990;28:205-215.

13. Nasser M. Comparative study of the prevalence of abnormal eating attitudes among Arab female students of both London and Cairo universities. *Psychol Med* 1986;16(13):621-625.

14. Furnham A, Alibhai N. Cross-cultural differences in the perception of female body shapes. *Psychol Med* 1983;13(4):829-837.

15. Striegel-Moore RH. A feminist perspective on the etiology of eating disorders. In: Brownell KD, Fairburn CG, eds. *Eating Disorders and Obesity: A Comprehensive Handbook*. New York, NY: Guilford Press; 1995: 224-229.

16. Nasser M. Culture and weight consciousness. *J Psycho Res* 1988; 32(6): 573- 577.

17. Richards PS, Hardman RK, Frost HA, et al. Spiritual issues and interventions in the treatment of patients with eating disorders. *Eating Disorders: The Journal of Treatment and Prevention* 1997;5(4):261-279.

18. Neeleman J, Persaud R. Why do psychiatrists neglect religion? *Br J Med Psychol* 1995;68(pt 2):169-178.

19. Crawford ME, Handal PJ, Weiner RL. The relationship between religion and mental health/distress. *Review of Religious Research* 1989; 31:16-22.

20. Bruch H. *Eating Disorders: Obesity, Anorexia Nervosa, and the Person Within*. New York, NY: Basic Books; 1973.

21. Rowland CV Jr. Anorexia nervosa: A survey of the literature and review of 30

cases. *Int Psychiatry Clin* 1970;7(1):37-137.

22. Baruchin A. Why Jewish girls starve themselves. *Lilith* 1998; Spring: 23(1): 5.

23. Frank G, Bernardo CS, Tropper S, Noguchi F, et al. Jewish spirituality through actions in time: Daily occupations of young Orthodox Jewish couples in Los Angeles. *Am J Occup Ther* 1997;51(3):199-206. 35.

24. Goldberg AD. The Sabbath: Implications for mental health. *Counseling and Values* 1987;31:147-156.

25. Heilman SC, Witztum E. Value-sensitive therapy: Learning from ultra-Orthodox patients. *Am J Psychother* 1997;51(4):522-541.

26. Loewenthal KM, Goldblatt V, Gorton T, et al. The social circumstances of anxiety and its symptoms among Anglo-Jews. *J Affect Disord* 1997;46(2):87-94.

27. Baruchin A. What can Orthodox girls control? *Lilith* 1998; 23(3): 8 (Ethnic News).

28. Neumark-Sztainer DM, Palti H, Butler R. Weight concerns and dieting behaviors among high school girls in Israel. *J Adolesc Health* 1995;16(1):53-59.

29. Cooper PJ, Taylor MJ, Cooper Z, Fairburn CG. The development and validation of the Body Shape Questionnaire. *Int J Eat Disord* 1987;6:485-494.

30. Cooper Z, Cooper PJ, Fairburn CG. The validity of the Eating Disorder Examination and its subscales. *Br J Psychiatry* 1989;154:807-812.

31. Heinberg LJ, Thompson JK, Stormer S. Development and validation of the Sociocultural Attitudes Towards Appearance Questionnaire. *Int J Eat Disord* 1995;17(1):81-89.

32. Rosenberg M. *Conceiving the Self.* New York, NY: Basic Books; 1970.

33. Stunkard AJ, Sorensen T, Schulsinger F. Use of the Danish Adoption Register for the study of obesity and thinness. In: Kety S, Rowland LP, Sidman RL, Matthysse SW, eds. *The Genetics of Neurological and Psychiatric Disorders.* NY: Raven Press; 1983: 115-120.

34. Hollingshead AB, Redlich FC. *Social Class and Mental Illness.* NY: Wiley; 1958.

35. Gluck ME, Geliebter A. Racial/ethnic differences in body image and eating behaviors. *Eating Behaviors* 2001;2:1-9.

36. Striegel-Moore RH, Silberstein LR, Rodin J. Toward an understanding of risk factors for bulimia. *Am Psychol* 1986;41(3):246-263.

37. Stormer SM, Thompson JK. Explanations of body image disturbance: A test of maturational status, negative verbal commentary, social comparison, and sociocultural hypotheses. *Int J Eat Disord* 1996;19(2):193-202.

38. Silberstein LR, Striegel-Moore RH, Rodin J. Feeling fat: A woman's shame. In: Lewis HB, ed. *The Role of Shame in Symptom Formation.* Mahwah, NJ: Lawrence Erlbaum Associates; 1987: 89-108.

39. Herzog DB, Pepose M, Norman DK, Rigotti NA. Eating disorders and social maladjustment in female medical students. *J Nerv Ment Dis* 1985;173(12):734-737.

40. Silverstein B, Perlick D. The Cost of Competence: *Why Inequality Causes Depression, Eating Disorders and Illness in Women.* NY: Oxford University Press; 1995.

41. Goldberg AD. The Sabbath as a dialectic: Implications for mental health. *Journal of Religion and Health* 1986;25:237-244.

42. Platte P, Zelten JF, Stunkard AJ. Body image in the Old Order Amish: A people separate from "the world." *Int J Eat Disord* 2000;28(4):408-414.

43. Sorbara M, Geliebter A. Body image disturbance in obese outpatients before and after weight loss in relation to race, gender, binge eating, and age onset of obesity. *Int J Eat Disord.* In press.

Psychosocial Adjustment Among Returnees to Judaism

Brian Trappler
Jean Endicott
Steven Friedman

Abstract: *Two groups of returnees to Orthodox Judaism who were among Lubavitcher Hasidim attending an outpatient mental health center were studied to investigate a relief effect upon returning. One group manifested lifelong serious psychopathology, and the members of the comparison group, who had undergone similar religious transition, had sought help for adjustment-type problems. The psychopathology manifested prior to religious change persisted for those who had exhibited a lifelong history of pathology, even after the radical transition. The lack of a relief effect and the lifestyles possibly unique to Lubavitcher Hasidim are discussed.*

Previous studies (Nicholi, 1974; Zaretsky & Leone, 1974) appear to highlight an assumption that radical religious transitions are symptomatic of, or at least associated with, serious psychopathology. In contemporary society, and even among secular mental health professionals, radical change in religious affiliation is believed to be necessarily associated with psychiatric disturbance. In the present study we compared two groups of returnees to Orthodox Judaism/ Lubavitcher Hasidim. One group had a history of serious psychopathology. The comparison group consisted of participants adopting a similar lifestyle who were, historically, relatively free of psychopathology. The lack of comparison groups in previous studies may have confounded any discussion of the implications of radical religious transformations and mental health (Larson et al., 1993). To the best of our knowledge, there are no previous studies on Jewish returnees to a Hasidic affiliation.

We studied returnees to Lubavitcher Hasidim, who may be a unique Hasidic group in a variety of ways. They closely follow the charismatic leadership of the Lubavitcher Rebbe, who directs the worldwide movement. The emphasis of the movement is on outreach and education of assimilated Jews throughout the world. The Lubavitcher Hasidim themselves adhere closely to the strict interpretation of *Halacha* (legal code based on the written books of the Bible and the oral traditions), but they have an open community and open their homes to secular coreligionists. Newcomers in the community are warmly embraced and provided with an intensive supportive social network.

A distinctive feature of this group is that religious returnees are, in general, encouraged by the Rebbe to return to their former professions rather than live a life dedicated exclusively to Torah study. Instead, returnees are encouraged to integrate a religious lifestyle with pursuit of previous career aspirations.

Other qualities in the Lubavitcher group distinguish it from other systems with intense group beliefs. Group members are not protected or buffeted against the materialism and competition of the outside world. Some members may spend 1 or 2 years full-time in Yeshiva (a school for religious studies); others may become religious on a gradual basis while continuing to work in a professional role. There is no effort to create a boundary between members of the group and the outside community. There is no sense of persecution or antagonism; members of the group are encouraged to interact with outsiders. Outsiders are, in fact, invited to experience the community life. Intellectual challenge is invited. Likewise, contact with a person's extended family is encouraged; for example, a new religious affiliate is encouraged to spend holidays with his or her family in a less religious environment so that the member's transition may be integrated into the life of significant others. During this process, considerable flexibility is shown in abdication of rules. Members are counseled against rigidity of beliefs and inflexible attitudes. Not only is dogma not rigidly enforced, but the format of education also encourages question and debate. This practice may differ sharply from the rigid and obsessional enforcement of dogma and coercion or dominance used by leaders in many other groups (Levine, 1984).

The critical period of religious transition described by Levine (1969) in other groups does not appear to occur in the Lubavitcher community. During this process in other groups the novices described by Levine (1969) become closed minded and happy true believers, and they emerge from a state of alienation. Levine described how members become alienated or estranged from parents and are not given the opportunity to mix with former groups. The pseudo-protection offered by the closed community provides an immediate relief effect, which may later crumble under challenge.

We decided to study the complex issue of psychosocial adjustment and new religious affiliations by comparing two groups of participants. Although both groups consisted of "returnees" (*Baalei Teshuvah*), one group had a long history of psychopathology, whereas the comparison group consisted of similar returnees with a relatively stable psychosocial history and adjustment.

Method

Participants

Although all of the participants were born Jewish, their previous religious involvement had been minimal. Lubavitcher Hasidim direct their efforts to "returning" fellow Jews to religious practice. They do not engage in outreach to convert non-Jewish members of society. The participants' backgrounds were uniformly upper and middle class, with families of origin relatively assimilated into secular American culture and of either Reform or Conservative Jewish background. After the new religious affiliation, all of the participants had undergone changes in name and dress, in accordance with Hasidic tradition, and they had moved in with the community of the Lubavitcher Hasidim in the Crown Heights section of Brooklyn.

Within the returnee group two distinct subgroups were selected. The patient subgroup (n = 15) consisted of persons in treatment at a community-based mental health clinic, which was run under the auspices of the Orthodox Jewish community. Members of this group were referred by their therapists if they (a) had experienced a psychosis or major depression/bipolar disorder with active symptoms within the past year, (b) were in weekly treatment, and (c) were on some form of psychotropic medication.

The comparison group of returnees (n = 14) consisted of clients referred from the mental health clinic with problems that were consistent with an adjustment disorder (either work or family related). This comparison group was receiving family therapy or supportive counseling. No members of the comparison group were receiving psychotropic medication.

Measures

Data were obtained from a self-report questionnaire, as well as from clinical judgments made by the clients' therapists on a variety of rating scales. A wide range of subjective feelings and functioning were studied, including items on adolescent turmoil and self-image, emotional control, previous substance and alcohol abuse, qualities of the family of origin, stress on Jewish education, and history of previous treatment.

Evaluation of present functioning included items on quality of marriage, connectedness to family members outside the community, social interaction patterns with friends and neighbors, job or role functioning, standard of living, use of community supports, perception of living environment, severity of symptoms, use of defenses and religious ritual, and ability to internalize religious values.

Some of the items of the self-report questionnaire were taken from other rating instruments, such as the Self-Image Questionnaire developed by Offer (1969) or the Personal Resources Inventory (PRI) developed by Clayton and Hirschfeld (1978). Other items were designed specifically for this study.

The second component consisted of clinical judgments by the patient's therapist (either a licensed social worker or a doctoral-level psychologist). This component consisted of global judgments on severity of psychiatric symptoms, quality of marriage, community functioning, nature of defenses, and maturity or flexibility in the use of religious beliefs and rituals.

Results

The two groups did not differ in age (patients M = 36.9 years, SD = 6.4; comparison group M = 37.0 years, SD = 11.3) or gender distribution (males = 57% and 71 %, respectively). They did differ significantly on a number of other demographic characteristics. The members of the control group were more likely to be married (93%) than the patients (64%), χ^2 (1, n = 29) = 3.4, p < .06. Only 14% of the patients' group were employed (versus 69% of the comparison group), χ^2 (1, n = 29) = 8.4, p < .004; and fully 50% of the patients' group (versus none of the comparison group) were receiving some form of public assistance (rent subsidy, food stamps, or Medicaid).

Members of the patients' group, not surprisingly, were more likely to have a psychotic or schizophrenic diagnosis (see Table 1 for clinicians' ratings on a variety of clinical characteristics on which the two groups differed). The patients' group was also rated by their therapists as having more severe symptoms, poorer community functioning, less ability to meet household responsibilities, and generally less ability to nurture their children and partners. In addition, they were seen as using more primitive defenses and were also viewed as being more "rigid" in their religious practices.

The participants' retrospective analysis of their childhood on a number of dimensions is summarized in Table 2. The patients were more likely than the control group to recall that they were treated poorly, were less confident, were more anxious, were less ambitious, had more problems with their temper, and generally felt "easily hurt."

Compared with the control group, the patients described their families as less closely knit, and they had a sense that their parents "did not care" (see Table 3). They also reported less sense of community ties while growing up, and a continued sense of fewer family ties.

TABLE 1: Clinicians' Ratings of Clinical Characteristics on which Two Groups Differed Significantly

Characteristic	% patients' group (n = 15)	% comparison group (n = 14)	χ^2	P
Diagnosis			9.9	.007
No mental disorder or problems	0	69		
Nonpsychotica	60			
Psychotic/schizophrenic	40	0		
Severity of symptoms			11.6	.008
None	0	38		
Mild	6	23		
Moderate	67	39		
Severe	27	0		
Community functioning			12.8	.001
Good	13	77		
Fair	20	15		
Poor	68	8		
Meets household responsibilities			19.8	.001
Well	7	92		
Fair	40	8		
Poorly	53	0		
Ability to parent			20.5	.001
Able	0	92		
Fair	58	8		
Problems	42	0		
Ability to nurture				
Able	14	100	19.1	.001
Fair	50	0		
Problems	36	0		
Use of defenses			15.4	.001
Flexible	7	69		
Neurotic	33	31		
Primitive	60	0		
Religious ritual			5.3	.072
Flexible	27	69		
Somewhat rigid	27	15		
Extremely rigid	47	15		
Adherence to religious rules			10.4	.005
Just adhering	53	0		
Gratifying	47	100		
Follow rules rotely or internalized values			9.3	.009
Rote	67	15		
Variable	13	8		
Internalized	20	77		

'Most had some form of depressive disorder.

TABLE 2: Differences Between Two Participant Groups in Reported Feelings While Child or Adolescent*

Feeling	Patients' group (n = 15)	Comparison group (n = 14)	χ^2
Treated badly	86	29	9.7
Felt relaxed	0	71	17.6
Felt confident	7	57	8.7
Felt comfortable with looks	33	86	9.1
Worried about health	33	50	8.1
Felt ambitious	47	79	5.9
Enjoyed life	13	64	8.5
Felt anxious	100	36	15.2
Feelings easily hurt	93	50	7.5
Lose temper easily	20	93	16.1

*p < .05.

TABLE 3: Differences Between Two Participant Groups in Description of Family of Origin*

Description	Patients' Group (n = 15)	(n Comparison group (n = 14)	χ^2
Closely knit	14	77	13.6
Mother cared	60	100	12.0
Father cared	40	79	7.8
Mother understood	33	71	7.8
Mother shared my success	36	100	14.3
Father shared my success	7	57	8.1
Mother encouraged independence	21	71	8.6
Family was connected to community	13	85	15.4
Was sent to Jewish day school/summer camp	20	71	8
Current close ties with family	40	92	10.5
Could count on family now	14	79	13.4

*p <.05.

Discussion

In this study of two groups of returnees to strict Jewish Orthodoxy, the patient group reported experiencing emotional distress going back to adolescence. For this group, this distress and lower functioning continued after their religious conversion. Of interest was that the patient group did not automatically endorse all negative statements. For instance, the patient group did not report feeling more inferior growing up than did the control group, nor did the patients report feeling more unattractive or less ambitious. However, 100% of the patients' group described feeling anxious in adolescence, and the majority reported feeling unhappy and easily hurt. This contrasted strongly with the comparison group of religious returnees, who reported feeling relaxed, happy, and much less vulnerable as adolescents. The frequency of alcohol or substance abuse prior to the religious change was of low frequency in both groups (patients, 13%; controls, 7%; ns), probably lower than that of the general population at large and consistent with the report of lower rates of alcoholism or substance abuse among Jews.

Another finding was that the comparison group of religious returnees reported that they had "closely knit" families, whereas the patients' group did not (7% vs. 26%, respectively, ns). In the patients' group, there was a much higher rating, though nonsignificant (26% vs. 7%, ns), of mothers as not "being available" or "not caring." Only 14% of the patients reported their families of origin as being "closely knit," compared with 77% of the comparison group.

The comparison group maintained better family integration in that they were more likely to be married and found their marriages to be happy, fulfilling, and comfortable, whereas more members of the patient group were unmarried, divorced, or involved in unhappy marriages. Other studies have found that new religious groups often discourage their members from maintaining close family contact (Levine, 1969). In our comparison group of religious returnees, 92% continued to maintain close family contact.

Most members of the patients' group were receiving one or more kinds of public assistance, such as rent subsidy, food stamps, and Medicaid. Therapists found that members of the patients' group were less involved in community affairs and less adaptive in their vocational functioning, and that their community functioning was more need gratifying than truly independent.

The patients' group also showed more difficulty with household responsibilities and the ability to nurture and parent. Offspring of members of the patients' group were also more likely to be reported as having problems in school or in their daily behavior. The therapists noted that the patients' group used more neurotic or primitive defenses, whereas the comparison group showed more mature and flexible defenses. The patients tended to adhere to rules in a rote-like way, whereas the comparison group showed greater internalization and experienced the religion in a more gratifying way.

Our findings indicate that new religious affiliates to Lubavitcher Hasidim who seek or are referred for assistance can be separated into at least two groups, which differ in functions both prior to and after joining the Lubavitcher. The higher functioning group, in our study, experienced better nurturance and were freer of psychopathology prior to religious involvement.

This group continued to function after the religious transition in a more independent way. They used religion in a flexible and ego-enhancing way. In contrast to the control group, the patients' group had experienced poorer nurturance; had manifested, early in their lives, symptoms of psychopathology; and, even after religious change, they continued to function in a more dependent way, following rules in a rote fashion with less internalization.

Other studies have emphasized (a) the relief effect of new religious affiliations (Galanter, 1978), (b) pre-existing turmoil or crisis, and (c) reduction of stress and improved psychological well-being as a result of a new religious affiliation (Kilbourne & Richardson, 1984; Wilson, 1972). Although both our patients' and comparison groups of religious returnees acknowledged that religion provided a sustaining and supportive role, no "relief effect" was noted. In general, previous patterns of adjustment continued. Those who showed lifelong histories of psychopathology and family dysfunction continued this pattern, and those who reported better parental nurturing and more stable adolescence achieved a high level of community integration and adaptive functioning even after their religious change.

The lack of a relief effect in this study may be attributed to our use of two preselected comparison groups or to certain characteristics of the Lubavitcher Orthodox Jewish lifestyle. Some characteristics of this community are shared with those of many other systems with intense group beliefs, but they also differ in important ways. In common with other groups is the belief system and commitment to its theology, the sense of belonging, and regulation of behavior through religious precepts and rules (Frank, 1987; Levine, 1984). However, our findings suggest that the continued stress of competitive materialism and the continued challenge of interpersonal relationships maintain the separateness of two groups—the well and poorly adjusted. Factors that determine the presence or absence of psychopathology during early development, and that influenced adjustment before the participant made the religious change, continue to operate and are not radically altered by religious conversion.

However, there were instances when a participant had benefited by becoming a member of a "therapeutic community," although the returnee patients' group generally continued to show significant psychiatric pathology after returning. Examples of the support system include learning groups, various hotlines, mothers' helpers from Yeshivas, and "*Mashpium*" (mentors who act as surrogate parents). Although these benefits were not systematically measured, the authors' impressions were, from individual case records, that several patients were on doses of medication that were lower than those they had been receiving, and that they had much less frequent hospitalizations after religious change (e.g., two patients who had been hospitalized 20 times each in the 10 years prior to their religious change were not hospitalized at all in the 10 years after joining the community). Employment, even part time, was often provided in neighborhood stores and may have had an additional stabilizing effect.

The senior author has treated several patients who received charity (i.e., an anonymous donor gave money to a storekeeper to be used as a salary conditional on a certain number of hours of weekly employment) in the guise of actual employment. Another patient, whose children had been removed from the house by the Department of Special Services prior to joining the community, was able to regain custody after the children received free day-care with door-to-door bus pick-up service. That patient's day was also structured by a friend from the community who ensured that she attended daily classes. In addition, for that patient, a homemaker was provided by the Jewish Community Council.

In summary, by studying two groups of participants who have undergone a radical religious transformation, we have demonstrated that the effect of this process is complex and often related to a person's early developmental history. Intense religious beliefs and experiences, which are often a sensitive topic for mental health professionals, have a profound impact on many people's lives. Simple approaches that predict either a relief from psychiatric symptoms or an eventual emotional collapse for those who join charismatic fundamental movements are misguided. Further study of the interplay between religious conversions, leadership characteristics, and community and individual dynamics are clearly warranted to understand this important and complex topic.

Acknowledgments

This work was supported in part by NIMH Mental Health Clinical Research Center Grant MH 30906.

References

Clayton, P., & Hirschfeld, R. M. A. (1978). *Personal Resources Inventory.* (Available from the second author).

Frank, J. D. (1978). Sources and functions of belief systems. In P. E. Diets (Ed.), *Psychotherapy and the human predicament* (pp. 260-269). New York: Schocken.

Galanter, M. (1978). The "relief effect": A sociobiological model and neurotic distress and large-group therapy. *American Journal of Psychiatry, 135,* 588-591.

Kilbourne, B. K., & Richardson, J. T. (1984). Psychotherapy and new religions in a pluralistic society. *American Psychologist, 39,* 237-251.

Larson, D. B., Thielman, S. B., Greenwold, M. A., Lyons, J. S., Post, S. G., Kimberly, A. S., Wood, G. G., & Larson, S. S. (1993). Religious content in the DSM-111-R glossary of technical terms. *American Journal of Psychiatry, 150,* 1884-1885.

Levine, S. V. (1969). Life in the cults. *Cults and New Religious Movements: A Report of the APA, 6,* 95-107.

Levine, S. V. (1984). Belief and belonging in adult behavior. *Perspectives in Psychiatry, 3,* 1.

Nicholi, A. M. (1974). A new dimension of the youth culture. *American Journal of Psychiatry, 131,* 396-401.

Offer, D. (1969). *The psychological world of the teenager: A study of normal adolescent boys.* New York: Basic Books.

Wilson, E. D. (1972). Mental health benefits of religious salvation. *Diseases of the Nervous System, 33,* 383-386.

Zaretsky, I., & Leone, M. (1974). *Religious movements in contemporary America.* Princeton, NJ: Princeton University Press.

Local Jewish Population Studies: Still Necessary After All These Years

Ira M. Sheskin

Abstract: Local Jewish population studies provide important information on issues that concern local Jewish communities. Because Jewish communities differ regionally, local (versus national) studies often offer a more accurate picture of the community.

Unequivocally, the 1990 National Jewish Population Survey (NJPS 1990) changed the agenda of the American Jewish community. All major American Jewish magazines, as well as Jewish publications around the world, have devoted articles or whole issues to the concerns about Jewish continuity implied by the study. It has become the topic of sermons in countless synagogues. It has become the subject of discussion even among American Jews who view themselves as somewhat marginal to the community. Particular attention has been paid to the findings on the intermarriage rate.

While one could argue from anecdotal evidence that we should have known about such matters as the high intermarriage rate even before the 1990 NJPS, it took such a scientific demographic study, with irrefutable results published by the coordinating bodies for all Jewish Federations in North America (the Council of Jewish Federations), to catch the attention of all and to obtain a commitment to address the various issues. Jewish communities now seek those types of programs that might be attractive to young Jews so that they will "opt in" rather than "opt out," and those that might attract young intermarried couples to identify with the Jewish community and to raise Jewish children.

Many of the issues raised by the NJPS are now being researched by members of the National Technical Advisory Committee of the Council of Jewish Federations and others. The national results, to some extent, may obviate the need for certain information at the local level. For example, we now have national information about Jewish fertility levels. Local Jewish federations, however, are not in a position (nor is it their mission) to try to increase the number of children Jewish couples are having. Information on attitudes on some matters of importance to Jews is also available from the national study and indicates that some have clearly changed over the past decades. It is hard to imagine, however, that the crosstabulations of these attitudes with age or with measures of religiosity will vary greatly from one community to the next, even if the attitudes themselves do.

Nevertheless, despite the existence of this invaluable national data set, it is quite clear that local Jewish community studies have, can, should, and will continue to be executed. New York, Chicago, South Broward, and Columbus all timed their local studies to be in the interviewing stage within a short time of the NJPS. Since 1990 studies have been completed or are underway in, among other places, Alaska, Amarillo, Detroit, Harrisburg, Las Vegas, Memphis, Middlesex County-NJ, Montreal, Orlando, Miami, Philadelphia, Sacramento, St. Louis, St. Paul, St. Petersburg/Clearwater, San Antonio, Sarasota-Manatee, Seattle, Southern NJ, Toronto, and West Palm Beach.

Just as a national study addresses issues of national concern that must be dealt with nationally, local studies provide significant information about a local community that a national study never could. The results of such studies can be useful to local communities. Horowitz (1994), for example, in her articulation of the "New York effect," points out that there are regional differences in the level of Jewishness. On the whole, there is less erosion of Jewishness in New York than has occurred nationally. Where Jews form a relatively high percentage of the overall population, as in New York, the generational erosion model applied to many local communities may not be as accurate as elsewhere.

In contrast, Sheskin (1994), in examining the southern Jewish community of Orlando, shows the significant decline in Jewishness in that community, with the results in Orlando mirroring the national survey relatively well. The results clearly suggest that "Jewish continuity" had to move to the top of the community's agenda, rather than their proceeding with earlier plans for a Jewish nursing home which had provided part of the initial impetus for the study.

Friedman (1994) makes the important point that data from the demographic study in Chicago were used as input to a Priorities Study, a Jewish Identity and Continuity Study, sub-regional planning studies, and the betterment of synagogue and Federation relations.

In a somewhat similar vein, Mott and Mott (1994) have noted that local planning needs to take account of local conditions. In particular, community planning in Columbus has to address the fact of increasing geographic dispersal and variation. The ability of the local community to render religious, social and communal services is greatly affected by such dispersal and variation. The logistic complications alone are considerable. Local population studies can enlighten discussions of such issues as the feasibility of serving outlying populations.

Methodological issues are addressed as well in local population studies. Sheskin, for example, in his study of the Jewish population in Orlando, Florida, addressed two issues with respect to sampling: improving both Random Digit Dialing (RDD) surveys and the use of Distinctive Jewish Names (DJNs). Mott and Mott examined differences between the Columbus RDD samples and the sample drawn from the federation's mailing list. Friedman addressed the problems created by ever decreasing response rates and raised the issue of the definition of "who-is-a-Jew" in the content of local demographic studies. Clearly, methodological issues still present themselves. Different communities may well find it best to opt for somewhat different methodologies.

Finally, it should be mentioned that many recent local community studies indicate that both the art and the science of Jewish demographic studies have advanced significantly in the past decades. As a group, researchers have improved methodology, recognized limitations of the methodology, and, in particular, learned the types of questions that do and do not "work" in a telephone survey. Many local studies also have proved to be important to local communities, and they indicate the value of communities repeating their studies at intervals that facilitate identifying and understanding trends in the American Jewish Community.

References

Friedman, Peter (1991). 1991 *Chicago Area Jewish Population Study: Survey Methods and Population Projections* (Chicago: Jewish Federation of Metropolitan Chicago).

Horowitz, Bethamie (1993). *The 1991 New York Jewish Population Study* (New York: UJA-Federation of New York).

Mott, Frank L. and Susan H. Mott (1990). *The 1990 Jewish Population Study of Greater Columbus* (Columbus: the Columbus Jewish Federation).

Sheskin, Ira M. (1993). *The Jewish Federation of Greater Orlando Community Study* (Orlando: The Jewish Federation of Greater Orlando).

Jewish Identity in the Sunbelt: The Jewish Population of Orlando, Florida

Ira M. Sheskin

Abstract: *This paper presents important results from a population survey of Orlando and compares its geographic, demographic, religious and philanthropic profile with the results of other Florida communities and with those of NJPS. Orlando appears to mirror the national picture relatively well, but is very different from the other Florida communities. In part, the differences from the other Florida communities are attributable to the fact that the population of Orlando is significantly younger.*

The 1990 Council of Jewish Federation's National Jewish Population Survey (NJPS) revealed that significant challenges exist as the American Jewish community moves into the next century. Although the survey found signs of strength within the community, and while evidence exists of a thriving American Jewish community (including strong synagogues and Jewish Community Centers, increasing numbers visiting Israel, and the growth of Judaic Studies programs), the study indicates that large numbers of Jews have assimilated completely into American society. Levels of religious practice and membership were shown to be low even among those who identify as Jews (Kosmin, Goldstein, Waksberg, Lerer, Keysar and Scheckner 1991).

The data from this study also reveal that significant geographic variation exists in the levels of Jewish identification. In general, Jews who live in more densely settled Jewish areas tend to be "more Jewish" (Sheskin forthcoming). They are more likely to follow more traditional branches of Judaism, join synagogues and other Jewish organizations, follow Jewish ritual practices, and give to Jewish causes.

Elsewhere, I (Sheskin 1993b) have defined three "ethnic homelands" for Jews in the United States: the metropolitan areas of New York, South Florida, and southern California. These areas are recognized by Jews and non-Jews alike as important areas of Jewish settlement. The infrastructure exists in all three regions for Jews to live a fully American Jewish life. Jews who choose to live in these areas (as well as other areas of dense Jewish settlement) do so, in part, because of the existence of a large Jewish community in the area. Jews who choose to live in locations outside areas of dense Jewish settlement include a disproportionate number of Jews who consider their Jewish identity to be marginal components of their lives. At the same time, those Jews who move to areas with few other Jews, but who have a strong Jewish identity themselves, often tend to be disproportionately active in their small local Jewish community. Perhaps they recognize the greater relative importance of their contributions in a small community.

Orlando, Florida is a small southern Jewish community in an area in which only about two percent of households contain one or more persons who identify themselves as Jewish. It lies outside any traditional area of Jewish settlement, at a significant distance (about four hours driving) from the closest large Jewish community in South Florida. The purpose of this paper is to report on the results of the Greater Orlando Jewish Community Study (Sheskin, 1993a).

Method

The methodology employed in this survey is relatively similar to that used in many recent Jewish demographic studies. About 670 15-minute telephone surveys were conducted in January, 1993. Two-hundred and three were produced via random digit dialing (RDD). An additional 468 surveys were completed with households with a Distinctive Jewish Name (DJN) listed in the Greater Orlando telephone directory. The survey covered topics related to geography, demography, religious practices and memberships, Jewish education, anti-Semitism, Israel, human and community services, health problems, and disabilities.

Two methodological issues are selected here for brief discussion: modifications to the RDD procedure that facilitate cost reduction and the use of DJNs to supplement the RDD surveys.

Modification of the RDD Procedure: The basic problem in any small, dispersed Jewish community (that is, one which is only a small percentage of the metropolitan area's total population) is to produce a representative sample of that Jewish population while keeping costs within reason. The accepted methodology is to use random digit dialing. Even with the help of a firm such as Survey Sampling, Inc. providing the RDD sample, only about 60% of the randomly dialed numbers reach a household. If only two percent of households contain someone who is Jewish, then every 100 random telephone numbers will yield, on average, the potential of only 12 interviews. Even assuming an 80% response rate implies that of every 100 numbers dialed, only one will yield a cooperative Jewish household. To complete just 200 RDD interviews requires that approximately 20,000 RDD numbers be dialed. To increase the "hit rate," this survey used the following procedure. The Jewish Federation of Greater Orlando's computerized list of households was examined to produce a table listing each telephone exchange code (the 3-digit prefix) and the number of households on this list with that exchange code. Only those exchanges that collectively accounted for 95% of the listed Jewish population were selected for random digit dialing. This improved the "hit rate" significantly by omitting areas that contained very few, if any, Jews. There was a small chance that there were significant numbers of unknown Jews in areas that were not surveyed, but the benefits of the greater hit rate far outweighed the disadvantages. In these types of surveys, a map showing the geographic distribution of a sample of Distinctive Jewish Names drawn from the telephone directory is helpful to make certain there is no significant Jewish population in the geographic areas represented by the five percent of the listings in exchange codes that are not called. In any case, in a sample of 200, if the other telephone exchange codes were called, about 10 surveys would come from those exchange codes. Clearly, those ten surveys could not have any significant impact on the results.

Use of Distinctive Jewish Names: Given the enormous expense of RDD surveys, completion of 400 such surveys (the number needed for a 95% confidence level and a 5% confidence interval) would have been overly expensive, particularly for a small Jewish community. In Orlando, we completed one RDD survey every three hours. Consistent with other Jewish demographic studies, the Orlando RDD sample was supplemented by a list sample. The two most likely lists were the Jewish Federation's mailing list and the Distinctive Jewish Names in the telephone directory. Each presented its own biases.

Any Jewish Federation's mailing list is biased significantly toward households that are in some way involved with the Jewish community. Thus, this researcher felt that the use of the sample, in an era when the leading issue in the Jewish community is continuity, was a particular problem.

The second list, the telephone directory, comes with its biases as well. New residents are not listed. Many professionals, such as doctors and lawyers, tend to not list their home address. Single women living alone are less likely to be listed. Intermarried households in which the husband is not Jewish and the wife does not keep her own last name are very unlikely to be in this sample. In addition, the most commonly used list of DJNs are of German and East European origin. Thus, in a community with significant numbers of Sephardic or Hispanic Jews, the DJN sample will certainly underestimate these populations.

For this survey, 467 interviews were completed with the use of Distinctive Jewish Names from the telephone directory.[1] Three biases were shown by the use of chi-square tests: The DJN sample was significantly older, less likely to belong to a synagogue, and less likely to be intermarried. Weighting factors were developed so that the age distribution and synagogue membership statistics in the DJN sample matched that in the RDD sample. After this step, a chi-square test showed that the difference in the intermarriage rate between the two samples was no longer significant, although the rate in the DJN sample was, of course, still somewhat lower.

It is not known whether the use of the Federation's mailing list would have produced a sample closer to the RDD sample than did the DJN sample. What is needed to determine the best sample is to design a test in which the RDD sample can be compared with both DJN and Federation's mailing list samples. Of course, the results of this type of a test may well depend upon the particular city in which it is executed, since the representative quality of the Federation's mailing list may vary significantly from Federation to Federation.

Table 1. Comparison of Orlando Survey Results with "Reality"

Factor	Survey Indicates	Actual Number
Number of Synagogue Members	(32%) 2,921	2783[a]
JCC Membership	(17%) 1,519	1550[a]
Read local Jewish Newspaper	(42%) 3,817	3,000[b]
Gifts To Federation	(30%) 2,713	2,744[a]

Source: [a] Organization's list   [b] Circulation figures.

Two recent studies suggest that DJN sampling does produce survey results which mirror reality. In Sarasota (Sheskin 1992) no weighting factors were needed. That is, the DJN sample was not significantly different from the RDD sample on any important variable. Moreover, as Table 1 shows, the results of the Orlando survey are quite close to reality on variables upon which it is possible to perform a "reality check," that is, to compare information based on the DJN list with that based on organization lists. While, as mentioned above, it was necessary to use weighting factors in Orlando to adjust certain biases, the overall results again mirrored reality well. Only for the reading of the Jewish newspaper does the survey number vary from "reality," the actual circulation figure. This variation may be explained by the fact that more than one household may read each copy of a newspaper.

Results

This section presents some of the most important findings of the Orlando Jewish Community Study. These findings are compared to other Florida Jewish communities, namely, Miami (Sheskin 1982), Palm Beach County (Sheskin 1987), Sarasota-Manatee (Sheskin 1992), and South Broward (Sheskin and Tobin 1991) and to NJPS results (Kosmin et al., 1991). While the survey covered the broad range of topics typical of Jewish community studies, the impetus for the study derived from the Federation's Elderly Services Committee, which was examining the possibility of developing a Jewish nursing home in the Greater Orlando area (Sher 1993). While the national study has helped to shape the overall agenda of the American Jewish community, local studies serve an even more specific purpose, with planning implications for local Federations, Jewish agencies, organizations, and synagogues.

Population Size and Geography: The Orlando Jewish community is unlike any other studied Florida Jewish community, including Miami (Sheskin 1982), South Broward (Tobin and Sheskin 1991), West Palm Beach (Sheskin 1987), and Sarasota-Manatee (Sheskin 1992), on a number of important dimensions. The other Florida communities include large numbers of transplanted elderly retirees from the Northeast (Sheskin 1985), producing age pyramids with narrow bases and broad tops. In some aspects, the other communities (with the partial exception of Sarasota-Manatee) are exurbs of the New York metropolitan area. Orlando is much more a typical southern town, with a mid-sized, assimilating Jewish population.

The Jewish Federation of Greater Orlando Jewish Community Study found 9,044 households containing at least one person of Jewish heritage. In all, the households surveyed included 23,413 persons, 18,848 of whom were Jews themselves, and 4,565 who were not. In part as a response to the overall growth in the metropolitan area, the Jewish population increased by 43% between 1985 and 1993. This growth has also come about as a result of the growth of the tourist industry in the southern part of Orange County, including the Disney theme parks. The movement of the movie industry (Disney/MGM and Universal studios) into the area has been particularly important to the recent growth.

While more Jews live north of the Orlando Central Business District than south, mapping the distribution of Jewish households shows that Orlando, unlike all other studied Florida communities, has no identifiable Jewish neighborhoods. Moreover, the current dispersed distribution shows little sign of changing: 31% of new residents are moving to North Orlando, 32% to Central Orlando, and 37% to South Orlando. These findings help to explain why the delivery of services to this community is particularly difficult. There is no readily identifiable single location for Jewish agencies and organizations wishing to serve the entire community.

Only 14% of Jews are born locally, although more than one-third were born in the South. About half were born in the Northeast and only eight percent in the Midwest. While this is the highest percentage of locally born Jews in any Florida community study so far, it is a very low figure compared with Jewish communities outside the state. In addition, about one-third of the population has moved to the area within the past five years. Two implications may be drawn from these findings.

First, because a large portion of the community is not native and a large portion is of recent origin, little feeling of commitment to local institutions—both Jewish and non-Jewish—exists. The local synagogue is not the one that people "grew up in," nor is it the one that they expect their children to join upon becoming adults. This situation in the long run likely acts to minimize synagogue membership as well as to minimize the commitment of members to a synagogue.

Second, we can expect to see an increase in synagogue membership and community involvement in Orlando in the near future because of the recent population growth. The impact of a recent immigration often has a delayed effect. For example, in Orlando about 40% of those in residence for 5 or more years are members of synagogues, versus only 22% who are in residence for less than 5 years. When people enter an area, they often live in temporary housing or simply desire to wait until they are more settled prior to joining community organizations.

One of the most important findings that bears on the issue of Jewish identity in Orlando, in comparison with that in other Florida communities, is that 73% of Jews are American-born of American-born parents (third genera-tion or higher). Twenty percent are American-born of foreign-born parents (second generation), and only seven percent are foreign-born. The percentage of third generation or higher (73%) compares to 23% in West Palm Beach, 27% in South Broward, 32% in Miami, and 43% in Sarasota-Manatee. The percentage of Jews who are third generation or higher compares with 62% for the core Jewish population in the 1990 NJPS. Clearly, the further away American Jews are from the European Jewish experience, the greater the rate of intermarriage and assimilation. Thus, generational status may be seen as a major explanatory variable in the examination of religiosity below.

Demography: As mentioned above, the age distribution for Jews in Orlando is significantly different from any other studied Florida Jewish community. Only 12% of the population is age 65 or over and only 15% is age 60 or over. This compares with 67% in West Palm Beach, 63% in Sarasota, 55% in South Broward and 19% for American Jews as a whole. This translates to 3,536 persons, only 866 of whom are age 75 or over. Of these, 468 are female, 389 of whom live alone. About one-third (130) of the women 75 or over and living alone earn less than $10,000 per year. These factors, combined with other findings, led to a recommendation of a "go-slow" policy with respect to the establishment of the proposed Jewish nursing home.

Table 2. Demography: Comparison of Orlando with NJPS

Category	Orlando[a]	NJPS[b]
Age 19 and under	25%	23%
Age 60 and over	15%	19%
Persons per Household	2.6	2.6
Married	68%	63%
Single	22%	22%
Widowed	6%	8%
Divorced	4%	7%
College Graduates	52%	51%
Employed Full Time	57%	52%
Employed Part Time	8%	11%
Retired	8%	9%
Median Income	$45,700	$39,000

[a]1993   [b]1990

The comparison of several other Orlando demographic indices (see Table 2) with the 1990 NJPS (Kosmin et al., 1991) is instructive. The Orlando community is slightly younger and the average household size in Orlando (2.6) is equal to that found in NJPS. Marital status shows only minor differences, with Jews in Orlando being somewhat more likely to be married than is the case for Jews nationally. The percentage of college graduates is approximately equal to the NJPS finding. Orlando Jews are more likely to be working full time. Finally, the median income in Orlando is significantly higher than the median income nationally. Thus, Orlando mirrors the national picture relatively well demographically, but is somewhat younger, 91ore apt to be married and of somewhat higher income.

Religiosity: In both Orlando and nationally, about two out of three Jews associate themselves with one of the three main religious denominations (Orthodox, Conservative, Reform). The lack of a significant local infrastructure for an Orthodox lifestyle has meant that this area has not attracted Orthodox Jews. However, the percentage of Conservative Jews in Orlando is six points higher than the national figures, while the percentage of Reform Jews is three

Table 3. Religiosity: Comparison of Orlando with NJPS

	Orlando	NJPS
Orthodox	2%	6%
Conservative	33%	27%
Reform	30%	33%
Just Jewish	35%	34%
Always Light Chanukah Candles	64%	57%
Always Attend Seder	54%	55%
Always Light Sabbath Candles	9%	14%
Kosher in Home	6%	15%
Always Have Christmas Tree	18%	22%
Never Attend Services	34%	27%
Attend Services Monthly or More	21%	22%
In-married Couples	59%	68%
Conversionary	9%	4%
Mixed Married	32%	28%
Synagogue Membership	34%	39%
Jewish Organizational Membership	30%	27%
JCC Memberships	17%	17%
Adults with Formal Jewish Ed.	65%	67%
Been to Israel	34%	26%

points lower. Thus, overall, Jewish identification in Orlando differs only marginally from the national picture.

Measures of home religious practices differ from the national picture. Only for lighting Chanukah candles is there a greater level of observance (64%) for Orlando Jews than is the case nationally (57%). Lighting Chanukah candles is a child-oriented activity. This finding may be the result of there being a greater percentage of married persons in Orlando and the somewhat younger population and, thus, more families with young children. Orlando compares favorably on this measure with other Florida communities (in which average age is considerably higher), with only 48 % in Sarasota-Manatee, 57 % in Miami, 58 % in West Palm Beach, and 64% in South Broward always lighting Chanukah candles.

The percentage (54%) who always attend a Passover Seder is about the same in Orlando as is the case nationally. Attendance at a Passover Seder remains one of the most observed Jewish religious practices. The Orlando figure compares to 54% in Sarasota-Manatee, 56% in South Broward, 60% in West Palm Beach, and 70% in Miami. The fact that the populations in the other Florida cities tend to include more elderly may help to explain these differences.

The other Jewish practices shown in Table 3 indicate that Orlando is less observant than Jews nationally. Only nine percent always light Sabbath candles, compared to 14% nationally. Only six percent keep a kosher home, compared to 15% nationally. Thirty-four percent never attend synagogue services, as contrasted to 27 % nationally. Orlando is well behind other Florida communities with respect to lighting Sabbath candles and keeping a kosher home. However, with respect to never attending synagogue services, Orlando's percentage (34%) is just about equal to that in Sarasota-Manatee (33%) and West Palm Beach (32%), but is much higher than Miami (24%), and South Broward (19%). The reason for non-attendance in Orlando, however, is likely to be the assimilation of the young, whereas the reasons for non-attendance in the other Florida communities are apt to be different. Much of the nonattendance elsewhere in Florida occurs among elderly who feel strongly Jewish, but whose transportation and health problems restrict attendance.

Attendance at services on a regular basis (once per month or more) in Orlando (21%) is about equal to the 1990 NIPS finding (22%). This figure can be compared with Sarasota-Manatee (24%), West Palm Beach (31%), South Broward (19%), and Miami (17%). Geography is one reason for the relatively high rate of synagogue service attendance on a regular basis in Orlando. As discussed above, and unlike any of the comparison Florida Jewish communities, there are no Jewish neighborhoods or geographic concentrations of Jews in Orlando. Thus, those who wish to establish a Jewish social network and to associate with other Jews on a regular basis must do so by regularly participating in a Jewish institution. In South Florida (Miami, South Broward, and West Palm Beach), in particular, one can develop a Jewish social network by simply becoming involved in condominium life. In many Florida condominiums up to 90% of the occupants are Jewish. Moreover, many have clubhouses with recreational, educational, and cultural activities that act much like Jewish Community Centers. Some condominiums have "synagogues" and minyon groups that meet in the condominium clubhouses. Such is far from the case in Orlando, where associating with other Jews takes some effort.

Orlando has a lower percentage (59%) of couples that are both born-Jews than is the case nationally (68%). On the other hand, nine percent of couples are conversionary (a born-Jew married to a Jew-by-choice). Thirty-two percent of married couples in Orlando are in mixed marriages, compared to 28% nationwide. In spite of this somewhat greater mixed marriage rate, Orlando has a somewhat lower percentage of households (18%) who always have a Christmas tree than is true nationally (22%). However, the percentage (18%) with a Christmas tree is much higher than is the case in South Broward (5%), Sarasota-Manatee (8%), and West Palm Beach (9%). This comparison clearly is affected by the differences in the age distribution and intermarriage rates among the Florida communities.

Turning to measures of Jewish institutional affiliation, we find that Orlando is close to the national average on synagogue membership (34% in Orlando, 39% nationally), organizational membership (30% compared to 27%), and JCC membership (17% for both). A similar argument can be made for the membership data as was proffered above for attendance at services: membership is more important in areas with no concentration of Jews if one wishes to maintain a Jewish identity.

Finally, a somewhat higher percentage of households in Orlando (34%) have had at least one household member visit Israel than is the case for Jewish households nationwide (26%). On the other hand, the percentage in Sarasota-Manatee (53%), South Broward (52%), Miami (45%), and West Palm Beach (45%) is considerably higher. That the Orlando percentage is higher than the national percentage may reflect differences in income. That the Orlando percentage is much lower than the other Florida communities doubtlessly reflects the age differences; older persons have had more years to make such a trip.

Philanthropy: Table 4 shows some comparisons between Orlando and the NJPS on three measures of philanthropy: overall giving to Jewish charities, giving to the Federation and giving to non-Jewish charities. With respect to overall giving to Jewish charities, the percentage in Orlando doing so (58%) is at about the same level as is the case nationally (56%). Compared to other Florida communities, however, the percentage is low: West Palm Beach (91%), Sarasota-Manatee (76%), and South Broward (68%).

Table 4. Philanthropy: Comparison of Orlando with NIPS

	Orlando	NJPS
Give to Jewish Charities	58%	56%
Give to Federation	30%	34%
Give to Non-Jewish Charities	71%	67%

With respect to giving to Federation, the percentage in Orlando (30%) is also just about at the national level (34%). Interestingly, in Orlando 46 % of in-married couples donate to Federation, but only 17% of the mixed married couples. This difference is similar to that found nationally, where 45% of all

Jewish households donate to Federation, compared to 12% of mixed households. Again, compared to other Florida communities, however, this percentage is low: West Palm Beach (56%), Sarasota-Manatee (43%), and South Broward (44%).

Finally, with respect to giving to non-Jewish charities, Orlando's results (71%) are also just about at the national level (67%) and, like the national results, display no significant difference between entirely Jewish and mixed households. West Palm Beach (84%) and Sarasota-Manatee (81%) are significantly higher, but South Broward (56%) is significantly lower in this regard than is Orlando.

Conclusion

This paper presents important results from a population survey of a southern Jewish community and compares its geographic, demographic, religious and philanthropic profile with the results of other Florida Communities and with those of the 1990 NJPS. Orlando appears to mirror the national picture relatively well, but is very different from the other Florida communities. In part, the differences with the other Florida communities are attributable to the fact that the population of Orlando is significantly younger. However, quite clearly, Orlando lies outside what has been called the South Florida Jewish homeland (Sheskin 1993b). Many of the younger people who chose to move to Orlando may have had less concern about the existence and the quality of the local Jewish community than did those younger Jews who moved to Southeast Florida (Dade, Broward, and Palm Beach Counties).

The NJPS has served its purpose of helping to set the agenda of the American Jewish community. Local studies will do the same for each federated Jewish community. In Orlando, it became clear that community priorities should include a strong emphasis on Jewish continuity and that, while the goal of a Jewish nursing home provided the initial impetus, it would not become economically feasible for about five to ten years (Sher 1993).

Notes

[1] The names are taken from the list provided in Chenkin (1971). For a discussion of the use of DJNs see: Massarik (1966) and Lazerwitz (1986).

References

Chenkin, Al. 1971. "UJA Demographic Kit." New York: Council of Jewish Federations. mimeo.

Kosmin, Barry A., Sidney Goldstein, Joseph Waksberg, Nava Lerer, Ariella Keysar and Jeffrey Scheckner. 1991. *Highlights of the CJF 1990 National Jewish Population Survey.* New York: Council of Jewish Federations.

Lazerwitz, Bernard. 1986. "Some Comments on the use of Distinctive Jewish Names in Surveys." *Contemporary Jewry* 7: 83-91.

Massarik, Fred. 1966. "New Approaches to the Study of the American Jew." *Jewish Journal of Sociology* 8:175-191.

Sher, Karen Wolchuck. 1993. *The Jewish Federation of Greater Orlando Committee on Services to the Elderly Program Selection Project.* Orlando: Jewish Federation of Greater Orlando.

Sheskin, Ira M. 1982. *Population Study of the Greater Miami Jewish Community.* Miami: Greater Miami Jewish Federation.

—. 1985. "The Migration of Jews to Sunbelt Cities." Sunbelt Conference, Miami.

—. 1987. *The Population Study of the Jewish Federation of Palm Beach County.* Palm Beach: Jewish Federation of Palm Beach county.

—. 1992. *Population Study of the Sarasota-Manatee Jewish Community.* Sarasota: The Sarasota-Manatee Jewish Federation.

—. 1993a. *The Jewish Federation of Greater Orlando Community Study.* Orlando: The Jewish Federation of Greater Orlando.

—. 1993b. "Jewish Ethnic Homelands in the United States." *Journal of Cultural Geography* 13: 119-132.

—. Forthcoming. *Jewish Geography.* Albany: State University of New York Press.

Tobin, Gary A. and Ira M. Sheskin. 1991. *The Jewish Federation of South Broward Community Study.* Hollywood, FL: The Jewish Federation of South Broward.

Working Women/Cloistered Men:
A Family Development Approach to Marriage
Arrangements Among Ultra-Orthodox Jews

Donna Shai

Abstract: This article uses the family development approach to examine a cultural marriage variant in which the wife supports the family during an early stage of the marriage, among ultra-Orthodox Jews. An educational program, "kollel," requires the husband to delay entry into the job market to participate in full-time religious study, placing the main responsibility for working, childrearing, and home management on the wife. The hypothesis is that, when family events are out of sequence from larger cultural norms, women in these families evidence stress, and that the women must develop adaptive coping and support mechanisms to deal with the stress. The data were obtained through participant observation and interviews with ultra-Orthodox women 21-47 years of age whose husbands either were in or had been in kollel, including Lubavitcher Hasidic women, Aish HaTorah women, and Yeshivish women. Results highlight the need for economic resources and adaptive strategies, including coping mechanisms and assistance from both relatives and the community, to help kollel families deal with the unusual sequence of life transitions.

Introduction

Women's labor force participation has been increasing both in the United States (Wilkie, 1991) and elsewhere (Richter, 1994; Meleis and Bernal, 1995; Mehra et al., 1996) as they take additional responsibility for the support of children and other kin. An important issue in family research has been the problem of stress among married women in the work force due to multiple roles and possible conflicting demands of husbands, children and employers (Affleck, 1985; Barnett and Baruch, 1985; Presser, 1988; Hochschild and Machung, 1989; Potucheck, 1992; Agarwal, 1994). Recent research in family development has focussed on the dual-earner family in comparison with the traditional one-earner family with a male provider, assessing how the articulation between work and family demands is affected by the timing and sequence of stages in the family career (White, 1999).

A less common but theoretically interesting variation is the family maintained by a woman with the husband present. Married women are not generally expected to take on the main financial support of the family unless the husband is disabled or temporarily unemployed (Voydanoff, 1987), in compulsory military service (Hogan. 1978), or in an occupation which requires long training such as law, academia and medicine (Fowlkes, 1980). This paper uses the family development approach to examine a cultural marriage variant in which the wife supports the family during an early stage of the marriage. A growing trend among ultra-Orthodox Jews, who number approximately 360,000 in the United States (Goldstein, 1992), is for the husband to delay his entry into the job market, often for years, in order to participate in full-time religious study. Unlike the professional school, however, the educational program or "kollel" does not usually lead to an advanced professional degree or provide the students with any skills readily transferable to the workplace. The long involvement of the husband in education, the norm of child-bearing early in the marriage (Friedlander and Feldmann, 1993), large family size and traditional gender norms, place the main responsibility for working, child rearing and home management on the wife. In such multiple-role situations, working women from a variety of backgrounds have turned to networks of support (Lee and Keith, 1999; Jarrett and Burton, 1999; Weiss. 1999). This article examines the consequences of timing norms and the resultant economic and normative pressures on women as well as their use of support networks as coping strategies for handling these pressures. The subjects of this study are present and past kollel wives who are currently U.S. residents.

The data are drawn from a larger study of women and kollel among three ultra Orthodox groups: Lubavitcher Hasidim, Aish HaTorah and Jews of the yeshiva world or the "Yeshivish." These groups differ in their organization, social structure, patterns of authority and. philosophical outlook, but share "an unswerving commitment to scrupulous Torah observance" and the view that, except for vocational training, all knowledge of importance lies in Torah (Jewish law) (Belcove-Shalin, 1995:15). The "Yeshivish" are the most committed to the ideal of a "society of scholars" and attempt to extend kollel as long as possible. In the United States this usually means up to seven or eight years. Lubavitcher Hasidim usually limit kollel to a year or two since their primary mission is outreach to secular Jews, although sometimes newly religious couples will remain in kollel longer, using it as an opportunity to "catch up" in religious education. Aish HaTorah, a relatively new movement founded in the 1960s, is made up almost exclusively of the newly religious and, like the Lubavitcher Hasidim, limits kollel to a few years after which students are expected to take on outreach activities.

Previous Research

A search of the literature on American kollel families reveals that there has been little scholarly attention to this topic. Women who support husbands in kollel are discussed, but not the main focus, in Bomzer (1985), Schwarcz (1985), Bunim (1986) and Mintz (1992). Helmreich (2000) devotes a chapter of a book on the yeshiva to kollel families. He notes the elite status of participating in a kollel for the husband and wife and its function as a ritual transition into married life. Given the lack of research on this topic, this paper is largely exploratory, with the intention of raising questions rather than giving definitive answers.

Historical Background

The kollel was founded in 1878 in Kovno, Lithuania, by Rabbi Israel Lipkin for the purpose of providing graduate education in a yeshiva to married men regardless of economic background (Eckman, 1975). Prior to that time only the sons of the wealthy could be supported by their families for advanced study. The innovation quickly spread among Jews throughout Eastern Europe and Russia (Eckman,1975). Many of the yeshivas that provided the framework for kollel were closed under the Bolshevik regime in Russia and later destroyed, along with most of their students, in the Holocaust (Trunk, 1979). Refugee scholars from the European yeshivas established the kollel in the United States in the 1940s as part of an effort to rebuild traditional Jewish culture and educational institutions in the West. Once limited to a scholarly elite, the institution of the kollel is now growing in number and popularity (Bomzer, 1985; Helmreich, 2000).

Timing Norms

According to Rodgers and White (1993), an important measure used in family development studies is the notion of events being "on time", i.e., following timing norms. "A timing norm is one that states that when an individual, relationship, or family is at a certain age, particular events or accomplishments are both expected and behaviorally followed in the society" (Rodgers and White, 1993:239). As Neugarten (1976) has argued, every society has a system of social expectations concerning when family events such as marriage, childbearing and retirement should occur. The sequencing and order of these events have important consequences for family life. "Cross-institutional norms" are created when norms from one social institution, for example, "work", articulate with another, e.g., "family", in order to establish an expected sequence of events such as "get a good job before you get married" (Rodgers and White, 1993:233).

Hogan (1978) demonstrated that men in U.S. birth cohorts subjected to compulsory military service, whose education had been postponed due to military service and completed after marriage, had higher rates of marital disruption than men whose life events followed a more normative sequence. He argued that a disruption in the normative course of events may have negative consequences later during the life course of the individual (Hogan, 1978). When transitions are "on time" they may be "more easily incorporated into one's identity and more supported by social institutions, therefore yielding more beneficial effects on well-being than transitions that are non-normative or 'off time'" (Marks and Lambert, 1998: 655). A transition that is in keeping with normative expectations may coincide with developmental readiness and resources on the part of the individuals making the transition (Marks and Lambert, 1998).

Goals of This Study

This study examines the hypothesis that when family events are out of sequence from the larger cultural norms, women in these families will evidence stress and that these women must develop adaptive coping and support mechanisms for dealing with this stress (Rodgers and White, 1993). One would expect that men also experience stress, but this article focuses on the expectations which accumulate on women due to the differential ordering of early married life.

Methods

Two qualitative techniques were used: participant observation and interviews. These methods are well suited to the investigation of areas of family life that are not well studied, and in which lack of research literature precludes the highly structured investigation used in quantitative techniques (Rosenblatt and Fischer, 1993). Qualitative techniques can focus on the meanings that a topic has for the population under study. Since the world of the kollel family was largely unstudied and highly complex, and the intent exploratory and descriptive, the design of the study was kept "loose" and inductively oriented (Huberman and Miles, 1994).

Participant Observation

Participant observation, the first technique, involved a neighborhood in an eastern city which has one of the largest Jewish populations outside of New York City, from December, 1995 to December, 1998. The main area of observation, "Rockingham,"[1] had an Orthodox population of approximately 100 families, including Lubavitcher Hasidim, Aish HaTorah and the "Yeshivish". I followed an approach that has been described best by Evans-Pritchard (1962), in which the researcher observes daily activities, everyday events as well as ceremonies, and takes part in those events where appropriate, trying to live, think and feel in the culture as much as possible. Despite the fact that I intended to write specifically about women who supported husbands in kollel, I did so, as far as possible, in the context of their cultural and social life as a whole. Any part of a people's culture must be seen "against the background of their entire social activities and in terms of their whole social structure" (Evans-Pritchard, 1962:80). Most importantly, I attempted to gain the perspective of ultra-Orthodox Jews, and particularly present and former kollel families. I spent two to three days or evenings a week in the Orthodox community which was approximately five miles from my home, making it possible to walk to the site on the Sabbath and holidays when religious norms would not permit driving. I attended classes held by each of the groups, synagogue services and activities, women's organization meetings and family events.

Outside the neighborhood I participated in a "Discovery Seminar" run by Aish HaTorah. I carried out fieldwork at summer camps for women in the Catskill Mountains of New York and in Blue Bell, Pennsylvania, run by Lubavitch. I traveled with a local family to visit the grave of the Lubavitcher Rebbe on Long Island, New York, an annual pilgrimage for Lubavitchers on the anniversary of his death.

I took field notes following each contact, although usually not in the presence of informants. Notes were coded according to larger themes following the methods of the "grounded theory approach" (Glaser and Strauss, 1967) in which conceptual categories are created from the data and new observations are used to develop these categories (Frankfort-Nachmias and Nachmias, 1992). The fieldwork component of the study was an opportunity to observe everyday interactions in families and in particular to gain the knowledge of the underpinnings of kollel in women's lives. With time, certain themes appeared as important. They included the normative expectations in the roles of men and women, preparation of daughters for marriage and kollel, the financial involvement of relatives in the life of a married couple before and after kollel, and links between family members and broader institutions.

Qualitative Interviews

Qualitative interviews, the second technique, involved a series of questions concerning the attitudes and experiences of women towards the role of supporting a husband in kollel as well as general social and economic data on the respondent (see Appendix for schedule of questions). Participants were first selected by word of mouth among the women encountered during participant observation. The sample was one of convenience in which the informants were asked to recommend other women who would qualify. The sample included seventeen Lubavitcher Hasidic women, seven Aish HaTorah women and six Yeshivish women. Eight of the husbands were currently studying, and the remainder had completed kollel. The women ranged in age from 21 to 47. All of them had at least one year of higher education. Thirteen had bachelor's and three had master's degrees. They had spent from six months to seven years married to men in kollel. At the time of interview they were residents of Boston, Chicago, Cleveland, Detroit, Los Angeles, Morristown (New Jersey), New York City, Philadelphia, Pittsburgh, and Saint Louis.

Three kinds of interviews were used. Whenever possible, I interviewed the respondent in person, resulting in fifteen interviews. These ranged from 30 to 90 minutes. The face-to-face interview had the advantage of unobtrusive observation of the setting and the opportunity to clarify questions or to encourage the respondent to answer more fully. Some women understood the face-to-face interviews to be an occasion for giving an account of a difficult and challenging situation, resulting in highly detailed stories about an exciting period in their lives. A few women were nervous about expressing any negative ideas that could reflect poorly on an institution that was central to their lives and therefore gave hesitant and abbreviated answers.

Telephone interviews are sometimes more convenient for the interviewer and the respondent and in my case there were five women who preferred to be interviewed by telephone (using the same schedule), with the limitation that less anecdotal information was given by phone than in the personal interview. However, women interviewed by phone tended to be surprisingly expressive about their personal lives. It is possible that not being face-to-face created some distance which made them willing to express strong emotions ranging from the pleasures of enabling a husband to study, to the loneliness and frustration of managing a job, child rearing and household alone.

Finally, ten women were contacted by mail, allowing sampling among women living in distant locations. Mailings permit a wider geographical area to be covered and also permit greater anonymity, but have the disadvantage of a lower response rate than the other two methods. In the written responses, some gave very brief answers, sometimes one word, while others wrote long and detailed accounts of their adjustment to kollel life. Some wrote of their transition from being perplexed by the situation to greater understanding. Others described the change from being overwhelmed by the problems of supporting a family to increased confidence in their own ability to be innovative and creative.

While the practical effects of asking the same questions by different means have not been fully determined, it has been suggested that the different methods can complement each other and provide more precise information (Frankfort-Nachmias and Nachmias, 1992).

Reliability and Validity

The problems of reliability, or the replicability of observations, and validity, the problem of gaining an accurate impression of the phenomenon being studied, take on special forms in qualitative research (Shaffir et al., 1980). These include reactive effects of the observer on the activities studied, the problems of selective perception and interpretation, and the inability of the researcher to view all relevant aspects of the phenomenon studied (Shaffir et al., 1980). In order to minimize reactive effects, care was taken so that interactions with individuals, families, and the broader community were carried out calmly and respectfully. Selective perception can occur when the researcher overidentifies with the informants and "goes native:" To prevent this I tried to maintain a friendly attitude while also maintaining objectivity. I made it clear to those informants who asked that I was there to learn and not to become Orthodox. In order to maintain a wide perspective on the kollel experience, data were collected from a broad range of women, of different ages, from three groups, and in a variety of settings. As a woman researcher, I was able to interact with and have informal interviews with men under the right circumstances, as rabbis, teachers and the husbands of the women studied. Therefore I was able to confirm some of the findings with men who had been in kollel. In general, findings were discussed with informants using their terminology as well as with colleagues.

Data Management

Following the method of data management outlined in Huberman and Miles (1994), observations from fieldwork were dated and entered into notebooks chronologically, with important themes and topics noted. At the completion of the fieldwork the contents of the notebooks were coded into themes and subject matter such as worldview, socialization, roles, and case histories. The interviews were transcribed and stored in files to facilitate analysis of specific data for the informants as a whole or for subgroups within the total group for purposes of cross-reference.

Results

The prolonged education of men, high family fertility, and women's employment create a need for economic resources and adaptive strategies to deal with this unusual sequence of life transitions. The results of the research will be presented in terms of "off-time" or "out of sequence" life transitions, normative pressures, and economic pressures. Adaptive mechanisms are then discussed including coping mechanisms, assistance from relatives and assistance from the community.

"Off-Time" and "Out of Sequence" Life Transitions

An elaborate set of timing norms within traditional Jewish culture is the result of the complex interplay of cultural, social and historical forces which create a distinct lifestyle with its own values, norms, goals, and standards of behavior. To protect and transmit this lifestyle, ultra-Orthodox Jews have created their own educational institutions from elementary school to higher education. These also provide them with employment and help to buffer them from the larger society. Therefore the timing and sequence of events which is "on schedule" in the social organization of the religious community may be regarded as "off-time" relative to the larger society. Since kollel families are dependent on the larger society for certain services, there are economic consequences to following their own cultural timing norms. Like other Orthodox Jews, kollel families tend to live in urban settings where housing is expensive, and during kollel they may depend on the larger society for public housing, government assistance programs, and educational loans. After kollel, as much as they may wish to remain apart from the larger society, they may need and utilize services such as vocational training, employment, mortgages, health insurance, medical services, social security and welfare. Being "off-time" or "out of sequence" relative to the larger society has other consequences as can be seen by the typical life course for kollel families as discussed below.

The Life Course

Marriage among ultra-Orthodox Jews is usually arranged by a matchmaker or semi-arranged by mutual friends. Courtship is kept very short and the age of marriage is typically in the late teens to the early twenties for the bride (Mintz, 1992), with the groom a few years older, while for the United States as a whole, the median age of first marriage for women is 24 and for men 26 (U.S. Census Bureau, 1999). Parents are usually financially involved in establishing and maintaining the young couple, although varying with the parents' financial means and religious traditionalism. The burden of support usually falls more heavily on the bride's parents who often undertake to support the couple fully or partially for a certain number of years of full-time study in a kollel. Depending on the level of support, the wife works full time, part-time or, less commonly, not at all. Since courtship is kept to only about a month, and the bride and groom have only had close friendships with members of their own sex prior to marriage, the kollel period is an opportunity to gain intimate familiarity with the particular partner, as well as with a member of the opposite sex outside of the family.

Normative pressures to begin childbearing in the first year of marriage (Friedlander and Feldmann, 1993) tend to foreshorten the stage between marriage and childbearing, a period in which couples in the broader society typically try to establish themselves financially with a car, furniture, consumer durables and perhaps the purchase of a home (Aldous, 1996). As the kollel family grows, the first economic crisis comes when the number of children exceeds the wife's capacity to work. As women acknowledged, children at different ages require different foods, care and levels of supervision, so that each additional child brings new complications into child care. Women interviewed often measured the difficulty of kollel by the number of children. "One or two" were considered easy to care for, while more were more difficult. In the interview sample the number of children ranged from none among the recently married to eight. The average number of children was three. By this time the couple is likely to have exhausted their savings and parental support may have ended. When their expenses outstrip their ability to generate income, the husband may be forced to "moonlight" by taking on part-time jobs at the yeshiva, analogous to married men in the larger society working overtime when expenses outstrip income (Dempster-McClain and Moen, 1989). Alternatively the economic difficulties may signal the end of the kollel period entirely. After leaving the kollel, the husband takes on the role of breadwinner, either as a religious functionary or at a vocational trade.

As children reach adolescence, the parents begin to save for their daughters' years as a kollel wife. In the larger society the "empty nest" stage is usually one of financial recovery. In kollel families, however, the "empty nest" stage comes late due to high fertility and there may be no financial recovery since social and economic pressures lead to support for married children in kollel.

Marriage is relatively stable so that remarriage is rare. While the divorce rate is not precisely known, it is considered to be lower than that of secular Jews and of the larger U.S. population (Farber et al., 1988; Goldstein, 1992).

Stressors

Economic Pressures

While women who support men in kollel cite financial difficulties as a major source of stress, several factors lessen its impact. Many of the women interviewed had saved for kollel or used their savings for that purpose. They acknowledged that they were giving up material possessions as well as "getting ahead" financially. The goal is redefined as "keeping your head above water." One woman said, "You have to value the spiritual over the material because there will be much more spiritual than material," and "You have to live on very little, but if you live among kollel people, then nobody has a lot." An analysis of the qualitative interviews showed that out of 37 separate responses given to "stress or practical problems" for women, lack of money was cited most frequently, 14 times (37.8 %). It also occurred most often (nine times, 27.3 %) of the responses to the disadvantages of kollel.

Most students in kollel receive a stipend, and the newer institutions offer more generous sums than the more established ones to attract well-qualified students (Helmreich, 2000). The stipend varies by family size (Bomzer, 1985) and in some cases the financial awards are linked to the student's progress. While all of the women interviewed mentioned the stipend, no couple was able to live on it entirely, since it was too small to constitute the total source of support. Therefore, unless the parents of the couple were well to do and willing to support them, the main burden of support fell on the wife. In the sample, education within the religious community was the most usual area of employment, although other work mentioned included sales, social work, secretarial work, occupational therapy, and babysitting. The difficulty in women supporting the family stems also from religious attitudes toward secular education. University education is usually coeducational and exposes students to relativistic thinking, both of which are seen as undermining ultra-Orthodox values. As women said during fieldwork observations, a religious person exposed to secular higher education "would come back a different person" and "Professors in universities don't have the right attitude." In this regard the newly religious may have an advantage since if the woman completed her education before becoming religious she can usually acquire a professional position.

A number of women interviewed mentioned income from enterprises that can best be described as the "informal economy," using skills developed through a hobby or skill to earn additional income (Voydanoff, 1987). For example, one woman from Aish HaTorah said, "We had numerous businesses on the side—my husband attended art school before yeshiva so he sold paintings, he baked cookies to sell in yeshiva, I sold headcoverings[2], we had a homemade challah business, [we did] editing, we had a boarder."

The literature on men in yeshivas shows that it is not unusual for a kollel student to be given work-study assignments such as remedial work with younger students, adult education classes, administrative work, kitchen work, library duties, handling the mail or cleaning the synagogue (Bomzer, 1985; Helmreich, 2000). In the interviews I carried out, women often expressed the idea that for the man to take a part-time job, even within the yeshiva, was counterproductive in that it took time from his studies. However, if there is too much stress on the wife or if she cannot manage financially, the man may need to work. This sometimes has other negative consequences because, as one woman interviewed pointed out, if he works at the kollel he may almost never be home and that may also prove stressful for the wife.

Normative Pressures

The interdependence of husband and wife is emphasized in Jewish law (Bulka, 1989). Together with the central value of religious learning, the division of labor between the husband-student and the wife-nurturer is seen as natural and supported by the community. Earning a living was not automatically assigned to one gender in traditional Jewish life and the prestige of supporting a husband in learning is a longstanding tradition (Zborowski and Herzog, 1969). During fieldwork observations, it was clear that both men and women are encouraged to see working as a way to earn a livelihood and not as an important sense of identity. Women in particular are socialized to stay out of the limelight and not to draw attention to themselves. Norms encourage a woman to work in a situation which is either restricted to females (e.g. women's educational institutions) or at least does not promote the mixing of sexes.

In response to the question in the interview concerning what characteristics and attitudes are important in a "kollel wife", out of 21 answers, the most frequently given responses were that a woman should value learning (29%), be supportive (19%), and be willing to work (14%). Other answers included being self-sacrificing (10%), uncomplaining (10%), suppressing her own needs (10%) and tolerating separation from her husband (10%)[3]. All of the responses emphasize the woman taking an enabling role vis-a-vis the husband. The following quote from an interview is a good summary of the ideal attitude:

> ... this is probably the only time he will learn full time. [A wife] has to exert as much effort as possible to get him to take advantage of it, whether it can be doing chores he might otherwise do, so he can learn in that time, or convince him to go to a farbrengen (men's religious and social gathering).

On the other hand, the desire to spend more time with the spouse was a common source of frustration indicated by the women interviewed. Even women who were adamant about marrying a man who would study in a kollel often expressed loneliness due to the husband's constant involvement in activities which exclude women. As one woman put it:

> It ends up being that your whole lifestyle is for the purpose of learning. But you feel it's for a worthwhile cause. You don't get to see your husband that much and my husband doesn't get to see my kids that much, which bothers me. Everything is always in a rush. I have to get supper ready because he has to get back on time. It's very pressured ... There are a lot of drawbacks. You're tired, doing a lot more on your own. You're with your baby alone. It's difficult. It's lonely sometimes. At eight o'clock [p.m.] he's gone back to the yeshiva and I'm alone. It's hard.

The women discussed here participate in what Hochschild and Machung (1989) have called "the second shift" or the struggle that married woman in the labor force have in dealing with both work and home. During kollel, the wife is expected to relieve the husband of all household responsibilities so that he can devote himself to learning:

> They don't have a phone [at the kollel]. If they have [one] they try not to answer it. You don't want to disturb him. You feel that you are taking him away from learning, so you have to be rather independent ... many times the wife has to take care of everything in the house. He has to be free from all burdens.

Coping

During the interviews women mentioned nine different ways they coped with demands on their time and energy. Out of 26 responses, the most frequent one was support from other women (31%). The second most frequent answer was getting organized (19%), followed by help from husband (15%). Other ways of coping included doing only necessary chores (12%), spending time with husband (8%), having a positive outlook (4%), being invited out for meals (4%), reading (4%) and exercise (4%). The ways of coping (using social networks for support, organizational strategies, pasttimes and optimism) are much more individualized and varied than the ideal characteristics and attitudes.

Assistance from Kin

After the wife's salary, money from relatives was the second most frequently mentioned source of income. It is difficult to generalize about the role of family support because a great deal depends on a family's motivation, ability to contribute, religiosity, experience with kollel or even personal experiences such as being Holocaust survivors. For religious families, a scholarly son-in-law may in itself be a reason to support the young couple. One woman interviewed explained, "My husband was a serious student so my parents wanted to support him. He was involved in publications. . . ."

For women who are newly religious, it is often difficult to convince their secular parents to contribute support for the family while their son-in-law studies, apparently indefinitely. One woman interviewed stated that secular parents can sometimes be convinced by reframing kollel in a more acceptable light by arguing that kollel would prepare the husband for the rabbinate, even though the couple didn't see that as the purpose. This comment shows that the value of learning is so strong that the young couple, in order to get support from the parents, emphasized the professional possibilities when in actuality they valued learning for its own sake.

Another woman got help from parents only when her financial situation had become extremely difficult. As she related in an interview, when her mother visited her apartment in Israel, where her husband was enrolled in a Lubavitcher kollel, her mother

> . . . went to pick up the phone to make a phone call and the phone was
> dead. . . We called from a neighbor's to find out why the phone was
> disconnected and [they] said, 'Look, you haven't paid for six months.'
> And my mother flipped her lid and said, 'Tomorrow morning we're

going down there and I'm paying for this, and why didn't you tell me?' So then she felt really bad. She decided that she would send us money regularly, so that the last six months there we had some help.

However, there were other secular parents who supported newly religious couples from the beginning such as an Aish HaTorah couple where the woman's family supported the couple for several years and a Lubavitch woman whose parents paid their rent and whose father-in-law gave the young couple his credit card to use as necessary. Gifts from the family constitute an important source of support. A woman from the yeshiva world reported that her family gave her sizable gifts on holidays and birthdays.

Assistance from the Community

A young couple usually receives gifts of money from relatives and friends at their wedding for the purpose of launching them financially. Wedding gifts in cash can often get the couple through the first year. Jewish charities are available to help couples cope with financial expenses. The "Sheltering of the Bride" charitable organization covers wedding expenses for those who need it. Other charities may provide furniture for an apartment. There are special stores where kollel families can get discounts or carry credit for long periods. In New York City, especially, couples may qualify for Section Eight (subsidized) Housing, welfare, WIC, Medicaid, and health insurance at student rates. American kollel families in Israel may get subsidized or free housing and may qualify for National Insurance (welfare) on behalf of the children.

Even with these resources, as time goes on, supporting the growing family during kollel may prove difficult. Wedding money and personal savings are eventually exhausted. Kollel families may take out formal or informal loans within the Jewish community. Free-loan societies offer no-interest loans. Needy students can also obtain short-term loans interest-free from a special fund usually repayable within a year (Helmreich, 2000). One woman interviewed, now a high school administrator, reported that she extends informal loans to her teachers who are supporting husbands in kollel. For one couple, when all else failed, help came from a rabbi in the kollel, as a woman recounted during an interview:

> A few times I had no money and the store [clerk] said. 'You can no longer buy anything on credit. If you don't pay today you can't buy any more food.' So I ran to the rav [rabbi] and said, 'What do I do?' And he gave me fifty dollars in cash or something like that, that was stuffed in a drawer somewhere and said, 'If you can ever pay it back, fine. And if you can't, well, G-d willing, be well!'

Given the functional interdependence in the traditional Jewish community, there is little stigma in receiving help, whether from others or from government agencies, since the kollel student by learning is fulfilling an important function in the community. Those who cannot study due to occupational pressures or lack of training often feel that it is only just to support the scholar. However, the lack of stigma and the variety of help available do not necessarily preclude the difficulty of dealing with intermittent and perhaps temporary sources of support.

Discussion

This study presents a complex picture of adaptive strategies used by women in a religious culture which emphasizes prolonged education for men, early marriage and high fertility. Both fieldwork and interviews showed the importance given to learning and the willingness of women to take a supportive role. The result is that women find themselves being the main financial support of the growing family, often with help from others.

Hogan (1978) hypothesizes that "the variable ordering of events in the life course is a contingency of some importance in the life cycle" (p. 573). He argues that among American males the completion of formal schooling is one of the most important markers of adult status, along with economic independence and marriage. Conformity in the patterning of these events in terms of age and order reduces the chances that a first marriage will end in separation or divorce. He concludes that an individual:

> will achieve maximum harmony between his own life style and the social context in which he lives when his life cycle events are ordered in a normative fashion. On the other hand, a man who lives through the sequence of these transition events in a disorderly fashion more frequently is in discord with the social setting (p. 574).

In our study. kollel families follow a set of timing norms indigenous to the religious community and therefore in harmony with their internal norms and values. Aspects of their economic lives, including employment, are usually contingent on the larger society. However, the kollel is not intended to prepare a man for employment except in cases where he plans to be a religious functionary, and the opportunities for these positions are limited. Does this delayed entry into the work force negatively affect the stability of the marriage as Hogan's research might predict? As mentioned above, the divorce rate of observant Jews in the United States is lower than that of secular Jews who are more likely to follow the life transitions of the broader society (Goldstein,

1992). Attending kollel emphasizes religious values, which support family stability. Therefore women see the "delay" as a worthwhile investment in the stability of the marriage especially given the relatively high divorce rates in the secular society. Attending kollel also gives a couple high status within the religious community, thereby bolstering self-esteem. This is a case where the timing norms of the subculture and those of the larger culture contradict each other and the stress and financial disadvantages involved in deviating from the larger norms are mitigated by adaptive mechanisms in the subculture. These include instrumental assistance such as financial help from relatives, coworkers, religious leaders, shopkeepers and the broader community, and emotional support in the form of advice and mutuality from other women. Furthermore, the kollel experience provides families with an ideology that downplays the economic sacrifices and interprets them as a sign of "spiritual investment" in the future, shaping the positive meaning of economic deprivation in this stage of life. As a result, kollel families do not appear to be at greater risk of separation and divorce because the husband delays entry into the work force.

Despite the social networks available and the mitigating effects of the meaning attached to the kollel experience, problems remain in terms of coping behaviors to deal with the lack of financial resources and the normative pressures to take responsibility for the household while the husband's energies are directed toward his learning. How do the coping mechanisms of the women studied here compare with those of other groups in American society faced with delays in entry into the work force? The findings on the kollel family are consistent with research on medical student couples in which the nonstudent spouse feels pressure to release his or her partner from many family roles and family life is organized around the student's work schedule (Fowlkes, 1980; Gabbard and Menninger, 1989). Medical families learn to postpone material rewards so that a temporary hardship for the medical student family (Gabbard and Menninger, 1989) is a sign of being a member of an elect for the kollel couple. Student marriages are common in graduate and professional schools and are often viewed as "inherently problematic" (Rohr et al., 1985:56). Researchers cite the competition between the student and the spouse for scarce time and personal commitment (Rohr et al., 1985), and the need for emotional support from spouses and the extended family (Spendlove et al., 1990). On the other hand, the kollel demonstrates that the deep integration of study and family life, the interdependence of the spouses, as well as time set aside for the family, can be extremely beneficial in creating a satisfying experience for both spouses in a graduate student marriage.

Our data show that in general women see the kollel period as a normative stage in the family life cycle with its benefits and stressors. The high status accorded the kollel period in the religious community and the subjective meanings of kollel are consistent with the notion that feelings of well-being in a role depend on how well the role identity is integrated with other role identities in an individual's life (Marks, 1998). During kollel, the conflict between a woman's roles is reduced by the ideology that her primary role is being a wife and mother. The wife is working only to support the family and to enable the husband to learn. These findings coincide with those found by Deutsch and Saxon (1998) in their research among working-class couples who do shift work and share child care but maintain a traditional gender ideology. The two cases differ in that kollel husbands do not share child care to the extent of the men studied by Deutsch and Saxon. However, this study of the kollel couple confirms that traditional gender ideology can be preserved and possible conflicts reduced by maintaining that a woman's primary sense of identity does not come from her work.

The strategy of gaining financial support from a variety of sources provides an interesting parallel to strategies used by other groups. While differing in family structure, socioeconomic level and available resources, poor African-American families also use mutual reliance on extended family networks (Jarett and Burton, 1999), as well as religious leaders and institutions (Weddle-West, 2000).

The methods of coping used by women in our study also coincide with those reported by Agarwal (1994) in his research on dual-career marriage in India where women traditionally have the primary responsibility for family demands. As among women married to kollel students, effective coping strategies used by Indian women to reduce stress included prioritizing demands, time management, compartmentalizing work and home roles and decreasing career involvement (Agarwal, 1994).

Conclusions

Sociologists have recognized that women's life cycle experiences may differ from normative models, depending on their place in the larger sociopolitical structure (Carter and McGoldrick, 1999), and that ethnic, racial and gender differences are often not incorporated in the theory (Rodgers and White, 1993). Family development among ultra-Orthodox Jews, in which the marriage precedes the economic readiness of the husband to support the wife, shows how the values of a religious culture can produce a pattern that challenges some of the basic expectations in American society concerning the assumed roles of husbands and wives.

A variable order of life cycle events does not always lead to instability of marriage. The kollel family constitutes an exception to Hogan's generalization that the change of, sequence and timing in the order of life events leads to the increased risk of divorce. This variant is not without its costs in stress and role overload on the part of women. While women come up with creative coping solutions to reduce distress, in many cases there appear to be limits to the extent that women can provide both economic support and caretaking for a large family. Unless more egalitarian child care norms are worked out, the length of such arrangements is limited by the number of children. Therefore kollel is likely to be, for most couples, only a stage in family development and not a permanent arrangement.

This study has several limitations. The sample is small and non-random making questionable generalization to the larger population. However, the goal here was to describe a group of women who are largely unstudied, whose life course differs in important ways from that of the larger society, and who have succeeded in constructing and perpetuating their own lifestyle despite the seemingly relentless forces of modernization and secularism in American society. It will be important to examine other groups in American society that have their own timing norms which may contradict those of the larger society. A step in this direction is a paper by Peters (1998) on Old Order Mennonites in Canada. Other possible subjects are the Amish and Mormons, both of whom are dependent on the larger society but maintain their own values, norms and sense of timing in family events. Such studies could enlarge the present efforts to understand the possibility of different models of family development.

Notes

1. The place-name is rendered pseudonymously for the purposes of privacy.
2. It is customary for married ultra-Orthodox Jewish women to cover their hair with wigs or head coverings such as scarves and hats.
3. Percentages are rounded up and therefore may not add up to 100%.

References

Affleck, M. 1985. "Feelings of time pressures and stress: husband-wife differences." *Free Inquiry in Creative Sociology* 13:27-30.

Agarwal, V. 1994. "Stress and multiple role women." *The Indian Journal of Social Science* 7:319-333.

Aldous, J. 1996. *Family Careers: Rethinking the Development Perspective*. Thousand Oaks: Sage.

Barnett, R. and G. Baruch. 1985. "Women's involvement in multiple roles and psychological distress." *Journal of Personality and Social Psychology* 49: 135-145.

Belcove-Shalin, J. (ed.). 1995. "Introduction: New World Hasidim." Pp. 1-30 in J. Belcove-Shalin (ed.), *New World Hasidim: Ethnographic Studies of Hasidic Jews in America.* Albany: State Univ. of NY Press.

Bomzer, H. 1985. *The Kollel in America.* New York: Shengold.

Bulka, R. 1989. "The dynamics of Jewish marriage." *Journal of Psychology and Judaism* 13: 73-86.

Bunim, S. 1986. *Religious and Secular Factors of Role Strain in Orthodox Jewish Mothers.* Doctoral dissertation submitted to Yeshiva University.

Carter, B. and M. McGoldrick (eds.). 1999. *The Expanded Family Life Cycle: Individual, Family and Social Perspectives.* Boston: Allyn and Bacon.

Dempster-McClain, D. and P Moen. 1989. "Moonlighting husbands: a life-cycle perspective." *Work and Occupations* 16: 43-64.

Deutsch, F. and S. Saxon. 1998. "Traditional ideologies, non-traditional lives." *Sex Roles* 38:331-362.

Eckman, L. 1975. *The History of the Musar Movement: 1840-1945.* New York: Shengold.

Evans-Pritchard, E.E. 1962. *Social Anthropology.* London: Cohen and West Ltd.

Farber, B., C. Mandel, et al. 1988. "The Jewish American Family." Pp. 400-437 in C. Mandel et al. (eds.) *Ethnic Families in America* (3rd ed.). New York: Elsevier.

Fowlkes, M. 1980. *Behind Every Successful Man: Wives of Medicine and Academe.* NY: Columbia University Press.

Frankfort-Nachmias, C. and D. Nachmias. 1992. *Research Methods in the Social Sciences.* 4th ed. New York: St. Martin's Press.

Friedlander, D. and C. Feldmann. 1993. "The modern shift to below-replacement fertility: has Israel's population joined the process?" *Population Studies* 47: 295-306.

Gabbard, G. and R. Menninger. 1989. "The psychology of postponement in the medical marriage." *Journal of the American Medical Association* 261: 2378-2381.

Glaser, B. and A. Strauss. 1967. *The Discovery of Grounded Theory.* New York: Aldine.

Goldstein, S. 1992. "Profile of American Jewry: Insights from the 1990 National Jewish Population Survey," Pp. 77-173 in D. Singer (ed.) *American Jewish Yearbook* 1992. Philadelphia: The Jewish Publication Society.

Heilman, S. 1995. *Portrait of American Jews: The Last Half of the 20th Century.* Seattle: University of Washington Press.

Helmreich, W. 2000. *The World of the Yeshiva: An Intimate Portrait of Orthodox Jewry.* Hoboken, N.J.: Ktav Publishing House.

Hochschild, A. and A. Machung. 1989. *Second Shift: Working Parents and the Revolution at Home.* NY: Viking Penguin, Inc.

Hogan, D. 1978. "The variable order of events in the life course." *American Sociological Review* 43: 573-586.

Huberman, A. and M. Miles. 1994. "Data management and analysis methods." Pp. 428-444 in N. Denzin and Y. Lincoln (eds.) *Handbook of Qualitative Research.* Thousand Oaks: Sage Publications.

Jarrett, R. and L. Burton. 1999. "Dynamic dimensions of family structure in low-income African American families: emergent themes in qualitative research." *Journal of Comparative Family Studies* 30: 177-188.

Lee, S. and P Keith. "The transition to motherhood of Korean women." *Journal of Comparative Family Studies* 30: 453-470.

Marks, N. 1998. "Does it hurt to care? Care giving, work-family conflict, and midlife wellbeing." *Journal of Marriage and the Family* 60: 951-966.

Marks, N. and J. Lambert. 1998. "Marital status, continuity and change among young and midlife adults: longitudinal effects on psychological well-being." *Journal of Family Issues* 19: 652-686.

Mehra, R., T. Du, et al. 1996. "Women in waste collection and recycling in Ho Chi Minh City." *Population and Environment* 18: 187-199.

Meleis, A. and P. Bernal. 1995. "The paradoxical world of daily domestic workers in Cali, Columbia." *Human Organization* 54: 393-400.

Mintz, J. 1992. *Hasidic People: A Place in the New World.* Cambridge, MA: Harvard University Press.

Neugarten, B. 1976. "Adaptation and the Life Cycle." *The Counseling Psychologist* 6:16-20.

Peters, J. 1998. "Development theory and the Canadian Old Order Mennonite family." Paper presented at the International Sociological Association, 1998.

Potucheck. J. 1992. "Employed wives' orientations to bread winning: a gender theory analysis." *Journal of Marriage and the Family* 54: 5-18-558.

Presser, H. 1988. "Shift work and child care among young dual-earner American parents." *Journal of Marriage and the Family* 50: 133-148.

Richter, K. 1994. "Living separately as a child care strategy: implications for women's work and family in urban Thailand." Paper presented at the American Sociological Association Annual Meeting.

Rogers. R. and J. White. 1993. "Family development theory:' Pp. 225-254 in P. Boss, W. Doherty, et al. (eds.) *Sourcebook of Family Theories and Methods: A Contextual Approach.* New York: Plenum Press.

Rohr, E., K. Rohr. et al. 1985. "Role conflict in marriages of law and medical school students." *Journal of Legal Education* 35: 56-64.

Rosenblatt, P. and L. Fischer. 1993. "Qualitative Family Research:" Pp. 167-177 in Boss, P., W. Doherty. et al. (eds.) *Sourcebook of Family Theory and Methods: A Contextual Approach.* New York: Plenum Press.

Schwarcz. M. 1985. *The Kollel: A Study in Traditional Knowledge and Community Life.* Doctoral dissertation submitted to the University of Pittsburgh.

Shaftir, W., R. Stebbins, et al. (eds.). 1980. *Fieldwork Experience: Qualitative Approaches to Social Research.* NY: St. Martin's.

Spendlove. D., B. Reed, et al. 1990. "Marital adjustment among housestaff and new attorneys." *Academic Medicine* 65: 599-603.

Trunk, I. 1979. *Jewish Responses to Nazi Persecution: Collective and Individual Behavior in Extremis.* New York: Stein and Day.

U.S. Census Bureau. 1999. *Statistical Abstract of the United States: 1999.* 119th edition, Washington. DC.

Voydanoff. P. 1987. *Work and Family Life.* Newbury Park. Ca.: Sage.

Weddle-West. K. 2000. "African-American Families: Trends and Issues Over the Life Course." Pp. 64-76 in S. Price, P. McHenry, et al. (eds.) *Families Across Time: A Life Course Perspective.* Los Angeles: Roxbury Publishing Co.

Weiss, L. 1999. "Single Women in Nepal: familial support, familial neglect." *Journal of Comparative Family Studies* 30:243-256.

White, J. 1999. "Work-family stage and satisfaction with work-family balance." *Journal of Comparative Family Studies* 30: 163-176.

Wilkie, J. 1991. "The decline in men's labor force participation and income and the changing economic support." *Journal of Marriage and the Family* 53: 111-122.

Zborowski, M. and E. Herzog. 1969. *Life is With People: The Culture of the Shtetl.* New York: Schocken.

Appendix

Questionnaire

Thank you for taking part in this study. I hope that you find it interesting and assure you that any personal information will be kept confidential. My purpose is to learn about the experiences of women married to kollel students, past or present.

1. How important was it to you that your husband study in a kollel and why?
2. What are some of the rewards of being a "kollel wife"?
3. What do you feel are some of the disadvantages, if any?
4. What are some characteristics and attitudes you feel are important in a kollel wife?
5. While every marriage has some degree of frustration, what are some of the special areas of stress or practical problems in a kollel marriage?
6. Were rabbis at the kollel an important influence on family relations? If so, how?
7. What do you (or did you) find useful in coping with demands on your time and energy?
8. What arrangements did you make for child care, if necessary? How many children did you have while in kollel?
9. If you have finished kollel, what is your husband working at now?
10. Did you work while your husband was in kollel? If so, was it full time or part-time?
11. What economic resources do or did you use to support your family besides your work? stipend? help from parents or relatives? wedding money? savings? other (please specify)?
12. Did you receive any help from the community or the government? Please specify.

13. Background information:

1. Age:
2. Highest year of education completed:
3. How long have you been married?
4. Number of children at present:
5. Year husband started kollel: year finished:
6. Were you born into a religious family or are you a ba'alat teshuva'?
7. Which of the following best describes your religious orientation?
   a. Chabad
   b. yeshiva world
   c. Aish HaTorah
8. Are you working now? What kind of work? Full time or part-time?

Examining and Responding to Conflict Between African American and Jewish American Students on a College Campus

Warren J. Blumenfeld
Lisa D. Robinson

Abstract: *The authors interviewed several undergraduate students of African and Jewish heritage at the University of Massachusetts-Amherst, to accumulate information focusing on the question, "What is the relationship on campus between African American and Jewish American students?" The results showed there were indeed tension, conflict, and misunderstanding between the two groups, which were particularly heightened when outside speakers were brought to campus. As a result of their research project, the authors designed and facilitated a full-weekend course at an off-campus conference site, bringing together undergraduate students of African and Jewish heritage. The authors share the results of their survey and the design, facilitation, and evaluation of their course, "African American and Jewish American Students Dialogue," within the historical background of race relations at the university.*

African Americans and Jewish Americans have a bittersweet history, fluctuating along a continuum from cooperation and alliance to tension and conflict according to historical, economic, political, cultural, social, and geographic circumstances. At times they are comrades in struggles for equality; at other times they are competitors for scarce resources. Sometimes they travel side-by-side working for common interests; at other times they stand alone, serving self-interest. Occasionally their goals merge. Sometimes identities and cultural styles collide in public conflict. And all too often, they do not regard one another at all.

    The University of Massachusetts-Amherst reflects in microcosmic perspective the events, alliances, and conflicts being played out in the larger U.S. society between African Americans and American Jews. In the spring of 1995, Lisa D. Robinson and Warren J. Blumenfeld, doctoral candidates in the Social Justice Education Program at the University of Massachusetts-Amherst, interviewed several undergraduate students of African and Jewish heritage. Through their conversations and interviews with these students, they were able to accumulate information focusing on the question, "What is the relationship on campus between African American and Jewish American students?" The results from this sample underscored the fact that there were indeed tension, conflict, and misunderstanding on campus between these two groups, which are particularly heightened when controversial outside speakers are brought to campus. Another common theme was that many of the students did not know much about the others' culture and history and expressed a desire to learn more. The participants in the study suggested a variety of strategies to improve intergroup relations and reduce conflict between African American and Jewish American students.

As a result of this initial research project, the authors decided to follow through on the students' suggestion of creating an opportunity to explore these issues in a safe and supportive environment. They applied for and were awarded a grant from the Chancellor's Commission on Civility in Human Relations at the University of Massachusetts-Amherst to design and facilitate a general education, two-credit course bringing together undergraduate students of African and Jewish heritage from the University of Massachusetts-Amherst (UMass.-Amherst). The course was held at an off-campus conference site (Bullard Farm in New Salem, Massachusetts) from late afternoon Friday, November 8, through late afternoon Sunday, November 10, 1996. In addition to the weekend, students were asked to attend a "debriefing session" at the university on Sunday, December 9, 1996.

This article explores the experiences of a group of students who participated in the intergroup dialogue on African American and Jewish American relations on the UMass.-Amherst campus. The instructors share the results of their initial student survey, and the design, facilitation, and evaluation of their course, EDUC 396J: African American and Jewish American Students Dialogue. To appreciate the climate of African American and Jewish American relations at the university, and to put the course into a historical context, we include an overview of intergroup conflict theory as well as a brief history of contemporary "race" relations there.

Intergroup Conflict Theory: An Overview

The term *intergroup relations is* sometimes used interchangeably with *intergroup behavior* or even *intergroup conflict,* though of course conflict is not necessarily an inevitable condition between groups. According to Gordon W Allport, not all relationships between groups from differing cultures result in conflict.

Hewstone and Giles (1986) emphasize that the context in which individuals and groups interact is crucial in understanding their relationships. Context involves the historical and ongoing relationship between social groupings. Intergroup conflict exists on the individual and interpersonal, organizational or institutional, and societal or cultural levels and must be viewed within its objective contexts—historical, economic, political, geographic, cultural, and social—and subjective contexts manifested in the form of stereotypes, belief systems, and value systems. "Intergroup conflict can be said to exist when groups attempt to achieve incompatible goals or when one group attempts to impose its values on another" (Stephan and Stephan, 1996, p. 144).

Researchers have subdivided intergroup conflict theories into varying taxonomies. Coser (1956) refers to two general categories: first, "realistic conflict" is one that arises from frustration of specific demands and is directed at the presumed frustrating object or group. The second, "unrealistic conflict," is not generated by the actual rivalries of the antagonists but rather by the need for release of tension of at least one of them. LeVine and Campbell (1972) divide their theoretical framework into three general categories: psychological-level, societal-level, and sociopsychological theories. Rothbart (1993) distinguishes four categories: motivational theories, cognitive theories, realistic conflict, and real group differences.

Blumenfeld (1998) discusses four categories: (1) realistic-group-conflict theory, which includes all the theories that posit the cause of intergroup strife and conflict as actual, or real, competition over limited resources between groups with incompatible interests (see, for example, Deutsch, 1994; Sherif and Sherif, 1969; and Sherif and others, 1961); (2) sociopsychological and perceptual theories of group conflict, which argues that denial of basic (and often intangible) psychological needs ("dispositional determinants") for security, identity, recognition, and participation underlie such conflicts (see, for instance, Burton, 1986; Cohen and Azar, 1981); (3) social identity theory, positing that conflict is activated whenever social categories and group divisions are present and emphasizes the social context as a cause of the conflict, in part because of the multiple processes of identification, comparison, and group differentiation to maximize self-esteem (see, for example, Tajfel, 1982; Tajfel and others, 1971); and (4) cross-cultural styles in conflict, which has an impact on the communication process between individuals and groups from varying cultures, sometimes resulting in miscommunication (see, for instance, Kochman, 1981, 1994; Weaver, 1994; Tannen, 1984, 1990, 1994).

Though many of the theorists do not emphasize broader social contexts, to fully understand intergroup conflict between two or more groups *within* a given society it is important to examine the larger contextual societal (or systemic) structures related to relative power differentials and inequities. These systemic inequities are pervasive throughout the society. They are encoded into the individual's consciousness and woven into the very fabric of our social institutions, resulting in a stratified social order privileging dominant (agent) groups while restricting and disempowering subordinate (target) groups based on ascribed social identities. This is the case not only in societies ruled by coercive or tyrannical leaders; according to Iris Marion Young (1992), it also occurs within the day-to-day practices of contemporary democratic societies.

Although fairly unique in some respects, the individual categories in all of these taxonomies should not be viewed as mutually exclusive or discrete processes, for at times it is extremely difficult to accurately distinguish between them. They often exert dynamic influence on one another, and at times they are mutually reinforcing. Moreover, one element (or concept) seems foundational and overarches each of the contributors to our understanding of intergroup conflict. This is the concept of *ethnocentrism*, defined by William Graham Sumner (1906), as "the view of things in which one's own group is the center of everything, and all others are scaled and rated with reference to it. . . . Each group nourishes its own pride and vanity, boasts itself superior, exalts its own divinities, and looks with contempt on outsiders. Each group thinks its own folkways the only right ones. . . . [T]he most important fact is that ethnocentrism leads a people to exaggerate and intensify everything in their own folkways which is peculiar and which differentiates them from others. It therefore strengthens the folkways" (pp. 12-13).

Each of the theories, taken individually and in concert, can help to explain intergroup conflict between African Americans and Jewish Americans, at various times and locations, depending on the context of the tensions.

A UMass.-Amherst Chronology on "Race" Relations

Responding to a number of anti-Semitic and racist incidents, including graffiti and slurs, the UMass.-Amherst administration established the Chancellor's Commission on Civility in Human Relations in 1980, composed of faculty members, college deans, staff, and students, to look into incidents of hate crimes on campus. The commission issued a list of recommendations, among them instituting "awareness days" on issues of racism, anti-Semitism, and sexism; including these issues in department curricula; and holding a campus conference on civility. From this conference came the UMass.-Amherst "Year Toward Civility," the 1981-82 academic year, to promote awareness of multiple forms of oppression.

Throughout the 1980s, a number of incidents placed the university in the media spotlight, giving it a reputation for being a "racist campus." The most infamous of these incidents occurred following baseball's World Series in 1986 between the Boston Red Sox and the New York Mets. After the Mets won the series, what could accurately be called a race riot developed in the southwest residential area of the campus on October 27. Angry white Red Sox fans, many of whom had consumed large amounts of alcohol, at one point numbering in the hundreds and headed by white members of the UMass.-Amherst football team, rampaged through the area and attacked a group of black Mets fans. One black student was hospitalized after suffering repeated blows to the body and being beaten unconscious.

This was not merely an isolated incident. Prior to this attack, interracial couples on campus suffered racial epithets hurled by other students, a number of students of color faced harassment in the residence halls, and racist and anti-Semitic graffiti appeared on campus. Some of the incidents involved non-UMass.-Amherst students who came to the campus.

Following the World Series confrontation, Judge Frederick Hurst from the Massachusetts Commission Against Discrimination investigated the riot and issued what has come to be called the Hurst Report, which concluded that (1) the incident in question was predictable owing to the hostile racial climate on campus, and it was also preventable; (2) there exists large-scale denial among white students and segments of the administration that race is indeed a problem on campus; and (3) the UMass.-Amherst administration interfered with the investigators' attempts to discover the truth surrounding this incident. The recommendations in the report to improve the racial climate on campus included:

- Criminal prosecution of students who violate the law
- Revision of current campus security procedures and annual in-service training for security police on criminal civil rights statutes
- Review and revision of UMass.-Amherst student alcohol policy
- Sensitivity training for football players and other student athletes
- Strengthening of the existing Chancellor's Commission on Civility in Human Relations
- Campuswide educational programs to maximize student awareness of racial issues
- Greater focus on black student and resident recruitment and retention

In response to the conclusions reached in this study, the campus coordinated a number of "civility weeks" during the 1987-88 school year, offering presentations and workshops to raise awareness of the many forms of oppression. In their desire to increase consciousness and expand campus discussion on the issue of race and racism, black students invited Minister Louis Farrakhan, leader of the Chicago-based Nation of Islam, to deliver a speech on February 3, 1989. In preparation for this event, the university's Office of Human Relations facilitated its first effort at education programs prior to and during the appearance of controversial speakers. The best-attended program was a joint presentation on issues of racism and anti-Semitism by black and Jewish faculty members.

More than eight hundred students and members of the Jewish Defense League (JDL) and the Jewish Defense Organization (JDO) held a candlelit march and vigil in protest outside the event. Most of the protesters peacefully carried signs reading "I Reject Racism and Anti-Semitism," "Unity!" and "Just Say No to Hate," but some members of the JDO and JDL chanted "Death to Farrakhan" and "Farrakhan Out!"

During his presentation, Farrakhan denied that he admires Adolph Hitler (as had previously been reported in the media), though he implied that Jews were ultimately responsible for the bombing of Pan American flight 103 over Lockerbie, Scotland, because of their oppressive treatment of the Palestinians. (Prior to Farrakhan's appearance on campus, during the late 1970s, the black student publication *Nummo* News—an insert in the UMass.-Amherst campuswide newspaper, the *Massachusetts Daily Collegian*— ran a series of antiSemitic articles and editorials. Actually, *Massachusetts Daily Collegian* has been and continues to be one battleground, providing a forum on campus for issues of race, ethnicity, class, gender, and sexual orientation.)

In 1988, black students took over the New Africa House in response to a number of campus incidents, among them white students harassing an inter-racial couple and, after a black man allegedly sexually harassed a woman, a large number of black male students being gathered and lined up by campus officials in a residence hall for identification. In addition, some black faculty refused to allow black students to maintain student organization offices in the New Africa House.

A black residence hall advisor was assaulted in 1992 by three white nonstudent visitors to the residence hall. Twenty students entered Washington Towers residence hall in protest. Also in that year, students took over the Whitmore Administration building and demanded that the university hire ten additional faculty of color.

Leonard Jeffries, a black professor at the City College of New York, spoke on campus November 12, 1992. The event was sponsored by Phi Beta Sigma (a black fraternity) and Afrik-Am and the New Black Agenda (two student groups). Jeffries had previously been removed from his post as chair of the Black Studies Department at CCNY following a speech in which he blamed "rich Jews" for financing the slave trade, and blamed Jews and the Mafia for negative portrayals of blacks in movies. Seventy protesters, organized by UMass.-Amherst Hillel students, demonstrated in the rain.

Following the speech, approximately one hundred African heritage and Jewish students convened for dialogue. The event was sponsored by the Black and Jewish Relations Committee of Hillel and the Black Mass Communications Project (a project of WMUA, the campus TV station, producing public access information for the black community at UMass.-Amherst). John Bracey, a black professor from the Department of History, and James Young, a Jewish professor from the Department of English, gave a presentation.

Minister Farrakhan was again invited to the campus in February 1994. The black student organizers of the event claimed they were bringing him in for the purpose of stimulating discussions on issues of racism, and to get the attention of the administration to finally hear their concerns. Their motivation, they contended, was not to slander Jews. They also stressed the issue of freedom of speech and asserted that blacks should be able to choose their own leaders without considering whether these leaders are acceptable to whites. The Office of Human Relations once again organized a number of educational programs, including a faculty presentation on the topic of black and Jewish relations, a meeting at the chancellor's house with black and Jewish students, and a dinner with black and Jewish faculty and staff to explore how the campus could respond.

Around this time in the spring of 1994, in the wake of concerns from the Jewish community about increasing anti-Semitism on campus (including growing tension between the black and Jewish communities), the university chancellor created the Chancellor's Task Force on Jewish Awareness and Anti-Semitism, which in turn recommended that an office be created, along the lines of the Office of ALANA (African American, Latino/a, Asian, Native American Affairs, to advocate for the needs of those students). The Office of Jewish Affairs was founded in May 1995. Among its many activities are informal conversations and formal collaboration with black leaders and organizations on campus, including a campus visit by Morris Dees Jr., founder of the Southern Poverty Law Center, who discussed the topic of hate crimes in America; a joint Jewish and African heritage delegation to a national conference in Washington, D.C., on black and Jewish relations on college campuses, and subsequent collaboration on an issue of pressing concern in the ALANA community (the perceived disproportionate attrition of ALANA students because of financial hardship).

Anthony (Tony) Martin, a Wellesley College African American professor, was invited by Phi Beta Sigma to deliver a speech titled "Black Leaders Under Siege" on December 6, 1994. However, during his presentation, he focused on Jewish oppression and enslavement of African Americans and often referred to his book, *The Jewish Onslaught: Dispatches from the Wellesley Battlefront.*

The Black/Jewish/Other Dialogue Group formed in the summer of 1995 and expanded into the Black/Jewish/Other Student Video Dialogue Project, sponsored by the Chancellor's Commission on Civility in Human Relations and the Office of Human Relations. By this time, with their history of conflict, Jewish and black student leaders were rarely talking face-to-face to resolve intergroup tensions. (On closer examination, however, it is quite remarkable to find how similar the groups were to one another within their differences. Most of the combatants involved in the intergroup conflict were male and held relatively conservative political and religious views.)

The video project was organized as an experimental program to begin the process of dialogue. It centered on taping three separate and simultaneously active homogeneous groups: one composed of black students with two black staff facilitators, a second made up of Jewish students facilitated by two Jewish staff members, and a third comprising students and facilitators who are neither black nor Jewish. Each group was separately videotaped in discussions of black and Jewish relations. After project staff edited the tapes, each group viewed the tapes of the other two. They were then taped in their responses to the other groups. The process continued for a second and then a third round, with these further discussions recorded, and then a final video was produced. This "reflective process" allowed participants to express their views honestly without fear of immediate reaction, and it permitted people to reflect on others' opinions before reflexively responding to what had been said. The project was completed in 1997 with production of the final video. The members of the three groups then all met for dinner and discussed their experiences.

In the fall of 1995, Maya Angelou and Elie Wiesel were invited to campus to present a dialogue on black and Jewish issues, sponsored by the university chancellor's office, Hillel, and others.

In 1996, an engineering student of African heritage was accused by university store security officers of stealing a package of Tums. It was later discovered that the student was innocent of the charges when he showed a receipt for the item. As a result of the incident, students of African heritage held protest demonstrations charging there was a pattern of harassment of blacks at the campus store. Store management agreed to hire more black employees and to institute diversity training for all its employees.

During the 1994-95 academic year, an employee at the university dining hall expressed a racial epithet: "Eeny, meeny, miney, moe, catch a nigger by the toe." This was said by a female employee who was reacting to a male student reciting the nursery rhyme "Eeny, meeny, miney, moe, catch a piggy by the toe" while choosing his lunch. As a result, the employee was reprimanded;

students protested her racist comment and demanded that the dining service conduct mandatory diversity training, which it later did.

A regularly scheduled Race Talks Forum focused specifically on black and Jewish issues in the spring of 1996 with a panel of UMass.-Amherst black and Jewish professors, staff, and students assessing the current campus climate.

Also in 1996, the Chancellor's Commission on Civility in Human Relations merged with the UMass.-Amherst Multicultural Advisory Board to become the Council on Community, Diversity, and Social Justice, acting in an advisory capacity to campus groups focusing on ethnicity, race, religion, gender, sexual orientation, and disability.

A faculty seminar on the history of black-Jewish relations was led by Maurianne Adams, professor in the Social Justice Education Program, and Bracey of the History Department in the 1996-97 school year. (Adams and Bracey were editing a book on the history of African American and Jewish American relations.)

The authors of this article were awarded a grant from the Chancellor's Commission on Community, Diversity, and Social justice to design and facilitate EDUC 396J, a two-credit course titled African American and Jewish Student Relations, in the fall of 1996.

ALANA and white students occupied the Goodell Building on campus in the spring of 1997, demanding an increase of ALANA students for the incoming class to 20 percent and at the graduate level to at least 14 percent; allocation of funds targeted for ALANA and low-income students as well as increased diversity of the staff in the Bursar's Office and throughout the administration, faculty, and staff; and upgrading to major department status for Irish Studies, Native American Studies, Latin American Studies, and Asian Studies.

In conclusion, a cycle seems to have emerged at the university. First there are antiracial or anti-Semitic incidents, leading to an administrative response, soon followed by a demonstration by students who charge that the climate on campus is intolerable, followed by recommitment on the part of the university, and the cycle is then repeated.

Survey: Methodology and Results

The authors designed a survey instrument for African-heritage and Jewish undergraduate students at the university to assess their perceptions of African American and Jewish American relations on the campus. Blumenfeld surveyed Jewish students, and Robinson simultaneously surveyed students of African heritage. The information gathered was used to determine whether a workshop or course on African American and Jewish American relations would be an appropriate tool in improving intergroup relations, and if so, if this data would aid in designing such a workshop or course.

The survey was organized into four basic subdivisions.

Identity. This section included students' demographic information: age, year in school, college major or area of concentration, native country or state of birth, permanent residence, campus residence, biological sex, racial or ethnic identity, religious identification if any, class background (poor, working-class, middle-class, owning-class), physical and mental ability (for instance, "temporarily able-bodied" or "disability"), and sexual identity (heterosexual, lesbian, gay, bisexual, other). The researchers emphasized that owing to the personal nature of many of the questions in this section, answering was optional.

Perceptions. Students were then asked to rate their perceptions, based on experiential knowledge, on issues related to African American and Jewish American relations on campus in a Likert-type survey. Questions included:

1. How would you rate the present state of African American and Jewish relations at UMass.-Amherst? (very good, moderately good, moderately bad, very bad, don't know)

2. On what information do you base your judgment?

3. What type of relationships have you had with African Americans [for Jews] or Jews [for African Americans] before coming to UMass.-Amherst? (school-related, neighborhood, work-related, social, other, none)

4. If you had a relationship, how would you rate it? (positive, neutral, negative, don't know)

5. If you did not have a relationship, was it mainly because: You were not interested; There were no African Americans or Jews around; There was a lack of opportunity; You did not feel comfortable; Other

6. How would you describe your relationship with African Americans or Jews since coming to UMass.-Amherst? (none, school classes, residence hall, work, social, other)

7. If you have had a relationship at UMass.-Amherst with African Americans, how would you rate it? (positive, negative, neutral, don't know)

8. How has your relationship with African Americans or Jews changed, comparing before you came to UMass.-Amherst to since coming to UMass.-Amherst? (better today, worse today, same, don't know)

Both groups reported that they perceived real tension, conflict, and misunderstanding on campus between African Americans and Jews, which are particularly heightened when controversial outside speakers are brought to campus. Six African American undergraduate students participated in the study.

Although four of the Jewish students stated they had had fairly good interactions with African Americans before coming to UMass.-Amherst, four rated the present state of African American and Jewish relations on that campus as "moderately bad," while two responded "very bad." They all stated that the heightening of tensions between the groups over the preceding few years was caused by African American student organizations inviting a number of what some of the Jewish students termed "anti-Semitic African American speakers" to the campus, most notably Farrakhan, Rev. Al Sharpton, and professors Jeffries and Martin. Most Jewish and African American students noted, however, that the tensions seemed primarily directed on the institutional level (between Jewish and African American *organizations),* rather than on the inter-personal level (between *individual* Jewish and African American students). The one exception was a Jewish student leader who reported being personally "targeted by African American students who called me 'bagel' and threw pennies at me." He said that African American students were successful in their attempts to have him expelled from his student government position "for allegedly being racist." None of the Jewish students interviewed acknowledged the role or responsibility of Jewish student organizations or individuals in creating the current state of affairs.

Knowledge. This section accessed the students' level of knowledge of the other group:

1. What courses have you had during or before high school that focused on or included [for Jews] African American studies or racism, or [for African Americans] Jewish studies or anti-Semitism? Please list.

2. What courses have you had in college that focused on or included [for Jews] African American studies or racism, or [for African Americans] Jewish studies or anti-Semitism? Please list.

3. Outside of a class setting, what other types of information have you read or seen related to [for Jews] African American studies or racism, or [for African Americans] Jewish studies or anti-Semitism? Please list.

4. Have you planned or attended any conferences, workshops, presentations, or other forums on the topic of [for Jews] African American studies or racism, or [for African Americans] Jewish studies or anti-Semitism? If yes, please list.

A common theme arising from both groups was that most of the students did not know much about the other's culture and history, though they did have a desire to learn more. All of the Jewish students had had some discussion of African American history in high school coursework, and many of the African American students had, at least, discussed the Nazi Holocaust in their coursework.

Goals. The final section of the survey related primarily to suggestions for improving the campus climate:

1. Are you aware of any antidiscrimination policies at UMass.-Amherst or at your workplace? (yes or no)

2. If yes, what groups does this policy cover? Please list.

3. What suggestions can you give to improve Jewish and African American relations at UMass.-Amherst?

4. If we were to design a workshop (or course) on African American and Jewish relations, what would you like to see included? Please list.

5. Would you come to the workshop if we gave it at a time that you could attend? (yes or no)

All the students, of African heritage and Jewish, suggested similar strategies to improve intergroup relations and reduce conflict between African American and Jewish American students. These included inviting progressive African American and Jewish American speakers to campus; instituting an African American and Jewish American relations course taught hy African Americans and Jewish Americans; developing more opportunities for dialogue and interaction, including a formalized dialogue course; continuing the Black/Jewish/Other Student Video Project then under way on campus; developing workshops emphasizing African American and Jewish history and culture; and generally offering opportunities for discussion to point out the similarities between the groups while acknowledging their differing cultural and historical perspectives.

EDUC 396J: African American and Jewish American Students Dialogue

The authors facilitated the full-weekend course at Bullard Farm, a converted farmhouse and barn in the pristine hills of New Salem, Massachusetts, approximately fifty miles northeast of the university, from late afternoon on Friday, November 8, until late afternoon on Sunday, November 10, 1996. Transportation to and from the conference site, food, and sleeping accommodations were provided. To enhance the overall group dynamics, and also because of insurance liability issues, students were required to remain at the conference site throughout the weekend. Students were also required to attend a debriefing session at the university one month later, on Sunday, December 9.

The instructors attempted to ensure an equal number of Jewish and African-heritage students. Eight Jewish students (three females and five males), eight African-heritage students (six females and two males), and the two authors as facilitators attended the weekend gathering.

All of these students were to receive academic credit for their participation and therefore made a personal commitment to engage in the process. To increase their knowledge on the issues that would be discussed in the course, the students were required to read the book *Blacks and Jews: Alliances and Arguments*, edited by Paul Berman (1994), before participating in the weekend. They were also required to complete and turn in a ten-to-twelve-page written assignment within three weeks after the weekend. The paper was composed of two parts: a summary of selective essays in the book, and personal reflection on the weekend.

The instructors listed the course goals in the syllabus:

- To learn more about our own and other individuals' and groups' culture and history
- To create an understanding of social justice and multicultural issues around the topics of racism and anti-Semitism
- To enhance intragroup and intergroup collaboration and dialogue
- To form and strengthen coalitions
- To train intergroup panels to facilitate campus workshops and forums
- To have some fun

On the first day, the students generated a number of guidelines to follow throughout the weekend:

- Anonymity (what is discussed here can be talked about outside these rooms, but please do not use people's names or other identifying characteristics).
- No hitting (physically or emotionally).
- Try to be as real as possible without being offensive.
- Try to be open and open minded.
- Respect others' opinions.
- Be honest.
- Take turns speaking.
- Take quick showers.
- Come on time.
- Ouch! (If someone says something you find offensive, say "ouch," and we can take time to discuss it.)
- Try not to hold grudges.
- Take care of personal needs.
- Chew gum and food quietly during group sessions.
- Don't just be negative; be balanced and constructive.
- No guilt or blame.
- Have self-control.
- Remember what you are trying to do.

The students filled out an "African American and Jewish American Questionnaire" designed by the instructors to access the background, goals, and attitudes of the students. The survey was very similar to the assessment tool the instructors distributed in their initial study in 1995. The current survey was divided into four basic sections: identity, perceptions, knowledge, and goals.

The students ranged in age from eighteen to twenty-two. The Jewish students and four African-heritage students were born on the U.S. mainland, and four were born in the Caribbean (Haiti and the Dominican Republic).

Though the instructors attempted to recruit participants with diverse experience on the topic of African American and Jewish American relations on the UMass.-Amherst campus and in the larger society, from information gathered on the student survey questionnaire and from personal observation the instructors determined that, though there was a range of experience, the students in general had little prior *direct* personal involvement with the topic. (The primary exception was one Jewish-heritage male student who has been involved in this issue for a number of years both personally and in his capacity as a staff member of the *Massachusetts Daily Collegian.)*

A sampling of the responses of the African-heritage students on the final evaluation suggests they previously perceived the tensions between the groups as primarily racial in nature (that is, between blacks and whites in general):

> *African-heritage woman no. 1:* Before the seminar *I* was in the dark about the conflict between blacks and Jews. All this time *I* was thinking that the only conflict was between whites in general and blacks.

> *African-heritage woman no. 6:* At first I didn't know what to think. Blacks and Jews? What do the two have in common? And what can they possibly be fighting about? I never thought that there was a problem between blacks and Jews. I had heard Minister Louis Farrakhan make anti-Semitic statements, but then again he made many statements that offended white people in general. I never really took the time to differentiate white people by their religion. Being Jewish to me was like being Catholic or Baptist. Now if someone told me that there was a class to discuss the relationship between Catholics and Jews, I would understand. But blacks and Jews ... that I couldn't quite understand.

> *African-heritage man* no. 1: I was truly unaware of the level of discontent and conflict between blacks and Jews until I read and viewed materials in preparation for this workshop. I was ignorant to

the facts and the degree that certain individuals perceived and reacted to events such as the Crown Heights [section of Brooklyn, New York, 1991] incident. I read about it, even saw short news clips about it, yet I was still oblivious to it. Why? I think it's probably due to two reasons, one of which was because I was simply detached from the event and I was living abroad. The other reason was that I just viewed the Jewish people on the news clips and articles as being white and simply dismissed it for classic racism, the type I was used to! I had "zero" knowledge of Jewish culture, history (besides the Holocaust), or current feelings on social interactions.

Many of the Jewish American students, though not having extensive personal involvement, were generally aware that tensions existed between the two groups:

> *Jewish-heritage woman* no. 1: Since my freshman year here at UMass. -Amherst, I had been hearing about the black Jewish tensions on campus. . . . I was glad to be given the opportunity to participate in this class because I wanted to see who was being affected by these tensions.

> *Jewish-heritage man no. 2:* One thing that was interesting was that many of the blacks never knew that there were problems between the two groups in society, while all the Jews knew there were problems. Does this mean it is the Jews hating the blacks? Is it that if the Jews never were to start certain situations they wouldn't happen? Or is it that just because of where some of these people grew up, they were not witness to the hate between the two groups? These extreme examples are things that I do not know the answers to since 1 personally have never witnessed any problems, but I definitely knew of their existence.

Before attending the weekend retreat, most students had discussions with family and friends, with mixed reactions:

> African-heritage woman no. 6: When I first told my friends and family that I was going on a retreat with Jewish students, their first reaction was "Why?" and to tell you the truth I didn't even know. They kept asking me all of these questions that I really could not answer. "Why are you going?" "Do you know a lot of Jewish people?" "What are you going to talk about?" "Do you have to sleep in the same room as them?" "Do you think that you will like them, or they will like you?" "What will you do if they say something racist?" The list goes on and on, but I guess that made me want to go even more. . . .

Jewish-heritage man no. 2: When I first signed up for the class I remember calling my parents and telling them that I was taking a new class which included going away for a weekend with a group of blacks and Jews. The first thing my mother said was, "Are they students, or are they from the ghetto?" This is a normal stereotypical question from a Jewish mother, but I did not even know the answer. I assumed that the black people on the trip were students as well, which is what I told her. My mother is not a racist person, and I do not come from a racist family. The media and society has made us think that the only type of black people are those that grow up in ghettos. . . . One of my friends, who is not Jewish, wanted to go [to this course] so badly that she teased of changing her last name from Stella to Stellaberg. I do not consider jokes like these as racist or slander, although some people do.

Hopes and Concerns

The course design included experiential and cognitive activities in a number of formats and covering a range of learning styles: large-group, small-group, dyad, and caucus groups divided by social identity; written, aural, visual, and kinesthetic; active, reflective, concrete, and abstract.

In the Hopes and Concerns activity on the first evening of the weekend course, students were asked to fill out a three-by-five card. On one side of the card, they were to anonymously list their hopes for the course (what they hoped to get out of it). On the other side, they were to list the concerns or fears they brought to the course. (The authors also filled out cards.) The facilitators (the authors of this article) then collected the cards, shuffled them, and redistributed them to the participants, who read them aloud to the group. Here are some samples:

- I hope to be able to meet and understand different people that I would normally not hang out with.
- To learn from one another; to understand each other.
- That the eighteen of us can all get along at the same time as discussing the problems.
- What I hope to get out of this? I hope to have a good time; learn a little bit more about the relationships between blacks and Jews over the years and present.
- That I learn something new and beneficial.
- Better understand differences and similarities between blacks and Jews and to close the gap.

- Learn more about black students and their concerns; meet interesting people; help resolve black Jewish tensions on campus.
- This gives me a better understanding of the relationship between blacks and Jews. Basically, what's the problem.
- To learn about black-Jewish tensions: do they exist and what causes them?
- To assess for myself the true level of antagonism between B/Js.
- We all get along, two credits, Days Inn.
- That this workshop be a positive experience for all of us.
- (1) Students remain open-minded on both sides; (2) learn more of both Jewish and African culture; (3) form new bonds with people; (4) learn more about myself.
- To get a better grasp on the Jewish religion.
- To get a better understanding of the Jewish religion.
- That we will leave knowing more about each other's group.
- I hope to learn more about the similarities between blacks and Jews.
- Hope people will work hard and also have a lot of fun.

Among concerns and fears:

- I have no major fears about this weekend. I just hope it will be fun and interesting.
- That we will all leave here thinking the same things about blacks and Jews.
- To leave the same way I came in, knowing nothing.
- I'm afraid I won't be able to wake up tomorrow morning that early. That a ghost will wake me up in the middle of the night.
- I'm afraid of not being honest so I won't offend. None really.
- We won't all get along. People may get offended about different issues discussed.
- Not getting anywhere.
- Transportation.
- We came through the back door earlier?
- Last week I was in class and we saw a video on Crown Heights incident in NYC (1991). It was very negative and it scared me. After seeing it I wasn't as excited to come to the seminar.
- (1) Tunnelmindedness of both groups; (2) isolation between two groups; (3) my little knowledge on both culture and its effect.
- That what people learn from this seminar will not take it back to UMass.-Amherst.

- That blacks and Jews will not realize that they have a lot in common.
- Concern that people will not participate.
- NOTHING.
- Fear that I will say something that someone might consider is rude or offensive.

Active Listening Exercise

The authors modeled active-listening skills that would enhance the learning experiences for the students. In front of the group, Blumenfeld told Robinson of an incident in which he experienced anti-Semitism. Active-listening concepts emphasized in this modeling included:

- Having the listener ask questions for clarification and for more information.
- Considering body posture and eye contact in reflecting active listening. (The facilitators gave a cultural disclaimer that in some cultures eye contact is not a form of respect.)
- The listener not talking about her or his similar personal experiences. The focus is on the person telling the story. Focus does not shift to the listener.

Students were then asked to pair up for ten minutes; in the dyad each person was given five minutes to practice active listening. Processing this activity, many students acknowledged that they had difficulty not turning the focus back on themselves as they listened to their partner. When they were listening, they often related a personal incident similar to the one they were told. This concept became a recurring theme throughout the weekend, where students caught themselves and others taking the focus from the speaker to themselves.

Some of the students commented on this activity in their final reflection paper:

> African-heritage woman no. 2: A big concept I came back from the class with was how to listen. It is so hard to just sit and listen to someone without interjecting any advice or antidotes. For the first time, when we sat down to do the exercise, I was able to just listen and really hear what the person was saying, instead of just thinking of what I was going to say next. That is probably one of the most important skills that I could ever hang on to and use later on in life. Using listening skills in race relations is a tool I think would help

alleviate a lot of the problems we have in this country today. Instead of shouting at one another needlessly, we could try to talk rationally with one another about specific incidents. This could help create a new level of understanding and compassion.

Jewish-heritage man no. 3: On the weekend we also learned how to be allies and active listeners. . . . To be an active listener one must ask clarifying questions. You must also give eye contact, and basically give the talker the feeling that you care and hear what they are saying. I can already see these things helping in my life today. 1 can see myself being a more active listener and people responding to me better.

Caucus Groups and "Fishbowls"

One of the purposes of a caucus group is to allow an opportunity for members of similar social identities to engage in open dialogue and check in with one another, before returning to the larger group. The authors structured the groups around answering six questions, which the participants would share later in a "fishbowl" exercise. Robinson facilitated the African-heritage caucus group, and Blumenfeld facilitated the Jewish-heritage group.

Many of the students found the caucus groups to be extremely worthwhile. From their reflection papers:

African-heritage woman no. 2: The caucus and the fishbowl had the greatest impact on me. During the caucus, I felt a sense of unity within our group. . . . There was a lot of hurtful stories and statements that were shared within the group. And I am glad that we were strong enough to recognize and speak about our feelings and how we are viewed in the world.

At the conclusion of the caucus group, participants reconvened as a large group for the fishbowl activity, arranged in two concentric circles, inner and outer. In the fishbowl, members of the inner circle speak and express their views while members of the outer circle listen to what is being said without responding—as if viewing fish within an aquarium. African-heritage students elected to go first in sharing their answers to the six questions discussed previously in their caucus group.

Robinson facilitated the African-heritage fishbowl. Here is a summary of excerpts from their responses:

1.   *What is it like to be black on the UMass.-Amherst campus?*

Deprived, targeted (aimed at), left-out (isolated), suspected, proud, pissed off, angry; a small number (only six hundred out of a total of seventeen thousand undergraduate students); there is uncertainty, lack of unity; paranoid of being paranoid.

2. *What I never want to hear said about blacks again:* name calling and the word NIGGER; that we are all here because of affirmative action; that we are lazy and that all we want to do is chill and do no work; that we are all welfare-dependent; we are not all drug dealers if we drive phat cars; we don't all love collard greens, chicken, watermelon, grits, chitlin, kool aid, cornbread; we don't all have weapons; that we are all criminals and thieves; that we are reckless and shiftless; that we're ignorant, stupid, and uneducated; that all we do is party; we don't all do drugs; that we all play ball; that we all could dance; we don't all listen to rap; not everyone is from the "hood."

3. *What are some critical incidents of racism you have witnessed or experienced personally?* The bad treatment of blacks by store personnel, especially either not getting help or being followed by security officers, like in our own university store on campus when an engineering student of African heritage was falsely accused of stealing a package of Tums; also the incident in one of our university dining halls where one of the workers expressed a racial epithet.

4. *What have you heard about Jews?* Stereotypes we've heard are that they are cheap, stingy; they smell [with] a peculiar odor; they don't change their clothes; they are friendly and generous; they are racist, religious, rich; they live on Long Island, they are doctors and lawyers; they are stuck-up; millions were killed in the (German) Holocaust; not all Jews are white; they are Kosher; they killed Jesus; they were forced to wear tattoo numbers in the concentration camps; they have horns and tails, big noses, and beards.

5. *Stereotypes that we think Jews have about blacks*: Their fear of our perceived "manness"/penis/manhood; they think we are savages, live in jungles, and are monkeys; they think we can't swim; we all have ghetto names; we have big lips and butts; we have bad attitude.

6. *How Jewish people can support me and be my ally*: We are too much alike to be so different; don't turn racism on us; respect each other as equals; talk to us; stick up for us-even in our absence.

Students in both the inner and outer circles were then given the opportunity to pair up with a partner and discuss what it was like for them and what issues and feelings came up when they either answered or heard the responses to the questions in the fishbowl.

The Jewish students then formed the inner circle and African-heritage students situated themselves on the outside of the fishbowl. Blumenfeld facilitated the discussion. Students chose to answer questions one and three together:

> 1. _What is it like being Jewish on the UMass.-Amherst campus?_ and
> 3. _What are some critical incidents of anti-Semitism you have
> witnessed or experienced personally?_ I don't usually make a point of
> letting people know [that I am Jewish] unless it comes up; some
> professors plan quizzes or tests on Jewish holidays like Yom Kippur,
> and when I say I can't be there, they say I have to take an essay test,
> which is harder than the multiple-choice test everyone else takes in
> class; I told a professor that I needed to get off for Yom Kippur, and
> he asked me if I go to Temple during the year, and said that if I
> didn't, and he asked why would I just go on Yom Kippur, I wasn't
> really paranoid about being Jewish until 1 read the book for this
> course, _Blacks and Jews: Arguments and Alliances_; a number of
> really anti-Semitic letters to the editor are printed in the
> _Massachusetts Daily Collegian_ in the guise of supporting the
> Palestinians against the Israelis; someone, whenever he sees me,
> throws a penny down on the ground to see if I would pick it up.
>
> 2.   _What 1 never want to hear said about Jews again_: That the
> (German) Holocaust didn't happen or that we are exaggerating it; that
> we are a separate "race"; "kike"; we are miserly; we dominate all
> these industries and institutions—entertainment, banks, the
> government.
>
> 3. _What have you heard about African Americans?_ Stereotypes are
> that they are savages; criminals; they are all in gangs; they take and
> sell drugs; they are graceful and athletic.
>
> 4.   _Stereotypes that we think African Americans have about Jews_:
> Jews had a major influence in the slave trade; we are miserly and
> cheap; we are controlling and have a lot of influence; all Jews are
> rich.
>
> 6. _How African Americans can support me and be my ally_: talk to us;
> ask us questions; realize that we have a lot in common, a lot of
> similarities.

Again, students were asked to pair up. The authors then facilitated a general
open discussion, asking first if anyone had a question for the other
group. Questions African-heritage students had for Jews:

- What is kosher?
- What is the prayer shawl [tallis] used for and what does it represent?
- Why do you wear the yarmulke?

Jewish students had only one question for African-heritage students: Do you want to be called "African American" or "black"?

One African-heritage woman began the general discussion by stating that she felt the black students were more open and honest in their portion of the fishbowl than the Jewish students—that they were more willing to take risks and expose the stereotypes they heard about Jews, but the Jewish students, on the other hand, seemed to be holding back, maybe for fear of offending or appearing to be racist. A number of other African-heritage students agreed.

A Jewish woman responded by saying that her family taught her to follow the important social convention that if you don't have anything nice to say about someone, don't say anything at all. A Jewish man proposed that maybe this is one of the cultural differences separating people of African heritage and Jews, positing that Jews might not be as willing to express their feelings in public for fear of offending. This controversy was echoed in students' reflection papers:

> *African-heritage woman no. 2*: I felt cheated when it was time for the Jewish group to speak. A lot was not said that would have been said. When it was time for them to list all the stereotypes about us, they basically read everything we had written up on the board. I think people were scared of saying things that might have hurt our group in any way. I perceived the whole activity as a card game: here's the table, lay all the cards down, and let's play. When we discussed the stereotypes against them, we were much more vocal than they were.

> *African-heritage woman no. 4*: The greatest impact I had from the workshop was that I was very disappointed that the Jewish students weren't as honest as we were during the fishbowl activity. They said that they were raised not to speak their minds; if they had nothing good to say, not to say it. I understand that but we did sign a paper [at the beginning of the weekend] saying we could make mistakes. I also felt that they were intimidated by us because we were so blunt. . . . Even after the fishbowl, we asked them questions and they kind of went around them. I guess they didn't want to hurt our feelings, they didn't feel comfortable, but at the beginning of the workshop we all asked for everybody to be honest and everybody agreed. I felt they were being dishonest because they wouldn't speak their minds.

> *Jewish-heritage woman no. 5*: Another thing that struck me was a comment someone ([African-heritage woman no. 3], I think) made at the end of the session. She said she felt the black students asked more questions and didn't hold back as much, which I think was true. The ensuing conversation helped me realize that I do hold back in these

situations for a few reasons. The first is that I don't want to offend anyone. Also, I think I've been trained to not notice or to try not to notice the difference between anyone. It is only when we don't notice the differences, I've been taught, that we can all come to accept each other. As the black students pointed out, however, they don't have the luxury, or even the desire, to ignore the differences.

Jewish-heritage man no. 4 did not raise contentious issues during the discussion but tackled them instead in his reflection paper:

> [The] dialogue allowed us to bring up controversial ideas on our own. However, I felt there could have been some more argument which would have come along with larger issues such as the Holocaust versus slavery, Afrocentrist support of the Palestinians, and "Pro-Afrocentrism" versus "Anti-Afrocentrism." In other words, how did blacks react to Afrocentrist movements and their praise of a better life and how did the Jews feel about the dehumanization of Jews?

The open discussion following the question-and-answer period centered on issues that have both separated and connected people of African heritage and Jews, drawn from their readings and personal experiences. Some of the *similarities:*

- Both groups have an "enemy memory"—collective historical memory of group oppression (Steele, 1994).
- The histories of African Americans and Jews are *similar* and *parallel* rather than *shared.*
- Both experienced diasporas (being forced out of their historical homelands and scattered throughout the world).
- Both groups have suffered abuse and violence.
- Both groups have suffered the silence (of others) in the face of their oppression.

Differences between the groups:

- Cultural differences.
- Many Jews are white, while African Americans are black.
- Jews can maintain their historical culture, while African Americans were severed from their historical culture.
- The United States for Jews meant freedom; though their choice to come here was often forced, it was a choice nonetheless. The United States for African Americans meant bondage, forced upon them and not a choice.

- Many Jews can hide the fact of their Jewishness; most African Americans cannot hide the fact of their color.
- White Jews have white privilege; African Americans don't have this privilege.

Some of the issues separating people of African heritage and Jews:

- Some African American leaders (Farrakhan and others).
- Israel and its treatment of the Palestinians.
- Issues of socioeconomic class.
- The perceived political influence of Jews.
- Affirmative action; many Jews see this as establishing *maximums* they cannot exceed, and they are therefore opposed, while many people of African heritage see this as establishing *minimums* under which they cannot fall and are therefore in favor.

Ally Action Component

To advance the process of understanding and help build alliances between students of African and Jewish heritage, the authors facilitated a multistep "ally action" exercise toward the close of the weekend course and concluded at the debriefing session one month later. They first asked students to brainstorm definitions of the term *ally* and to read the handout "Becoming an Ally." Students were asked to answer the question, "What are the qualities you treasure in an ally?" They were requested to write within an outline drawing of a person on newsprint in front of the group. Qualities included "friend, companion, gives time, understanding, educate yourself, respect, honesty, stand up for someone else, consistency, support, active listening, awareness, advocate, advisor, not holding back, acceptance, consideration, help, being there, take everything into relation, perspective."

The facilitators gave a lecturette on the "Action Continuum," outlining the continuum of actions in formulating allies, from actively joining in oppressive behavior or no response, to educating oneself, interrupting the oppressive behavior, interrupting and educating, and initiating an organized response.

Students were asked to take a copy of the "Action Strategy Planning Sheet" and bring it to the debriefing session with as many boxes filled in as possible to improve relations between people of African and Jewish heritage. Some of the general strategies they recommended:

- Inviting progressive African American and Jewish American speakers to campus.
- Instituting an African American and Jewish American relations course (another one like the weekend course, as well as a full-semester course) taught by African Americans and Jewish Americans.
- Develop more opportunities for dialogue and interaction, including a formalized dialogue course.
- Continue the Black/Jewish/Other Student Video Project then under way on campus.
- Develop workshops on African American/Jewish history and culture.
- Provide opportunities to discuss similarities between groups while acknowledging different cultural and historical perspectives.

Here is a sampling of personal initiatives (for the African-heritage students):

- Learn more about the Jewish culture and its people.
- Educate those who are ignorant about Jewish American and African American relations.
- Initiate and organize workshops on Jewish American and African American relations.
- Teach my children about culture and diversity, the similarities and differences between African Americans and Jewish Americans.
- Offer a day (Cultural Day) where all groups come together.
- Reach out to my peers and teach them what I've learned.
- Discuss the problems that exist within our communities and try to come up with ideas to help each other in our own communities.
- Start having Jewish and black dances and other social events.

And personal initiatives for Jewish-heritage students:

- Stop ignorant comments and jokes.
- Educate myself when questions arise.
- Quell comments; stand up for both groups.
- Write a movie on African American and Jewish American relations. (screenwriting major)
- Discuss racism in the workplace.
- Talk to the older generation about African American and Jewish American issues.
- Write positive stories for the campus newspaper and elsewhere.
- Form my own group with similar interest as me in black Jewish relationships.

Discussion

The African heritage and Jewish students who participated in the retreat attended classes on the same campus, but at times it seemed they lived in two separate realities and had differing cultural communication styles. Jewish students were more comfortable about writing their true feelings and perceptions on paper, white the African-heritage students were more than willing to verbally state how they were feeling. This was seen even in the context of agreeing to guidelines about being open and honest in the beginning of the workshop.

During the retreat, several African-heritage students questioned how Jewish students could be Jewish if they weren't religious. "Isn't Judaism a religion?" they asked. On the other hand, some of the Jewish students questioned how the African-heritage students could be so direct: "Isn't it wrong to say what you mean if it is offensive?" Although some of these concerns were stated out loud, others were brought up in personal journals and in small groups. In whatever case, it clearly showed that there were some personal, cultural, and stylistic differences among this group of students.

Many of the African-heritage students felt that they needed to deal with the issue of race directly because the color of their skin leaves them no choice. Even if they do not acknowledge their blackness, they feel that others react and respond to it anyway. Their overall sentiment was that they suffer and deal with racism and whatever other consequences result from having black skin, regardless of whether or not they open their mouths. Some of the Jewish students, however, because of their white skin, stated that they could make choices about when, how, where, or if they should reveal their Jewish identity. Thus, if they choose not to reveal their true identity, others may mistake them for something other than Jewish. This distinction is important to note because although many Jewish students may assimilate into the larger white society, many African Americans may not have that opportunity. For Jews, the so-called privilege of not identifying as Jewish and therefore accepting the benefits of whiteness (including gaining access to resources) sets up a dynamic between others, such as those of African heritage, who cannot always receive the same access.

From the outside, this may seem like an easy remedy to discrimination. Yet many Jewish students often have to pay the price of relinquishing their Jewish cultural traditions and identity (at least outside of Jewish community circles). Moreover, from an outsider's perspective (non-Jewish), it may seem that it is not a problem; but from the inside, Jewish students expressed that this buffering is sometimes used to protect themselves from the stereotypes, the shame, and the humiliation of being discriminated as a Jew. The reality is that Jewish students feel that they must always be on guard against anti-Semitism, never knowing who to trust, as blacks must always be on guard for racism.

Nearly all the students lacked knowledge about the history and culture of the other group. This lack of information led to curiosity to learn about the other group, so long as it was done in a safe environment or in response to a required class assignment. No student had voluntarily enrolled in a course pertaining to the other group prior to the weekend course. Thus information they previously received was passed down to them from families, school, friends, the media, etc. Some of the students stated that they did not realize the extent of the history and conflict between blacks and Jews until they completed the assigned readings or signed up for this course.

Another theme was that many of the students were drawn to this course to satisfy their curiosity, in spite of some of the stereotypes and warnings they had heard from family and friends. Few of them had actually been involved in the conflicts on campus, but they were willing to make the effort to help alleviate tensions by actively engaging in dialogue.

Overall, the students cordially participated in the weekend assignments and activities; but not surprisingly, total trust was never established between the African-heritage and Jewish students. This was evidenced by the fact that tensions and conflict arose when the African-heritage students named numerous stereotypes they thought Jews held of blacks, which the Jewish students later repeated without articulating their own thoughts about this question. It was decided by both groups and the facilitators that the African-heritage students could choose whether to present their information first or second. The reason the African-heritage students chose to present first during this sharing exercise was to prevent the appearance of having the Jewish students go first (that is, allowing white privilege to play out in the dialogue weekend).

In retrospect, there was some resentment from the African-heritage students because they felt they were forthright in their answers, while (they believed) the Jewish students were simultaneously holding back some of their true feelings about racial stereotypes toward blacks. Jewish students, on the other hand, did not feel safe in reporting this information in this venue because of "the way we were raised." The seemingly small gesture of which group went first in reporting out of the caucus groups led to an open and tense discussion about how these two cultures were taught to publicly speak the truth or remain silent on such sensitive issues as race and stereotypes.

In addition, although the group was of mixed gender, most of the conflict on campus seems to be between members of African American fraternities and male Jewish student leaders. Thus, the participants in our group did not necessarily reflect the students on campus who were entangled in the conflict.

At the end of the course, it was apparent that the students had bonded as a group and had crossed over into new territory by questioning each others cultures, history, and values. The small-group discussion, large-group activities, and one-on-one interactions allowed participants deeper understanding of themselves, their own cultural group, and the other group. Although all of their questions were not answered, participants concluded the course with greater appreciation and.critical analysis of the complexities of black and Jewish relations.

The African-heritage students were confronted with the reality that all students who looked white were not necessarily so in the overall historical construction of race, and Jewish students were confronted with the reality that they did have white-skin privilege that they consciously and unconsciously used in their daily lives. Both groups realized how much more they needed to learn about the other group—and about their own cultures. Moreover, each group was pushed to acknowledge that even if they were not personally involved in actively perpetuating forms of racism or anti-Semitism, their mere presence in an oppressive society played a part in this ongoing relationship.

Implications for the Future

The fact that overt tensions seem to flarc up only when an African American speaker comes to campus needs to be addressed. There have not been protests by African American students when a Jewish speaker is invited to campus. Does this imply that no Jewish speakers are making racist comments? Or does it follow the pattern of what the authors noticed in their course and what one of the Jewish students voiced (about not saying anything not nice), as well as the response from the African-heritage student who said she felt cheated during the workshop because she was brought up to speak her mind and felt that the Jewish students were not as honest as the African-heritage students?

On the UMass.-Amherst campus, in general, women (of African heritage or Jewish) tend not to be as vocal about these issues as men. We need to explore whether college women are more concerned with issues of gender than about issues of race or ethnicity, or whether male styles of communication make it likely that intergroup conflicts develop.

Several of the students who participated were of African heritage but born outside the United States, and they had different cultural values and experiences from those of U.S.-born African Americans. Are there unique factors acting between African Americans and Jews that West Indians do not share, or are the tensions between Jews and all black people of African heritage similar?

To fully address the issue of blacks and Jews, we need to examine the relationship at times other than when a controversial African American speaker comes to campus to understand how these relationships are playing out organizationally (institutionally) and on an individual level. We also need to study the role of the media in creating or exacerbating intergroup conflicts. Because of the willingness of this group of students to explore these issues, the facilitators suggest more classes (or at least some type of cross-cultural dialogue) on college campuses. The eagerness of these students indicates that many others around the country would also have an interest in continuing this process.

Note

This essay is an edited version of a paper presented at the conference Conflict Studies: The New Generation of Ideas, University of Massachusetts-Boston, Oct. 23, 1998. The authors would like to thank the following persons from UMass.-Amherst for their help and guidance in designing their course and writing this paper: Ximena Zuniga, Maurianne Adams, and Pat Griffin from the Social Justice Education Program; Grant Ingles from the Office of Human Relations; Larry Goldbaum from the Office of Jewish Affairs; and Judy Davis from the Office of Counseling and Assessment.

References

Allport. G. W. (1954). *The Nature of Prejudice*. Reading, MA: Addison-Wesley.

Berman, P. (1994). *Blacks and Jews: Alliances and Arguments*. NY: Delacorte Press.

Blumenfeld, W. J. (1998). *African American and Jewish American Relations Projected Through an Intergroup Conflict Theory Lens*. Unpublished comprehensive examination paper. Social Justice Education Program, University of Massachusetts-Amherst.

Burton, J. (1986). "The Procedures of Conflict Resolution." In E. Azar and R. Burton (Eds.). *International Conflict Resolution: Theory and Practice*. Boulder, CO: Lynne Reiner.

Cohen, S. P., and Azar., E. E. (1981). "From War to Peace: The Transition Between Egypt and Israel." *Journal of Conflict Resolution, 25*, 87-114.

Coser, L. A. (1956). *The Functions of Social Conflict*. New York; Free Press.

Deutsch, M. (1994). "Constructive Conflict Resolution: Principles, Training, and Research." *Journal of Social Issues, 50*(1). 13-32.

Hewstone, M., & Giles, H. (1986). "Contact Is Not Enough." In M. Hewstone and R. Brown (Eds.). *Contact and Conflict in Intergroup Encounters. Oxford*. UK: Blackwell.

Kochman, T. (1981). *Black and White Styles in Conflict*. Chicago: University of Chicago Press.

Kochman, T. (1994). "Black and White Cultural Styles in Pluralistic Perspective." In G. R. Weaver (Ed.). *Culture, Communication, and Conflict: Readings in Intercultural Relations*. New York: Simon & Schuster.

LeVine, R. A., & Campbell, D. T. (1972). *Ethnocentrism: Theories of Conflict, Ethnic Attitudes, and Group Behavior*. New York: Wiley.

Rothbart, M. (1993). "Intergroup Perception and Social Conflict." In S. Worchel and J. A. Simpson (Eds.). *Conflict Between People and Groups*. Chicago: Newlson-Hall.

Sherif, M., Harvey, O. J., White, B. J., Hood, W. R., & Sherif, C. W. (1961). *Intergroup Conflict and Cooperation: The Robbers' Cave Experiment*. Norman: Univ. of Oklahoma Press.

Sherif, M., & Sherif, C. W. (1969). *Social Psychology*. New York: HarperCollins.

Steele, S. (1994). "Breaking Our Bond of Shame." In P. Berman (Ed.). *Blacks and Jews: Alliances and Arguments*. New York: Delacorte Press.

Stephan, W. G., & Stephan, C. W. (1996). *Intergroup Relations*. Boulder, CO: Westview Press.

Sumner, W. G. (1906). *Folkways*. New York: Ginn Press.

Tajfel, H. (1982). *Social Identity and Intergroup Relations*. Cambridge, UK: Cambridge University Press.

Tajfel, H., Billig, M. G., Bundy, R. F., & Flament, C. (1971). "Social Categorization and Intergroup Behavior." *European Journal of Social Psychology, 1*. 149-177.

Tannen, D. (1984). *Conversational Style: Analyzing Talk Among Friends*. Norwood, NJ: Ablex.

Tannen, D. (1990). *You Just Don't Understand: Women and Men in Conversation*. New York: Ballantine Books.

Tannen, D. (1994). *Talking from 9 to 5*. New York: Morrow.

Weaver, G. R. (1994). "Contrast Culture Continuum." In G. R. Weaver (Ed.). *Culture, Communication, and Conflict: Readings in Intercultural Relations*. New York: Simon & Schuster.

Young, I. M. (1992). *Justice and the Politics of Difference*. Princeton, NJ: Princeton University Press.

Do They Want Their Children to Be Like Them?: Parental Heritage and Jewish Identity[1]

Arnold A. Lasker
Judith N. Lasker

Abstract: *The concept of "parental heritage" focuses attention on the deliberate transmission of parents' values and characteristics to their children, yet little empirical research has considered this dimension of the socialization of children. The importance of parental heritage is demonstrated in this study of 815 parents whose children were attending Jewish day or afternoon schools. The parents' ratings of the importance of nine dimensions of Jewish identity in their own lives and in the lives of their children when they grow up show remarkable consistency between the two. Yet several striking differences also exist: parents place greater importance on knowledge and less on friends for their children than for themselves. The meaning of these findings is discussed along with the value of this method for understanding parents' transmission of values and identity to their children.*

Social scientists have a long tradition of seeking to understand the ways in which children acquire their attitudes, characteristics and values. For example, a large literature considers the acquisition of specific characteristics such as sex role behavior (e.g., Mussen and Rutherford, 1963; Hoffman, 1972; Eisenberg *et al.*, 1985). Socialization and social learning theories have been developed to explain the mechanisms of transmission of personal qualities from parents, peers, and other significant influencers to children as they grow (Bandura and Walters, 1963; Bandura, 1977; Mischel, 1973; Aronfreed, 1969; Goslin, 1969). In this connection, there have been attempts to explain both the similarities and the differences between parents and their children (Acock, 1984). Yet, as Kohn (1983, p. 7) points out, ". . . despite decades of research in developmental psychology and in the sociology of socialization, all too little is known about the processes by which parents' values are communicated to their offspring."

Those studies that relate to the process of socialization by parents tend to focus either on the characteristics and values of the parents or on those of the children (Kohn, 1977; Bacon and Ashmore, 1986). Some go further, considering the degree of agreement between parental values and those of the children, assessing how much the children share the parents' opinions or behavior

(Bengtson and Troll, 1978; Russell and Russell, 1982; Glass *et al.*, 1986). Melvin Kohn (1983), among others, has developed a model for understanding the complex process of value transmission in the family. Nevertheless, surprisingly lacking in this whole literature is research on the extent to which parents *intentionally* attempt to transmit their own characteristics to their children and on which characteristics (or values, attitudes, etc.) of theirs they most wish to develop in their progeny.

Since parents are principal socializing agents, the seemingly complete absence of such studies is surprising. It would be most helpful to know what goals and aspirations guide parents in the upbringing of their children. To what extent do they want their children to replicate their own personalities, their own values and their own characteristics? On the other hand, to what extent do they intentionally attempt to develop in their children values and qualities which are *different* (or which are more or less intense) than what they perceive their own to be?

The reasons why people want to have children include the opportunities for companionship and the pleasure of associating with youngsters, as well as the desire to have someone they can teach and who will carry on the family name and the family line. Children serve as an extension of the parents' lives and personalities (Hoffman *et al.*,1978). Bengtson and Kuyper (1971) use the term "developmental stake" to describe one generation's investment in another, with the parent generation seeking a form of immortality through their children. Yet if there is indeed a tendency for parents to want to perpetuate themselves in their children, further research is necessary to determine the precise qualities desired in order to achieve that objective.

We know that some parents specifically try to ensure that their children will *not* be like themselves. Sennett and Cobb's study of working class adults (1973), for example, found that they wanted something better for their children than that which they themselves had achieved. They therefore denigrated their own accomplishments in attempting to convince the children not to follow their example. Moss *et al.* (1980) refer to this phenomenon of parents wanting their children to become what they themselves could not as "deficit-filling." [2]

To what extent do parents consciously seek to replicate their own values and characteristics in their children? Under what conditions do they wish their children to surpass them (or to have less than they do) for particular characteristics, abilities, and values? These are questions which virtually cry out for empirically derived answers.

Moss and Abramowitz (1982) call for empirical research on "the parent's conceptualization and intentional transmission of valued material or psychological assets to the child," which they call "parental heritage" (p. 358). In contrast to social learning theories, "parental heritage" focuses on the "deliberate choice" of the parent in the transfer of a legacy of values and characteristics. One area of needed research, they say, is that of intergenerational continuity: "Research to date has equated intergenerational continuity with intergenerational similarity but has done little to answer questions concerning the processes by which certain agents within a culture assume such continuity. Thus, previous research has overlooked the possibility that the parental motive to convey a heritage may be an important contributing factor" (p. 364).

It is not that interest in parental goals has been entirely lacking. LeVine (1969) writes of the role of parental goals in "deliberate socialization," but he sees the source of parents' values and preferences as being largely unconscious (pp. 529-30). Others have identified a variety of goals which parents have for their children, including sex roles, personality, political and religious values, and ethnic or cultural identity (e.g. Himmelfarb, 1980; Jennings and Niemi, 1968). What is still missing is a clear understanding of the parents' own characteristics and values, and how, and to what extent they purposively want their children to acquire them. Although Moss and Abramowitz call for such empirical investigation, to our knowledge, none has yet appeared which tests this important concept.

The use of the constellation of values and characteristics which comprise Jewish identity lend themselves to such an investigation. As Himmelfarb (1980) points out, "One of the most consistent findings in the Jewish identification literature is the positive relationship between an individual's Jewish identification and that of his parents . . . However, we actually know very little about the process of parental socialization" (p. 55).

In this paper we offer an illustration of the kind of study which would contribute to further delineation of the concept of "parental heritage." The study to be described here shows how parents' perceptions of their own Jewish identity relate to their goals for their children. What is of interest here is both the similarities—what parents want their children to be like Jewishly that is similar to their own Jewish identity—and the differences—the dimensions of Jewishness that the parents would prefer their children to emphasize either more or less than they themselves do in their own lives.

The Study

The data reported here were collected as part of an investigation of what parents want their children to derive from Jewish education with regard to Jewish identity (Lasker, 1976; Lasker, 1976/77). The study was predicated on the proposition that Jewish identity reflects a variety of characteristics or dimensions which, while not independent of each other, vary considerably in their strength among individual Jews. A multi-dimensional approach has been widely used in the study of Christianity, much of it drawing on the work of Glock and Stark (Glock, 1962; Stark and Glock, 1968; see also King, 1976; Spilka *et al.*, 1985). It was applied to Jewish identity by Lazerwitz (1973, 1978), and a number of other scholars have investigated specific aspects of Jewish identity (e.g., Herman, 1977; Cohen, 1983; Goldscheider and Zuckerman, 1984).

Based on previous work in this area, we identified nine dimensions of Jewish identity. They are listed below, as they appeared on the questionnaire used in the study. A term precedes each by which it is identified throughout the remainder of this paper.

1. *People* Feel part of the Jewish people.
2. *Heritage* Have a high regard for the value of the Jewish heritage.
3. *Knowledge* Have a background of Jewish knowledge.
4. *Ethics* Live in accordance with Jewish ethical standards.
5. *Faith* Have faith in God.
6. *Religious Proficiency* Know how to take part in Jewish religious practices.
7. *Community* Take part in the Jewish community.
8. *Friends* Have Jewish friends.
9. *Observance* Observe Jewish religious practices.

Parents whose children were attending eight schools in the Boston area were sent questionnaires. The schools included those under Orthodox, Conservative, and Reform auspices; two were day schools, and the other six were afternoon schools. Since one of the schools, an Orthodox day school, had many children from non-Orthodox families enrolled, the parents from this school were divided into Orthodox and non-Orthodox for the sake of analyses in which school units were compared; hence we will refer later to nine school groupings. Respondents were 368 fathers and 447 mothers, for a total of 815 subjects. Husbands and wives were asked to complete the questionnaires independently of each other.

The parents were asked, "How important is it to you that, when your children grow up, they shall. . . ." Later in the questionnaire they were asked, "To what extent do you feel that Jewishness plays a part in your life?" Both of these two questions were followed by the nine dimensions, and subjects were asked to respond on a Likert-type scale with four points, ranging from "None" (1) to "Very greatly" (4).

Hypotheses

Based on the concept of "parental heritage," that parents wish to transmit valued aspects of themselves to their children, we hypothesized that parents in the study would want their children to resemble themselves. Thus, if a parent described him/herself as highest on a particular dimension, it was expected that he or she would also value it most for the child. If, on the other hand, a dimension was not important in the parents' lives relative to other dimensions of Jewish identity, it was anticipated that this dimension would also be ranked low in hopes for the children's future.

It was also considered likely that there would be dimensions in regard to which the parents hoped their children would attain a higher level than they themselves did. This "deficit-filling" pattern would be most likely for those dimensions which the parents might feel they had not been able to achieve adequately on their own. These were expected to be "Knowledge" and "Religious Proficiency," both involving learning processes from which the parents may not have had the opportunity to benefit. This was particularly to be expected in a sample of Jewish parents who chose to send their children to Jewish schools. It was also considered that, in contrast to the other dimensions, "Knowledge" would be most likely to be considered a "possession" as well as a value, thus adding to the likelihood that parents would want it to be increased for their children.

Method of Analysis

Several strategies were used to determine whether the parents wanted their children to be like them—or different from them—on each of the components. First, the median score for "Children" was compared to the median for "Self" on each of the nine dimensions. Similar medians would indicate that the sample as a *whole* wanted their children to be similar to them. If, on the other hand, the medians for children were higher or lower than for the parents, this would indicate that the parents as a group wanted their children to have more or less of the particular dimension than they themselves had.

The second step was to consider whether these group results were true for individual parents as well, and this was done by correlating responses for "Self" with those for "Children" on each of the nine dimensions. This would indicate whether individual parents' self-ranking (relative to other parents) on a particular dimension corresponded to their ranking for their children on that same dimension.

Finally, we checked for consistency within the sample by comparing results for eighteen subsamples—mothers and fathers in each of the nine school units. Consistency across these subsamples would indicate that, regardless of religious denomination, gender, and type of schooling provided for the children, the relationship between the parents' own values and their hopes for their children—the degree of concern for parental heritage—was the same. If all of these diverse parental groups agreed that they wanted their children to share the dimensions of Jewish identity which were most important to them, we would have further support for the importance of "parental heritage."

Results

Table 1 presents the results for the comparison of medians on each of the nine dimensions.

Table 1
Comparison of Medians of "Self" and "Children" on
Nine Dimensions of Jewishness
(n=815)

Dimension	"Self"	"Children"	Difference
People	3.883	3.88	-.003
Heritage	3.882	3.853	-.029
Knowledge	3.061	3.728	.667
Ethics	3.569	3.648	.079
Faith	3.447	3.439	-.008
Religious Proficiency	3.103	3.128	.025
Community	2.887	3.025	.138
Friends	3.488	2.902	-.586
Observance	2.937	2.844	-.093

On six of the nine dimensions, the medians for "Self" were less than 0.1 point different from the medians for "Children." On the average, parents seemed to want their children to have the same levels on each of those six dimensions as the levels that characterized the parents themselves. For these aspects of Jewish identity, they apparently wanted their children to be very similar to themselves.

Three dimensions, however, do indicate some differences between "Self" and "Children." The largest contrasts come in regard to "Knowledge," for which "Children" is higher than "Self," and "Friends," for which "Self" is higher. A lesser discrepancy is found on "Community," which the parents ranked higher for their children than for themselves.

Table 2 gives the results of correlational analysis for the nine dimensions. Aside from the correlation for "Knowledge," all correlations are high enough to assure us that parents who scored highest on a dimension for themselves tended to want their children also to be high on that dimension, and the reverse in the case of those who scored lowest on that dimension.

Table 2

Pearson Product-Moment Correlations Between "Self" and "Children" on Each of the Nine Dimensions

Dimension	r
People	.478
Heritage	.543
Knowledge	.270
Ethics	.543
Faith	.787
Religious Proficiency	.425
Community	.553
Friends	.538
Observance	.635

All correlations are significant at a level of <.001

The results presented in Tables 1 and 2 indicate that, in regard to six of the nine dimensions, there is a strong association between parents' perceptions of the characteristics of their own Jewish identity and those which they considered important for their children to value. The exceptions to this pattern are "Knowledge," which has a much higher median for children but a low correlation, "Friends" with a substantially lower median and a high correlation, and "Community," which has a somewhat higher median as well as a high correlation.

We then considered the third test of similarity, that of consistency across subsamples for each of the dimensions. An examination of the pattern of consistency for the three dimensions on which there are differences between

"Self" and "Children" should give further clues as to the importance of these differences. Table 3 presents the results for consistency among the eighteen subsamples.

For five of the nine dimensions, there is considerable agreement among the subsamples, with more than half appearing in one column. With regard to "Heritage" and "People" the parent groups agreed that they want their children to be just like them. A smaller majority also wanted their children to resemble them in their level of "Faith," with the other groups more likely to downgrade the importance of "Faith" for their children. All groups wanted their children to exceed them on "Knowledge" and to value Jewish "Friends" less than they do.

Table 3
Differences in Self-Child Medians by Subsample

Dimensions	Self >.3 higher	Self between .1 & .3 higher	Difference between -.1 and +.1	Children between .1 & .3 higher	Children > .3 higher
People*	0	1	17	0	0
Heritage*	0	1	17	0	0
Knowledge	0	0	0	1	17
Ethics	0	3	8	5	2
Faith	2	3	11	1	1
Religious Proficiency	1	3	9	4	1
Community	0	1	8	6	3
Friends	17	1	0	0	0
Observance	3	5	9	0	1

Since almost every subsample had medians for "Self" on these items of more than 3.7, it would not be possible for "Children" to be more than .3 higher.

There is also substantial agreement on "Ethics" and "Community" for which the parents in almost all subsamples wanted their children to either resemble or exceed them, and on "Observance," which almost all groups wanted their children to value less than or the same as they do. "Religious Proficiency" is the only dimension for which the distribution of responses is not skewed in one direction or the other.

The most striking findings are those with regard to "Knowledge" and "Friends." In every single subsample, the difference between "Self" and "Children" on "Knowledge" is higher than the difference between "Self" and

"Children" on any other dimension in that subsample—in most cases, more than twice as high as any other. Similarly, the drop from "Self" to "Children" in medians for "Friends" is far greater in almost every subsample than the negative difference on any one of the other dimensions.

Discussion

The hypothesis that parents would want their children to have a Jewish identity whose dimensions are similar to the ones which they themselves value is confirmed for the sample as a whole for six of the nine dimensions—People, Heritage, Ethics, Faith, Religious Proficiency, and Observance. All six have similar medians and moderate to high correlations in the comparison of Self and Children. Friends and Community were hypothesized to fit this pattern but did not; however, the "self"-"children" difference in medians for Community is small, the correlation is high, and the majority of subsamples wanted their children to value Community the same or more than they do. Therefore, Community may be seen as being close to the pattern of the other dimensions.

People and Heritage, the highest ranked values for the sample (see Table 1), also show the most consistent pattern across groups. Almost every one of these diverse groups of parents placed the highest value on their Jewish heritage and their affiliation with the Jewish people, and they all wanted their children to perpetuate those values.

The hypothesis that parents would want their children to exceed them in regard to "Religious Proficiency" because it is a characteristic which they might not have been able to acquire, was not confirmed for the sample as a whole. "Religious Proficiency" is apparently a possession which they did not consider valuable, because they saw it as a resource needed only for "Observance," which they rate very low. There are several indicators producing this interpretation. "Religious Proficiency" is closely related to "Observance" ($r = .672$ for "Children"). It is also the only dimension other than "Knowledge" which does not correlate most highly, across the "Self"-"Children" divide, with its equivalent. Whether from "Self" to "Children" or the reverse, the highest correlate is "Observance," with "Religious Proficiency" coming second in both cases. The parents' disinterest in the value of "Observance" is evident in Table 1, which shows that it ranks lowest of all the dimensions among the parental values for their children and second lowest for themselves.

"Religious Proficiency" also fails the test of consistency, inasmuch as it is the only dimension in which subsample scores are not skewed. Five groups wanted their children to observe more than they did, nine wanted the same, and the four others rated "Children" lower than "Self." However, the differences among groups in this instance are quite revealing. All five groups which wanted their children to demonstrate more "Religious Proficiency" than they did were women; three out of the four who wanted less are men. It is likely that the women in this sample did not receive what they consider to be adequate religious training. For these women, then, our expectation that "Religious Proficiency" would follow the "deficit-filling" pattern of parents wanting for their children what they themselves could not attain, was apparently confirmed.

Since the response patterns for "Friends" and for "Knowledge" differ most strikingly from those of the other dimensions, with parents wanting their children to value "Knowledge" more and "Friends" less than they do, we will examine each of these in turn in order to understand further the reasons for these findings.

Friends This is the only dimension on which parents' goals for their children represented a substantial drop from their own self-descriptions. This finding is consistent across every subsample. Yet a number of observers (e.g., Liebman, 1973,1976; Sklare and Greenblum, 1979) have claimed that the essence of Jewish identity in America is social ties with other Jews. When the parents described the importance for themselves of having Jewish friends, they were referring to a reality—the actual friends they had and whom they liked. Those who rated this dimension high can be assumed to have Jewish friends and to find satisfaction in the feeling of a shared identity with fellow Jews. On the other hand, thinking of their children, they most likely concerned themselves more with their ideal of the kind of friends they thought their children should have. That ideal derives partly from the non-discriminatory demands of liberal democracy, calling for treating members of all religions as equals. Marshall Sklare (1967-68) referred to this apparent contradiction between practice and ideals when he wrote, "even those [Jews] who say Jews should not associate with each other tend to associate with fellow Jews" (p. 6).

Knowledge The fact that parents wanted their children to exceed them in "Knowledge" is consistent with our hypothesis. Not only was the median for "Children" substantially higher than the median for "Self" in the entire sample (Table 1); the same was true for each of the subsamples as well. This can perhaps be explained as being due to the fact that knowledge is regarded as a valuable possession which parents wanted their children to have more of than they themselves had. However, while parents generally wanted their children to have a greater background of Jewish knowledge than they themselves possessed (Table 1), the degree of desired knowledge was only moderately correlated with their own individual degree of knowledge, in contrast to much higher correlations for the other dimensions (Table 2).

Further analysis shows the reason for this discrepancy. "Knowledge" for parents, it turns out, represents a somewhat different concept from

"Knowledge" when considered for children. When parents referred to their own "Knowledge," they were thinking of the kind which supports religious practice or observance. The kind of "Knowledge" they meant when thinking about their children, however, is a knowledge which supports pride in the Jewish people.

This interpretation is confirmed by comparative correlations. When each dimension of "Self" is correlated with all nine dimensions of "Children" and when each dimension of "Children" is correlated with all the dimensions of "Self," the like dimensions in both questions have the highest correlation in practically every case. The major exception, however, is "Knowledge." Parental ranking of "Knowledge" for themselves is most highly correlated with "Observance" for their children (.339), and only secondly with "Knowledge" for children (.270). Also, the highest "Self" correlate with "Knowledge" of "Children" is "Heritage" (.336). "People" scored second (.287), and "Knowledge" (.270) is third.

Thus the parents' own "Knowledge" was most closely related to their hopes for the childrens' "Observance" while their wishes for their children's "Knowledge" was most associated with their own value of "Heritage" and "People." This finding is further demonstrated by comparing the correlations of "Knowledge" for "Self" with the other eight dimensions of "Self" and the correlations of "Knowledge" for "Children" with the other eight dimensions for "Children." The result is that the highest correlations with "Knowledge" for "Self" are with "Religious Proficiency" ($r = .61.2$) and "Observance" ($r = .433$). Parents who think of themselves as knowledgeable do so because they have knowledge regarding religious observance and are generally more observant; they would like their children to be observant also. Those with little such knowledge are less concerned about having their children observe Jewish. ritual.

When it comes to comparing "Knowledge" on the part of children with other dimensions of "Children," the highest correlations are with "Heritage" ($r = .521$) and "People" ($r = .407$). The parents apparently saw "Knowledge" for their children as being knowledge of their Jewish heritage, leading to a pride in being part of the Jewish people and identification with that heritage. Only to a limited extent would an increase in such knowledge be related to their observance.

This helps explain why there is so little correlation between the degree of Jewish knowledge of the parents and their desire for Jewish knowledge by their children. In the two contexts, the words, "Jewish knowledge," have different referents.

Conclusion

The Yiddish saying, *"Der apfel falt nit veit fun boim"* (the apple doesn't fall far from the tree) or the French expression, *"tel père tel fils"* (like father, like son) are indications of the common attitude that children resemble their parents. Moss and Abramovitz (1982) call for research to indicate whether this similarity may be intentional on the part of the parents; in this study, we have seen that, for most dimensions, the hypothesis that parents as a group want their children to resemble themselves is confirmed. The similarities found between parents and children in research on intergenerational continuity and socialization are likely to result at least in part from intentional transmission by the parents of qualities and values which they consider to be important to themselves. The similarity between what the parents in this study perceived to be central dimensions of their own Jewish identity and what they wanted their children to experience as adult Jews is quite striking.

In addition, the expectation that they would want their children to be higher than themselves on "Knowledge" was also sustained, although the content of such knowledge may be different for their children than it was for themselves. In fact, a striking finding was the marked increase of "Knowledge" of "Children" over that of "Self." The difference between "Knowledge" and the other dimensions is supported by correlational and consistency analyses as well. We had expected that difference to be the result of the parents' desire for their children to "possess" more of what they regarded as a worthwhile acquisition— very likely an important factor. More important, however, seems to be the change in meaning of "Knowledge" as possessed by the parents themselves to the "Knowledge" they want for their children. The "Knowledge" of "Self" is most highly correlated with "Religious Proficiency" and "Observance," which are in sixth and last places respectively on Table 1. By contrast, the , "Knowledge" of "Children" is most highly correlated with "Heritage" and "People," which are in the two highest places on Table 1. The change in the meaning of "Knowledge," to which we referred above, has undoubtedly given it greater importance in the eyes of the parents as a goal for their children.

"Religious Proficiency" was not valued more for children than for "Self" as hypothesized (except for five groups of mothers). This was apparently because "Religious Proficiency" was interpreted more as a matter of "Observance" than of "Knowledge."

An unexpected finding was that association with Jewish friends seemed to be less important in parents' goals for their children than it was in their own lives. It may be that their own friends were part of their existing reality, while the idea that in the future, their children might choose to concentrate on having Jewish friends would be indicative of a socially undesirable parochialism. This was not related to attitudes toward intermarriage, since those who offered the comment (elsewhere in the survey) that they were opposed to intermarriage were no more likely to want their children to value Jewish friends (Lasker, 1976).

These findings are consistent with the concepts of "parental heritage," "developmental stake," and "deficit-filling." They indicate that similarities between children and their parents, at least with regard to specific dimensions of Jewish identity, are desired by the parents. These parents did not simply want their children to be similar to them in having a Jewish identity; rather they made distinctions as to the elements of that identity which were important to them and which they also wanted their children to consider important. Thus for the more secular dimensions of Jewish identity—People, Heritage, Ethics, Community, and Knowledge (seen here to be a knowledge of people and heritage rather than of religious practice)—the parents wanted their children to value these traits as much as ("parental heritage") or even more than ("deficit-filling") they themselves do. For the more religious dimensions— Religious Proficiency, Faith, and Observance—there was also evidence of a desire for a "parental heritage" to be conveyed, but there is considerably more variation among the groups and a tendency toward being satisfied if children have less of these qualities. The very strong evidence of parents' wanting their children to value Jewish friends less than they did fits with this secularizing tendency within the sample. This is also an example of "deficit-filling"; wanting their children to value Jewish friends less indicates a desire for the children to be more diversified, more cosmopolitan, more American, perhaps, than they are themselves.[3]

This study provides one illustration of how research on parental heritage might be approached. Although parents' intentionality can only be inferred from such data, the results do demonstrate the existence of systematic and consistent similarities between self-identity and desires for childrens' identities, as well as specifying dimensions on which parents consistently wish their children to place either greater or less value than they do. Such research needs to be replicated to discover if the priorities of this particular sample, surveyed in the 1970's, have changed as the American Jewish community has changed. The results reported here indicate the value of such research for understanding how parents think about which of their values and characteristics they most want their children to adopt. It also can be helpful to schools and other agents of socialization which seek to collaborate with parents in the transmission of values to children.

Further research should consider other aspects of parents' values and characteristics and the extent to which they desire that these qualities be replicated in their children. In addition, it would be valuable to study in depth the actual processes by which parents actively and intentionally transmit these values and characteristics. Presumably such actions go beyond a general hope that somehow or other the children will become like their parents. To what extent do parents teach and model particular aspects of their identity in a conscious effort to perpetuate what is important to them? Such questions require detailed empirical research, but they offer the possibility of greater insight into the process by which children are socialized and the ways in which group identities are transmitted and transformed.

Notes

1. This study was carried out under the auspices of the Hebrew Teachers' College in Brookline Mass. We are grateful to Dr. Eli Grad of that institution for his support and assistance. Also, the University of Miami Department of Sociology provided invaluable support in the data-analysis phase. Thanks go as well to Stuart Kelman and Dr. Abraham Lavender for their assistance, and to Don Campbell, Kevin Christiano, Dana Dunn, Larry Greil, and Joan Spade for their helpful comments on earlier drafts. An earlier version of the paper was presented at the Society for the Scientific Study of Religion meeting, Virginia Beach, VA, November 1990.
2. Sometimes parenthood itself can be seen as part of a "deficit-filling" phenomenon. Peters (1985, pp. 925-26) suggests that "Parents often look to their children for affirmation of having successfully fulfilled their role of parenthood . . . This is particularly important when they perceive themselves as having been unsuccessful in other areas."
3. One might speculate that the increase in intermarriage and decline in religious affiliation in the Jewish community today may be in part an unintended result of what parents wanted for their children in earlier years.

References

ACOCK, A. C. (1984) "Parents and their Children: The Study of Intergenerational Influence" *Sociology and Social Research* 68:151-171.

ARONFREED, J. (1969) "The Concept of Internalization." In D.A. Goslin, *Handbook of Socialization Research,* Chicago: Rand McNally.

BACON, M. and ASHMORE, R. D. (1986) "A consideration of the Cognitive Activities of Parents and their Role in the Socialization Process." In Richard D. Ashmore and David M. Brodzinsky, eds., *Thinking about the Family: Views of Parents and Children.* Hillsdale, N.J.:Erlbaum, 3-33.

BANDURA, A (1977) *Social Learning Theory.* Englewood Cliffs, N.J.: Prentice-Hall.

BANDURA, A. and WALTERS., R.H. (1963) *Social Learning and Personality Development.* New York: Holt, Rinehart, and Winston.

BENGTSON, V.L. and KUYPERS, J.A. (1971) "Generational difference and the developmental stake." *Aging and Human Development* 2:249-260.

BENGTSON, V.L. and TROLL, L. (1978) "Youth and their Parents: Feedback and intergenerational influence in socialization," in R.M. Lerner and G.B. Spanier, eds. *Child Influences on Marital and Family Interaction,* New York, Academic Press, 215-240.

COHEN, S. M. (1983) *American Modernity and Jewish Identity.* N.Y.: Methuen Books.

EISENBERG, N., WOLCHIK, S., HERNANDEZ, R., and PASTERNACK, J. (1985) "Parental Socialization of Young Children's Play: A Short-term Longitudinal Study," *Child Development* 56:1506-1513.

GLASS, J., BENGTSON, V. L., and DUNHAM, C. C. (1986) "Attitude Similarity in 'Three-Generation Families: Socialization, Status Inheritance, or Reciprocal Influence?'" *American Sociological Review* 51:685-698.

GLOCK, C.Y. (1962) "On the Study of Religious Commitment," *Religious Education Research Supplement* 57:98-110.

GOLDSCHEIDER, C. and ZUCKERMAN, A .S. (1984) *The Transformation of the Jews.* Chicago: University of Chicago Press.

GOSLIN, D. A., ed. (1969) *Handbook of Socialization Theory and Research.* Chicago: Rand McNally.

HERMAN, S. (1977) *Jewish Identity; A Social Psychological Perspective.* Beverly Hills, CA: Sage.

HIMMELFARB, H. S. (1980) "The Study of American Jewish Identification," *Journal for the Scientific Study of Religion* 19:48-60.

HOFFMAN, L. W. (1972) "Early Childhood Experiences and Women's Achievement Motives," *Journal of Social Issues* 28:129-155.

HOFFMAN, L.W., THORNTON, A and MANIS, J.D. (1978) "The Value of Children to Parents in the United States" *Journal of Population* 1:91-132.

KING, M.B. (1976) "Measuring the Religious Variable: Nine Proposed Dimensions" *Journal for the Scientific Study of Religion* 6:173-190.

KOHN, M. (1977) *Class and Conformity; A Study in Values,* 2nd ed., Chicago: University of Chicago Press.

—. (1983) "On the Transmission of Values in the Family: A Preliminary Formulation" *Research in Sociology of Education and Socialization* 4:1-12.

LASKER, A (1976) "What Parents Want from the Jewish Education of their Children" *Journal of Jewish Communal Service* 52:393-403.

—. (1976-77) "Parents as Partners: Report of a Research Project" *Impact* 35.: 4-16.

LAZERWITZ, B. (1973) "Religious Identification and its Ethnic Correlates: A Multivariate Model" *Social Forces* 52:204-220.

LEVINE, R. A. (1969) "Culture, Personality, and Socialization: An Evolutionary View." In Goslin, D., ed., *Handbook of Socialization Theory and Research,* Chicago: Rand McNally,503-541.

LIEBMAN, C. (1973) "American Jewish Identity and Affiliation." In David Sidorsky, ed., *The Future of the Jewish Community in America.* Philadelphia: Jewish Publication Society.

—. (1976) *The Ambivalent American Jew: Politics, Religion, and Family in America.* Philadelphia: Jewish Publication Society.

MOSS, N. E., ABRAMOWITZ, S. I., and KASCHAK, E. (1982) "From Mother to Daughter: Conceptions of Family Heritage" *Smith College Studies in Social Work* 53:1-14.

MOSS, N.E. and ABRAMOWITZ, S.I. (1982) "Beyond Deficit-filling and Developmental Stakes: Cross-disciplinary Perspectives on Parental Heritage" *Journal of Marriage and the Family* 44: 357-366.

MUSSEN, P. and RUTHERFORD, E. (1963) "Parent-Child Relations and Parental Personality in Relation to Young Children's Sex Role Preferences" *Child Development* 34:589-607.

PETERS, J. (1985) "Adolescents as Socialization Agents to Parents" *Adolescence* 20: 921-933.

RUSSELL, A and RUSSELL, G. (1982) "Mother, Father, and Child Beliefs about Child Development" *Journal of Psychology* 10:297-306.

SENNETT, R. and COBB, J. (1973) *Some Hidden Injuries of Class.* New York: Alfred Knopf.

SKLARE, M. (1967-68) "Problems of the Contemporary Jew" *The Torch.*

SKLARE, M. and GREENBLUM, J. (1979) *Jewish Identity on the Suburban Frontier; a Study of Group Survival in the Open Society.* Chicago: University of Chicago Press.

SPILKA, B., HOOD, JR., R.W., and GORSUCH, R.L. (1985) *Psychology of Religion; An Empirical Approach.* Englewood Cliffs, N.J.: Prentice-Hall.

STARK, R and GLOCK, C.Y. (1968) *American Piety: The Nature of Religious Commitment,* Berkeley, CA: University of California Press.

Jewish and Arab Perceptions of
Civil Rights in Israel

Rita J. Simon
Jean Landis
Menachem Amir

Abstract: *The authors compare the opinions of Jewish and Arab Israeli citizens about the status and importance to them of freedom and democracy in their country—the former based on two national surveys (N = 1,174 and 573 respondents [Rs]) conducted by the Israel Institute of Applied Social Research, and the latter derived from two smaller surveys (N = 200 Rs each), using the same instrument, conducted in 2 Muslim Arab villages, Baqa El Garbiya and Jat. The substantive issues focused on freedom of expression, police power, confidence in social institutions, beliefs about the importance of democratic rule, and satisfaction with the way "democracy" works in Israel. Jewish and Arab Israelis agreed on many of the free speech items, but disagreed on "how things are run in Israel." The Arab Rs showed less opposition to police intervention than did the Jews. The main thrust of other differences was that, in contrast to the Arabs, the Jews believed the outside threat to their country was much greater and that democracy was in better shape. With the growing possibility of a Palestinian state, it is becoming increasingly apparent that the Israeli Arabs would prefer to cast their lot with the Arab kinsmen rather than retain their citizenship with their Jewish countrymen.*

This paper compares opinions of Jewish and Arab Israeli citizens about the status, and importance to them, of freedom and democracy in their country. The source of the Jewish Israeli opinions are two national surveys conducted first in the summer of 1986 and then in the spring of 1987 by the Israel Institute of Applied Social Research, a major survey agency comparable in the United States to the Harris or Gallup polls. Israeli Arab opinions are derived from two much smaller surveys, using the same instrument, conducted in two Muslim Arab villages of Baqa El Garbiya and Jat. The Arab survey was supervised and administered by Israeli Arabs. The first "national" survey had 1,174 Jewish respondents who were located in the major urban areas plus smaller cities and rural areas. The second had 573 respondents, all of whom were located in major urban areas. Each of the two surveys of Arab opinions contains 200 respondents. They were conducted at approximately the same time as the national polls.

The substantive issues focus on freedom of expression, police power, political tolerance, confidence in social institutions, and beliefs about the importance of democratic rule and satisfaction with the way "democracy" works in Israel. The current surveys included items that had been asked in a 1975 poll of Israeli attitudes toward civil liberties and that have also appeared on recent surveys of U.S. public opinion.

Background

Like Great Britain, Israel has no constitution. Shortly after independence in 1948, the first Parliament entertained, but rejected, the idea of drafting a constitution to insure civil liberties. Instead, it instructed a Constitutional Law and Judicial Committee to draft the present basic laws that would eventually form a constitution. Such laws were expected to articulate the fundamental powers of state institutions and to define the relationship of the state to the individual.

After conducting a national survey of Israeli attitudes toward civil liberties in 1975, Simon and Barnum (1978, p. 98) commented as follows on the results:

> There is a high degree of awareness and respect for fundamental individual civil liberties among the Israeli public. The data indicate a high degree of tolerance for criticism of social conditions, a consciousness of the need to respect politically deviant viewpoints, a preference for limiting police activity in favor of private rights, and a marked support for involvement of judicial processes where an individual's rights are limited.

> In several important instances public opinion shows a greater desire to protect individual rights than is reflected in existing legislation. Considering that there is no formal constitutional statement of individual civil liberties, that existing legislation permits substantial incursions into individual civil liberties, and that objective security conditions require restriction on individual freedoms, the level of expressed belief in individual liberties and freedoms is high.

Noting the absence of a constitution, they emphasized that the passage by the Israeli parliament of laws pertaining to civil liberties are likely to be much more in response to public sentiments because the range of options available to the legislative branch is very wide; much greater, for example, than under the U.S. system.

In the twelve years that have elapsed between the 1975 survey and the ones mentioned at the beginning of this paper, Israel experienced its longest and least popular war. There were widespread public demonstrations against the Lebanese war, the formation of "peace now" groups and even acts of disaffection within the Israeli Defense Forces (IDF). Israel has also experienced a resurgence of religious and nationalist fervor which has manifested itself in greater restrictions of activities on the Sabbath, passage of religious laws, especially in Jerusalem, the expansion of Jewish settlements in the West Bank, and the election to parliament of representatives of "extremist" right wing and religious parties.

To what extent will we find these events and changes in Israeli society reflected in public attitudes about freedom of expression, political tolerance, trust in institutions and support for democracy in the 1986 and 1987 surveys? We included items on our questionnaire that also appeared on recent U.S. national surveys of attitudes toward civil liberties in order that we might compare Israeli opinions against those held by Americans. Comparisons with American opinions are appropriate because the United States provides constitutional guarantees on many of the issues in question; and, because in the United States individual freedom and political differences have been both protected and, in large measure, respected.

Freedom Of Expression

Jewish and Arab Israelis agreed on many of the free speech items included in the survey, but they disagreed on "how things are run in Israel." Thirty-seven and 42% of the Arab respondents in 1986 and 1987 said that "people are too restricted in what they are allowed to think and do" compared to 12% and 11% of the Jewish respondents. Most of the Arab respondents (49% and 60%) believe it is "never justified" to refuse to hire a professor because of his political beliefs as opposed to 30% and 38% of the Jewish respondents. Along the same lines, Arabs are more likely to believe that the government never has the right to fire a person because of disloyalty to the country; 19 and 35% as opposed to 3 and 4% of the Jewish respondents. About half of the Arab respondents in contrast to a third of the Jewish ones believe the government "never has the right to punish someone for a particular speech."

Each of these disagreements consistently places the Arab community on the side of greater freedom and greater support for the right of dissent than the Jewish community. Of course these opinions must be seen in the context of the position that Israeli Arabs occupy in the state. Formerly the majority community, they now occupy minority status within a Jewish state, but hold ethnic, religious and political ties to Israel's enemies in the surrounding area.

Thus, for example, the political beliefs that a professor is likely to hold, which would make hiring him a questionable decision, are likely to be beliefs sympathetic to the Arab cause. These differences of opinion should also be seen in light of the shared views that are held on related items such as:

Books that preach the overthrow of the government should be made available by the library just like any book.

	Jews		Arabs
1986	1987	1986	1987
45.9	53.4	49.5	65.8

Freedom to worship as one pleases applies to all religious groups regardless of how extreme their beliefs are.

	Jews		Arabs
1986	1987	1986	1987
49.9	38.4	32.0	37.6

Free speech should be granted to everyone regardless of how intolerant they are of other people's opinions.

	Jews		Arabs
1986	1987	1986	1987
58.7	57.9	54.5	45.5

In Israel today, too much emphasis is placed on conformity and obedience to the community.

	Jews		Arabs
1986	1987	1986	1987
25.0	18.3	23.5	31.7

Items pertaining to book censorship, freedom of worship, a professor's political beliefs, and granting free speech to intolerant people had been included in a national survey conducted in the United States in 1979 (McClosky and Brill 1983). Only on the freedom to worship item did the American public express stronger support for civil liberties than did the Israelis (Jewish and Arab). Sixty-nine percent of the U.S. respondents said it should apply to all groups. Only 18% of the Americans polled believed that refusal to hire a professor because of his/her political views is never justified; and 32% believed that books that preach the overthrow of the government should be available in the library. American public opinion matched Jewish Israeli views on the item that stated: Free speech should be granted to everyone regardless of how intolerant they are of other people's opinion (U.S. 58%).

Police Interference

The role and power of the police are significant measures of the amount of restrictions a society places on its citizenry. Initially in 1975, and again in 1986 and 1987, we included a series of questions about various forms of police surveillance and intrusion into the activities and movements of the populace. The format for the specific items reads as follows:

> How strongly do you support or oppose the police listening to telephone conversations, reading mail, maintaining surveillance, limiting freedom of movement, and forbidding demonstrations on the part of a wide range of political groups in Israeli society, including leftists (Racah) and rightists (Kach, Jewish underground movements) and religious groups that oppose the state (Netora Karta).

The figures in Table 1 report the respondents who supported, opposed, and had no opinion about police intervention for *all* the political and religious movements cited above. On the whole, and especially in 1987, the Arab respondents showed less opposition to police intervention than did the Jews.

Contrary to expectations that might have been gained from stories in the popular media, Jewish Israeli opposition to police interference vis-à-vis all of the groups tended to increase or remain at about the same level from 1975 to 1986/87 on all of the activities shown in Table 1.

The same issues, with different political groups as illustrations, were included on a national U.S. poll in 1975 (Simon and Barnum 1978). Unlike in the United States, where constitutional guarantees forbid most of these activities, in Israel, legislation exists that provide a legal basis for the execution of each of these activities by administrative bodies that are essentially free from judicial review. The American responses differed from the Israeli's on three issues. Americans were more opposed than Israelis to direct invasions of privacy such as tapping of telephones (69%) and opening mail (80%), and to forbidding demonstrations (70%). But they expressed less opposition than Israelis to placing persons under surveillance (17%). On placing limitations on internal movements, the American public shared similar views to those of the Jewish Israelis (53% compared to 50%).

So, once again, we have a basis of comparison between Israeli and American support for civil liberties. We found that while the American public demonstrated greater support for the personal rights of privacy (i.e., via telephone and mail), a majority of the Israelis also demonstrated their respect for privacy and a concern for limiting police interference in public as well as personal activities, even though in Israel such activities are legally mandated.

Table 1. Opinions Supporting and Opposing (In Percent)

Activities	1975	*Jews* 1986	1987	*Arabs* 1986	1987
Listening to Telephone Conversations					
Support[a]	20	28.9	24.6	5.5	10.4
Oppose[b]	43	48.2	50.1	56.5	37.1
No Opinion	11	5.8	6.6	4.5	15.3
Opening Mail					
Support	20	23.8	22.2	6.5	9.4
Oppose	45	54.4	53.8	51	40.6
No Opinion	12	6	6.6	3.5	15.3
Surveillance					
Support	31	35.1	30.2	6	10.4
Oppose	26	37.6	40.1	44.5	27.7
No Opinion	11	6	5.9	6	19.8
Limiting Movement					
Support	15	20.2	21.3	4.5	9.9
Oppose	50	53.8	52.9	44	33.2
No Opinion	9	6.3	6.6	6.5	17.3
Forbidding Demonstrations					
Support	14	26.1	19.2	9	8.4
Oppose	56	48.8	58.6	40.5	36.1
No Opinion	7	6.1	5.6	8.5	15.3

Notes: [a] Proportion of respondents who approve of the activity for all groups.

[b] Proportion of respondents who disapprove of the activity for any group.

Political Tolerance

One indication of how much respect or support there is for civil liberties is the extent to which the public tolerates expressions of unpopular beliefs and opinions about important and controversial public issues. In a U.S. national survey of civil liberties conducted by Stouffer (1957) in 1955 (a period marked by widespread fear of internal subversion, suspicion of disloyalty, and emphasis on political conformity), tolerance was measured by asking respondents how suspicious they were of various political sentiments: for example, persons who say they would refuse to sign an oath of loyalty to the United States, or persons who talk against religions. We adopted the same format in the 1975 Israeli survey and used it again in 1986 and 1987. The higher the percentage of "not at all suspicious" responses to each of the items, the greater the level of tolerance, which in this context indicates acknowledgement of the legitimacy of the views expressed.

Items in Table 2 are arranged such that in the first version Jewish respondents were judging Jewish views and Arab respondents were judging Arab views. In the second version Jewish respondents were judging the same opinion when it was expressed by an Arab, and Arab respondents were judging that same opinion, but this time it was expressed by a Jew. The substantive issues and the positions espoused did not vary. The only alterations were in the identity of the persons espousing the views.

Given the issues covered by most of the items in Table 2, it is not surprising the Jewish respondents were more suspicious of the views expressed than were Arab respondents. But note that especially in 1987, Jewish respondents distinguished hardly at all by the source of the opinion: Jews and Arabs were viewed with the same degree of suspicion by Jewish respondents. Arab respondents, on the other hand, perceived Jews who espoused these views with much greater suspicion, indeed with as much suspicion as did the Jewish respondents and with greater suspicion than when the same views were espoused by Arabs. For both communities, the level of tolerance decreased from 1986 to 1987. The items about which Jews were most suspicious concerned the establishment of an independent Palestinian state on the West Bank, the transformation of Israel into a bi-national state, and support for direct talks with the PLO. Arab respondents were most suspicious of persons who favor Jewish settlements in the West Bank in the midst of Arab communities, and who want Jewish religious law to have priority over secular law.

Three of the tolerance items were included in the 1975 Israel survey: "discrimination against Israeli Arabs," "persons who favor talks with the PLO," and "establishment of a Palestinian state of the West Bank" (Simon and Barnum 1978). In 1975 only 5% of the Jews polled viewed Jewish opinions

Table 2.   Percent Not At All Suspicious of Statementd
Voiced by Jewish and Arab Citizens (In Percent)

Statements	Jews		Arabs	
	1986	*1987*	*1986*	*1987*
A (Jewish/Arab) citizen claims that a Palestinian State should be established on The West Bank	27.8	14.1	59.5	80.2
An (Arab/Jewish) citizen claims that a Palestinian State should be established on The West Bank	14.9	15.2	40.5	40.1
A (Jewish/Arab) citizen objects to imprisonment of soldiers who refuse to serve in certain areas	35.9	29.5	36.0	57.4
An (Arab/Jewish citizen) objects to imprisonment of soldiers who refuse to serve in certain areas	25.7	28.4	34.5	29.2
A (Jewish/Arab) citizen declares that there is discrimination in Israel against Arabs	46.0	32.1	51.0	73.3
An (Arab/Jewish) citizen declares that there is discrimination in Israel against Arabs	40.7	37.3	47.5	44.6
A (Jewish/Arab) citizen declares that Israeli Arabs should have equal rights to welfare aid	51.6	44.0	54.0	82.7
An (Arab/Jewish) Citizen declares that Israeli Arabs should have equal rights to welfare aid	51.3	49.6	53.5	45.0
A (Jewish/Arab) citizen claims that Israel should be a Bi-National State	24.8	14.7	53.0	63.4
An (Arab/Jewish) citizen claims that Israel should be a Bi-National State	22.1	18.2	31.5	38.1
A Jewish citizen declares that there should be direct talks with representatives of the PLO[a]	23.1	16.4	51.5	48.0
A Jewish citizen claims that religious law should have priority over those of the state[a]	39.8	31.8	26.5	7.9
A Jewish citizen claims there is discrimination against Jews in Israel, such as not being allowed to settle everywhere[a]	59.2	49.7	28.0	15.3
A Jewish citizen claims that Jews should settle in the midst of Arab towns in Judea and Samaria (for example, Nablus and Hebron)[a]	65.2	57.6	27.0	14.4
An Arab citizen objects to settlement of Jews in the area of Arab towns in Judea and Samaria (for example, Nablus)[b]	27.3	28.4	53.0	74.8

Notes: [a] No Arab Citizen Counterpart.
         [b] No Jewish Citizen Counterpart.

about discrimination against Israeli Arabs with "great suspicion," compared to 12% in 1986 and 17% in 1987; in 1975, 19% were "very suspicious" of persons who favored direct talks with the PLO, compared to 39% in 1986 and 43% in 1987; and in 1975, 22% were "very suspicious" of persons who favored the establishment of a Palestinian state on the West Bank, compared to 33% in 1986 and 46% in 1987. Over a 12-year time span, the level of suspicion increased quite a lot, especially on the extremely sensitive issues involving direct talks with the PLO and the establishment of a Palestinian state.

Confidence In Public Institutions

In two national surveys conducted in Israel in January and July 1987, Israeli sociologists Ephraim Yuchtman Yaar, Yohanan Peres, and Mira Freund, of Tel Aviv University, reported responses to items that asked about the extent of trust in central institutions in Israeli society (Yaar, Peres, and Freund 1987). In discussing the implications of their study, they observed:

> Without a firm, wide base of support and trust, the political system's ability to function is weakened, and the danger arises of anti-democratic forces and currents being generated which challenge the existing system and which counterpose alternative forms of movement supposedly more "just" and more "efficient." Such dangers, whose bitter lessons have already been learned by a number of western democracies in the recent past, are especially evident in times of crisis, when the society is engaged in existential struggles such as those characterizing Israeli society since its beginnings (p. 31).

> The amount of trust felt by the public toward the institutions of a society based upon democratic principles constitutes one of the most important indicators of the vigor of that type of society and of its prospects for persevering in its democratic character. Indeed, the existence and stability of democracy, more than any other type of political regime, depend upon the degree of support and legitimacy which governmental and other central social institutions receive from the public (p. 34).

In our second survey, we included items that also asked about trust in many of the same institutions. The Jewish responses on our survey match closely those reported by Yaar et al. (1987). For example, they, as we, found that the military was the institution that received the highest degree of support: 76 and 66% answered "a great deal of confidence" on their survey and 73% of our respondents answered "a great deal of confidence." In their, and our surveys, the courts ranked second with 56 and 57% on theirs and 52% on ours answering "a great deal of confidence."

The question we look at now is how similar are the Arab and Jewish respondents. The answer, as shown in Table 3, is that *except* for the military to which only *one* percent of the Arab respondents expressed a great deal of confidence, Jewish and Arab ratings matched closely on important institutions that were not directly political: for example, the courts, the universities, the trade unions, banks and financial institutions. They disagreed in their confidence of the police, the government, and the Likud party. Unlike the Jewish respondents, the Arabs expressed much more confidence in the Labor party than they did in the right of center, Likud party.

In 1987, we also asked Arabs and Jews which groups and movements they believed posed threats to Israeli democracy and to its internal security (see Table 4). For the Arab respondents, threats to democracy are most likely to emanate from rightist groups, religious groups, and the movement for a greater Israel. For the Jews, the greatest threats to democracy emanate from Arabs in the occupied territories, leftist groups, and Israeli Arabs. Both Jewish and Arab respondents agree that the military and the police do not pose a threat to democracy.

As described in Table 5, Jews are more selective about which groups they perceive as threats or dangers to internal security. On that issue, the Arabs in the occupied territories outdistance any other group. Only the Israeli Arabs and leftist groups are mentioned by more than 20% of the Jewish respondents. The Arab respondents do not focus on any one group, but rate the movement for a greater Israel, rightist groups, and religious groups higher than any of the others.

Especially on the matter of "internal security," the Jewish respondents make a big distinction between Israeli Arabs and Arabs in the occupied territories; clearly perceiving the latter as the more serious threat. The Arab respondents distinguish hardly at all between themselves and the Arabs in the occupied territories.

Attitudes About Loyalty, Security, and Conformity And Democracy

More than any other democratic society in the past quarter of a century, Israel has had to evolve policies and respond to situations in which there were strong tensions between the need to maintain national security and a desire to sustain democratic institutions and respect the right of protest. The items in Table 6 describe respondents' assessments of the threat to Israeli security, the extent to

Table 3. Degree of Confidence in Israeli Institutions, 1987 (In Percent)

Institutions	Jews	Arabs
Military		
A great deal	73.1	1.0
Some	18.2	10.9
Only a little	4.9	33.7
Almost none	1.7	19.8
None at all	1.7	32.7
No answer	0.3	2.0
Courts		
A great deal	52.2	39.6
Some	25.8	25.7
Only a little	12.9	18.8
Almost none	3.0	8.9
None at all	3.8	6.4
No answer	2.3	0.5
Universities		
A great deal	21.1	24.3
Some	34.6	36.6
Only a little	27.4	19.8
Almost none	5.2	9.4
None at all	5.9	9.4
No answer	5.8	0.5
Police		
A great deal	15.7	4.5
Some	25.1	10.4
Only a little	32.5	41.1
Almost none	13.1	23.8
None at all	11.9	18.8
No answer	1.7	1.5
Government		
A great deal	4.9	1.0
Some	17.6	5.4
Only a little	43.5	26.2
Almost none	20.2	41.1
None at all	13.1	25.2
No answer	0.7	1.0
Trade Unions		
A great deal	9.6	12.4
Some	19.7	19.8
Only a little	32.8	34.2
Almost none	17.6	16.3
None at all	17.6	15.3
No answer	2.6	2.0

(*continued*)

Table 3. (*Continued*)

Institutions	Jews	Arabs
Religious Parties		
A great deal	6.1	3.5
Some	9.4	5.9
Only a little	24.8	17.3
Almost none	22.9	33.2
None at all	34.7	39.6
No answer	2.1	0.5
Banks and Financial Institutions		
A great deal	7.0	9.9
Some	23.7	24.8
Only a little	38.7	32.2
Almost none	15.9	18.3
None at all	14.3	13.4
No answer	0.3	1.5
Small Business		
A great deal	3.1	2.0
Some	17.5	15.3
Only a little	41.9	40.6
Almost none	21.1	30.2
None at all	12.6	9.9
No answer	3.8	2.0
The Likud Party		
A great deal	10.1	2.0
Some	18.0	3.0
Only a little	25.3	16.8
Almost none	20.6	23.8
None at all	23.4	54.0
No answer	2.6	0.5
The Labor Party		
A great deal	12.7	5.9
Some	20.6	23.3
Only a little	27.7	34.2
Almost none	16.1	18.8
None at all	20.6	17.3
No answer	2.3	0.5

Table 4. Degree of Threat Posed To Israeli Democracy by Various Political Movements or Groups, 1987 (In Percent)

Political Movements or Groups	Jews	Arabs
Leftist Groups		
Very big danger	30.4	6.4
Quite big	18.8	5.0
Some	18.2	17.8
Little	10.1	32.2
No danger at all	20.8	37.1
No answer	1.7	1.5
Israeli Arabs		
Very big danger	22.7	3.0
Quite big	19.5	1.5
Some	24.6	12.4
Little	14.7	30.2
No danger at all	17.8	52.5
No answer	0.7	0.5
The Military		
Very big danger	1.7	8.4
Quite big	1.0	15.3
Some	3.5	19.8
Little	6.1	32.7
No danger at all	86.7	23.3
No answer	0.9	0.5
Religious Groups		
Very big danger	9.8	27.7
Quite big	17.5	22.3
Some	30.0	24.8
Little	19.7	15.3
No danger at all	22.2	9.9
No answer	0.9	0.0
Groups for "The Whole of Eratz Israel"		
Very big danger	8.9	39.1
Quite big	15.2	21.3
Some	26.5	23.3
Little	17.3	9.9
No danger at all	30.0	5.4
No answer	2.1	1.0
Arabs in the occupied territories		
Very big danger	39.6	4.0
Quite big	22.7	12.4
Some	14.7	33.2
Little	9.2	24.8
No danger at all	12.2	25.2
No answer	1.6	0.5

(*continued*)

Table 4. (*Continued*)

Political Movements or Groups	Jews	Arabs
"Peace Now" Groups		
Very big danger	16.1	1.0
Quite big	19.0	4.5
Some	23.2	18.8
Little	13.3	35.1
No danger at all	26.4	40.6
No answer	2.1	0.0
Rightist Groups		
Very big danger	13.3	29.7
Quite big	16.2	19.8
Some	26.0	29.7
Little	17.3	14.4
No danger at all	25.7	5.4
No answer	1.6	1.0
The Police		
Very big danger	2.3	4.5
Quite big	1.9	8.9
Some	12.0	30.2
Little	15.7	27.2
No danger at all	67.2	28.7
No answer	0.9	0.5

which, in their views, civil liberties and personal freedom are observed in Israel, their satisfaction or lack of it with the way democracy works, the importance that they attach to democracy in Israel, and the likelihood that they will remain faithful to Israel.

The main thrust of the differences is that Jews believe that the threat to their country is much greater than the Arabs do, that democracy is in better shape, that both Arab and Jewish civil rights are well protected, but should there be conflict, security must take precedence over civil rights. Jews are also more pessimistic about the likelihood of peace with their Arab neighbors but are unshaken in their loyalty to their country. The Arab responses provide almost a mirror image on each of the issues cited.

The sad and depressing conclusion that must be drawn from these responses is that in the forty years that Jews and Arabs have lived side by side

Table 5.   Degree of Threat Posed To Israel's Internal Security by
Various Political Groups, 1987 (In Percent)

Political Movements or Groups	Jews	Arabs
Leftist Groups		
Very big danger	22.7	6.4
Quite big	21.3	3.5
Some	22.2	14.9
Little	14.0	38.1
No danger at all	18.0	36.6
No answer	1.9	0.5
Israeli Arabs		
Very big danger	27.1	1.5
Quite big	26.4	3.0
Some	22.5	10.4
Little	13.4	33.7
No danger at all	9.2	50.5
No answer	1.4	1.0
The Military		
Very big danger	0.2	5.4
Quite big	0.5	10.4
Some	1.2	15.8
Little	5.4	33.7
No danger at all	91.6	32.7
No answer	1.0	2.0
Religious Groups		
Very big danger	5.6	21.3
Quite big	12.6	22.3
Some	25.7	30.7
Little	22.5	16.8
No danger at all	32.6	7.9
No answer	1.0	1.0
Groups for "The Whole of Eratz Israel"		
Very big danger	5.8	29.7
Quite big	13.8	20.3
Some	29.1	25.7
Little	18.5	14.9
No danger at all	31.8	7.4
No answer	1.0	2.0
Arabs in the occupied territories		
Very big danger	52.0	5.4
Quite big	21.1	11.4
Some	16.2	32.7
Little	6.8	27.7
No danger at all	2.6	21.3
No answer	1.2	1.5

(continued)

Table 5.   (*Continued*)

Political Movements or Groups	Jews	Arabs
"Peace Now" Groups		
Very big danger	12.9	0.5
Quite big	18.2	5.0
Some	25.3	16.8
Little	17.5	39.1
No danger at all	24.4	38.1
No answer	1.7	0.5
Rightist Groups		
Very big danger	9.4	22.8
Quite big	15.4	25.7
Some	25.1	29.2
Little	22.2	15.8
No danger at all	25.3	5.9
No answer	2.6	0.5
The Police		
Very big danger	0.7	6.4
Quite big	2.1	4.5
Some	6.6	16.3
Little	12.2	30.2
No danger at all	77.5	41.1
No answer	0.9	1.5

Table 6.   Opinions about Democracy, Loyalty, Security, and Peace (In Percent)

	Jews		Arabs	
Items	1986	1987	1986	1987
How important to you is it that the state of Israel be a democratic country?				
Very important	75.1	76.4	43.5	59.9
Fairly important	19.5	16.1	21.0	22.8
Hardly important	3.1	3.0	15.5	8.9
Not important	0.9	1.0	13.0	6.4
Does not know	0.9	2.6	6.0	1.0
No answer	0.5	0.9	1.0	1.0
On the whole, how satisfied are you with the way democracy works in Israel?				
Extremely satisfied		11.2		6.9
Very satisfied	(not	35.1	(not	14.4
Fairly satisfied	asked	40.1	asked	26.7
Not very satisfied	in	7.9	in	24.8
Not at all satisfied	1986)	4.5	1986)	14.9
No answer		1.2		12.4

(*continued*)

Table 6. (Continued)

	Jews		Arabs	
Items	1986	1987	1986	1987
Do you believe you will remain faithful to the state of Israel under any conditions?				
Positively	74.1	75.0	26.5	26.7
Probably	22.1	19.5	38.0	48.0
Probably not	2.6	3.0	22.5	15.3
Positively not	0.5	1.2	12.0	7.4
No answer	0.7	1.2	1.0	0.5
Would you say that Israel is seriously threatened by terrorists these days?				
Definitely		46.8		30.7
Probably	(not	35.1	(not	27.2
Probably not	asked	11.3	asked	29.2
Definitely not	in	5.9	in	11.4
No answer	1986)	0.9	1986)	1.5
To what extent are Arab citizens' rights in Israel safeguarded today?				
To a great extent	30.9	24.8	7.5	3.0
To a certain extent	44.8	40.0	15.0	14.4
Hardly at all	17.9	19.9	40.0	34.2
Not at all	1.0	3.1	32.5	42.6
Does not know	4.7	11.5	3.0	5.0
No answer	0.7	0.7	2.0	1.0
To what extent are civil liberties observed in Israel today?				
To a great extent	29.0	20.4	9.5	3.0
To a certain extent	49.3	54.3	21.5	29.2
Hardly at all	16.6	15.7	42.5	36.6
Not at all	2.6	3.3	24.0	27.2
Does not know	2.3	4.9	1.5	2.5
No answer	0.2	1.4	1.0	1.5
In your opinion, is there a contradiction between safeguarding the security of Israel and safeguarding citizens' rights?				
A great contradiction	11.8	11.5	26.0	39.6
A certain contradiction	42.5	42.1	28.5	21.8
No contradiction	19.3	20.9	18.0	15.3
No great contradiction	17.7	11.7	18.5	13.4
Does not know	8.1	11.9	6.5	8.9
No answer	0.7	1.9	2.5	1.0

(*continued*)

Table 6.   (*Continued*)

Items	Jews		Arabs	
	1986	*1987*	*1986*	*1987*
In case of conflict should Israel give priority to security or to the protection of civil rights?				
Definitely to security	68.9	64.7	23.4	22.8
Probably to security	23.6	24.4	32.0	23.3
Probably to civil rights	3.3	5.1	23.5	21.8
Definitely to civil rights	2.1	0.9	19.5	26.2
No answer	2.0	4.9	1.5	5.9
Do you think that most of the Arab countries are likely to sign a peace treaty with Israel in the next five years?				
Definitely		5.4		22.3
Probably	(not	31.6	(not	29.2
Probably not	asked	41.2	asked	19.3
Definitely not	in	18.5	in	27.2
No answer	1986)	3.3	1986)	2.0

as citizens of the same country, little has happened to forge a common identity or sense of unity. They share the same citizenship, elect representatives to the same parliament, but they remain separate and suspicious of each other. With the possibility of a Palestinian state becoming more of a reality, the likelihood that the Israeli Arabs would prefer to cast their lot with their Arab kinsmen rather than retain their citizenship with their Jewish countrymen becomes more apparent.

Commenting on the status of the Israeli Arabs, *Jerusalem Post* reporter Yehuda Litani wrote in 1987:

> The Israeli Arabs no longer feel any great difference between themselves and their brothers from the occupied territories. True, the former enjoy more rights than the latter, but both feel they are being discriminated against by the Jewish majority (as quoted in Brinner 1987, p. 21).

Forty years has had little impact on healing wounds or forging a sense of commonality and unity. The dream of some of the early leaders of the new state, Judah Magnes and Martin Buber, in particular, is no closer to realization today than it was more than half a century earlier.

Acknowledgment

Funds for this project came from the Ford Foundation. Their support is gratefully acknowledged.

References

Brinner, W. M. 1987. "The Arabs of Israel: The Past Twenty Years." *Middle East Review* (Fall): 13-21.

McClosky, H. and A. Brill. 1983. *Dimensions of Tolerance.* New York: Russell Sage Foundation.

Simon, R. J. and D. Barnum. 1978. "Comparative Assessment of Public Support for Civil Liberties in the United States and Israel." *Research in Law and Sociology* 1:81-100.

Stouffer, S. 1957. *Communism, Conformity and Civil Liberties.* New York: Doubleday.

Yaar, E. Y. 1987. "Public Trust in Social Institutions." *Israeli Democracy* 1(3):31-34.

Assessing African-American and Jewish Intergroup Perceptions and Attitudes

Martin S. Fiebert
Lara Horgan
Edger Peralta

Abstract: *To study intergroup attitudes of 203 African-American (93 men, 110 women) and 127 Jewish-American (55 men, 72 women) college students, two versions of a 39-item scale were developed. One version assesses anti-Semitic attitudes held by African Americans, the other focuses on anti-Black attitudes held by Jews. Scales were completed in 1996-1997. Analysis indicated that, over-all, the African-American group responded significantly more negatively to Jews than the Jewish group responded to African Americans. This effect was more marked for African-American men than women in the group.*

Currently perceived tensions between the African-American and Jewish communities are receiving increasing scholarly attention (e.g., Berman, 1994; Friedman, 1995; Kaufman, 1995; Lerner & West, 1995; Salzman & West, 1997). In an earlier paper Fiebert (1996) examined the history of African-American and Jewish relations in the United States from prior to the Civil War to the present. Specifically, five eras were outlined to understand better the genesis of conflicts and periodic transitions toward cooperation between the two communities. A number of interrelated psychological and sociological hypotheses were provided to account for the intensity of contemporary African-American and Jewish intergroup conflict.

Social science survey data (e.g., Martire & Clark, 1982) have shown a marked decline in anti-Semitism on the part of Euro-Americans but indicate that African Americans, particularly young ones, have apparently increased their negative views of Jews. Blauner (1994, p. 28) attributes this increase in anti-Semitism to include "not only streetwise youth of the urban centers, but those college educated blacks who have been influenced by Afrocentric perspectives." The present investigation was designed to assess current intergroup attitudes and perceptions of African-American and Jewish college students.

Method

Participants

A total of 203 African-American (93 men, 110 women) and 121 Jewish-American (55 men, 72 women) students participated. Data were collected during the academic year 1996-1997 and the Fall of 1997. Most subjects were enrolled in general psychology or Black Studies classes at California State University Long Beach or at California State University Fullerton. The ages of participants ranged from 18 to 52 years, with a mean of 24.9 years. Subjects' education ranged from 12 to 18 years, with a mean of 15.5 years. Age and education of the two groups did not differ significantly. Subjects were informed that their participation was voluntary and their responses anonymous.

Procedure

A 39-item attitude survey was developed from a pool of questions previously used to measure anti-Semitism and racism in studies reported by Smith (1990, 1994) and Rosenfeld (1982). Questions that measured anti-Semitism were rewritten to assess attitudes towards African Americans; questions that measured prejudice against African Americans were rewritten to assess attitudes towards Jews. Items dealing with affirmative action, Israel, the Holocaust, and intergroup social relations, among others, were added to examine contemporary attitudes between the two communities. (See Table 1 below for a complete listing of items.)

Two separate surveys were assembled: the first assessed anti-Semitic attitudes and was completed by African Americans, while the second focused on anti-black attitudes and was completed by the Jewish students. To facilitate a comparison between groups, items in the two surveys were presented in similar formats as shown in the table.

Scoring

Subjects responded to items on a 4-point scale anchored by Strongly Agree and Strongly Disagree. Items presented positively, e.g., "the more contact a person has with black people, the more one gets to like them," and endorsed Strongly Agree were scored 1 and considered as indicating low prejudice, while items endorsed Strongly Disagree were scored 4 and considered as indicating high prejudice. Items framed negatively, e.g., "Jews don't care about what happens to anyone but their own kind," were evaluated in a reverse manner so that Strongly Agree received a score of 4 and was considered high prejudice while items endorsed Strongly Disagree were scored 1 and considered low prejudice.

Results

Analysis indicated that over-all the African Americans responded more negatively to Jews (M = 2.4, SD = .4) than Jews responded to African Americans (M = 2.1, SD = .4): t_{330} =5.61, p <.001). Comparisons of the mean responses of Jewish men to African-American men and Jewish women to African-American women showed the same pattern of differences. The mean response of Jewish men was 2.2 (SD = .4), while the mean for African-American men was 2.5 (SD = .4: t_{146} = 4.01, p <.001). The mean response of African-American women was 2.3 (SD = .4), while the mean for Jewish women was 2.1 (SD = .3:t_{180} = 3.92, p <.001). It might also be noted that AfricanAmerican men evaluated Jews more negatively than African-American women (t_{201} = 2.75, p <.01).

A comparison of participants' responses indicates that there were significant differences between the African-American and Jewish groups on 31 of the 39 survey items. Given the possibility that some of these differences may have emerged by chance (Type 1 error), only *t* tests with values of p <.001 may be reliably interpreted. As to the direction of the differences more prejudiced responses were endorsed by the African Americans on 28 items, while the Jews' scores suggested more prejudiced responses on Items 13, 15, and 29, dealing, respectively, with affirmative action, intelligence, and a general attitude toward intermarriage. There were, however, a number of items dealing with specific and personal reactions to intermarriage (e.g., "I can hardly imagine myself marrying a. . ." and "I would be distressed if a close relative of mine married a . . .") and intergroup socialization, e.g., "I try to avoid socializing with . . . ," which suggested a pattern of nonsignificant differences between the groups.

TABLE 1

MEANS, STANDARD DEVIATIONS, AND STATISTICAL SIGNIFICANCE OF AFRICAN-AMERICAN AND JEWISH-AMERICAN STUDENTS' RESPONSES TO 39 ITEMS

Question	Jewish American n = 127		African American n = 203		
	M	SD	M	SD	
1. Jews (Blacks) have suffered from persecution and discrimination throughout history, and that is wrong.	1.45	0.56	1.89	0.87	5.62†
2. In general, do you favor or oppose the busing of Jewish (Black) school children from one school district to another?	2.52	0.81	2.76	0.92	2.40†
3. Jews (Blacks) have too much power in the U.S.	1.76	0.62	2.36	0.98	6.74†
4. If your political party nominated a Jew (Black) for president, would you vote for him or her?	2.01	0.67	2.22	0.70	2.69†
5. Jewish (Black) employers go out of their way to hire other Jews (Blacks).	2.66	0.64	3.16	0.79	6.10†
6. Jews (Blacks) have contributed much to the cultural life of America.	1.82	0.67	2.35	0.72	6.79†
7. The Jewish (Black) congressional lobby in this country is far too powerful for the good of the U.S.	1.90	0.56	2.65	0.88	9.11†
8. Jews (Blacks) are more loyal to Israel (Africa) than to America.	1.86	0.67	2.89	0.82	12.12†
9. Jews (Blacks) have supported rights for minority groups more than other white people.	2.60	0.67	2.57	0.80	0.32
10. Do you think that anti-Semitism (racism) is a serious problem today for American Jews (Blacks)?	1.80	0.75	2.40	0.74	6.88†
11. In order to maintain a nice residential neighborhood it is best to avoid living close to Jews (Blacks).	1.76	0.74	1.70	0.65	0.66
12. Jews (Blacks) may do a certain amount to help their own people, but they don't do much to assist others.	2.44	0.67	2.69	0.75	3.07†
13. I support affirmative action.	2.53	0.92	1.38	0.70	12.06†
14. I become upset when Jews (Blacks) criticize Afrocentric studies (Israel).	3.33	0.67	3.41	0.81	0.98
15. Compared to most Americans, Jews (Blacks) are Less, More, About the Same with regard to intelligence.	2.13	0.36	1.94	0.36	4.62†
16. Jews (Blacks) are warm and friendly people.	2.02	0.61	2.30	0.69	3.74†
17. Jews (Blacks) are more willing than most to use shady practices to get what they want.	2.10	0.68	2.44	0.79	4.13†
18. Jews (Blacks) stick together too much.	2.49	0.79	2.64	0.82	1.61
19. Jews (Blacks) don't care what happens to anyone but their own kind.	2.10	0.74	2.40	0.79	3.49†

(continued on next page)

*$p < .05$, †$p < .01$, two-tailed.

TABLE 1 (CONT'D)

MEANS, STANDARD DEVIATIONS, AND STATISTICAL SIGNIFICANCE OF AFRICAN-AMERICAN AND JEWISH-AMERICAN STUDENTS' RESPONSES TO 39 ITEMS

Question	Jewish American $n=127$		African American $n=203$		
	M	SD	M	SD	
20. The more contact a person has with Jewish (Black) people, the more they get to like them.	2.03	0.71	2.22	0.65	2.37*
21. Jews (Blacks) are too pushy.	2.15	0.62	2.40	0.69	3.31†
22. When it comes to choosing between people and money, Jews (Blacks) will choose money.	1.96	0.63	2.56	0.83	7.18†
23. How would you feel if a member of your family wanted to bring home a Jewish (Black) dinner guest?	1.85	0.57	2.03	0.59	2.76†
24. If you and your friends belonged to a social club that would not let Jews (Blacks) join, would you try to change the rule?	1.33	0.62	1.81	0.73	6.30†
25. How would you feel if a Jew (Black) attended your place of worship?	1.59	0.66	1.92	0.62	4.39†
26. Do you feel that Jews (Blacks) are trying to get ahead at the expense of people like you?	2.10	0.70	2.51	0.86	4.68
27. Have you personally experienced racial discrimination (anti-Semitism)?	2.07	0.50	2.34	0.62	4.27†
28. There are a few exceptions, but in general Jews and Blacks are pretty much alike.	2.62	0.81	2.88	0.88	2.63†
29. It is wrong for Jews and Blacks to marry each other.	2.22	0.90	1.98	0.84	2.45*
30. I try to avoid socializing with Jewish (Black) people.	1.70	0.66	1.82	0.74	1.60
31. Would you accept from a Jew (Black) the statement, I know how you feel because I have been discriminated against, too?	1.74	0.63	2.01	0.60	3.83†
32. I can hardly imagine myself marrying a Jew (Black).	2.87	0.94	2.74	0.99	1.21
33. While the Nazi Holocaust was terrible for Jews, the holocaust of slavery was equally terrible, if not worse, for Blacks.	2.57	0.89	3.40	0.80	8.54†
34. As an African American (Jew), deep down, I have an admiration of Jews (African Americans) and their culture.	2.12	0.62	2.35	0.79	2.84†
35. I would not feel comfortable if most of my coworkers were Jewish (African American).	2.02	0.71	2.19	0.77	2.06*
36. Because of long term experience with anti-Semitism/racism, Jews (Blacks) have a special understanding of suffering and concerns.	2.38	0.78	2.54	0.81	1.77
37. I would not mind if my immediate supervisor at work was Jewish (Black).	1.66	0.63	2.02	0.70	4.69†
38. In my experience, Jews (Blacks) are overly sensitive when discussion focuses on Jewish (Black) behavior and values.	2.73	0.84	2.63	0.81	1.07
39. I would be distressed if a close relative of mine married a Jew (Black person).	2.23	0.75	2.13	0.77	1.12

*$p < .05$, †$p < .01$, two-tailed.

Discussion

These findings indicate that this sample of undergraduate African Americans held slightly but significantly more negative attitudes towards Jews than the undergraduate Jews held toward African Americans, with a more marked effect for African-American men than for African-American women. In evaluating these results it should be noted that the subjects, young urban Southern California Jews and African Americans, were constituted as a convenient rather than as a representative sample. In the absence of a normative sample of Euro-American or other minority group, the relative prejudice expressed by the African Americans is uncertain. Nevertheless, the findings are of interest. It appears that African Americans may hold negative stereotypical perceptions of Jews. These include viewing Jews as pushy, willing to use "shady" business practices, exercising too much political and economic power, and only willing to help other Jews. Consistent with these findings, Martire and Clark (1982) reported that 37% of African Americans compared to 20% of Euro-Americans scored high on anti-Semitic attitudes, particularly in economic areas. In addition, the data suggest that Euro-American students were not as willing as were the Jewish students to acknowledge similarities in personal or historical discrimination. The Jewish students, for their part, tended to view the African Americans more negatively in terms of their intelligence and were less supportive of affirmative action than were African Americans, and they also held a more negative general view toward intermarriage than did the African Americans. These differences in attitudes and perceptions may be partly accounted for by the fact that contemporary African Americans and Jews live in vastly different worlds, psychologically, socially, and economically (Friedman, 1995; Kaufman, 1995). Given residential divisions there are, compared to the 1950s and '60s, few social or personal interactions occurring between the two communities so cultural (and historical) stereotypes are reinforced and most likely influence current findings.

Acknowledgment

The authors thank J. Robert Newman and Scott Hershberger for their assistance with data analysis and Margo Kasdan for valuable comments on a draft of this manuscript. An earlier version of this paper was presented at the 9th International Conference on Personal Relations, June 23, 1998, at Saratoga Springs, New York.

References

Berman, P (Ed.) (1994) *Blacks and Jews, alliances and arguments.* New York: Delacorte.

Blauner, B. (1994) That Black-Jewish thing: what's going on? *Tikkun,* 9(No. 5), 27-32, 103.

Fiebert, M. S. (1996) Collaboration and conflict: five phases in Jewish and Black relations and an analysis of tension between the two communities. Paper presented at the annual meeting of the American Psychological Society, San Francisco, CA.

Friedman, M. (1995) *What went wrong? The creation and collapse of the Black-Jewish alliance.* New York: Free Press.

Kaufman, J. (1995) *Broken alliance: the turbulent times between Blacks and Jews in America.* New York: Touchstone.

Lerner, M., & West, C. (1995) *Jews and Blacks, let the healing begin.* New York: Putnam.

Martire, G., & Clark, R. (1982) *Anti-Semitism in the United States: a study of prejudice in the 1980s.* New York: Praeger.

Rosenfeld, G. (1982) The polls: attitudes toward American Jews. *Public Opinion Quarterly,* 46, 431-443.

Salzman, J., & West, C. (Eds.) (1997) *Struggles in the promised land: toward a history of Black-Jewish relations in the United States.* New York: Oxford University Press.

Smith, T. W. (1990) Jewish attitudes toward Blacks and race relations. *Jewish Sociology Papers.* New York: American Jewish Committee.

Smith, T. W. (1994) Anti-Semitism in contemporary America. *Working Papers on Contemporary Anti-Semitism.* New York: American Jewish Committee.

Permissions

The articles in the anthology appear with the permission of the authors or publishers of the journals in which the articles originally appeared. Original citations are as follows:

Blum, M. "The Influence of Austrian Humanism in Theodor Herzl's Vision of a Jewish State." *European Journal of Law and Economics, 1996, 3, 2, 175-92.*

Blumenfeld, W. & Robinson, L. "Examining and Responding to Conflict between African American and Jewish American Students on a College Campus." *Mediation Quarterly, 2000, 17, 3, 231-263.*

Bodo, K. & Gibson, N. "Childbirth Customs in Orthodox Jewish Traditions." *Canadian Family Physician, 1999, 45, 682-686.*

Carlton, D. & Weiss, A. "The Economics of Religion, Jewish Survival, and Jewish Attitudes Toward Competition in Torah Education." *Journal of Legal Studies, 2001, 30, 1, 253-275.*

Ferber, A. "Of Mongrels and Jews: The Deconstruction of Racialised Identities in White Supremacist Discourse." *Social Identities, 1997, 3, 2, 193-208.*

Fiebert, M., Horgan, L. & Peralta, E. "Assessing African American and Jewish Intergroup Perceptions and Attitudes." *Perceptual and Motor Skills, 1999, 88, 1, 253-258*

Fishman, J. "Interwar Eastern European Jewish Parties and the Language Issue." *International Journal of the Sociology of Language, 2001, 151, 175-189.*

Glazer, N. "American Jewry or American Judaism?" *Society, 1990, 28(1), 14-20.*

Gluck, M. & Geliebter, A. "Body Image and Eating Behaviors in Orthodox and Secular Jewish Women." *Journal of Gender-Specific Medicine, 2002, 5(1),19-24.*

Horowitz, I. L. "Minimalism or Maximalism: Jewish Survival at the Millennium. *Sociological Papers, 1998, 6, 1-18.*

Lasker, A. & Lasker, J. "Do They Want Their Children to Be Like Them?: Parental Heritage and Jewish Identity." *Contemporary Jewry, 1991, 12, 109-126.*

Lipset, S. M. "Some Thoughts on the Past, Present and Future of American Jewry." *Contemporary Jewry, 1994, 15, 171-181.*

Lyman, S. M. "Postmodernism and the Construction of Ethnocultural Identity: The Jewish-Indian Theory and the Lost Tribes of Israel." *Sociological Spectrum, 1997, 17,3, 259-282.*

Newsome, Y. "International Issues and Domestic Relations: African Americans, American Jews and the Israel-South Africa Debate." *International Journal of Politics, Culture and Society, 1991, 5, 1, 19-48.*

Shai, D. "Working Women/Cloistered Men: A Family Development Approach to Marriage Arrangements Among Ultra-Orthodox Jews." *Journal of Comparative Family Studies, 2002, 33, 1, 97-115.*

Sheskin, I. "Jewish Identity in the Sunbelt: The Jewish Population of Orlando, Florida." *Contemporary Jewry, 1994, 15, 26-38.*

Sheskin, I. "Local Jewish Population Studies: Still Necessary after All These Years." *Contemporary Jewry, 1994, 15, 1-3.*

Simon, R., Landis, J. & Amir, M. "Jewish and Arab Perceptions of Civil Rights in Israel." *Studies in Law, Politics, and Society, 1990, 10, 245-262.*

Sorotzkin, B. "Understanding and Treating Perfectionism in Religious Adolescents." *Psychotherapy, 1998, 35, 1, 87-95.*

Stern, D. "The Significance of Jewishness for Wittgenstein's Philosophy." *Inquiry–An Interdisciplinary Journal of Philosophy, 2000, 43, 4, 383-402.*

Sublette, S. & Trappler, B. "Cultural Sensitivity Training in Mental Health: Treatment of Orthodox Jewish Psychiatric Inpatients." *International Journal of Social Psychiatry, 2000, 46(2), 122-134.*

Thomas, L. "The Matrices of Malevolent Ideologies: Blacks and Jews." *Social Identities, 1996, 2, 1, 107-133.*

Toback, P. "The Public Debate on Life and Death Choices: A Response from a Jewish Hospital Chaplain." *Journal of Pastoral Care, 2000, 54(1), 23-32.*

Trappler, B., Endicott, J. & Friedman, S. "Psychosocial Adjustment Among Returnees to Judaism." *The Journal of Psychology, 1995, 129(4), 433-41.*